Samuel M. Behloul, Susanne
Andreas Tunger-Zanetti (eds.
Debating Islam

global local Islam

Samuel M. Behloul, Susanne Leuenberger,
Andreas Tunger-Zanetti (eds.)

Debating Islam

Negotiating Religion, Europe, and the Self

[transcript]

Bibliographic Information published by the Deutsche Nationalbibliothek
The Deutsche Nationalbibliothek lists this publication in the Deutsche Natio-
nalbibliografie; detailed bibliographic data are available in the Internet at
http://dnb.d-nb.de

© 2013 transcript Verlag, Bielefeld

Cover layout: Kordula Röckenhaus, Bielefeld
Proofread & Typeset: Ursina Marty, Andreas Tunger-Zanetti,
  Saskia Weidmann, Diego Wider
Printed by Majuskel Medienproduktion GmbH, Wetzlar
ISBN 978-3-8376-2249-2

Contents

PART III

Epilogue

On relating religion to society and society to religion

Foreword

In the last two decades, and with increased intensity since the key event of 9/11, Islam has become a dominant concern, structuring national debates on immigration, integration, democracy, liberalism and secularism Europe-wide. Adapting an interdisciplinary outlook, this volume presents a comparative analysis of debates on Islam and Muslims in different West-European national contexts. Introducing Switzerland as an under-researched object of study to the academic discussion on Islam in Europe, this volume offers a fresh perspective by putting recent case studies from diverse national contexts together. We are interested in scrutinising both the specificity as well as the exemplary test-case nature of its trajectory in a European comparison.

The research perspectives gathered together in this volume were largely developed in the course of the international conference "Debating Islam: Switzerland – Europe" held at the University of Berne during 29th of September to 1st of October 2011. It was organised co-operatively by a number of members of the SGMOIK (Schweizerische Gesellschaft Mittlerer Osten und islamische Kulturen) and the Groupe de recherche sur l'Islam en Suisse (GRIS), and was financially supported by the Swiss National Science Foundation, the Swiss Academy of Humanities and Social Sciences, the Mittelbauvereinigung der Universität Bern (MVUB) as well as the Bernese Institute of Advanced Study in the Humanities and the Social Sciences (IASH).

This volume consists of papers discussed during the conference, complemented by fresh contributions from interlocutors and discussants on questions also raised during the event. The overarching idea that informs this book project is to bring together case studies on various national Muslim debates and apply a comparative perspective on Europe and its specific perception of Islam. The chapters should allow to see similarities and differences between for example the Danish cartoon crisis and the Swiss anti-minaret campaign, or between the self-positioning of converts to Islam in different national contexts. By reading the chapters of this volume against each other we hope the reader will be able to develop a more thorough understanding of the imaginary, the mechanisms and the objectives which are at work in the different yet related debates on Islam.

Expertise brought together in this volume ranges from a wide field of academic approaches such as sociology, political science, religious and Islamic studies. This interdisciplinary approach as well as the procedure to hand in working papers in advance that were to be discussed in plenary sessions led to fruitful discussions and debates during the international conference, that have also been taken up in the articles collected in this book project.

The volume is arranged into subsections under the headings "Rules and roles"; "The one facing the many"; "The many facing the 'other' (within)". It goes without saying that this subdivision is at most a makeshift attempt to orient the reader and bundle various discussion foci which are, however, closely intertwined.

We want to use this foreword to acknowledge all the people and institutions which have contributed to the realisation of this volume. Firstly, our thanks go out to Astrid Meier, Frank Peter and Petra Bleisch Bouzar who conceived and organised the conference with us and to Barbara Luder for her important practical assistance. Further, we would like to thank the authors of this volume for their fruitful cooperation in realising this book project. We also would like to mention our editorial helpers Diego Wider, Saskia Weidmann and Ursina Marty. Zoë Lehmann Imfeld is owed our special thanks for copyediting the entire volume. Finally, our thanks go out to several institutions for their financial support: the Research Commission of the University of Lucerne (Forschungs-kommission der Universität Luzern), the Department for Migration Affairs of the Reformed Churches of Bern, Jura and Solothurn (Bereich OeME-Migration der Reformierten Kirchen Bern-Jura-Solothurn, www.refbejuso.ch/migration), the Swiss Society for the Study of Religions (Schweizerische Gesellschaft für Religionswissenschaft) and a private foundation, Stiftung Dr. phil. Josef Schmid Staatsarchivar von Luzern und Frau Amalie Schmid-Zehnder.

Berne/Lucerne, September 2013

Samuel M. Behloul   Susanne Leuenberger   Andreas Tunger-Zanetti

Introduction

SAMUEL M. BEHLOUL

The now extensive research on Muslims in Western Europe has undergone several changes in its processes in recent decades. Before the new quality of the – no longer temporary – Muslim presence in Western Europe was pointed out in the 1980s (Gerholm/Lithman 1988), it was almost exclusively migration sociologists who dealt with the immigrants from Islamic societies in Western Europe.

Research focused on issues of social integration, family reunification, labor laws, living conditions, and education. The immigration and multiculturalism discourse mainly took place without explicit reference to religion. Initiated by the Rushdie Affair in Britain and the first *affair du foulard* in France, both taking place as early as 1989, the religious difference of migrants from Islamic societies only gradually entered the consciousness of science, politics, and the public in the 1990s. In general, studies that have emerged since that time can be assigned to the following five groups with regard to their content and focus:

1. One type of study provides insight into the origin, development, and goals of Islamic organizations in Western Europe (Feind-Riggers and Steinbach 1997; Lewis 1994; Amiraux 2001; Jonker 2002; Lemmen 2002; Humayun 2004).

2. From the mid-1990s and especially after 9/11, questions about the socio-political dimensions and implications of the presence and dealings with Muslims in Europe increasingly became the focus of scientific and public interest. Keywords such as 'Islamism' and 'fundamentalism' became the particular focus of attention (Heitmeyer et al. 1997; Bielefeldt/Heitmeyer 1998; Roy 2002; Ulfkotte 2003).

3. Closely linked to this question is the question of the emergence of a 'European Islam' and its future institutional form, which has long been the focus of

research on Islam (Dassetto 1996; Roy 1998, 1999; Ramadan 1999c, 2001; Levau et al. 2001; al-Sayyad and Castells 2002; Tibi 2002; Leggewie 2004; Bielefeldt 2003). In recent years, this research context has seen a consolidation and incorporation of various debates and issues: from the value and integration debate to educational and legal issues to questions of internal security (Bundesministerium des Inneren 2003).

4. While these debates more or less circle around the question 'Europeanisation of Islam?' or 'Islamisation of Europe?', more recent, mostly sociologically oriented studies are predominantly based on an qualitative approach. They particularly emphasise dialectical interaction processes between Muslims and their respective majority societies (Cesari 2004) and empirically elaborate on the development of individual Muslim identities (Schiffauer 2000; Tietze 2001; Frese 2002; Göle and Ammann 2004; Jonker and Amiraux 2006). In recent years, studies and individual contributions related to gender have also emerged in this thematic context, focusing on the explicit life practices and processes of religious identity formation of Muslim women in the West (Klein-Hessling et al. 2000; Klinkhammer 2000; Karakasoglu-Aydïn 2000; Nökel 2002; Gerhard and Jansen 2003; Jonker 2003a, 2003b).

5. The concept of 'transnational migration' introduced by Bash et al. in the US in the 1990s (Bash et al. 1994), according to which migrants interact and identify with several nation states or communities through cross-border and transnational practices of communication and mobility, thus contributing to the development of transnational communities or to the formation of transnational spaces, was also taken up in the area of research on Muslim immigrant groups in the West. In recent years, studies on the effects of 'societies of origin' on Muslim immigrants in Western Europe and their transnational connections have emerged (Mandaville 1999, 2001; Trautner 2000; Allievi and Nielsen 2003; Salih 2003).

These thematic foci show that the production of knowledge about Islam and Muslims in the West is not just a purely academic discourse. Rather, it encompasses virtually all socially relevant topics. The immigration and integration discourse, inter-religious dialogue projects, discourse on the religious education of children, naturalisation, the identification of the relationship between religion and state, the freedom of art, the religious and cultural heritage and identity of Europe, the architectural design of public spaces, and, not least, discourse on security issues – all of these individual discourses – and this applies particularly to the period after 9/11 – have been linked in one way or another to the 'Islam issue.'

THE AIM OF THIS VOLUME

Conspicuously, Islam has become a key issue in most European societies with respect to issues of immigration, integration, identity, values and inland security. As the mere presence of small Muslim minorities (usually ranging between 3 and 7%) fails to explain these debates convincingly, new questions need to be asked: How did 'Islam' become a topic? Who takes part in these debates? How do these debates influence both individual as well as collective 'self-images' and 'image of others'?

The very title of this volume, *Debating Islam: Negotiating Europe, Religion and the Self*, contains two key insights. On the one hand, it is drawing on the fact that current Western-European Islam debates have a totalising character with regard to the discussed content and questions. On the other hand, the book's title should express that this debating is not a mere 'discussing.' Rather, debating here has a normative character, insofar as 'discussion' implies the presupposition and (re)production of certain subjectivities, categories and matters. Therefore, 'debating' is understood as a discursive social practice characterised by power relations and whose actors follow and shape certain epistemic conditions of speaking about and reflecting on religion, and thereby develop certain strategies for (re)producing the self and other(s). The empirical examples from different social contexts in Western Europe which are discussed in this volume, show that in secular Western Europe, religion plays a pivotal role for normative demarcation and identity building strategies. This applies both at the individual and the collective level. To exemplify what power relations dominate the current Western-European Islam debates and how these debates influence individual and collective self-images and images of others, the book is divided into three thematic areas (more specific overviews precede each of the three parts).

In the first part, "Rules and roles", the diversity of socio-political contexts and conditions under which current Islam debates take place – from laicism and republicanism to gender dimension and criminal law – is analysed and discussed, using selected Western-European countries as examples (Switzerland, Britain and France). As well as highlighting the question of women's rights as one of the more powerful normative regulators of Western-European debates on Islam, this section also shows that seemingly clear concepts such as French laicism and British multiculturalism may trigger unexpected self-representation and boundary making strategies in the context of the Islam debates.

The contributions of the second part, "The one facing the many: Conversion to Islam and transformation(s) of identity", focus on the phenomenon of conversion to Islam. Due to the ambivalent perception of converts to Islam as bridge-builders or radical 'newborns,' the issue of conversion in recent years has gained increasing attention both in academic research and among policy makers. The contributions in this part analyse the role and strategies of converts to Islam in terms of their respective reconfiguration of religious difference, religious authority, and political loyalty in the context of the normatively charged demarcation between 'us' and 'them' specific to debates on Islam.

The contributions of the third part, "The many facing the other (within)", centre on the question of the collectivist images of self and others within the Islam debates. The contributions stem from one of the most striking discursive patterns of Western-European debates on Islam: the construction of a supposedly homogeneous 'we' vis-à-vis a supposedly homogeneous 'other.' The contributions critically examine the alleged uniqueness and homogeneity of these constructions. Using the example of three different national contexts with various forms of political control regarding religious and minority issues (Austria, Switzerland, and Denmark), unexpected dynamics of discursive interaction and communication processes are presented both among the various actors within a 'we' as well as between the actors of a 'we' and an 'other' for collectivities otherwise perceived as homogeneous.

Compared to the previous research on debates on Islam in a Western-European context, the innovative approach of this volume consists of the following two features: First, it introduces the under-researched case of Switzerland into broader European research about Islam in Western-European countries, and especially about the different Islam debates going on in these countries. In doing so, this volume offers a fresh perspective on the issue of Islam debates by putting recent case studies from diverse national contexts into comparative perspective. Second, the book specifically addresses the epistemic conditions under which Islam is generally thematised and perceived as a problematic religion within Western-European Islam debates.

The research done so far about the Western debates on Islam – as mentioned above – has been distinguished by a variety of analytical approaches. Numerous studies have repeatedly shown that in the aftermath of the events of 9/11, religious affiliation abruptly became the centrally perceived criterion of otherwise very culturally disparate migrant groups from Muslim countries in the West (cf. Sen 2006; Tezcan 2006; Spielhaus 2006; Behloul 2010). Nevertheless, few attempts have been made to ask, on the one hand, why has become a unifying interpretive category of differing ethno-cultural migrant groups in secular democracies in the context of dealing with immigrants from countries shaped by Islam religion, and, on the other hand, to explore which understanding of religion in general underlies the Western debates on Islam.

The following analytical introduction therefore attempts to present the specific epistemic anchoring of Western-European debates on Islam. It specifically addresses the understanding of religion which the current debates on Islam are based on, and defines the development of this understanding within the context of Western-European religious and church history. A diachronic comparative perspective will demonstrate how a particular understanding of religion took shape in Western Europe starting in the seventeenth century, the core of which was no longer the question regarding the truth of religious dogmas or the authenticity of the holy scriptures. Due to traumatic experiences with religious conflicts in the seventeenth century, questions concerning the development potential of a religion increasingly took centre stage, namely in terms of their potential for peace or conflict and their compatibility with modern development. This evolutionary-essentialist understanding of religion, which stems from an ideal image of a 'real' religion, I argue, also forms the epistemic context of current debates on Islam in Western Europe.

'REAL' RELIGION AND PERCEIVED 'DEFICITS' OF ISLAM

Muslim and non-Muslim participants alike in the Islam debates repeatedly stress that Europe has a particular view and image of Islam that has been influenced by historical experience with the Islamic world on the one hand (for example the Crusades and the expansion of the Ottoman Empire), and socio-political developments in the Islamic world over the last decades (such as religious radicalisation and terrorism) on the other. They go on to assert that this image and understanding of Islam is the main reason why Muslims are perceived in the way they are in the Western Europe of today, and why they have become the subject of heated and emotional public debates in the first place. However, a less frequently asked question pertains to the understanding of religion in general which underpins the current preoccupation with Islam and Muslims, and categorises them as problematic. This is astonishing inasmuch as what has now become a massive proliferation of literature on Islam in the West repeatedly comes to the critical conclusion that, in the wake of the events of 9/11, religious affiliation has become the central homogenising criterion of the way ethnically and linguistically heterogenious groups of migrants from Islamic countries are perceived in the West (cf. Sen 2006; Tezcan 2007; Spielhaus 2006; Tiesler 2006; Behloul 2010) and that the issue of religion per se has come to feature ever more prominently in societal discourse as a whole.

The most striking characteristic of the debates on Islam in Western Europe is their tendency to emphasise its deficits. They focus on Islam's perceived shortcomings in relation to the expected level of developmental timeliness of a religion today in terms of its compatibility to secular notions of peace, gender equality, freedom, individuality and integration into secular legal systems.[1] This pertains both to the significance of religion within society and the relationship between individuals and religion.

It is notable that within the framework of the 'Islam Issue', people in the West generally do not talk about Islam in the same way as it is factually presented by the presence of immigrants possessing a Muslim perspective, i.e. multifaceted in terms of culture and language. Rather it is discussed according to the political perspective, merely how it is expected to become or how it cannot become at all. Although such forms of positive and negative essentialisation of the Islam perspective differ from one another in a diametric sense, they both follow the postulate of a 'real religion' which, following a linear modernisation pattern in terms of the acceptance of new normative paradigms (individuality, gender equality, freedom), inevitably stands in a constitutive relationship to the societal developments and achievements of modern times. What is striking in this respect is the way in which public debates often refer to 'moderate' Islam as distinct from radical Islam or Islamism. This is in striking contrast to the extreme rarity of references to 'moderate Buddhism' or 'moderate Hinduism'. So what are the structural preconceptions and criteria for such characterisations? It is inadequate to simply ask which specific image of Islam, conditioned by negative experiences with the Islamic world in history and the present time, underpins Western-European debates on that faith. Such an approach does not take into account that within the framework of the current debates on Islam the issue of religion per se, rather than merely that of Islam, has become a new focus of attention. One must therefore go a step further and try in general to identify the normative presuppositions that govern the way people talk about and reflect on religion which are informing the current debates. Debates on Islam in Western Europe must therefore be analysed from the perspective of an understanding of religion that has its roots in the specific religious and, in particular, Christian history of Western Eu-

---

1   In this respect Islam is faced with four definitions of itself: 1) Islam as a deficient religion because it has not yet reached the levels of enlightenment of Christianity; 2) Islam is and will remain deficient because its very nature, which makes it more than merely a religion, means that it is, unlike Christianity, fundamentally unsuited to such a development; 3) by its very nature Islam has already anticipated modern social developments. It does not require further development, needing only to return to its primordial roots, and 4) Islam is a social, moral and ethical alternative in a society whose values have decayed. This position in particular is specific to converts to Islam and to young and old Muslims alike who rediscovered their faith in God, experiencing religious and spiritual awakening.

rope. After all, the tradition of religious criticism, which was so influential in the emergence of modern Europe, gave rise to plausibility structures in respect to the way religion is regarded and its significance within a state. These plausibility structures shape a society's perception of its own religion just as profoundly as that of foreign religions. What is more, they establish the society's 'own' religion as the normative model for foreign religions, in this case for Islam.

To help the reader understand the structural presuppositions behind the debates on Islam in the West post-9/11, the focus of this book will thus be on the following key issues: How do 'religion'/'Islam' and 'religiousness'/'Islamicity' become topics of socio-political debate? Under what historical and ideological conditions do such debates occur? Who takes part in the debates and dictates them in a normative and content-related sense? And how are these debates ultimately incorporated into an individual and a collective 'self-image' and 'image of others' by Muslims and non-Muslims respectively?

A view of current Western-European debates on Islam as a discourse (in the Foucauldian sense) on religion gives rise to two essential implications. The first of these is that different political and academic discourses have at different times taken place in Europe in connection with the concept of religion and have shaped the object of discourse –namely, religion – accordingly and filled it with normative content. With regard to European religious history in particular, Friedrich Tenbruck stresses that "by virtue of a shared general conception of all religions [Europeans were able to] talk in general terms about religion and its nature and function amongst themselves and across linguistic barriers" (Tenbruck 1993: 37).[2]

The second implication consists in investigating the question of pre-structure, that is, the epistemic conditions behind discourses on religion that manifest themselves in current debates on Islam.[3] After all in post-9/11 debates on Islam the issue of religion per se, rather than merely that of Islam, gained a completely new and, for many observers, unexpected discursive intensity as a

---

2   The translation from the German original is mine here and for all following citations unless otherwise indicated.

3   According to Michel Foucault, a specific epistemological configuration underlines all discourse, causing the discourse to always follow certain thought and knowledge structures. Such structures regulate, at a given point in time, how something is spoken about and how it is not. Debates do not form any self- contained entities, thematically or chronologically, in and of themselves. Current debates are much more likely to reproduce earlier debates and, at the same time intersect with thematically different debates (cf. Foucault 1973: 261).

specific model for explaining societal processes and behaviours amongst both individuals and groups. Above all from the Western-European perspective, the question of the 'how' of religious understanding in the context of current debates on Islam appears still more relevant. The relevance becomes apparent, if, on the one hand, reference is made to the problem of the exclusively religious categorisation of migrants from Muslim backgrounds and their descendants in the West. The relevance of posing this very question lies, on the other hand, in the fact that, as Rolf Schieder indicates, in a Europe profoundly influenced by the devastating consequences of the Thirty Years' War, "the necessity of a definition of the relationship between politics and religion for the preservation of the peace [forced] the formation of a discursive space that continues to this day to define the effects of statements on religion." As Schieder goes on to say by way of conclusion, "Since the seventeenth century the concept of religion has been a political one" (Schieder 2001: 11).

Possibly the most significant characteristic of the transformation undergone by the post-Reformation Western-European understanding of religion, i.e. from the sixteenth century onwards, was the increasing displacement of dogmatic theological doctrine, of true versus false worship, by ideas concerning the contribution of religion(s) to the general good of society and the cause of modernisation. This new-era Protestant, secular understanding of religion subsequently became the normative framework for European religious discourse, initially at the inter-denominational (Protestantism v. Catholicism) level and then, from the nineteenth century, increasingly also between religions. It goes without saying that we also come across the normative criterion of the compatibility of a 'true' religion with the generally accepted societal secular values (freedom of opinion, democracy, tolerance, peacefulness, individual freedom) in the context of Western-European debates on Islam in the post-9/11 era.

If we are to locate current debates on Islam in the historical context of European arguments over the phenomenon of religion in general and the institution of the Church – the Catholic Church in particular –, in the wake of which a specific religious understanding emerged that continues to manifest itself in the current debates on Islam, we need look no further than the period since the early seventeenth century. For ecclesiastical politics in the period from the end of the sixteenth and, in particular, the seventeenth century were characterised by constant disputes within the Protestant churches and between the denominations. What became known as the Thirty Years' War came to define almost the entire first half of the seventeenth century. That the Thirty Years' War was not a purely religious conflict is beyond doubt (cf. Krusenstjern 1999). However, the permanent legacy of its devastating effects was the emergence of a specific discourse about religion. This discourse revolved primarily around the key question of how to define religion and politics in such a way as to maintain peace. And, as far as occidental religious discourses are concerned, it remains dominant to this day. Likewise specific to the reflections on religion taking place in the current era is the accentuation of individual and political rationality versus tradition and dogmatism as an indispensable foundation for reliable understanding and action.[4] The ascent to the pre-eminence of rationality, which was conditioned by the political-religious developments of the seventeenth and eighteenth century, and the question of perfect compatibility between 'rational insight' and 'religion' as a generally indispensable criterion for the truth of a religion – in this instance meaning the socio-political usefulness of a religion – offer key insights into the location of current debates about Islam in the historical context of Western religious discourses. This development does more than just bear witness to the discursive interweaving of socio-political framework conditions on the one hand and the definition of the functional content of religion on the other. It also permits to draw a parallel to the current debates on Islam that are likewise being conducted against a background of socio-political and religious-cultural conflict and are exercising a decisive influence on the way religion is understood. This influence makes itself felt, for instance, in the fact that the criteria by which a religion is judged as being true today are its potential to bring peace and its compatibility with secular democracy rather than the truth of its scriptures or of its images of God.

The emergence of the correlation between reason and religion as an essential normative criterion for the 'rightness' of a religion led also in the eighteenth century to the development of a general concept of religion as a generic term, against whose normative content every historical formation of positive religions was to be measured. The use of a general conception of religion from the eighteenth century as a generic term must likewise be viewed in the context of the specific European religious-political situation of the age. In view of the denominational fragmentation of European Christianity, one of the purposes of this development was to create a unifying generic understanding of what Christianity actually was. On the other hand, this meant that it was possible to speak appro-

---

4   In particular the heated debate on ritual circumsicion of Muslim boys in 2012 in Germany made it clear how Islam is perceived as being a (still) archaic and irrational religion. In the wake of such debates in which religions are being assessed on the basis of their adaptability to modern social developments, religions become quickly designated as 'good' and 'evil' (cf. a series of articles by renowned authors under the common caption "Was ist eine gute Religion?" [What makes a good religion?] in the *Neue Zürcher Zeitung,* March 2006 to May 2007).

priately of the non-Christian religions and cultures which were emerging ever more strongly into popular consciousness, albeit only in relation to 'the religion', which stood above the religious diversity of individual faiths (cf. Wagner 1986; Feil 1997; Haussig 2003; Matthes 2005).

Although the generic term 'religion' came to occupy an inherently critical position with respect to all historical forms of positive religions, Klaus Hock emphasises a consistent ambivalence in the concept of religion in the age of Enlightenment. This ambivalence was to be found in the fact that on the one hand an ideal type of religion, i.e. a 'religion per se' became a medium of criticism for every specific form of positive religion whilst, on the other, having no tangible historical form itself, it was immune to any religious criticism, allowing it to be reinterpreted as the medium of justification for a claim to absoluteness (cf. Hock 2002: 12). Hock cites the specific example of the application of the general concept of religion to the history of Christianity in the nineteenth and twentieth centuries:

> On the one hand, the use of the general concept of religion is fundamentally opposed to the claim of Christianity to a position of supernatural, 'absolute' preeminence outside of history, and the Christian religion is relegated to the same level as all other specific religions and represented within the framework of the same world history. On the other, historical evolutionism in combination with the notion of 'religion' as a general concept in the singular led to the emergence of new ways of justifying Christianity's claim to absoluteness: through the assumption that 'religion' undergoes a linear process of development and strives in this manner for realisation in the world, the claim being that Christianity, as the most highly civilised and developed form of religion, comes closer to this ideal than all other world religions.   (Hock 2002: 12)[5]

The normative scheme that was created here and that represents Christianity – at least with regard to its degree of enlightenment and general modernity – as superior to all other religions played a decisive role as the epistemic framework of the religious discourses of the nineteenth century. However, the actual distinguishing feature of this understanding of religion shaped by new-era

---

5   According to Friedrich Schleiermacher, Christianity represents 'the' religion of religions, the religion of mature and responsible humanity, in comparison with which all other religions – Schleiermacher uses the example of Judaism – are characterised by an immaturity in contradiction to the ideal of the actively religiously mature individual (cf. Ehrhardt 2005: 55).

Protestantism was that 'religion', in the course of its transformation into a generic term as an autonomous Christian way of life, began to oppose itself to the 'church' as the upholder of the religious order. 'Religion' gradually became a term used to denote a lived Christian reality alongside the established 'church' (cf. Matthes 1989: 198). So, in connection with the Reformation concept of a direct relationship between the divine and the Christian individual, 'religion' as a generic term across the denominations became an internal Christian medium of normative demarcation between individual piety and faith on the one hand and an institutionally (ecclesiastically) defined and administered faith that permitted no exercise of individual freedoms on the other.

At this point it is interesting to observe how this new-era Protestant, secularised understanding of religion defined the Western-European perception of the Islamic world and the discourses between Catholics and Protestants in the nineteenth century. Some of the semantics and normative demarcations between what is one's own and what is foreign encountered there are also to be found in the current Western-European debates on Islam.[6] The following brief historical

---

6   In this context, it is revealing to note that the nineteenth-century expansion of European colonial powers, especially France and Great Britain into the Arabic-Islamic world constituted more than merely a military and political challenge to this area. Surely of much greater significance was the cultural challenge that accompanied the colonial powers, spurred on as they were by their optimistic confidence in technical and scientific progress.

This new shift in the balance of power led to the forcible opening of a new discursive space between the Western and Arab-Islamic worlds. This came to be essentially characterised by the antagonistic juxtaposition (defined and pursued by the West) of enlightenment and scientific-technical progress on the one hand and Islam on the other. The ideals of the Enlightenment and the French Revolution became the new normative *tertium comparationis* for the definition of the relationship between Islam and the West. As is the case in the current Western-European Islam-Debates, the Western-European perception of Islam in the nineteenth-century payd scant if any attention to questions of theological truth, correctness of the portrayal of the divine and authenticity of revelation that were characteristic of Christian-Islamic religious discourses up until the Reformation. Instead it revolved around the question of the capacity or incapacity of a religion to modernise and the ability or inability of its adherents to integrate into modern society. The frame of reference was increasingly provided by temporal values. This phenomenon also clearly manifests in argumentation of the most prominent Arab reformist thinker of the nineteenth-century

comparative overview of the anti-Catholic discourse in the Protestant-dominated countries of Europe in the nineteenth century is relevant to an understanding of current debates on Islam for the following reason above all. For, in the nineteenth century, we observe in Western Europe the same kind of synchronicity of two opposing tendencies that is also discernible in the Europe of today. The beginnings of the emancipation of many parts of society in the nineteenth century from the religious (i.e. ecclesiastical) context, especially in matters of world view, went hand in hand with a 'religious turn' in respect of ways of dealing with new and radical socio-political changes. The need for a reinforced sense of superiority and normative self-view led, as we will see below, in the denominationally mixed societies of nineteenth century Western Europe, to an intensification of the role of religious denominational criteria of belonging in the way people perceived both themselves and those alien to them.

We can observe, as explained further below, a similar development in the Western Europe of today: a historically unique loss of relevance of religion, i.e., of ecclesiastical religiosity above all, on the one hand and, on the other, an 'Islamic turn' in respect of the perception of immigrants from societies shaped by Islam.

AN ECHO FROM THE NINETEENTH CENTURY

In the interests of a comparative historical perspective it should at this point be noted that the understanding of religion at issue here also dominated the discourse between Catholics and Protestants in the same period, i.e. the nineteenth century. Clear examples of this are furnished by the nineteenth century anti-Catholic discourse in the Protestant-dominated countries of Europe, particularly in Germany and Switzerland, and the contentious issue of Catholic immigration into the USA in the same period. It must be admitted that the German and American Catholicism discourses of the nineteenth century took place under different socio-political conditions. And yet, what both discourse contexts had in common was, on the one hand, the situation of Catholicism as a minority denomination – much like the Western-European Islam of today – and, on the other, the suspicion directed against Catholics that they were by virtue of their religion somehow disloyal and anti-modern. The double exclusivity of the new understanding of religion, according to which the religion of free and mature citizens could find

Muhammad Abduh (1849-1905). For more details see Gunnar Hasselblatt 1969, Hossein Nasr 1961.

full expression only in Christianity and, to be more precise, in its Protestant form, led to the normative exclusion of Catholics (and, for that matter, Jews) from the project of civil society in the nineteenth century (cf. Behloul 2012).

From a general point of view it can be seen that in the nineteenth century in Europe, against a backdrop of profound social and political changes, a new area of tension opened up for the phenomenon of religion: a simultaneous crisis of religious relevance (especially of church-bound religion), on the one hand, and religious renaissance, conditioned by discourses on modernity, identity and nation state, on the other. There can be no doubt that the sustainable changes in modern society brought about by migration, urbanisation, industrialisation and, last but by no means least, the emergence of competing world views, created new kinds of legitimacy problems for religion. In the nineteenth century therefore, the need for reinforcement of a sense of superiority and a normative self-view led – in spite of the increasing loss of the relevance of religion – to a hardening of denominational lines in the area of perception of self and other.

A similar synchronicity of two opposing tendencies can also currently be observed in Western societies. While many parts of society have for some decades now been emancipating themselves increasingly from their religious (in Europe, Christian) context, the religious scene is becoming more pluralised and complex. Most recently, as the Western-European preoccupation with and problematisation of Islam and Muslims has shown, the overemphasis of religious affiliation in various fields of public discourse has gained fresh relevance from a normative point of view.

In current Western-European debates on Islam in the post-9/11 era, we are again encountering the essentialist-evolutionist understanding of religion that emerged, as we have seen, under the specific ecclesiastical-political conditions of European religious history since the sixteenth century and defined the content of the discourse on religion in the nineteenth century on both inter-faith and inter-denominational levels. The question of the social usefulness of religion corresponds to the linear development and modernisation model that is characteristic of this understanding of religion. In other words, the question is as to how a religion should be constituted if it is to be capable of inclusion into a modern society.

This understanding of religion is being deployed in various ways as a discursive weapon in current debates on Islam and can be found in the internal and external ascription strategies of the participants in the discourse.

It may be conceded that current debates on Islam in individual Western-European states such as Germany, France, the United Kingdom, Scandinavian countries, Austria and Switzerland are expressive of different political positions and reveal different thematic emphases. And yet all of them are based on the same reactive pattern: an ultimate defence of liberal and democratic societies against the fundamentalist and patriarchal customs of a religion that is perceived as alien and non-European. This defensive reflex does not in all cases take exactly the same form. It is either exclusivist, in cases where, for instance, Islam is generally held by virtue of characteristics immanent to its system to be resistant to modernisation, or it takes an inclusivist approach, where, in accordance with the modernising schema discussed above, any reference to the possible inclusion of Islam in society assumes that it must undergo modernisation in accordance with the Christian model. What both the exclusivist and inclusivist strategies of the political regulation of the Islam issue have in common, however, is the discovery of religion as a new identity marker.

NEGOTIATING ISLAM

'Real' Islam as a threat

In terms of their content, Western-European debates on Islam are dominated by specific normative terms of reference that fix Islam in either an antagonistic or a constitutive relationship to the values of modern European societies. Where earlier discourses on religion were characterised in general by their restriction to intellectual elite circles, in late modern, democratic society European/Western debates on Islam have become a subject of general public concern. Therefore follows that a vastly greater number of actors – not just the scholars or religious authorities, whether Muslim or non-Muslim – are participating in the process of negotiating what constitutes 'real' Islam.

In the context of the 2009 Swiss minaret initiative, for instance, every citizen with voting rights was called upon to decide whether or not the building of minarets should be forbidden in Switzerland. The vote on 29 November 2009 had been preceded by months of debate on socially acceptable interpretations and practices of Islam. The minaret debate in Switzerland was a particularly revealing example of the phenomenon of the link between religion and socio-politically relevant issues, based on the very question of the 'nature' of an socio-politically 'acceptable' religion, which is so characteristic of the understanding of religion in the modern era.

The question of the visible presence of religious symbols, whether buildings or garments, in the immigration countries of Western Europe not only accounts for big headlines, but it also engages courts and political institutions. The increasingly visible infrastructural and symbolic presence of Muslims in the public spaces of Western societies is perceived varyingly in each of those societies as provocative or even as a threat to the survival of the normative framework of society. Since 2006 the issue of building minarets in Switzerland gradually became a political issue. On May 1, 2007, a Swiss popular initiative/referendum, entitled "Against the building of minarets" (the "Minaret Initiative") was officially launched by the populist Schweizerische Volkspartei (SVP; Swiss People's Party) and the very small evangelical Eidgenössisch-Demokratische Union (EDU; Federal Democratic Union). In July 2008 the initiative was formally established.

The initiators of the minaret ban (the Egerkingen Committee) saw it as their mission "[to] *prohibit a religious-political symbol of power that rejects religious tolerance, so that religious freedom be guaranteed to all* (Anon., n. d.: 2; my translation; original emphasis]". These few lines indicate that the initiators were acting on the assumed opposition of Islam – understood as a socio-political order – to the normative framework of the Swiss majority society. On the initiative's own website (www.minarette.ch), posted in a compilation of texts under the title of Argumentarium gesamt (Body of arguments), a simplistic causal connection was made between Islam – which is already represented as inherently problematic – and the minaret as its most visible expression (Egerkinger Komitee 2007, 1sqq.).

In summary, the "Body of arguments" relied on four levels of reasoning (Qur'an, *sunna,* Sharia and *jihād*), which were placed in a mutually conditional relationship. By means of selectively chosen content from the Qur'an and historically contingent claims from *sunna*[7] there was demonstrated both the unalterable and normatively exclusive nature of Islam and the absolute obligation those contents impose on every Muslim regardless of his or her origin or cultural background. Islam as defined in the Argumentarium in its alleged essence inevitably corresponds with normative conflict as a result of the presence of Muslims in the West in general. This was then exemplified in a generalising perspective by means of deliberately selected individual cases, such as the bombings in London (7 July 2005) and the riots in the Parisian suburbs between the police and youths originating from the Maghreb (October/November 2005). Special emphasis was placed on the fact that the criminals of London and the rampaging youth of Paris were third generation migrants (ibid. p. 7; p. 28-30). In this way, apparently, the allegedly unconditional commitment to Islam (essentially reduced to individual, historically conditioned assertions) would gain ever more importance for its followers (regardless of location, time and generation; id., 6f.). The exclusivity and absolutism of Islam now find their most visible expression in the minaret: "The minaret is, so to speak, the spearhead of Sharia – of another law, one diametrically opposed to our own democratically created rule of law" (ibid.). Thus, so goes the conclusion, minarets "[…] are not to be rejected due to build-

---

7   E.g. on the relationship of Islam to Judaism and Christianity, and the relationship between man and woman; id., 14-24.

ing code considerations but because they are symbols of religious and political claims to power that threaten religious peace" (id., 12).

Once the causal link between minarets and Islam's 'claim to power' is accepted along with the latter's social and political consequences, one must conclude according to the minaret opponents, that not supporting a minaret ban means acting irresponsibly towards one's own country's concerns. The promoters even formulate this 'civic duty' positively: "Those who reject minarets as a sign of religious and political claims to power are stating that they respect freedom of religion and worship and also that they concede an equally high priority to the safeguarding of religious peace in Switzerland" (ibid). Accordingly, the federal government and the cantons were also reminded by the initiative committee, citing Article 72 of the Swiss Federal Constitution, of their duty to "safeguard religious freedom in the country" (ibid.).

'Real' Islam as an opportunity

A second approach to the issue of Islam to be found in the negotiation of what makes a real, i.e. socially and politically acceptable religion is the position paper of the Christlich-Demokratische Volkspartei (CVP; Christian Democratic People's Party), published under the title "Freedom of religious beliefs and integration – using the example of Swiss Muslims" (CVP 2006).

Like the initiative for the prohibition of minaret-building, the position paper also expresses a commitment to the maintenance of religious peace. In contrast to the exclusivist orientation of the 'argumentarium' of the initiative for the prohibition of minaret-building, this position paper takes an inclusivist approach. This is evinced as early as the introduction, in which it is stressed that "the actual threats to our culture [...] do not come from the values of others" but from "indifference, loss of moral compass, unbridled consumerism and materialism"(id., 3). Religious communities are accordingly called upon to "participate in a spirit of partnership" in a "public discourse" on socio-politically relevant questions (ibid.).

The approach of the position paper reflects the party's aspiration at strengthening prevention and dialogue at one and the same time. Its rationale therefore combines the generally observed potential for conflict inherent in globalisation processes and with the specific reference to the issue of the political instrumentalisation of this potential for political ends as it has already been the case in Switzerland.[8]

---

8   The 'Islamisation' of immigrants from Muslim societies corresponds to an 'Islamisation' of public debates in Switzerland on issues which in themselves are not

In contrast to the 'Body of arguments' of the anti-minaret initiative, the CVP's position paper is characterised by a clear attempt to reflect the issue of Islam's socio-political place in Switzerland in a more subtle and sophisticated way. This strategy with its inclusivist leanings finds clear expression in the position paper where the difference between Islam and fundamentalism or, as the case may be, between religion and cultural tradition is constantly stressed. This is the case, for instance, with regard to the issues seen in public debates on Islam as pertaining specifically to that faith, such as religiously motivated violence, the relative positions of men and women, child-rearing and, in general, the disposition toward modernisation in Islam.

Now, irrespective of such differentiation – or perhaps precisely because of it, – the position paper, like the 'argumentarium', albeit from an opposing position, is basically characterised by an attempt to define the essential nature of religion. The introduction to section 3, whose declared aim is the explication of the principles of Islam, stresses that "a distinction must be made between religion and cultural tradition" (id., 9). Possible value-based conflicts, such as regarding the position of women in Muslim societies, are accordingly attributed to tradition rather than identified with the religion itself. As it negotiates the spectrum of differences between 'religion' and 'tradition', the position paper is at all times at pains to stress, as the heading of 3.3 indicates, the "clear difference between Islam and Islamic fundamentalism" (id., 10).

---

directly related to religion or concretely to Muslims. In recent years in Switzerland the so-called 'Islamic question' has not only dominated initiatives and votes on different issues but has also had a significant influence on their outcomes. This was very clearly expressed, to give an example, in 2004 in the context of the referendum on two proposals for naturalisation reform. The proposals concerned facilitating naturalisation for the second generation of foreign youths descended from migrants and the automatic acquisition of Swiss citizenship at birth for the third generation. Although the referendum did not concern Islam and Muslims, the opponents of the proposed reform reduced the vote to the issue of the future presence of Muslims in Switzerland based on the growth in the number of Muslims in Switzerland over the last thirty years. In numerous newspaper advertisements, the opponents of the reform (especially the Swiss People's Party, SVP) warned that, in the event of the adoption of both naturalisation proposals, a radical shift in demographic majorities in Switzerland in favor of Muslims by 2040 would occur. Thus, according to their reasoning, Muslims would make up seventy percent of the Swiss population by the year 2040.

The analogy between the religious discourses of the nineteenth century and the current debates on Islam reveals a reproduction in the Western-European debates on Islam of the social, ecclesiastical-political and cultural motives that established themselves in the post-Reformation European understanding of religion and that the ideas of 'authentic' religion to its socio-political usefulness or, alternatively, potential for risk. The dominant issue here is not the question of the theological truth of a religion but, instead, the issue of its capacity or incapacity to modernise and, by association, the question of the normative capacity or incapacity of a religion and its followers to integrate into society. True to this linear modernisation schema, the CVP also emphasises in its position paper that ('real') Islam and secular modernity are not mutually exclusive. We encounter the same epistemic framework for the language used to discuss religion, as exemplified above, in the discourses on the Islamic world and Catholicism in the nineteenth century.

'ISLAMIC TURN' AND MUSLIM ACTORS

As has been stated and illustrated above, the new-era Protestant secular understanding of religion has been incorporated into the current debates on Islam as a discursive weapon by participants in the discourse through various lines of argumentation, all expressing a certain perception of the self and others. The 'Islamic turn' which abruptly began in the wake of 9/11 in the context of an explicit perception of immigrants from societies shaped by Islam in line with the criterion of religious affiliation, is having a transformative effect on the action and self-presentation strategies of Muslim participants in the discourse. Irrespective of their relationship to Islam and the diversity of its traditions, immigrants from societies shaped by Islam are in the context of the 'Islamic turn' being confronted with the explicit or implicit demand that they should offer 'specificly' Islamic solutions to 'specificly' Islamic problems. The majority society dominating the discourse is in the process setting the criteria for the negotiation of what a socially and politically acceptable Islam actually is, a trend which is ultimately reflected in the self-presentation strategies of Muslim actors to the public and their communication with that same public. A good example of this is the self-presentation of Muslim organisations on the internet. The following shows an example from the Swiss context.

The Vereinigung Islamischer Organisationen in Zürich (VIOZ, Association of Islamic Organisations in Zurich) conducts intercultural and inter-faith dialogue on its internet site as one of its central tasks, in the execution of which it intends, as the site explicitly says, "to make a contribution to social and religious peace in and around Zurich".[9] In its declaration of principles, adopted by the VIOZ in March 2005, the organisation states its objective of representing Islam's view of itself within Swiss society. The principles state the organisation's engagement "1. For democracy and the rule of law, 2. For peace, 3. Against violence, 4. For human rights, 5. For equality of opportunities, 6. For integration, 7. For inter-religious dialogue" followed by "8. Our faith, 9. Our religious duties, 10. Our aims". It is striking that the first seven principles, beside supplying the normative context of action of the VIOZ, are at the same time placed in a constitutive relationship with the Islamic faith. This not only places 'authentic' Islam in an affirmative relationship with the canon of values of the Swiss majority society, it is even seen to be founded in those same values (VIOZ 2005; 2).

However, along the distinguishing criterion of 'authentic' and 'abused' religion, expression is given not only to the view that 'authentic' Islam must necessarily be in a constitutive relationship with the normative framework of the majority society. It can even be said that the requirements of 'authentic' Islam give rise to a call to mission to Muslims when, in the text of the declaration of principles, they are called upon as Muslims to "actively serve the common good in their daily lives" (id., 3). Likewise basing their stance on the idea of 'authentic' Islam, the initiators of the anti-minaret initiative cited above came to the opposing view that Islam actively prevents Muslims from accepting the values of the majority of Swiss society.

DEBATING ISLAM AS A SEISMOGRAPH FOR SOCIAL CHANGES

The comparative historical contextualisation of current debates on Islam within European arguments about religion in the post-Reformation era shows that phases of social and political changes and crisis are also always articulated in discourses on religion. As was the case in the European and American Catholicism discourse of the nineteenth century, a specific situation of social changes and unease in Europe is also being articulated in the current debates on Islam. The immigration of people from societies shaped by Islam to Western Europe has since the late 1990s increasingly triggered discourses on the consequences of this immigration for the future religio-cultural, political and normative identity of Europe. As was the case in the discourses on religion of the

9   http://www.vioz.ch/4748.html (Accessed 3 July 2013).

nineteenth century, the current discourses on Islam are not purely religious. They are instead revealing themselves to be loci of intersection of different discourses of socio-political relevance.[10] When viewed from this perspective, discourses on religion also represent a kind of seismograph of social changes and transformational processes.

In the nineteenth century, in the wake of the dramatic changes to the socio-cultural and socio-political situation at the level of overall societal discourse, religion was forced into the straitjacket of a new normative relationship with the spirit of the age. At the denominational level this triggered, on the one hand, a new dynamic in the discourse on the 'essence' of religion: the question at issue was the constitutive contribution of religion to the newly emerging normative framework of a secular society in the throes of transformation. On the other hand, the requirement imposed on members of minority denominations and religions (Catholics and Jews) to declare their loyalty to this framework went hand in hand with the constitutive contribution at issue here.

Just like the Catholics of previous centuries in societies dominated by Protestants, the minority groups in Western Europe of people from societies shaped by Islam, extremely heterogeneous in their cultural and religious practices, are confronted with the challenge of being required to offer 'specifically' Islamic solutions to problems identified as pertaining 'specifically' to Islam so that they may win the prize of normative inclusion in their respective societies of residence as 'Muslims' (and not just as Turks, Albanians, Pakistanis or Arabs etc.).

The fact that religious affiliation has in the post-9/11 age become the sole category of perception and judgement of a particular minority may well appear confusing for at least two reasons. The first of these is that most of the problem areas attracting such intense interest in the context of current Western-European debates on Islam do not actually bear much relation to the cultural diversity of groups and the broad spectrum of individual ways of life followed by people of Muslim origin in the West. The second is that Western-European democracies see the separation of religion and politics as one of the unique features of their normative self-conception. The members of a society are accordingly not perceived in the first instance or even exclusively in terms of their religious affiliation or assessed for their capacity or incapacity to integrate on the basis of religious criteria. In this light, the reduction, specific to debates on Islam, of individuals and groups to a religious affiliation that has ossified into normative essentialism appears at first glance even to be anachronistic. Religion in the West

---

10 For more on the inter-relation between the anti-minaret initiative and the immigration or foreigner discourse in Switzerland cf. Behloul 2009.

may very well have become one sub-system among many and no longer be in a position either to symbolically represent or to use its authority to establish the normative nature of overall societal relations. Nevertheless, religion – or, to be more precise, its discursive appropriation by a great number of actors – appears in times of increasing uncertainty with regard to concepts like the nation or the secularisation of final boundaries that give rise to images of self and other – as a useful tool for boundary making strategies beyond ethnic origin and skin colour.

Seen in this light, especially under the conditions of dwindling cultural certainty, the increasing tendency to call into question previous ideological narratives and the pressure of social change, the medium of a detraditionalised and deculturalised 'real' religion is an appropriate indicator. It indicates one's own degree of progress and enlightenment and is at the same time suitable for use as a projection screen vis-à-vis the 'other' which, precisely for religious reasons, cannot attain to this degree of development or, in the best-case scenario, can but has yet to do so. When viewed from this perspective, religion might also in the future retain its relevance as a medium of cultural and normative self-affirmation and understanding. Against this backdrop, the empirical examples discussed in this collection under the programmatic title Debating Islam. Negotiating Europe, Religion and the Self show us the way Europe is handling religious and cultural diversity today.

REFERENCES

AlSayyad, Nezer / Castells, Manuel (eds) (2002): *Muslim Europe or Euro-Islam: Politics, culture, and citizienship in the age of globalization*, Lanham: Lexington Books.

Allievi, Stefano / Nielsen, Jørgen (eds) (2003): *Muslim networks and transnational communities in and across Europe*, Leiden/Boston: Brill.

Amiraux, Valérie (2001): *Acteurs de l'islam entre Allemagne et Turquie: Parcours militants et expériences religieuses*, Paris: L'Harmattan.

Anon. (n. d. [2007]): Das Minarett und seine Bedeutung. Pamphlet of the Egerkingen Committee. [online] Available at: http://minarette.ch/downloads/flyer-d.pdf (Accessed 27 July 2013).

Basch, Linda / Glick Schiller, Nina / Szanton Blanc, Cristina (1994): *Nations unbound: Transnational projects, postcolonial predicaments and deterritorialized nation states*, Lanhorne, PA.

Behloul, Samuel M. (2009): "Minarett-Initiative. Im Spannungsfeld zwischen Abwehr Reflex und impliziter Anerkennung neuer gesellschaftlicher Fakten", in: Tanner, Mathias et al. (eds), *Streit ums Minarett: Zusammenleben in der religiös pluralistischen Gesellschaft,* Zürich: Theologischer Verlag, pp. 103-122.

— (2010): "Religion und Religionszugehörigkeit im Spannungsfeld von normativer Exklusion und zivilgesellschaftlichem Bekenntnis. Islam und Muslime als öfffentliches Thema in der Schweiz", in: Allenbach, Birgit / Sökefeld, Martin (eds), *Muslime in der Schweiz,* Zürch: Seismo, pp. 43-65.

— (2012), "Negotiating the 'genuine' religion. Muslim diaspora communities in the context of the Western understanding of religion", in: *Journal of Muslims in Europe,* 1, pp. 7-26. [online] Available at: http://booksandjournals. brillonline.com/content/10.1163/221179512x644033 (accessed 18 July 2013).

Bielefeldt, Heiner (2003): *Muslime im säkularen Rechtsstaat: Integrationschancen durch Religionsfreiheit,* Bielefeld: Transcript.

Bielefeldt, Heiner / Heitmeyer, Wilhelm (eds) (1998): *Politisierte Religion: Ursachen und Erscheinungsformen des modernen Fundamentalismus,* Frankfurt a. M.: Suhrkamp.

Bundesministerium des Inneren (ed.) (2003): *Texte zur Inneren Sicherheit: Islamismus,* Berlin.

Césari, Jocelyne (2004): *When Islam and democracy meet: Muslims in Europe and in the United States.,* New York: Palgrave Macmillan.

CVP (2006): Religionsfreiheit und Integration – am Beispiel der Musliminnen und Muslime der Schweiz. Verabschiedet vom Parteivorstand der CVP Schweiz am 28. April 2006. [online] 28 April. Available at: http://www.cvp. ch/fileadmin/Bund_DE/downloads/positionspapiere/2006-05-Religionsfreiheit-d1.pdf (accessed 8 July 2013).

Dassetto, Felice (1996) : *La Construction de l'Islam européen: Approche socioanthropologique,* Paris: L'Harmattan.

Egerkinger Komitee (2007): Islam-Argumentarium. [online] 4 May. Available at: http://www.minarette.ch/downloads/argumentarium-komplett-d.pdf (accessed 8 July 2013).

Ehrhardt, Christiane (2005): *Religion, Bildung und Erziehung bei Schleiermacher: Eine Analyse der Beziehungen und des Widerstreites zwischen den "Reden über die Religion" und den "Monologen",* Göttingen: V&R unipress.

Feil, Ernst (1997): *Religio: Die Geschichte eines neuzeitlichen Grundbegriffs zwischen Reformation und Rationalismus (ca. 1540-1620),* Bd. 2, Göttingen: Vanenhoeck & Ruprecht.

Feindt-Riggers, Nils / Udo Steinbach (eds) (1997): *Islamische Organisationen in Deutschland: Eine aktuelle Bestandsaufnahme und Analyse,* Hamburg: Deutsches Orient-Institut.

Foucault, Michel (1973): *Archäologie des Wissens*, Frankfurt a. M.: Suhrkamp.

Gerhard, Ute / Jansen Mechtild M. (eds) (2003): *Facetten islamischer Welten: Geschlechterordnungen, Frauen- und Menschenrechte in der Diskussion*, Bielefeld: Transcript.

Gerholm, Thomas / Lithman, Georg (eds) (1988): *The New Islamic Presence in Western Europe*, London/New York: Mansell.

Göle, Nilüfer / Ammann, Ludwig (eds) (2004): *Islam in Sicht: Der Auftritt von Muslimen im öffentlichen Raum*, Bielefeld: Transcript.

Hasselblatt, Gunnar (1969): *Herkunft und Auswirkungen der Apologetik Muhammed Abduh's (1849-1905), untersucht an seiner Schrift: Islam und Christentum im Verhältnis zu Wissenschaft und Zivilisation*, Göttingen: unpublished ThD thesis.

Haussig, Hans-Michael / Scherer, Bernd (2003) (eds): *Religion – eine europäisch christliche Erfindung?*, Berlin/Wien: Philo.

Heitmeyer, Wilhelm (1997): *Verlockender Fundamentalismus: Türkische Jugendliche in Deutschland*, Frankfurt a. M.: Suhrkamp.

Hock, Klaus (2002): *Einführung in die Religionswissenschaft*, Darmstadt: Wissenschaftliche Buchgesellschaft.

Humayun, Ansari (2004): *The infidel within: Muslims in Britain since 1800*, London: Hurst.

Jonker, Gerdien (2002): *Eine Wellenlänge zu Gott: Der Verband der islamischen Kulturzentren in Europa*, Bielefeld: Transcript.

— (2003a), "Islamic knowledge through a woman's lens. Education, power and belief", in: *Social Compass*, 50, 1, pp. 35-46.

— (2003b): "Vor den Toren. Bildung, Macht und Glauben aus der Sicht religiöser muslimischer Frauen", in: Rumpf, Mechthild / Gerhard, Ute / Jansen, Mechtild M. (eds), *Facetten islamischer Welten: Geschlechterordnungen, Frauen- und Menschenrechte in der Diskussion*, Bielefeld: Transcript, pp. 219-241.

Jonker, Gerdien / Amiraux, Valérie (eds) (2006): *Politics of visibility: Young Muslims in European public spaces*, Bielefeld: Transcript.

Karakasoglu-Aydïn, Yasemin (2000): *Muslimische Religiosität und Erziehungsvorstellungen: Eine Untersuchung bei türkischen Pädagogikstudentinnen in Deutschland*, Frankfurt a. M.: Verlag für Interkulturelle Kommunikation.

Klein-Hessling, Ruth et al. (eds) (2000): *Der Neue Islam der Frauen*, Bielefeld: Transcript.

Klinkhammer, Gritt Maria (2000): *Moderne Formen islamischer Lebensführung: Eine qualitativempirische Untersuchung zur Religiosität sunnitisch geprägter Türkinnen der zweiten Generation in Deutschland*, Marburg: Diagonal-Verlag.

Leggewie, Claus (2004): *Die Türkei und Europa,* Frankfurt a. M.: Suhrkamp.

Lemmen, Thomas (2002): "Aktuelle Entwicklungen innerhalb islamischer Organisationen in Deutschland", in: Stanisavljeviç, André / Zwengel, Ralf (eds), *Religion und Gewalt: Der Islam nach dem 11. September,* Potsdam: Mostar Friedensprojekt e.V., pp. 129-156.

Leveau, Rémy et al.(2001), *L'islam en France et en Allemagne,* Paris: La Documentation Française.

Lewis, Philip (1994): *Islamic Britain: Religion, politics and identity among British Muslims: Bradford in the 1990s,* London: I. B. Tauris.

Mandaville, Peter, (1999): "Territory and translocality: Discrepant idioms of political identity", in: *Millenium,* 28, 3, pp. 653-674.

— (2001): *Transnational Muslim politics: Reimagining the umma,* London: Routledge.

Matthes, Joachim (2005 [1989]): "Reflexionen auf den Begriff 'Religion'", in: Matthes, Joachim, *Das Eigene und das Fremde: Gesammelte Aufsätze zu Gesellschaft, Kultur und Religion,* edited by Rüdiger Schloz, Würzburg: Ergon Verlag, pp. 195-208.

Meier, Andreas (1994): *Der politische Auftrag des Islam: Programme und Kritik zwischen Fundamentalismus und Reformen: Originalstimmen aus der islamischen Welt,* Wuppertal: Hammer.

Nasr, Hossein (1961): "Religion and secularism, their meaning and manifestation in Islamic history, in: *The Islamic Quarterly,* 6:4, pp. 118-126.

Nökel, Sigrid (2002): *Die Töchter der Gastarbeiter und der Islam: Zur Soziologie alltagsweltlicher Anerkennungspolitiken: Eine Fallstudie,* Bielefeld: Transcript.

Ramadan, Tariq (1999): *To be an European Muslim: A study of Islamic sources in the European context,* Leicester: The Islamic Foundation.

Roy, Olivier (1998) : "Naissance d'un islam européen", in: *Esprit,* 239, pp. 101 135.

— (1999) : *Vers un islam européen,* Paris: Esprit.

— (2002) : *L'Islam mondialisé,* Paris: Seuil.

Salih, Ruba (2003): *Gender in transnationalism: Home, longing and belonging among Moroccan migrant women,* London/New York: Routledge.

Schieder, Rolf (2001): "Zivilreligion als Diskurs", in: id. (ed.), *Religionspolitik und Zivilreligion,* Baden-Baden: Nomos (Interdisziplinäre Studien zu Recht und Staat 20), pp. 8-23.

Schiffauer, Werner (2000): *Die Gottesmänner,* Frankfurt a. M.: Suhrkamp.

Sen, Amartya (2006): "Welcher Multikulturalismus?", in: *Lettre International,* 72, pp. 104sqq.

Spielhaus, Riem (2006): Religion und Identität. Vom deutschen Versuch, 'Ausländer' zu 'Muslimen' zu machen. [online] March 2006. Available at: <http://www.islam.de/5337.php> (Accessed 8 July 2013).

Tenbruck, Friedrich H. (1993): "Die Religion im Maelstrom der Reflexion", in: Bergmann, Jörg / Hahn, Alois / Luckmann, Thomas (eds), *Religion und Kultur*, Opladen: Westdeutscher Verlag, pp. 31-67 (special issue no. 33 der *Kölner Zeitschrift für Soziologie und Sozialpsychologie*).

Tezcan, Levent (2007): "Kultur, Guvernementalität der Religion und der Integrationsdiskurs", in: Wohlrab-Sahr, Monika / Tezcan, Levent (eds), *Konfliktfeld Islam in Europa*, Baden-Baden: Nomos, pp. 51-74.

Tibi, Bassam (2002): *Islamische Zuwanderung*, Stuttgart: Deutsche Verlags-Anstalt.

Tiesler, Nina C. (2006): *Muslime in Europa: Religion und Identitätspolitiken unter veränderten gesellschaftlichen Verhältnissen*, Berlin: Lit.

Tietze, Nikola (2001): *Islamische Identitäten*, Hamburg: Hamburger Edition.

Trautner, Bernhard (2000): Eine 'Ver-Zivilgesellschaftung' des Islam in Deutschland? Türkische Muslime und islamische Organisationen als soziale Träger des transstaatlichen Raumes Deutschland-Türkei [online] Available at: http://www-user.uni-bremen.de/~bjtraut/transstaat.pdf (accessed 14 August 2013), printed as: "Türkische Muslime, islamische Organisationen und religiöse Institutionen als soziale Träger des transstaatlichen Raumes Deutschland-Türkei", in: Faist, Thomas (ed.): *Dazwischen und doch verortet: Transstaatliche Räume in und zwischen Deutschland und der Türkei*, Bielefeld: Transcript, pp. 57-86.

Ulfkotte, Udo (2003): *Der Krieg in unseren Städten: Wie radikale Islamisten Deutschland unterwandern*, Frankfurt a. M.: Eichborn.

VIOZ (2005). Grundsatzerklärung der VIOZ. [online] 27 March. Available at: http://www.vioz.ch/2005/20050327_VIOZ_Grundsatzerklaerung.pdf (accessed 3 July 2013).

von Krusenstjern, Benigna / Medick, Hans (eds) (1999): *Zwischen Alltag und Katastrophe: Der Dreißigjährige Krieg aus der Nähe*, Göttingen: Vandenhoeck & Ruprecht (Veröffentlichungen des Max-Planck-Instituts für Geschichte 148).

Wagner, Falk (1986): *Was ist Religion? Studien zu ihrem Begriff und Thema in Geschichte und Gegenwart*, Gütersloh: Gütersloher Verlagshaus.

Part I

Rules and roles

Rules and roles

SAMUEL M. BEHLOUL

Thematic approaches to the Islam question and normative enquiries about the Muslims in the context of Western European debates on Islam are characterised by a totalising tendency, as has been outlined in the introduction. This corresponds to the totality of the systematic binarism which, in the context of these debates, is constructed between concepts such as 'secularism and Islam,' 'democracy and Islam,' 'Islam and laicism,' and 'Islam and modernity'. Undoubtedly the most central feature of this hegemonic discourse on Islam is the implicitly or explicitly stated normative-juridical advantage of the West on the one hand and the expectations towards Islam to catch up on the other, with the aim of a possible 'integration' of Muslims into Western-European societies. The contributions in the first thematic section, "Rules and roles", exemplify not only the diversity and ambivalence of socio-political and normative-juridical conditions under which the Western-European debates on Islam take place, but also express the variety of reactions and positions of the actors involved in these debates within the specified conditions.

The wide range of analytical approaches to the "Rules and roles" of the Islam debates is introduced by David Tyrer's contribution. Tyrer attends to the phenomenon of Islamophobia that has been a contested topic for years and analytically places it in the context of the racialised setting which, viewed from a historical perspective, has been characteristic of the Western treatment of ethnic minorities inside and outside of Europe. He critically examines the now widespread and popular practice of using anti-Semitism as a metaphor for Islamophobia. This metaphorisation, as the author convincingly argues, is problematic not only in formal terms, but it also blinds out the respective singularity of both Islamophobia and anti-Semitism. In contrast to earlier forms of racism that were based on highlighting certain physical traits, Tyrer interprets

Islamophobia as a post-racial racism. It is no longer linked to a particular physiognomy or skin colour, but interprets the visual appearance of a religion and its members (minaret, *burqa,* hijab, beard) as a threat. Muslims are thus turned into more than a mere religious minority. They are constructed as a collective which, unable to practice their religion in a 'modern' way, instead turn it into a political programme, thereby threatening the normative-juridical framework of Western societies.

In the academic discourse on Islam and Muslims in Western Europe it is frequently pointed out that, with regard to the presence of Muslims in Western Europe, the number of Muslims in the West poses a novelty for Muslims and a new challenge for the West itself. At no time in the history of the Islamic religion have such large numbers of Muslims lived in secular, predominantly non-Muslim societies as they do today. This is a situation that neither the Qur'an nor the Sharia had foreseen.

Using the example of France, Frank Peter critically discusses this understanding which is widespread in debates on Islam in academic research circles as well as in intra-Muslim discourses, namely that Muslims in Europe are living in, for them, a special context (laicism, secularism, republicanism, ideological pluralism, etc.). On the basis of an analysis of the Union des Organisations Islamiques de France, the author highlights the structural ambiguity of the system of French laicism and republicanism, usually perceived as stable and coherent. In his view, the challenge of integrating Muslims in the French context is not found in the question regarding the compatibility of Sharia and laicism. The real difficulty lies rather in a totalising understanding of this context as a clearly and precisely contoured legal framework for the organisation of the life of Muslims in France. For Peter, the fundamental question as to what extent the intense academic and political discourses about the integration of Muslims into specific normative contexts of Western Europe are even relevant for the social reality of Muslims arises against this background.

Gender dimension plays a central and dominant role in the context of the intensely and controversially discussed question regarding the integration of Muslims into the juridical-normative context of Western-European societies. Independently from the respective regulation of the relationship between religion and state in the individual Western European countries, the question of the status of women in Islam has become a universal discourse topic in the context of debates on Islam. The veiled Muslim woman has not only become a symbol of the generally alleged oppression of women in Islam, but it is also perceived as a visible sign of the alleged Islamisation of Europe. Using selected European countries as examples, Amélie Barras discusses the necessity of considering the 'gendered dimension' of European debates on the Muslim 'other' and asks about the implications of such a perspective. The contextualisation of the gendered dimension within a historical continuity of the importance of women in the context of community and nation building processes in both European and Islamic societies proves to be a particularly insightful and revealing point in Barras' analysis. By means of this diachronic-comparative and cross-cultural view of women as the addressees of multifaceted policy measures, the author showcases the complexity of current debates on Islam with regard to their 'gendered dimension.'

While the topic of religion had seemed to be gradually losing its relevance in the socio-political discourses in Europe from the second half of the last century, since the mid-1990s it has ultimately reemerged to prominence in public debates due to the increasingly visible religious and cultural pluralism of Western societies.

As noted in the introduction to this volume, the essential characteristic of this 'religious turn' is that religion here is used as a discursive tool for explaining behaviors at both the individual and the collective level. It is striking that crime and anti-social behavior in general among Muslim adolescents and adults is often explained along the criterion of their religious affiliation. This is exemplified using statistics on the number of Muslim prisoners in European prisons. Based on her research conducted on Muslim inmates of Swiss prisons, Mallory Schneuwly Purdie analyses the construction of the Muslim 'Other' in the context of the prison. She places particular importance on the question regarding the influence of the totalising public discourse on Islam on the – at first sight – closed and non-public world of a prison as, in the sense of Goffman, a 'total' institution with regard to the totality of control and standardisation of the life of its inmates. Accordingly, her analysis centers on the question of whether the topos of the Muslim 'Other' so characteristic of the public debates on Islam also dominates how Muslim prisoners are perceived by both non-Muslim inmates and the prison staff. This analysis clearly demonstrates the penetration of the public image of Islam into the strictly regulated life of prison inmates. The normatively negative image of the Muslim 'other' in public debates on Islam influences not only the mutual perception of prison inmates, but also affects the significance Muslim inmates strategically attach to their religion.

The contribution by Kathy Sian constitutes the conclusion of the first thematic part of the volume. Sian takes a perspective on the Western-European Islam debates that does not center on the relationship between the Muslim minority and non-Muslim majority, but on the mutual perception between two ethno-religious minorities (Pakistani Muslim and Sikhs in the UK) in the context of current Western-European debates on Islam. The selection of these two communities is very revealing. Sian's analysis of the reasons for Islamophobia among Sikhs shows very clearly how old identity-constructing narratives are reactivated under the socio-political conditions of life in the multicultural diaspora on the one hand and in the context of the problematisation of Islam on the other. Considering the fact that British Sikhs define their identity along a sharp and radical demarcation from the Muslim community, the author asks whether this Islamophobic trait of identity definition among the Sikhs represents an expression of general Islamophobia or can be characterised as a 'Sikh-specific' Islamophobia. By comparing it to the historical example of Islamophobia in Russia that began in the seventeenth century, during which Russia increasingly distanced itself from the Islamic part of its cultural and religious history and stressed its exclusive affiliation with the European cultural space, Sian works out the historical roots of the Sikhs' Islamophobia. The interesting result of this comparative analysis is that the causes of postcolonial Islamophobic identity constructions in the Sikh diaspora are not found in British multicultural policy. Rather, they are related to the complex history of the relationship between Muslims and Sikhs on the Indian subcontinent. As such, they are rearticulated in the diasporic context.

Racial grammar and the green menace

DAVID LLEWELYN TYRER

INTRODUCTION

The strange thing about colours is that even as they confront us, they are not always so easy to recognise. Take Welsh, for example. The word *glas* normally means blue, but in certain contexts it can also mean grey, and can even signify green in place of the more usual *gwyrdd*. Umberto Eco reminds us of Gladstone's suggestion that Greeks could not tell blue from yellow, and of other claims that speakers of Latin had no means of drawing a distinction between blue and green (Eco 1985: 158; see also Deutscher 2010). One way of approaching this is to suggest that the signifiers we use are not unproblematic mirrors of nature, but that they provide a set of conventions which enable us to organise external phenomena. As such, we do not just know how to name a given colour, but we also know how to treat it, how to visualise it, how to work with it, and how to understand its relationship to other colours... That such conventions become naturalised to the point at which, within a given cultural formation, we may become unaware of them, does not mean that they are absent, but simply indicates the success of a given ontology. Where a difficulty might arise is the point at which some unforeseen occurrence interrupts these discursive operations to demonstrate their contingency and limits. Much of the time it seems unlikely that this will happen; for example, the prospect of a Welsh uprising against the naming of green grass as *glaswellt* (blue grass) (or even to challenge its Anglocentric naming as 'green') appears remote. But once we accept that the language of colours is not innate to the objects it describes, then we also have to accept the possibility that terms for colours can also be deployed in other ways. In other words, what happens when a sedimented label such as 'green' is suddenly applied to institute a new set of social relations around the naming of something that has not hitherto been named as such?

Such acts of radical institution can be understood as being fundamentally political (cf. Laclau/Mouffe 1985), and this metaphor helpfully illustrates the problem of race in so far as the grammar of colours that has been so central to modern racial discourse can often appear natural and unproblematic, even though the shoehorning of a great range of human diversity into categories such as 'black', 'red', 'white', 'brown', or 'yellow' is the product of a discursive operation which was centrally political. But what happens when the contingency of this radical institution is highlighted by the presence of subjects who appear to interrupt this now routinised ascription? Do we abandon the grammar of colours in the wake of this challenge to its naturalcy? Do we simply apply a previous naming? Or do we coin a new colour with which to conjure them forth? Such questions illustrate the challenges posed by Muslims. I find them a helpful way of opening a reflection on the question of Muslim raciality, for they force open the question of who Muslims are when conceived in the context of racialised societies. This can shed light on the epistemic conditions surrounding Islamophobia and historicise its emergence. So – who are Muslims?

RACE AND INVISIBILITY: ARE MUSLIMS WHITE?

The modern grammar of colours does not simply provide a label of convenience with which to deal with others, but it conjures them forth as subjects rendered hypervisible and particular by their racial marking. In this it is helpful to note that, just as whiteness has historically been figured within the western canon as a void; as an invisible absence of colour (see for example Batchelor 2000), whiteness as raciality comes to signify an invisible horizon. This makes the values marked as white universalisable as the basis for a hegemonic politics of racialised governmentality – what Hesse (1997) has termed "white govern-mentality". In this, to be white is to be racially neutral, in contrast to the status that comes with being racially marked as 'black', 'brown', 'red', or 'yellow'. In the case of Muslims, a problem is introduced because Muslim identity politics has involved a large scale move through which subjects previously made legible through the ascription of a range of racial or ethnic markings have supplanted these with a seemingly self-selected identity that does not appear to have its origins within the hegemonic discourse of race (Tyrer/Sayyid 2012). This identity politics appears, then, to unsettle and reveal the contingency of racial naming, and in the context of societies organised around such namings, it has the effect of placing the ontology of the social into crisis (ibid.). One reflection of this tension introduced into modern racial politics by this identity move is the continued dispute over the most fruitful way of understanding Islamophobia. The hegemonic way of responding to Islamophobia has involved rejecting its racist nature through a retreat into phenotypal logic and the argument that because Muslims are not a phenotypal racial group, they cannot be considered to experience racism. This logic has been critiqued elsewhere (cf. Patel/Tyrer 2011; Tyrer 2011), and needs no further elaboration here, save to note that it entails a fundamental misunderstanding of racism, which does not simply target already raced subjects, but racialises them.

Another reflection of this tension can be witnessed in the emphasis upon visibility in discussions about Muslims. For example, Deltombe (2007: 269) notes the construction of Muslims as an "invisible enemy" that disturbs us all the more because of its ability to take advantage of globalisation, as well as the wider trope of the double life of the apparently integrated terrorist Other. But this difficulty is not only a question of the problem of recognising the threat, because it is underpinned by a more fundamental problem of recognising Muslims (whether threatening or not) that is thrown up by their constitution as inadequately racialised subjects. The founding problem of Muslim visibility is that raciality is a principle coordinate for complete subjecthood in racialised social settings, but also that it dictates our understanding of the materiality of bodies. We can say that race is symbolic; it provides us with a way of organising the innumerable forms that life takes into bodies, species and populations in ways that suppress certain modalities of bodily difference and emphasise others as a means of organising them under a limiting rubric that is historically contingent. Race therefore comes to structure fields of visibility, which in turn helps naturalise racial logics (Alcoff 2006: 103). Subjects constituted as inadequately racial therefore run the risk of being invisible.

In this problematic, 'Muslim' offers an interesting counterpoint to 'white'. Like all other racialised identities, it has no positive ontic racial status. Yet like white, Muslim appears racially invisible. We can thus ask: are Muslims white? The answer, of course, is that the contemporary discourse which problematises Muslim minorities categorises them in opposition to whiteness. But the seeming invisibility of Muslims underscores the challenges posed by the Muslim question. A subject position that appears racially invisible opens out the possibility for a universalisable racial politics capable of transcending the opportunities traditionally presented by the particularisation of the racially and ethnically marked through colour marking. Muslimness is thus problematic for hegemonic racial politics, for it is another universalisable politics that goes racially unnamed, and in this it has the capacity to undo the ontological possibilities of whiteness by retaining its own ability to undo racial namings, to unwork racialised visibilities, to uncolour colour...

Yet at the same time, Muslims are not figured within this discourse as explicitly 'black'. Race is not static, so in different contexts it operates to name and render visible different groups in different ways. One way of looking at this in relation to the question of Islamophobia is by noting that race has never simply been a question of difference, but of how a seemingly inconceivable array of differences can be organised to create a viable basis on which populations can be administered. As such the question is not simply one of how raciality can be read from the surfaces of racialised subjects, but rather how it is inscribed, and phenotypal characteristics such as skin pigmentation and bodily features have been central to the marking and problematisation of the bodies of the racialised (Jackson 2006).

Although the hollowness of racism's scientific claims is well established, the cultural racisms which emerge in the wake of this debunking do not displace modern ideas of phenotypal race but supplement them, so that the idea of a hardwired difference between groups is elaborated through notions of binding, monolithic culture – strange habits, smelly food, alien clothing. Culture does not displace biology because as Hall (2000) notes, it is constructed as though it is biologised. Race thinking thus reduces the agency of the racialised and denudes them of proper being; as recipients of inherited traits, whether phenotypal or cultural, they are also passive bearers of them. In Fanonian terms, racialised selfhood can be read as a libidinal lack in being, so that the logics of modern colonial racism construct the raced other as a black skin, or mask, with a void within. Even the hyperinflation of racialised difference – for example, the figure of the hypermasculine Black male – has the effect of transforming the other into a giant void. In contrast to this, Islamophobia is marked by the perverse racialisation of Muslims as inadequately racialised (Tyrer 2011). This apparently incomplete raciality interruputs and unsettles such bodily inscriptions because Muslim corporeality seems more troubling as a consequence of their apparently incomplete raciality. The putatively inadequate raciality of Muslims implies a certain incorporeality (Tyrer/Sayyid 2012), so that in contrast to the representation of the colonial raced subject as a an amplified or inflated black surface containing a void within, the proposition is reversed in Islamophobic discourse, as Muslims are represented through the logics of a phenotypal absence/void without, and a hyperinflated difference within.

Are Muslims 'the new Jews'?

If Muslims are not figured in terms of traditional colour-marked racial identities, then is it possible that those who would oppose the recognition of Islamophobia as racism are in fact correct, and that they can be better understood as purely religious (and, by extension, Islamophobia as simply religious, rather than racist)? One way of approaching this might be through the introduction of another precedent in which a seemingly religious minority has experienced racism. This seems sensible insofar as different expressions of structural racism appear to share certain family resemblances. However, this also runs the risk of dehistoricising racisms, one result of which is that it becomes difficult to recognise the 'whatness' of Islamophobia. This difficulty is perhaps best illustrated by the tendency to note ostensible similarities between anti-Muslim racism and anti-Semitism. Among Muslim public figures the comparison has been drawn in the face of wider reticence to recognise Islamophobia. In its most basic form the parallel therefore acts as a rhetorical device intended to draw on historical precedent in order to draw attention to the possibility of Islamophobia existing and worsening (cf. Sardar 2005). The increasing purchase of such comparisons has been illustrated by their rehearsal among British Muslim public figures and even by Shahid Malik, a British Labour Member of Parliament (Doughty 2008). A piece by liberal columnist and commentator Yasmin Alibhai-Brown illustrates its emotive appeals to history:

> Since the organised massacres of Muslim males in Bosnia, we 16 million European Muslims live with a menacing whirr at the back of the head, ghostly fears that the fires next time will burn with our bodies. We are today's despised "other", blamed for all the ills of the world which is still largely controlled by Christians. We have to atone ceaselessly for the Taliban and al-Qa'ida and home grown men of violence. We are expected – just as Jews were in the thirties – to bend our heads and take the slurs, looks of hatred, to accept the burden of shame. By remembering the Holocaust with past victims, we remind ourselves of what could happen in the future [...]. When the boots kick down the doors and they come for us Muslims or our children, perhaps good Jews will not speak up and we will rue the day we callously refused to pray for their lost generations.
>
> (Alibhai-Brown 2006)

Such comparisons also find their expression through attempts to describe Muslims as the 'new Jews', either explicitly (Hellyer 2009: 112; Ma'oz 2010: 24), or implicitly through the narration of anti-Semitism as the template for Islamophobia. This draws attention to the problematic historicity of racism. One way of approaching this problematic parallel is to note that the difference between Islamophobia and anti-Semitism lies partly in the expansion of the former in a context marked by Islamist terrorism (cf. Cesarani 2008), although this line of argument is undermined both by the fact that Islamophobia emerged prior to the

growth of this security threat, and the fact that Islamophobia does not discrimi-
nate between the terrorist minority and wider Muslim populations, since any
Muslim can be fair game. In a further complication, Tibi (2008: 212) notes that
Muslim descriptions of themselves as 'new Jews' reflects a hypocrisy in the face
of Muslim silences over Islamist anti-Semitism, although this also fails to account for Muslim objections to anti-Semitism or the ways in which Islamophobia
does not simply target anti-Semites, but all Muslims.

A more fundamental difficulty with the description of Muslims as 'the new
Jews' can be found in the fundamental question at stake in its expression – for
what happened to the 'old Jews' (whoever they may be)? This line of argument
leaves us to assume that the 'old Jews' were those who experienced anti-
Semitism. Here a rupture is introduced, reliant upon the problematic assumption
that the 'new Jew' does not experience anti-Semitism. Of course, since Muslims
are held to be the 'new Jews', the assumption is that s/he actually experiences Islamophobia. At the heart of the description of Muslims as the new Jews is therefore a double violence. On the one hand, 'old Jews' are written out as subjects,
inscribed only as the objects of anti-Semitism rather than through, say, Jewish
remembrance of the humanity and agency of survivors, while 'new Jews' are
written out as subjects and displaced by the insertion of 'Muslim' as a shorthand
for abjection. On the other hand, Muslims are also written out as subjects, both
because they are written through this anti-Semitic logic, and because the description of them as 'new Jews' is simultaneously Islamophobic in as much as it reflects the inability to engage analytically with the Muslim presence without reading it through other historical metaphors.

The irony at the heart of descriptions of Muslims as the 'new Jews' is thus
that if on the one hand this superficial comparison dehistoricises anti-Semitism
and Islamophobia, on the other hand its deployment also points to a peculiar en-
tanglement of the two forms. This articulation of anti-Semitism with Islamophobia does not occur as a result of some primordial similarity between Muslims
and Jews or Islamophobia and anti-Semitism, but rather as an expression of a
post-racial logic that underpins exceptionalising conceptions of racism as having
been eradicated following horrors such as the Holocaust (cf. Hesse 2000), and
therefore as not being a contemporary concern. This argument exceptionalises
anti-Semitism as something experienced up to the mid-twentieth century by 'old
Jews', but not by the post-Holocaust 'new Jews'. At the same time, what we
speak of as Islamophobia is not contemporary in any substantive sense since it is
simply a residue of older forms of anti-Semitism. As a consequence, the very
conception of contemporary expressions of racism is hollowed out – neither contemporary anti-Semitism nor Islamophobia can be said to exist in any meaningful sense.

Despite such difficulties, twentieth-century anti-Semitism persists as a metaphor for explaining contemporary expressions of racism and Islamophobia. To illustrate this it is helpful to consider Žižek's conceptualisation of anti-Semitism as a template for subsequent racisms:

> In classical racism, anti-Semitism functions as an exception: in Nazi discourse, for example, the attitude towards Jews (who are the *unheimlich* double of the Germans themselves and, as such, have to be annihilated) differs radically from the attitude towards other 'inferior' nations, in whose case the aim is not their annihilation but only their subordination – they have to assume their 'proper place' in the hierarchy of nations. Jews are the disturbing element that incites other inferior nations to insubordination, so that it is only through the annihilation of Jews that other nations will accept their subordinate place. Here also, however, a specific inversion is taking place today: we are dealing with *universalised anti-Semitism* – that is, every ethnic 'otherness' is conceived of as an *unheimliches* double that threatens our enjoyment; in short, 'normal', non-exceptional, non-anti-Semitic racism is no longer possible. The universalisation of the Holocaust metaphor (apropos of every ethnic cleansing it is asserted that it is comparable to the Nazi Holocaust), excessive as it may appear, is therefore founded in the inherent logic of the thing itself, in the universalisation of anti-Semitism.
>
> (Žižek 2005: 79; original emphasis)

Of course, one could substitute anti-Semitism with Islamophobia in this account, and replace Jew with Muslim, and also replace the historical references with a contemporary framing and it might be possible to read from this a condition of banalised contemporary anti-Muslim racism. Indeed, Žižek has elsewhere noted that "today it is the Muslims, not the Jews, who are perceived as a threat and an obstacle to globalization" (Žižek 2006: 257). This again confronts us with the problem of historicity: anti-Semitism as a modern form, and Islamophobia as a postmodern emergence. A superficial means of reconciling this difficulty might be to posit Islamophobia as a dislocated modern anti-Semitism; this, however, still leaves us with the difficulty that by establishing anti-Semitism as the template for another form, we either end up losing the specificity of anti-Semitism or that of Islamophobia.

When modernity has presented us with so many variations on a centrally racist theme – genocide in the Americas, lynchings, millions killed in the Bengal famine thanks in part to colonial policy, extinction of the Tasmanian Aborigines... – it does not seem unreasonable to ask why Žižek selects anti-Semitism as the defining form of racism. To Žižek, what really differentiates anti-Semitism is the representation of Jewish people as "the disturbing element that incites other

inferior nations to insubordination" (ibid.), though in this there is ample historical precedent from other forms of racism throughout the modern history of Europe to suggest that this feature is not established by anti-Semitism as a template
for racism, but rather that it is a logic of racism that establishes the template for
anti-Semitism. Žižek's analysis is also predicated on the recognition that anti-
Semitism takes the neighbour as its object, and in this there is clearly a parallel
between Europe's pogroms and the Holocaust, say, and ethnic cleansing or anti-
Muslim hate crimes in the West. However, this also ignores a common misunderstanding of racism, namely that it works not through distance but through the
possibility of proximity. Even the deployment of the racial frontier through colonisation and empire was an attempt to regulate boundaries and to institute preferred modes of distance and permitted forms of proximity. In this, fear or hatred
for neighbours is not a template established by anti-Semitism, but rather one
provided by racism across a range of expressions including anti-Semitism. In the
case of Islamophobia, the problem of proximity is perhaps best reflected in the
claims of the Islamophobic right that Europe is becoming Islamised. But this in
itself needs to be historicised as part of a postcolonial problem attendant upon
the proximity of those traditionally held at a distance. In a postcolonial world,
the racial frontier is deployed domestically (Hesse 1997). This is a postcolonial
problem and the attempt to reduce contemporary racisms to an anti-Semitic logic
elides this historicity.

   This problem is important, for the presence in the West of peoples traditionally held at a distance is not simply a manifestation of decolonisation and globalisation, but it also has symbolic dimensions. The apparent porosity of borders in
the contemporary world is not simply an institutional problem but it is also
bound up with a crisis in the symbolic boundaries which moored traditional notions of 'us'/'them', 'neighbour'/'other', 'westerner'/'foreigner'. In a Foucauldian sense, race facilitates the operation of biopower precisely because it enables
the attempt to close a population around the exclusion of threatening others
(Foucault 2004). The presence within the population of previously marked and
excluded elements creates an ontological difficulty met through the domestic deployment of the racial frontier and associated technologies of the raced body
predicated upon 'integration' and 'assimilation' (cf. Sayyid 2004) to make
'them' more like 'us'. In the case of Jews, this was possible because modern anti-Semitism was contingent upon the hegemony of modernity's racial grammar,
so that in spite of its earlier roots in religious hatred, modern anti-Semitism
could construct Jews in distinctly racial terms. In contrast to this, Islamophobia
has emerged in the wake of postcolonial challenges to the hold of a modern racial grammar, and in the wake of a wider unraveling of the notion of phenotypal
race itself.

These difficulties are exacerbated by the ways in which Muslim identity politics interrupts traditional modes of racial inscription (Tyrer/Sayyid 2012), through the assertion of a self-selected mode of subjectivity which privileges religious affiliation over ascribed race. Here the obvious distinction between the two forms is thus that whereas anti-Semitism constructed Jewish people as a bounded race, Islamophobia constructs Muslims as lacking proper raciality. Whereas stereotypes about Jewish physiognomy abounded, contemporary Islamophobia figures Muslims as a lack and an absence; a central incorporeality. This returns us to our original question: are Muslims the 'new Jews'? In this we can perhaps reprise a question asked by Sander Gilman which in many ways resonates through the questions I seek to ask in this chapter. In *The Jew's Body*, Gilman (1991) asks "are Jews white?" A clue lies in the proper title of the chapter; "The Jewish Nose: Are Jews White? Or, the History of the Nose Job". To Gilman the question is, when framed "in a slightly less polemical manner, how has the question of racial identity shaped Jewish identity in the Diaspora?" (id., 149).

We can introduce an immediate distinction between the terms on which modern anti-Semitism racialises Jews through bodily inscriptions and those on which Muslims are racialised: Gilman notes that in contrast to German Aryans, Jews were constructed as racially impure, as bearers of blackness; a race with distinctive physiognomy, and as hybridised (id., 174). These descriptions are all contingent upon a particular mode of raciality which contrasts with the contemporary post-racial construction of Muslims: if anti-Semitism fetishised Jewish physiognomy, Islamophobia constructs Muslim incorporeality, focusing instead on the vessels without that contain the difference within *(burqa...)*; if anti-Semitism constructed Jews as mongrels contingent upon the mixing of phenotypal races, the Islamophobia of far right discourse constructs Muslims not as mongrelising, but as dissolving phenotypal race, not hybridising blackness but as undoing it... For these reasons, as well as the moral problem that to describe Muslims as new Jews involves occupying an anti-Semitic position that renders Jews invisible (or only visible through the lens of anti-Semitism itself) and banalises the Holocaust, it is unhelpful to view Muslims as the 'new Jews', and equally unhelpful to inscribe a simple relationship between anti-Semitism and Islamophobia.

The superficial attraction of the comparison between anti-Semitism and Islamophobia lies as much in the apparent parallel between discriminations faced by two apparently religious groups as in superficial comparisons between the forms taken by racism. But this ignores the ways in which anti-Semitism did not simply take the form of religious discrimination, but racialised Jews. It also ignores Islamophobia's perverse racialisation of Muslims as incompletely racial.

Perhaps the greatest paradox of descriptions of Muslims as the 'new Jews' is this: on the one hand they reflect a routinised and banalised anti-Semitism that renders Jews invisible; on the other hand they can be read in the context of a banalised Islamophobia that underwrites Muslim invisibility and a failure to grasp the racial politics at stake in Islamophobia through its problematic naming and conceptualisation. These distinctions point to a particular problem in our understanding of the relationship between Islamophobia and anti-Semitism, which also holds for wider expressions of modernist racism. In doing so it also helps historicise the emergence and form of Islamophobia as an emblematic form of post-racial racism. Still, if Muslims are this difficult to place in racial terms, perhaps we ought to revisit Gilman once more, this time to ask: Are Muslims Muslim?

ARE MUSLIMS MUSLIM? OR: THE GREENING OF MUSLIMS

So, if Muslims are not the 'new Jews', and if they are not 'black' or 'white', but in fact their identity politics has the effect of placing into question the hold of hegemonic notions of race, what are they? The most obvious way of refuting a reading of Islamophobia as racism would involve noting that the signifier Muslim has not been embedded in historical racial formations. Even under the most heavily institutionalised and regulated systems of racial segregation such as Jim Crow and Apartheid, the incredible array of racial classifications formally and informally instituted in western plutocracies lacked specific reference to Muslims. But such a claim immediately runs into two difficulties. First, it fails to acknowledge that this recognition merely draws attention to the reasons for the emergence of Islamophobia as a provisional means of solving the problem presented by the emergence of an increasingly subscribed to subject position which seems to elude conventional racial classification. If the signifier Muslim has not previously been part of the *lingua franca* of institutionalised race, this does not demonstrate that Islamophobia is not a form of racism, but rather, why it has been needed in order to reconcile this jarring presence with the apparatus of race. Second, following this, it also fails to recognise the ways in which Muslim is being deployed within contemporary racial discourse.

The most obvious example of this can be found in the hardening of debates about Muslim integration and assimilation over recent years. The greening of Muslims is not simply an attempt to institute a naming integrable within the hegemonic field of conventional racial politics, but also an attempt to constitute them as subjects in particular ways. As such it is also consistent with the wider formal attempts to insert 'Muslim' into formal institutional arrangements traditionally concerned with regulating the bodies of the ethnically and racially marked. Such attempts give lie to the superficial observation that formal racial politics has not historically engaged the Muslim question, and have most notably been witnessed in the marshalling of immigration control and the mobilisation of assimilation and integration measures to regulate Muslim difference. The hardening of integration and assimilation rhetoric has centred around the problematisation of difference and the notion of an excess of alterity (cf. Grillo 2007) seen as threatening to the closure of the nation (Tyrer/Sayyid 2012). In the case of Muslims, the excess of difference is not simply a question of excessive Muslimness, but equally one of the excess of unregulated difference. Racial ascription works through the naming of difference as a way of rendering it intelligible and governable, domesticating and taming difference just as it names it and marks it as threatening. In the case of Muslims, the identity politics through which racial ascription is interrupted is read as an excess of difference not least because it appears to have eluded these regulatory practices.

This also demonstrates that the signifier 'Muslim' has no single essential meaning, but its meanings are contingent. Here it is worth noting Yalçin-Heckmann:

> Migrants are perceived by the majority non-Muslim society as Muslims in certain contexts and instances. For example, Muslims are identified primarily as such when they are visible in public (with headscarves, beards, mosques, butchers etc). They are perceived as Muslims more at certain moments of political and historical development than others.   (Yalçin-Heckmann 1998: 168)

If the signifier Muslim has no single, authoritative meaning, then it is more helpful to note that its meanings are fixed through the ways in which it is articulated with other discursive elements. It is thus superficial to assume that the signifier Muslim only ever takes on a purely religious meaning. In racialised social settings it would be unconvincing to suggest that while, say, residential settlement, criminal justice, education, or media production might be racialised, religion somehow exists in a pure form unfettered by the workings of race. As the emphasis on dealing with the Muslim question through techniques such as immigration control and integration demonstrate, the signifier Muslim is frequently articulated with a wider range of metaphors and techniques for managing racially marked populations.

In this context it is helpful to note a familial similarity between Islamophobia and anti-Semitism, even if the conditions of their emergence and the forms of racialisation differ. Gilman (2006: 67) observes that, like the Jewish Diaspora before them, as Muslims have integrated into western societies, national differences among Muslims are being elided so that "Muslims seem to be everywhere and are becoming 'all alike'". One way of looking at this is to note that it introduces the possibility of a split reading of integration. Integration does not merely efface difference through acculturation and incorporation, but it also has the effect of elaborating and amplifying difference, partly because it involves the boundary work through which a notion of 'we' is shored up, a move contingent upon the construction of a 'they'. The signifier Muslim is thus deployed both as a marker for a subject position that seems to unsettle traditional modes of racial ascription by cutting across boundaries and, therefore, as a provisional reclassification.

A helpful metaphor for this process is the greening of Muslims. Indeed, a striking feature of contemporary Islamophobia is the coining of 'green menace' (Abu Sway 2006: 17; Cole 2011: 127; Haddad 2004: 99; Husain/Rosenbaum 2004: 171) as a metaphor for the threat Muslims are often said to pose to the west. 'Black menace' (hooks 2004: 241); 'yellow peril' (Clegg 1994; Ono/Pham 2009); 'green menace'. The greening of Muslims resonates with a wider way of managing racially and ethnically marked populations by visualising and organising their assumed difference under the terms of the colour grammar. Green menace is therefore a provisional naming which points to racial and post/colonial dis/continuities. The greening of Muslims also points to a particular mode of visualising Muslim difference that is common to Islamophobia.

Here the emphasis upon visibility as played out in tensions over signs of Muslim presence and proximity, notably through campaigns over religious spaces and clothing. For example, although Switzerland's Muslim population had hitherto been thought of as well integrated (Seib/Janbek 2011: 112), in a 2009 referendum over 50 per cent voted in favour of a move to ban the erection of new minarets on mosques. The importance of this case lies in the way in which it explicitly conflated the notion of excessive Muslim difference with politicality so central to Islamophobia, for the ban was based on the notion that minarets are political rather than religious symbols (Doe 2011: 167). In this the opposition between the naturalcy of race and the politicality of religion was curiously displaced by a distinction between religion proper and symbols of Islam as political rather than religious, which was necessary to ensure that the ban could not be construed as an attack against religion. This belies the unproblematised notion that Islam and Muslims are treated simply 'religious' categories. At the same time, the minaret issue was framed by the problem of visibility, and it played out in a wider process of securitisation of immigration. For example, while campaigning for re-election in 2007 the Swiss People's Party (SVP) infamously used a campaigning poster that depicted a black sheep being kicked off the Swiss flag by a white sheep, so that only white sheep remained on the flag (Paterson 2009). During the campaign to ban minarets two years later, the iconic campaigning poster depicted a threatening, darkened figure of a *niqāb*-clad woman standing like a threatening black ghost in front of a Swiss national flag that was penetrated by a number of stylised minarets resembling missiles (see illustration on p. 300). In this the political threat posed by minarets was conflated with an existential threat to the survival of the nation, and the juxtaposition of a recognisable, if heavily essentialised, Muslim figure served to link the notion of threat posed by Islam with the presence of Muslim populations. The Swiss minaret ban was significant for it represented an attempt to squeeze out of public space and visibility this jarring, alien presence. The deployment of the *niqāb*, incorrectly termed *'burqa'*, was equally telling in so far as it rendered visible the incorporeal raced subject of Islamophobia through the device of full veil.

In fact, full veil is worn by a tiny number of women in Europe; figures suggested by Moors (2011: 157) indicate that it is worn by about 0.003 per cent of the population of the Netherlands, while in the wake of moves towards banning the full veil in Italy Izzedin Elzir, head of the Union of Islamic Communities in Italy, remarked that he had only seen ten women wearing full veil throughout his two decades living in the country (Faris 2011). It is reported that only thirty women in Belgium wear *burqa* or *niqāb* (BBC News 2010) in spite of which the Vlaams Belang has made the *'burqa'* an important feature of its anti-immigration and anti-Muslim politics. Unsurprisingly, given the position of vestments as a site for the inscription of Muslim lack in excess, Donnell notes advice issued by the Muslim Women's League in America that warned:

> In the current climate of escalated religiously-motivated violence since the terrible attacks of September 11, Muslim women in hijab (headscarf) are particularly vulnerable because, for many years, western media and literature have consistently portrayed covered women as the predominant image of Islam. As a result, Muslim women in headscarves and other Muslim-style clothing are often the first and easiest targets of hate violence. (Donnell 2003: 123)

Although this refers largely to the hijab rather than the *burqa* or *niqāb*, it is nevertheless a helpful illustration because of the ways in which hijab and any type of full veil tend to be conflated and mistaken for one another in popular discussions about Muslims. The warning issued by the Muslim Women's League also illustrates the ways in which women and their clothing have been given a particular prominence in the politics of Islamophobia, so that the contests over *'burqa'* cannot simply be read as mobilisations over women's rights as they are appropriated in wider anti-immigrant and anti-Muslim racial politics, and become a means of visualising the incorporeal subject of Islamophobia. In April 2010 a law was passed in Belgium to ban the wearing of full veil in public, while a similar ban was introduced in France a year later. Moves towards similar legislation have occurred in the Netherlands, and in February 2011 Hesse became the first state in Germany to introduce a full veil ban for public sector workers. In Italy a draft law to ban the full veil was approved by a parliamentary commission in August 2011.

In February 2012 Vlaams Belang politician Filip Dewinter initiated a 'women against Islamisation' campaign accompanied by a poster in which an attractive young woman (his daughter) posed in bikini and *niqāb*, emblazoned – the poster, not the model – with the slogans: "Vrijheid of islam? Durven kiezen!" (Freedom or Islam? Dare to choose!). In an interview in *De Standaard* under the headline "Dochter van Filip Dewinter is een boerkababe" (Filip Dewinter's daughter is a burkababe), An-Sofie Dewinter explained her decision to participate in the campaign on the grounds that "women are fighting against the Islamisation of society. We must dare to choose between freedom and Islam" (Anon. 2012). This provided a justification of the campaign as simply a legitimate engagement over women's rights pursued through criticism of Islam in the abstract. But there was more to the campaign than simply a critique of religion, and it also involved Filip Dewinter taking to the streets with two *niqāb*-clad women bearing posters emblazoned with the slogan "Stop immigratie" (Stop immigration). In her interview with *De Standaard*, An-Sofie also claimed that white women are subjected to pressure over their attire by ethnic minority youth, and noted the prospect that they may eventually have to wear a headscarf, shifting the emphasis away from a critique of religion to the threat of Others. In this the ability of Muslims to engage in a seemingly universalisable politics by stepping outside the confines of racial ascription gives way to a fear of the green menace, and of the Islamisation of the west which has been a popular trope among the far right (cf. Fekete 2012).

Thus the figure of a young white Flemish woman in a bikini and *niqāb* simultaneously reintroduces an eroticised orientalist aesthetic underpinned by an investment in the corporeality of whiteness and ascribed raciality while rendering invisible and absent the troubling figure of the Muslim who threatens to interrupt these processes of racialised desire formation. Such anxieties produce racial visibility as a remainder that guarantees the integrity of the racial signifier, which is to point out that the scandal of the inadequate raciality of Muslims is reworked through this discourse as a means of keeping open the possibility of the properly racially marked subject. We thus see emerging from the problematisation of race by Muslims a range of strategies to shore up racial ascription and introducing means of naturalising race and rendering Muslims visible, and particular, while simultaneously fixing them as inadequately racial, incorporeal, and invisible.

Hellyer (2009: 113) notes that Muslims in Europe are integrated through their incorporation into a range of other categories, though not as a religious community *per se*. But this only tells us part of the story, because it is contingent upon a stable notion of Muslim underwritten by a stable understanding of identities which can in turn inform and be interpolated through stable practices of recognition. But what identities are not stable and fixed, but contested, and recognition is an act of power? Muslims are inscribed in the public sphere as non-racial (even though they are racialised), and this non-raciality is contingent on the absence of ontic racial purity, and the implication of ontic religious purity. As such, a particular status is inscribed, one which positions Muslims in very particular ways in relation to other groups, institutions of civil society, and the state: any attempt to politicise over the racism that they face is immediately displaced (because they are seen as not biologically racial), yet at the same time they are constructed as religious subjects (as minorities within states that have varying degrees of secularity), while their presence is regulated through their incorporation into categories that are not in themselves strictly religious. Muslims are therefore an awkward presence, and this move does two things. First, it has the effect of closing the political possibilities that are attendant upon those who describe themselves as Muslims or are ascribed by others an identity as Muslim. That is to say, it positions them as an improperly racial group, foreclosing certain kinds of politicisation over racism. Second, despite their perverse racialisation as incompletely racial, a further indeterminacy is introduced by dint of the fact that Muslims are not constructed as a purely religious group, but rather as a group that has perverted and politicised religion, blurring further categorical boundaries.

CONCLUSION

Another way of approaching the contingent and political nature of colour can be found in *White Chess Set*, a piece of political artwork by Yoko Ono produced in 1966 at the heart of the Cold War. This posed a fundamental question concerning power and antagonism, and involved dissolving the difference between antagonists, thus causing the game itself to collapse.[1] In doing so it illustrated the ways in which the contingency of boundary drawings and ascriptions can be radically highlighted. This helps to illustrate the epistemic conditions which underwrite the emergence of Islamophobia. Racial ascription facilitates the exercise of biopower both by introducing a boundary around the population and delineating

---

1   I would like to thank Salman Sayyid for drawing my attention to the chess metaphor.

its others (Foucault 2004). The presence of Muslims unsettles attempts to regulate bodies based on the deployment of a racial frontier. In encounters structured around the logic of colour, the implications of subverting one of the colours in play are not felt simply by those who make this move, but they have wider implications including for the dominant (non-)colour. The attempt to find new ways to integrate the new subject position within the rules of the game that has been challenged is an attempt to reassert the rules of the game, and in this sense Islamophobia cannot be viewed as occurring outside the play of racial politics, but as central to its extension.

This does not, however, mean that Islamophobia can be read as a simple throwback to older forms of racism. The epistemic conditions in which it has emerged are marked by three developments. First, there has been a wider unraveling of the hold of ideas about phenotypal racial difference. Second, this process has been radicalised by a Muslim identity politics which steps outside traditional modes of racial ascription. Third, in the context of the debunking of race, the emergence of a post-racial logic has been an attempt to hegemonise a response to this. Racism in post-race times emerges in the horizon opened by the formal critique of race and takes the form of racisms which can be expressed without the need for a stable ontic racial referent: racisms without race (Bonilla-Silva 2010). Islamophobia emerges in this context as an emblematic mode of post-racial racism which seeks provisional answers to the questions posed by the contingency of racial grammar. As such, if on one hand Muslims appear to make good the promise of post-racial society, on the other hand they illustrate its hollowness. Islamophobia thus emerges under specific epistemic and political conditions. At stake in the struggles over Islamophobia is therefore a complex politics of race. Contemporary Islamophobia can in this sense be best understood as a series of attempts to recentre a hegemonic racial grammar as a project concerned with restabilising a racial order which is unsettled by this display of agency by racialised subjects over the terms of their subjectification. Within the terms of Islamophobic discourse, much is therefore made of the inadequate raciality of Muslims; as seemingly inadequately racialised subjects and as void spaces residing behind the beards and veils which so act as obstacles to their racial knowability, Muslims are frequently represented as incompletely realised subjects within the terms of a hegemonic discourse which conflates subjecthood with racial classification in the case of minorities. This exploration points towards the ways in which Islamophobia constructs the Muslim other in terms of degrees of deviance from whiteness, as an incomplete subject, and draw attention to the ways in which this discourse also naturally works on the one hand to disavow its own racisms through the argument that these (apparently) incompletely raced subjects can be legitimately denied protection against anti-Muslim racisms while on the other hand working to more thoroughly race Muslims.

At the same time, grasping the wider work performed by Islamophobia is contingent upon first historicising its emergence and then recognising its complex interaction with, and differentiation from, wider forms of racism. It is only possible to deny the racist nature of Islamophobia if we assume racism has a once-and-for-all form from which anti-Muslim racisms deviate. As history shows, this is not the case: in differing contexts, different forms of racism emerge as emblematic – Jim Crow, anti-Semitism, moral panics about Black mugging. In this sense the attempt to reframe Islamophobia through dehistoricised comparisons with an exceptionalised and sanitised notion of anti-Semitism not only misses the point of what is at stake in post-racial racism, but reflects post-racial logics itself. Despite its obvious family resemblance to other racisms, its difference from earlier forms of racism historicise Islamophobia as a distinctly contemporary phenomenon and establish it as the emblematic racism for these supposedly post-racial, neoliberal times.

REFERENCES

Abu Sway, Mustafa (2006): "Islamophobia: Meaning, manifestations, causes", in: Schenker, Hillel / Abu-Zayyad, Ziad (eds), *Islamophobia and anti-Semitism*, Princeton: Markus Wiener, pp. 13-24.

Alcoff, Linda M. (2006): *Visible identities: Race, gender, and the self*, Oxford: Oxford University Press.

Alibhai-Brown, Yasmin (2006): "Why Muslims must remember the Holocaust", in: *The Independent*, [online] 23 January. Available at: http://www.independent.co.uk/opinion/commentators/yasmin-alibhai-brown/yasmin-alibhaibrown-why-muslims-must-remember-the-holocaust-524187.html?printService=print (accessed 12 March 2013).

Anon. (2012): "Dochter van Filip Dewinter is een boerkababe", in: *De Standaard*, 4 February. [online] Available at: http://www.standaard.be/cnt/dmf20120203_148 (accessed 12 March 2013).

Batchelor, David (2000): *Chromophobia*, London: Reaktion Books.

BBC News (2010): Belgian lawmakers pass burka ban. [online] 30 April. Available at: http://news.bbc.co.uk/1/hi/8652861.stm (accessed 12 March 2013).

Bonilla-Silva, Eduardo (2010): *Racism without racists: color-blind racism and the persistence of racial inequality in the United States*, Lanham: Rowman & Littlefield.

Cesarani, David (2008): "Muslims the 'new Jews'? Not by a long way", in: *The Jewish Chronicle*, [online] 17 January. Available at: http://www.thejc.com/comment/comment/muslims-new-jews%E2%80%99-not-a-long-way (accessed 12 March 2013).

Clegg, Jenny (1994): *Fu Manchu and the yellow peril: the making of a racist myth*, Stoke-on-Trent: Trentham Books.

Cole, Juan (2011): "Foreign policy rhetoric: The Bush years and after", in: Esposito, John L. / Kalin, Ibrahim (eds), *Islamophobia: The challenge of pluralism in the 21st century*, Oxford: Oxford University Press, pp. 127-142.

Deltombe, Thomas (2007): *L'Islam Imaginaire: La construction médiatique de l'Islamophobie en France, 1975-2005*, Paris: La Découverte.

Deutscher, Guy (2010): *Through the language glass: why the world looks different in other languages*, London: William Heineman.

Doe, Norman (2011): *Law and religion in Europe: A comparative introduction*, Oxford: Oxford University Press.

Donnell, Alison (2003): "Visibility, violence and voice? Attitudes to veiling post-11 September", in: Bailey, David A. / Tawadros, Gilane (eds), *Veil: Veiling, representation and contemporary art*, London: Institute of Visual Arts, pp. 120-135.

Doughty, Steve (2008): "'We Muslims are the new Jews' says MP who has been victim of a hit-and-run and a firebomb attack", in: *Daily Mail*. [online] 4 July. Available at: http://www.dailymail.co.uk/news/article-1031697/We-Muslims-new-Jews-says-MP-victim-hit-run-firebomb-attack.html (accessed 12 March 2013).

Eco, Umberto (1985): "How culture conditions the colours we see", in: Blonsky, Marshall (ed.), *On signs,* Baltimore: The John Hopkins University Press, pp. 157-175.

Faris, Stephan (2011): "In the burqa ban, Italy's left and right find something to agree on", in: *Time,* [online] 4 August. Available at: http://www.time.com/time/world/article/0,8599,2086879,00.html (accessed 12 March 2013).

Fekete, Liz (2012): "The Muslim conspiracy theory and the Oslo massacre", in: *Race and Class*, 53:3, pp. 30-47.

Foucault, Michel (2004): *Society must be defended*, London: Penguin.

Gilman, Sander (1991): *The Jew's body*, London: Routledge.

— (2006): "Can the experience of diaspora Judaism serve as a model for Islam in today's multicultural Europe?", in: Schenker, Hillel / Abu-Zayyad, Zaid (eds), *Islamophobia and anti-Semitism,* Princeton: Markus Wiener, pp. 59-74.

Grillo, Ralph (2007): "An excess of alterity? Debating difference in a multicultural society", in: *Ethnic and Racial Studies,* 30:6, pp. 979-998.

Haddad, Yvonne (2004): "The shaping of a moderate North American Islam: Between 'mufti' Bush and 'ayatollah' Ashcroft'", in: Geaves, Ron / Gabriel, Theodore / Haddad, Yvonne / Smith, Jane I. (eds), *Islam and the West post 9/11*, Aldershot: Ashgate, pp. 97-114.

Hall, Stuart (2000): "Conclusion: The multi-cultural question", in: Hesse, Barnor (ed.), *Un/settled multiculturalisms: Diasporas, entanglements, 'transruptions'*, London: Zed Books, pp. 209-241.

Hellyer, H. A. (2009): *Muslims of Europe: The 'other' Europeans*, Edinburgh: Edinburgh University Press.

Hesse, Barnor (1997): "White governmentality: Urbanism, nationalism, racism", in: Westwood, Sallie / Williams, John M. (eds), *Imagining cities: Scripts, signs, memory*, London: Routledge, pp. 85-102.

— (2000): "Introduction: Un/Settled multiculturalisms", in: id. (ed.), *Un/Settled Multiculturalisms: Diasporas, entanglements, 'transruptions'*, London: Zed Books, pp. 1-30.

Hooks, Bell (2004): "Reflections on Race and Sex", in: Torres, Rodolfo D. / Darder, Antonia / Baltodano, Marta (eds), *The critical pedagogy reader*, New York: RoutledgeFalmer, pp. 238-245.

Husain, Zohair / Rosenbaum, David M. (2004): "Perceiving Islam: The causes and consequences of Islamophobia in the Western media", in: Saha, Santosh C. (ed.), *Religious fundamentalism in the contemporary world: critical social and political issues*, Oxford: Lexington Books, pp. 171-206.

Jackson, Ronald L. / Hopson, Mark C. (2006): *Scripting the black masculine body: identity, discourse, and racial politics in popular media*, Albany: State University of New York Press.

Laclau, Ernesto / Mouffe, Chantal (1985): *Hegemony and socialist strategy: Towards a radical democratic politics*, London: Verso.

Ma'oz, Moshe (2010): "Introduction", in: id. (ed.), *Muslim attitudes to Jews and Israel: the ambivalences of rejection, antagonism, tolerance and cooperation*, Eastbourne: Sussex Academic Press, pp. 1-28.

Moors, Annelies (2011): "Fear of small numbers? Debating face-veiling", in: Sayyid, Salman and Vakil, AbdoolKarim (eds), *Thinking through Islamophobia: Global perspectives*, London: Hurst, pp. 157-164.

Ono, Kent A. / Pham, Vincent N. (2009): *Asian Americans and the media*, Cambridge: Polity Press.

Patel, Tina G. / Tyrer, David (2011): *Race, crime and resistance*, London: Sage.

Paterson, Tony (2009): Swiss move to ban minarets as 'symbols of Islamic power', in: *The Independent* [online] 14 August. Available at: http://www.independent.co.uk/news/world/europe/swiss-move-to-ban-minarets-as-symbols-of-islamic-power-1771879.html (accessed 12 March 2013).

Sardar, Ziauddin (2005): The next Holocaust, in: *New Statesman* [online], 5 Dezember. Available at: http://www.newstatesman.com/node/152128 (accessed 24 March 2013).

Sayyid, Salman (2004): "Slippery people: The immigrant imaginary and the grammar of colours", in: Law, Ian / Phillips, Debora / Turney, Laura (eds), *Institutional racism in higher education*, Stoke-on-Trent: Trentham Books, pp. 149-160.

Seib, Philip / Janbek, Dana M. (2011): *Global terrorism and new media: The post Al-Qaeda generation*, Abingdon: Routledge.

Tibi, Bassam (2008): *Political Islam, world politics and Europe: Democratic peace and Euro-Islam versus global jihad*, Abingdon: Routledge.

Tyrer, David (2011): "Flooding the Embankments: Race, biopolitics and sovereignty", in: Sayyid, Salman / Vakil, AbdoolKarim (eds), *Thinking through Islamophobia: Global perspectives*, London: Hurst, pp. 93-110.

Tyrer, David / Sayyid, Salman (2012): "Governing ghosts: Race, incorporeality and difference in post-political times", in: *Current Sociology*, 60:3, pp. 353-367.

Yalçin-Heckmann, Lale (1998): "Growing up as a Muslim in Germany: religious socialization among Turkish migrant families", in: Vertovec, Steven / Rogers, Alisdair (eds), *Muslim European youth: reproducing ethnicity, religion, culture*, Aldershot: Ashgate, pp. 167-192.

Žižek, Slavoj (2005): *The Metastases of Enjoyment: On Women and Causality*, London: Verso.

— (2006): *The Parallax View*, Cambridge MA: MIT Press.

The ambiguity of law and Muslim debates about the contextualisation of Islam in France

FRANK PETER

INTRODUCTION

The present article examines a presupposition widely found in studies about Islam in Europe, namely the notion that Muslims, whether reference is made to European Muslims or Muslims in a European state, live in a particular 'context'. References to the context in which Muslims live are frequent and feature prominently both in academic studies and in Muslim discourses. Various terms are used to describe this context, often in combination: secular, republican, liberal, pluralist, or racist. In scholarly literature, opinions differ as to the appropriate terms to use, but the terms 'secularism' *(laïcité)* and 'Republic' and a reference to the French legal order are indispensable elements of the analysis. The definition of these terms is controversial, but most studies today share an assumption that a relatively stable (but not unchanging) context exists, and that this context can be totalised – that is, it can be represented as a system which is both relatively coherent and stable. The possibility that the intellectual act of identifying or defining this context might itself be problematic for believers is rarely taken into account. In other words, little thought has been given to the possibility – not so implausible *a priori*, one would say – of describing such a context as difficult to characterise in a totalising manner and in terms of stable and relatively coherent properties.

In this article, I intend to demonstrate the usefulness of this second analytical option. Based on a case study of the Union des Organisations Islamiques de France (henceforward, UOIF or simply the Union), the following remarks are a plea for rethinking the way in which studies refer to the French context. The critical dimension of my argument concerns a particular way of characterising this context, namely in relation to French law. Reference to French law is inevitable in definitions of *laïcité* and of the Republican constitution of France, and is central to the act of imagining this context as relatively stable and coherent. I will analyse three authors and their conceptualisation of the law as one aspect of the French context. The analysis will focus on a central feature of the French context as it emerges in the discursive milieu of the UOIF, namely its structural ambiguity. Structural ambiguity here refers to the fact that the category of law and the language of law are, for Muslims, both necessary and insufficient when it comes to making sense of their life in France and legitimating and defending living in France in the first place. The structural ambiguity of the law designates a condition whereby it is indispensable for Muslims to rely upon legal categories in discourses about living in France, despite the fact that the legal order often appears to be ineffective in ensuring the equality of Muslims and, secondly, despite the fact that it is difficult to unequivocally determine the force of the law to shape the conditions of life for Muslims in France.

Such an approach opens up a different perspective on the multi-level debate – 'Islam and *laïcité*', 'Islam in the Republic', 'Islam and modernity' – about the oft-contested feasibility of living in France as a Muslim. As I will show here, to the extent that the French context is problematic for Muslims in the UOIF, it is not simply because this context is secular and/or republican and thus presents certain constraints on what Muslims can do as religious subjects. What renders it problematic, rather, is the very difficulty of totalising this context intellectually and, more particularly, of determining unequivocally the status of the French legal order in shaping the lived reality of French Muslims. The debate within the Union is not only about 'how to live Islam in the French context', or 'how to reconcile Islam and Sharia with citizenship'. While these questions are indeed often debated by members of the Union, this analysis will show that they imply, in different ways, a clarification of the status of French law as one factor among others which determines the conditions of Muslim life in France. In other words, in order for Muslims to contextualise Islam in France, it is necessary not only to adapt Islam to the French context in such a way that the integrity of the Islamic tradition is respected, but also to first make this context intelligible in a coherent way. Studies on Sharia in Europe, which often depend on the notion of a variously defined context in which Islamic jurisprudence is currently exercised, could be enriched through the perspective I want to suggest here.

The alleged challenge for French Muslims does not consist merely in bringing together Islamic normativity and French law. For this reason, it is problematic to focus the public debate on Islam in France solely on whether or not a secular and/or republican order allows sufficient space for Islamic practices. This question, which is of course important, takes the secular order of France as a given, whereas my analysis will show that this order has to be defined by Muslim intellectuals. More importantly, it will show that in the act of defining the French context, Muslims are led beyond the law to situate it in a broader context of power and to connect the acceptance of French law to different modes of subjectivity and ways of relating the self to law. Second, this chapter sets out to suggest a new way of thinking about the challenges often mentioned in connection with the new Muslim presence in Europe. I would like to suggest here that one of these challenges is apparent in the specific difficulty of re-narrating the Islamic tradition as coherent in a context marked by structural ambiguity. This ambiguity constitutes a recurrent threat for the coherence of the Islamic tradition in France. Asad has underlined that the Islamic tradition strives for coherence as much as any other discourse – a coherence which is hard to achieve for internal as well as external reasons (Asad 1986). In the French context, this tradition is weakened not only by the 'constraints' on Muslim practices usually associated with the secular and/or republican context in which the Muslim minority lives, but in part also by the inadequacy of these terms to decipher this context.

THE STRUCTURAL AMBIGUITY OF THE LAW

When I say that the French context ought to be characterised by its structural ambiguity, this refers to the French context as a normative space, i.e. as a social space where humans, in society or alone, consider what *is* in relation to what *should be*. France, as a normative space, is thus a social space that contains a certain number of public criteria – that may be contested and changing – to evaluate what is (or will be) in the light of what should be. This normativity need not be confined to the law – the constitution, constitutional principles and the legal order – and to the legal and political institutions founded upon it. There are of course many practices and individual behaviours that are not directly governed by law, but that can nevertheless be subject to various normative assessments. In fact, the authority of some fundamental principles of law – such as the principle of civic equality – depends on an existing ethic that establishes these very principles as norms that rule without imposing constraints on the free behaviour of individuals. If this principle of civic equality is often contradicted and regularly held in contempt through the way individuals behave, the authority of the judicial norm might dissolve in the widening gap between norms and social practices. The continuous debate on political and legal measures that ought to be taken to counter discrimination is one indicator of the structural relationship between law and ethics which is widely acknowledged in France. We will come back to this point, but for the moment let us note that the space of normativity extends *a priori* to the entirety of social practices assessed through public norms. It is also clear that state institutions play a central part in structuring and defining normativity, since they are frequently considered and presented as the only ones able to decide in an authoritative, binding manner what has the 'force of law' in France.

Now, if France, as a normative context, needs to be characterised by a structural ambiguity, this means in the first place that this normative context is ambivalent: its elements (the laws and norms and the state institutions founded upon them) assume different meanings for Muslims depending on the situation and produce diverse effects that cannot easily be integrated into a single coherent normative system which is identified with France. The problem, from the point of view of Muslims in the Union, consists in identifying, in particular contexts, the processes that bestow the 'force of law' on some laws and norms and not others. Hence, from the viewpoint of these Muslims, law as a central element in a comprehensive normative system meant to produce an inseparable connection between what should be and what is, again and again risks failing in its task so that it becomes hard to imagine the law as a unified and effective entity – effective in the sense of a force shaping social life in a particular manner. A distinction between law as a set of provisions and law as it is enforced becomes plausible in daily life.

More specifically, it is difficult on the one hand (for Muslims associated with the Union) to define French society or its State institutions as simply discriminatory and unegalitarian. It is impossible for them to consider French law and the republican principles the State claims to represent as mere ideologies that obscure the actual functioning of the State. On the other hand, it is difficult not to see the numerous cases in which these laws are ineffective or, to put it another way, simply do not have the 'force of law'. This structural ambiguity refers to the fact that sometimes law produces the expected effects and sometimes its effects are to various degrees unexpected and contrary to the entitlements people believe they have. It means that, admittedly, at times law seems to function as a simple ideology that obscures the actual mechanisms of a society in which Muslims experience discrimination, whilst this very law and its guarantee of rights is nevertheless essential, from a Muslim point of view, for anyone who wants legitimate, long-term residency and citizenship for Muslims in France. This structural ambiguity makes it essential to work on educating the public, which task, in this case, is assumed by the UOIF, with the aim of resolving the ambivalence and of rendering the French normative universe coherent and intelligible from a Muslim point of view.

My claim that the normative context of France requires a specific effort of rationalisation begs the question: Who, exactly, considers it important for the normative context in France to be coherent? Is this coherence a necessity not only for intellectuals, but also for 'ordinary believers', i.e. for those to whom the texts and sermons analysed below are addressed? It is important to mention this point as it raises the question of status for the discourses I examine in this essay: are they scholarly (or pseudo-scholarly) discourses, as is sometimes claimed, whose basic theme – the citizenship of Muslims – and approach bear no relevance to the life of most Muslims? The analysis that follows will show that this point of view is not sustainable. To put it in simpler terms, one thing the analysis of these discourses will show is that all of them, albeit in different ways, refer sooner or later to some notion of 'social reality' and reflect upon the limits of the law in explaining it. While I cannot dwell here on the reception of these discourses among French Muslims, it is clear that in crucial respects they are constructed with direct reference to the experience of Muslims living in France. The tensions and contradictions to be observed in the discourses analysed here demonstrate the weakness of their autonomy. If we discover tensions in the discourses, it is because the authors are obliged to confront the problems caused by the structural ambiguity of the law and are not always able to resolve them.

THE CASE OF THE UNION OF ISLAMIC ORGANISATIONS OF FRANCE

Building on the above, let me start my analysis of one of the largest Muslim federations in the country: the Union of the Islamic Organisations of France (for this organisation see Amghar 2008; Maréchal 2008; Bowen 2009; Peter 2011). This case seems worth considering, as it is an important French organisation that claims a practice fully compatible with the republican framework. It is active in associations of mosques, in education and in public debate. Despite its limited number of publications (books, videos, audios) and its restricted web presence, the UOIF has enjoyed a prominent visibility in the mass media since the late 1980s. One of the principal goals of the UOIF is to 'normalise' the Muslim presence in France (for French Muslims, Muslims from other countries and non-Muslim citizens). A question is often raised about its capacity and will to present a discourse bridging its vision of the Sharia and the republican framework. This question is based on the hypothesis that the commitment to Sharia – in its 'Islamist' understanding – is highly problematic if one wishes to endorse the Republic as a political form. And yet this criticism is in many regards flawed, and one of its faults is linked precisely to conceptualisation of the French context. In fact, what emerges from analysing the discourses of the UOIF is legitimating the citizenship of Muslims in the French Republic within the Islamic tradition is a perfectly feasible task, but that there is not one single legitimation for citizenship, since the understanding of the republican context can vary considerably.

While it is tempting, on the basis of writings, sermons and addresses by members of the Union, to ascribe to the organisation its own discourse about the citizenship of Muslims in the French Republic, this presupposes a regularity and boundedness which is made virtually impossible by legal ambiguity. In the light of this, it would be more accurate to speak of discursive strands which are central to the ways in which members of the Union present Islamic positions on citizenship (and the term 'discourse' should be understood here in this sense). These discursive elements combine differently and with varying emphasis in statements by the Union's members arguing for the compatibility of Islam and French citizenship. As a full analysis of these discursive strands would go beyond the scope of this essay, I would like to briefly sum up some of the elements. These discursive strands function in interrelation with the social imaginary of the Republic, three main aspects of which are treated from an Islamic perspective: sovereignty; civic virtues in relation to the common good (or public interest); and the public sphere.

The sovereignty of the State is addressed in this context as the recognition by Muslims of the authority of the legal order. In the first place, members of the Union seek to authorise French law from the perspective of Sharia, the obvious implication being that respecting French law becomes an obligation for Muslims. French law is recognised and its legitimacy is affirmed in a double manner. On the one hand, the duty to respect laws is constantly reaffirmed as a Qur'anic imperative. On the other, law is recognised and its respect is asserted as necessary only in so far as it is also presented as an adequate frame for the practice of Islam. Civic virtues are discussed in relation to the education of the citizen as a moral being who needs to cultivate certain civico-Islamic virtues necessary in order to motivate a strive towards the common good and public interest and avert the threat of a fragmented nation. The notions of public interest and common good are essential to the social imaginary of citizenship: it is not enough to respect law, citizens also have to aspire to contributing to the common good. Hence, there is recognition of a motivational sphere of citizenship that goes beyond respect of the law, and recognition of such civic virtues as solidarity and loyalty. In this respect, a central task of the Union consists in convincing Muslims that the creation of strong bonds with non-Muslims is not only licit, but in fact required by Islam. This also implies conceiving a religious pluralism – including the so-called situation of minority of Muslims – as something of positive value and part of the divine creation. Finally, the third overlapping dimension concerns the public sphere as a space of deliberation. The public space is considered in relation to the discursive abilities and the volitional disposition conducive and necessary to encounters and debates. These reflections, as above, do not refer to scholarly theories on public space, but rather to the simple idea that communication in public requires vocabulary to be adapted to the recipient of the message. This idea is also very present in the discourse of the Union. The need is regularly affirmed to develop a discourse that reaches beyond the specificity of Islam and creates a universal message.

These discursive strands are very important in statements by the Union's members. However, they are often edited and modified, and this is what I would like to elucidate now. The argument that I would like to make here is, briefly, that the discourse of the Union displays a tension. As the description above has shown, the Union has developed central elements of what in many respects is a clear-cut discourse about citizenship, a discourse which strives to give a total representation of France as a coherent and stable space. The law, in the sense of a code of rights and duties which are brought to bear upon actions exercised by an individual, is central to this discourse, which seeks to demonstrate both the compatibility of Sharia and citizenship and the possibility of practising Islam in France in the spaces of liberty defined by law. The heavy reliance on categories of the law is noteworthy, but not surprising. Any debate about citizenship is always (even if not exclusively, as we will see) about the individual's submission to state power. The primary means for representing the latter – as well as unifying and legitimating it – is the law (Foucault 2001: 1001-1020). It should be added that the notion of law which underlies this approach to citizenship, i.e. rules applied to human acts, has a certain affinity with the tradition of *fiqh* in which the normative evaluation of human acts is crucial, in both its legal and ethical dimensions (Johansen 1999). This essentially normative, i.e. rule-based, argument extends into a more teleological one by incorporating a number of values, notably the common good and public interest, and the virtues which favour their attainment. To some degree, this dimension of the Union's discourse responds to the emphasis on national unity and the moral education of citizens so characteristic of Republican thought.

However, this is not the whole story. The wish to represent the French context in a total manner in discussions about the conditions of life for Muslims in France faces an obstacle, and the discursive elements which I have described above are edited and modified in response to the structural ambiguity of the law. The three following case studies illustrate three ways in which legal ambiguity is dealt with in discourses on citizenship.[1]

---

1   All translations from the Arabic or French texts are mine unless otherwise indicated.

MODALITY NUMBER 1: AHMED JABALLAH

The first case study concerns Doctor Ahmed Jaballah, director of the Institut Européen des Sciences Humaines (IESH) in Saint-Denis in France (see www.ieshdeparis.fr). Teacher, imam and writer, Jaballah was president of the UOIF from 2011 till 2013. I will analyse Jaballah's position based on an article by him published in Arabic in 2008 by the European Council for Fatwa and Research (Jaballah 2008). In this article, Jaballah addresses the question of citizenship on two levels.[2] In the first part, he examines in detail why French Muslims can and must accept as licit the democratic form of the State and positive law. In this case the argumentation remains on a quite general level. For instance, the author does not mention any specific country. He starts by building an Islamic genealogy of citizenship with reference to the constitution of Medina – the first State, in his view, built on the recognition of religious pluralism. In this connection, he draws attention to the fact that the contractual model underlying this constitution represents the common denominator of all civilisations in the world. Then, he shows that the principle of "God's sovereignty" *(hākimīyat Allāh)* does not contradict recognition of the State's authority. In the second part, a number of more specific questions are examined, and the author studies concrete conflicts between Islamic prescriptions and civic obligations. For instance, he analyses the question of loyalty toward non-Islamic states and concludes that it is possible and licit. Jaballah encourages Muslims to criticise laws or policies that are in contradiction with Islam, whilst insisting on the duty to respect the law. Another question he examines concerns conflicts between the duty to denounce acts that are contrary to Islam on the one hand, and the civic duty to respect everyone's freedom. In this case, Jaballah admits that there can be discrepancies between the Muslim perception and evaluation of certain acts and the assessment a court will give them. It is possible that Muslims will consider certain acts (like

---

2 The article constitutes only one amongst Jaballah's statements which address in various ways the question of Muslims living in the French or European context. This article was chosen because it presents a systematic and comprehensive attempt to define the legal status of Muslim citizenship in Europe. It is evidence for the fact that the ambiguity of law also has far-reaching effects in scholarly discourses. A survey of Jaballah's speeches from 2000 to today shows that the phenomenon of ambiguity is addressed there too. See for example Jaballah's speech entitled "La présence musulmane en France: une réalité sociologique et une responsabilité collective" given at the 10th Rencontre Annuelle des Musulmans du Sud, Marseilles, 27 May 2011 or "Dans quelle mesure la pratique de l'Islam s'adapte-t-elle au contexte?" (Jaballah 2000).

the Danish cartoons) to be Islamophobic and racist, whilst the court rules that they are protected by the freedom of expression.

This text is not a naive plea in favour of Muslim citizenship. Nevertheless, as becomes clear in the last part of the article, the argumentation is based on a clear separation between law and the rights of citizens on the one hand, and social reality on the other. Thus, in the last section of his essay, the author moves on to deal with what he calls the "European Muslim reality" *(wāqi' al-muslimīn fī ūrūbbā)*. How is this reality described? Jaballah tries to emphasise the positive aspects: he notes that there have been changes allowing "more interaction with society and positive integration" (id., 269), but he adds immediately that many obstacles remain in the exercise of citizenship rights. Jaballah mentions a set of complex factors that play a role in this. One cause is the lack of openness of Muslims, especially among those who were immigrants to France ("the first generation") and those with limited linguistic skills; another derives from the ethnic links that continue to divide Muslims and stand in the way of integration in French society. Jaballah also notes that certain "societal" factors work against the exercise of citizenship rights and mentions the negative image of Islam propagated by the media and the political strategies that contribute to racism and Islamophobia. Nevertheless, he concludes with an optimistic remark by signalling two positive developments: the emergence of a new generation of Muslims engaged in many walks of life, and secondly he maintains that there is broader acceptance of Islam nowadays. For instance, it is relatively easy to build mosques.

In brief, what Jaballah describes and assesses here – and this constitutes an essential part of his defence of Muslim citizenship – is the current state of social conditions for citizenship. He presents as self-evident the fact that certain conditions should be fulfilled for citizenship to be better or fully exercised: education, acceptance of pluralism and a certain knowledge of Islam are presented as conditions to be fulfilled by non-Muslims, linguistic skills, and the practice of a so-called moderate Islam are conditions ascribed to Muslims. At first sight, the reflections I have summarised so far seem trivial, and this impression is not entirely wrong. The way the author reflects on these non-legal conditions of citizenship is quite common: it is a widely held view that educating the population will contribute to a multi-religious society that functions better; it is also frequently argued that certain forms of identity – such as those of Muslims born outside of Metropolitan France – pose an obstacle to 'integration' in France. While these ideas often seem self-evident and natural, it is important to note how they configure citizenship. In the perspective adopted by Jaballah, the full exercise of citizenship is not only potentially impeded by the media and certain forms of (legal) political mobilisation. His argument also implies that a specific use of individual freedom by Muslims is desirable or necessary. For example, Muslims are of course perfectly free to identify as a member of an ethnic group, but this, according to Jaballah, is detrimental to social integration. This also applies to certain practices of Islam that lead believers to isolate themselves from the society they live in.

In other words, what the author examines and legitimates in an Islamic perspective is not French citizenship understood simply as a legal order or a political philosophy. In fact, this is not how Jaballah conceives 'Islam in the Republic'. What he describes is a legal order that functions on the basis of a wider set of governmental mechanisms. Governmental mechanism designates here a way to regulate domains (such as civil society, the economy or cultural production) whose functioning cannot, and should not, be subject to direct regulation by the State. Rather, the State, in its own interest, ought to respect certain limits that are imposed on the ways it governs these areas, which obey their own laws and are by their very nature external to it. Hence the State has a certain interest – which is always bound to be understood differently – in respecting the freedom of those it governs. However, this does not mean that this freedom marks a limit which condemns the State to passivity. The State can regulate these domains by establishing certain ways of functioning, or by working on the way citizens rationalise their actions in these fields, or again by coordinating its politics – and thus all political, legal and disciplinary mechanisms – with non-State actors. Beyond the State, there is a diversity of actors who partake in this coordination, whose main goal is to regulate what people do within the limits of individual freedom. It is through this perspective that Jaballah's argument for citizenship has to be analysed. In trying to legitimise Muslim citizenship, not only does Jaballah provide a new foundation for the French legal order and place it within the Islamic tradition. He also outlines a governing ensemble that integrates this legal order and makes necessary, or at least desirable, a number of practices on the part of the Muslims.

To come back to the question of ambiguity, the argumentation described above is also an attempt to resolve this ambiguity. Jaballah seeks to create a particular reading of law 'in itself' as the normative grounding of Muslim life in France, and at the same time he offers an interpretation of the process through which law acquires force. From this perspective, one can say he tries to solve the ambiguity through a paradoxical figure, namely law 'in itself' as the ground of citizenship that depends on external factors. The ambiguity is not resolved on a conceptual level, but a way to resolve it on the practical level is clearly indicated.

MODALITY NUMBER 2: TAREQ OUBROU

There are of course other ways to address the challenge implied by the acknowledgment of this ambiguity. The second example concerns the imam Tareq Oubrou from Bordeaux. Oubrou was born in Morocco in 1962, studied in France and has worked as an imam since the 1990s (Caeiro 2005). He has written a number of articles and books (two of them book-length interviews) and is a well-known speaker in France. Oubrou is sometimes invited to participate in media debates. A series of his sermons has been released on audiotapes and he regularly gives public lectures in France.

Since the end of the 1990s, Oubrou has published articles on what he calls "the Sharia of minorities" (1998). In some regards, his positions are not very different from those of Jaballah. Oubrou believes that the presence of Muslims is not a problem in terms of law and the "values of the Republic". However, he believes this presence is extremely problematic on a cultural level "particularly with regard to mentalities, culture, and the *tectonics* of their evolution" (id., 27; original emphasis), as he writes in 1998. Oubrou has upheld this – fundamental – thesis in his later work. It should be added that Oubrou's basic notion that France cannot be reduced to its laws and constitution is shared by other Muslims who may or may not arrive at conclusions concordant with his. In 2012, a group of 'Muslim patriots' close to Oubrou created a movement named *Fils de France* in order to work for the 'acculturation' of Islam.[3] Tariq Ramadan is also among the critics of those who consider the problems confronting Muslims only in relation to the French legal order and, more specifically, the assumed conflict between French laws and Islamic normativity. Instead, he argues that it is necessary to write Muslims into the "shared narrative" of the nation-state and work for the recognition of Muslim cultures as constitutive of France (Ramadan 2012).[4]

In contrast to Ramadan, Oubrou conceives of French culture as a monolithic culture that cannot be easily changed. The diversity that Muslims have introduced into the French landscape is a real threat to the cohesion of French society and Oubrou continues to encourage Muslims to engage in a process of cultural integration. Oubrou has not offered a systematic adaptation programme yet. However, it is clear, on the one hand, that this view of France as a cultural entity is in tune with his attempt to reassess the place of theology in the Islamic tradition (Oubrou 2007) and with his re-reading of Sharia, emphasising its flexibility and the primordiality of its ethical dimension; on the other hand, the question of visible practices remains a central concern of his. Indeed, he often virulently criticises the hijab and the women who wear it. Oubrou has stated that it was a "mis-

---

3   Cf. www.filsdefrance.fr (accessed 20 April 2013).

4   In his earlier publications, Ramadan had recognised that the judiciary sometimes functions as a two-tier system, but had insisted primarily upon the important guarantees for the defence of rights which national legal order provides (Ramadan 1998).

take" to support practices like the "veil which is erroneously called 'Islamic'" and which can be dispensed with, particularly given its negative perception in France (Oubrou 2009: 70). With regard to covered women, he has claimed that "many of them are very unstable" and that their practice is "sometimes" motivated "unconsciously" by a will to "stand up" to society and not always part of a "sincere spiritual approach". I should add that Oubrou criticises the prohibitions on wearing headscarves in France as curtailing individual liberties (id., 80sq.).

There is no denial that the adaptation process that Oubrou presents is intended to address a context conceived to a large degree in cultural terms. Oubrou writes that "the practice of Islam in this new cultural niche has to adapt itself in order to access the status of a natural religion as much as Christianity and Judaism" (1998: 27). From his point of view, "the necessary integration of the cultural dimension" is a way to strike roots "consciously and willingly in a place, a history, a political space, a shared national destiny, a society, a language" (Oubrou 2009: 204).

Oubrou's intellectual project is centrally concerned with reconciling Islam with the French context and Oubrou implies (and, sometimes, asserts) that it is perfectly possible to define this context (see, for example, id., 39). To some degree, his efforts to reconstruct Sharia and theology as well as his criticism of visible practices constitute, from this perspective, a plausible attempt to embed Muslim religiosities in the context as he understands it. This is not all that can be said, however. Indeed, it can be argued that by his own standards, he is not able to fully embed Islam in France and that he is actually proposing to Muslims two distinct, but not necessarily incompatible, ways of relating to the French context. One takes shape in a wide-ranging project for rethinking the Islamic tradition, the other concerns the kind of subject able to live in a society which manifests hostility towards Islam and Muslims in various ways.

Indeed, there is a tension within Oubrou's statements. On the one hand, his incessant calls for reconstructing Muslim religiosities in France derive from a wish "to simplify the life of Muslims" and "to contribute to living together in a society in which Islam is not a majority [religion] and is not destined to become one" (Oubrou 2012: 47). Many of his statements suggest or directly claim that Muslims have contributed to the fear of Islam and that this fear can be reduced and life made easier by introducing certain changes to Muslim practices.[5] It is

---

5 See for examples this statement where Oubrou claims that the fear of Islam in France grew in proportion to the "religious visibility" of Muslims: "Or, la peur de l'islam dans la société française n'a cessé d'augmenter proportionellement à la visibilité religieuse des musulmans, même s'il y a eu d'autres facteurs liés aux grands bouleversements de notre monde et à la montée de l'islamisme violent…" (2009: 70).

this logic which justifies the effort of rethinking the Muslim tradition. On the other hand, Oubrou has to acknowledge that in the current context Muslims are regularly confronted with experiences of racism which will persist to some degree independently of what they do. When directly addressing the question of racism, the capacity of Muslims to influence their conditions of life in France through their own conduct is evaluated differently. Oubrou is in fact extremely reluctant to address the question of racism[6] and rather calls upon believers to concentrate on themselves and sometimes deliberately forget their environment instead of criticising it.

In a recorded sermon entitled *La volonté* (The Will; n.d.), Oubrou starts his address by observing that this is a "very demanding time for all Muslims in general, and for European Muslims in particular". He suggests addressing these demands by working on oneself to achieve an emotional distance between the individual believer and the social environment. For him, this is the priority. He criticises those who focus on problems in the way French Muslims are treated:

> [...] there are many Muslims who spend their time criticising others and thinking that, by insulting and criticising others, we will change our conditions of life. To this I say: be careful, if we have detected evil, we may still prescribe a cure that does not reflect the Qur'anic way. The antidote to this evil is to first lead an internal fight, and then sometimes to deliberately forget a little what happens in the world, and to concentrate on oneself. (Oubrou, n.d.)

According to Oubrou, Muslims see themselves facing a "society" that often shows hostility and fear of Islam. The cure he suggests does not consist in reflecting on any direct means to change this situation. He rather calls upon Muslims to step back, practice forgetting and focus on themselves. On the one hand Oubrou defends cultural adaptation and asserts that "the Muslim has to be given norms that do not handicap him in social, emotional, spiritual and economic aspects of life" (Oubrou 2009: 40). The construction of a Muslim subject culturally integrated in the French space is a central aim of his work. The aim of reducing antagonisms towards Muslims by changing Muslim practices is crucial for this adaptation project. On the other hand, Oubrou is forced to admit that the factors

---

6   Oubrou admits the existence of "racial discrimination", which he considers to be "unfortunately so obvious" that there is no need for him to talk about it. At the same time, he cautions against "systematically finding the reasons for one's failures in racism and exclusion" and "constest[s] the fact of mixing a social situation which is unfavourable with the affiliation with Islam" (id., 71).

that "handicap" Muslims in their daily life lie, at least currently, partly beyond their power to change. Hence, Oubrou can only advise Muslims to create an emotional distance to their society.

MODALITY NUMBER 3: AMAR LASFAR

The third case is that of Amar Lasfar, *recteur* of Al-Imane mosque in the south of Lille and since 2013 president of the UOIF. Originally from the north of Morocco, he has been very active in Islamic associations in France since the 1980s. This case illustrates yet another possible position with respect to legal ambiguity, a position that introduces a fracture in the author's discourse. Before embarking upon the analysis, I would like to underline the fact that Lasfar subscribes to the discourse of the Union described at the beginning of this chapter. He is keen to ensure that Muslims respect French law. Likewise, he insists on the fact that it is a duty for Muslims to act for the good of society as a whole and not only that of the *umma* (Lasfar 2011). There is no doubt that Lasfar seeks to enable Muslims to act in society, which presupposes that citizenship is legitimated and that the compatibility between Islamic tradition and the normative framework in France can be demonstrated. However, the legitimation of French citizenship may turn out to be problematic since it has to be justified in relation to the ambivalent status of the legal order. At times, when this ambivalence manifests itself in concrete incidents, discourses become more complex and sometimes even contradictory. An example can be found in a sermon given in Arabic by Lasfar at Al-Imane mosque (Lasfar 2007).

Note that this sermon was delivered in a specific context. In 2007, in the middle of the presidential campaign, the Socialist Party had published a document in which it criticised the Minister of Interior Affairs of the time, Nicolas Sarkozy, for his policies towards Islam. In this document, a Muslim high-school initiated by the Al-Imane mosque was denounced as fundamentalist. Later on, this part of the report was removed. From the point of view of Lasfar, this attack was the climax of a whole campaign against Islam in the context of the elections. Lasfar uses strong words to describe the situation of Muslims: he considers that Muslims are subjected to humiliation. In this context, his vision of the relationship between Muslims and the Republic changes in many regards. He emphasises the obligation for Muslims to protect themselves and strengthen their religion *(ta'zīz al-dīn)*. In addition, he asserts several times that Muslims should build a "fence" *(siyāj)* to protect their community According to him, this obligation follows from the practice of the Prophet Muhammad and more specifically his emigration to Medina, the anniversary of which was commemorated on the day of this sermon. In brief, the imam's thoughts radically exceed what the representative of a Muslim association can say in France without risking a vehement response. The position adopted here by Lasfar would be considered *communautariste* in France, i.e. as fragmenting the unity of the community of citizens. He addresses and tries to resolve the structural ambiguity of the normative context by simply choosing to reduce the reliance of Muslims on law and State institutions and to strengthen the community structure as a means to defend Muslims against injustice.

In the course of his address, he also expresses his views on the question of French citizenship from the Islamic standpoint. According to Lasfar, these debates (which, as we recall, are very important to the UOIF) should be abandoned. He is ironic about those – Muslims or not – who question the validity of republican laws for Muslims and affirms that there are simply no other options when one is subject to the laws of the Republic. He adds that one does not have to love the law, but to respect it. For him, the debate around Islam and the laws of the Republic is not only useless, but also problematic to the extent that it contributes to turning Muslim citizens into an exceptional group.

Clearly, the discourse of Lasfar is less complex than those of Ahmed Jaballah and Tareq Oubrou. What is important, though, is that it is comparable to the extent that it reacts to the same problem, namely the ambiguity of the normative context. At the time of the sermon, in a campaign aimed at Muslims and Islamic institutions, Lasfar temporarily moves away from the common discourse of the Union – to which he otherwise subscribes – and describes the citizenship of French Muslims as based on a *modus vivendi* agreement with the State order that cannot be changed. The ambiguity is thus resolved, but at the price of an incoherence in his own discourse.

CONCLUSION

I have argued for a different perspective on the 'context' in relation to which French Muslim religiosities are studied. Numerous studies have considered how to approach this context analytically. The notion of a (French) context is crucial not only for the study of changing Muslim practices and jurisprudence, but also for that of State policies, perceptions of Islam and public debates. My analysis has focused on how members of the Union of Islamic Organisations of France conceptualise the French context in relation to what is one of the most powerful modes of universalisation, the law. The UOIF has undertaken great efforts to reflect upon the compatibility of French law and the Sharia, and it has had a decisive impact on the debate and the emergence of a *fiqh* of minorities (Bowen 2009; Caeiro 2011). Members of the UOIF regularly regard France as a unified normative space which centres around the constitution and the law. However, the analysis has shown that the wish to represent the French context in a totalising manner is impeded by specific obstacles. The fundamental problem, not always explicitly stated, with which all the cases presented here struggle is that of the ambiguity of the law. Legal categories are indispensable elements of discourses about Muslim lives in France. At the same time, the law repeatedly seems ineffective when it comes to achieving equality for Muslims and it is difficult for Muslims to unequivocally determine the force of the law to shape the conditions under which French Muslims live their lives. It follows from this that part of the work of 'contextualising Islam' is invested in solving this ambiguity and defining a properly unified context which can take on different shapes.

The perspective outlined here shifts attention to another kind of challenge to be confronted by Muslims. This challenge resides not in the difficulty of legitimating French law and citizenship from within Sharia, but in the difficulty of grasping what kind of order is effectively determined through the law. More importantly, it suggests that the question of how Muslims relate Islamic normativity to French law is not simply a legal issue. Nor can secularism as it is enshrined in the law be restricted to the latter when one seeks to understand its effects. As these analyses have shown, the structural ambiguity of the law is one factor which gives rise to a both intellectual and practical endeavour by Muslims to re-shape, in a broader context of power, how law acquires force. The examples have indicated that this endeavour implies a movement to other fields, e.g. education, culture, or the social, which become related to the law. At the same time, it leads to a definition of proper modes of conduct and subjectivity for Muslims in this context. The structural ambiguity of law thus triggers some of the processes through which law, power, and subjectification become related in multiple ways. In this sense, the legal edifice of secularism as a central element of the French context stimulates Muslims to transcend it.

REFERENCES

Amghar, Samir (2008): "Europe puts Islamists to the test: The Muslim brotherhood", in: *Mediterranean Politics,* 13:1, pp. 63-77.
Asad, Talal (1986): *The idea of an anthropology of Islam.* [online] Georgetown University, Center for Contemporary Arab Studies: Occasional Papers. Available at: https://gushare.georgetown.edu/ContemporaryArabStudies/ CCAS%20publications/Talal%20Asad%20OP.pdf (accessed 20 April 2013).
Bowen, John R. (2009): *Can Islam be French? Pluralism and pragmatism in a secularist state*, Princeton: Princeton University Press.

Caeiro, Alexandre (2005): "An imam in France: Tareq Oubrou", in: *ISIM Review*, 15, pp. 48sq.

— (2011): *Fatwas for European Muslims: The minority fiqh project and the integration of Islam in Europe*, PhD thesis, Utrecht University.

Foucault, Michel (2001): *Dits et écrits*, vol. 2: 1976-1988, Paris: Gallimard.

Jaballah, Ahmad (2008 [1429]): "al-wasaṭīya bayna muqtaḍayāt al-muwāṭana fī ūrūbbā wa-l-ḥifāẓ ʿalā l-huwīya al-islāmīya", in: *al-majalla al-ʿilmīya li-l-majlis al-ūrūbbī li-l-iftāʾ wa-l-buḥūṭ*, 12/13, pp. 257-272.

— (2000): *Dans quelle mesure la pratique de l'Islam s'adapte-t-elle au contexte?* [video] Paris.

Johansen, Baber (1999): *Contingency in a sacred law: Legal and ethical norms in Muslim fiqh*, Leiden: Brill.

Lasfar, Amar (2007): *L'Hégire: Leçons et enseignements* [videos online] Sermon at Al-Imane mosque (in three parts). Available at: http://www.daily motion.com/video/x14izc_preche-lasfar-02-02-07_school (part 1); http://www. dailymotion.com/video/x14j59_preche-lasfar-02-02-07-partie-2_school?ralg =int.meta2-only#from=playrelon-1 (part 2); http://www.dailymotion.com/ ali59155#video=x14k69 (part 3) (accessed 20 April 2013).

— (2011): *Hommage à sheikh Fayçal Mawlawi* [video online] Sermon at Al-Imane mosque, 20 Mai. Available at: http://www.mosqueelille.fr/index.php? option=com_content&view=article&id=162:preche-du-vendredi-du-22042011 -sheikh-abdallah-nhari&catid=7:preches-du-vendredi&Itemid=24 (accessed 20 April 2013).

Maréchal, Brigitte (2008): *Muslim brothers in Europe*, Leiden: Brill.

Oubrou, Tareq (n.d.): *La volonté* [Audio-cassette] La Courneuve: Gedis.

— (1998): "Introduction théorique à la Charîʿa de minorité", in: *Islam de France*, 2, pp. 27-37.

— (2007): *L'unicité de Dieu: Des noms et attributs divins: At-tauhid: al-asmāʾ wa-s-sifāt*, La Courneuve: Gedis.

— (2009): *Profession imâm: Entretiens avec Michael Privot et Cédric Baylocq*, Paris: Albin Michel.

— (2012): *Un imam en colère: Entretien avec Samuel Lieven*, Paris: Bayard.

Peter, Frank (2011): "Die Union des Organisations Islamiques de France und die Tradition der Muslimbrüder im Zeitalter der Integrationspolitik", in: Reetz, Dietrich (ed.), *Islam in Europa: Religiöses Leben heute*, Münster: Waxmann, pp. 145-169.

Ramadan, Tariq (1998): *Les musulmans dans la laïcité*, Lyon: Editions Tawhid. Second revised edition.

— (2012): *Islamophobie en France: actions et perspectives.* [video online] Available at http://www.youtube.com/watch?v=Tm5VDN_7PjE (accessed 20 April 2013).

'Muslim women' marking debates on Islam

AMÉLIE BARRAS

> The body of the Oriental woman, a body that must be
> consistently unveiled and modernized, confirms the
> Western subject as a person of knowledge and reason.
>
> (Razack 2008b: 109)

> Perhaps the conversation we should be having, in this
> 'post-feminist' era, is about the resilience of patriarchy,
> about the global oppression of women in all of the forms
> that it takes. Although we would like to imagine that our
> 'culture' does not support this 'sort of thing', the statisti-
> cal data as well as the stories of women, should we
> choose to hear them, offer another version of the truth of
> the equality of women.   (Beaman 2012: 244)

INTRODUCTION

In his writings on Algeria in 1959, Frantz Fanon dedicated a whole chapter entitled "l'Algérie se dévoile" (Algeria unveiled) to the importance given to Algerian women and their veils by colonial powers. To shed light on why they were so
central to the colonial project, Fanon cites the colonial administration: "Si nous
voulons frapper la société algérienne dans sa contexture, dans ses facultés de résistance, *il nous faut d'abord conquérir les femmes; il faut que nous allions les
chercher derrière le voile où elles se dissimulent et dans les maisons où l'homme*

les cache" (1959: 20, my emphasis)[1]. Re-reading Fanon in an era marked by the events of 9/11 and the war on terror is particularly enlightening. One realises that the imagination of Western states is haunted by many of the same preoccupations that marked the colonial endeavour and the last years of the Algerian war – preoccupations that are often articulated around the bodies and predicaments of 'Muslim women'[2]. While there are several reasons for this, which cannot all be explored in this chapter, the aim of this piece is nevertheless to provide some insights into why women have been and continue to be at the centre of debates and policies on Islam in Europe, and elsewhere.

This paper seeks to do so by discussing a body of literature that looks at *why* women have frequently found themselves at the centre of national and community building projects, and linking this discussion to policies and discourses on Muslim women today[3]. While scholars studying Islam in the West have recently started to challenge the frequently assumed discursive connection made between secularism and gender equality (e.g. Hurd 2012; Jackobsen 2010; Razack 2008a and b; Fassin 2010; Scott 2007) and have explored the implications of tropes articulated around the need to 'save' Muslim women (e.g. Razack 2008a and b; Beaman 2012; Abu-Lughod 2002), bringing the aforementioned body of literature on gender and nationalism into the discussion has the benefit of highlighting how these narratives play a central role in the (re)production of borders of different political formations. That is: how they participate in imagining stable and cohesive polities.

---

1   "If we want to strike Algerian society in its structure, in its faculty of resistance, we first have to conquer its women; we have to look for them behind their veils where they hide themselves and in their house where a man hides them" (my translation).

2   The expression 'Muslim women' will be used throughout this chapter indicating that efforts are rarely made in public discourses on Islam to deconstruct and complexify this category. The usage of this category is interesting, in so far as it should push us to reflect on what it "produces" and what it "erases" (Razack 2008a: 86).

3   Similarly to the approach embraced in the edited volume by Morin and Guelke, while this chapter focuses mainly on women, gender differences (along with other social divisions) are considered to be central in shaping women's experiences (2007: xxiii).

WOMEN AS BAROMETERS OF NATIONAL AND COMMUNITY PROJECTS

> One of the great paradoxes of modernity has been that the moment of 'universal' emancipation was also the moment of female subordination and exclusion.
>
> (Yuval-Davis/Werbner 1999: 6)

Exploring the connection between gender, nation and citizenship has been at the centre of the work of several scholars, including Yuval-Davis (1997a and b); Yuval-Davis/Werbner (1999); McClintock (1996) and Kandiyoti (1991, 1997). Yuval-Davis argues that women have been given and play an important role in ethnic and national processes, including as biological, cultural and symbolic re-producers of collectivities (1997b: sqq.). For instance, because of their 'natural' role they are understood as being the biological (re)producers of the nation, as being responsible for bearing a certain 'type' of collective. This explains why they are frequently affected by policies aiming at regulating their reproductive rights (e.g. How many children they can have? Whom they can marry?; 1997b: 22). They are also responsible for (re)producing particular cultural codes, as they are perceived as the "border-guards" of their group (Yuval-Davis, 1997b: 23), ensuring that they protect and transmit values to future generations: "Women are often constructed as the cultural symbols of the collectivity, of its boundaries, as carriers of the collectivity's 'honour' and as its intergenerational reproducers of cultures. Specific codes of regulations are usually developed, defining who/what is a 'proper man' and a 'proper woman'" (Yuval-Davis 1997b: 67). In a sense, women have to ensure that boundaries are not blurred – a process that could de-stabilise the identity of their collectivity.

It is important to note that because these 'rules' are not fixed but change along with the ideology of who is in power, who is the dominant group, women also find themselves at the center of these changes and are therefore often the first ones to be the target of new regulations ensuring that they perform and symbolise a change in values through their bodies and actions. This is visible, for instance, in several countries in the Middle East where at the turn of the last century in contact with the European gaze, the unveiled woman came to symbolise modernity and progress, while the veiled woman came to be associated with family, authenticity and traditions (Moghadam 1999: 139; Kandiyoti 1991). The 'condition of women', in fact, became a direct marker of modernity and has been used by different groups to signal where they stand ideologically – using women's bodies as "sites of interventions" (Cinar 2005: 21)[4].

This focus on women is, therefore, particularly relevant as it not only highlights their importance in the construction of the identity of a nation and other types of collectivities, but it also clearly underscores how women are in that process subject to specific rules, which they are required to (re)produce, enact and perform:

> On the one hand, nationalist movements invite women to participate more fully in collective life by interrelating them as 'national' actors: mothers, educators, workers and even fighters. On the other hand, they reaffirm the boundaries of culturally acceptable feminine conduct and exert pressure on women to articulate their gender interests within the terms of reference set by nationalist discourse.
>
> (Kandiyoti 1991: 432)

As such, challenging what is 'acceptable' generally leads to a restriction of citizenship rights or entitlements in a community (id., 7). McClintock, in her analysis of the gendered character of nations and nationalism, discusses this paradox as well (1996: 354). She argues that while women are responsible for protecting 'specific' rules and regulations, they are not however understood as setting and defining those regulations. Rather they are perceived as being passive followers who have to be defended by an active 'male' political body.

In order to fully comprehend this connection between women and citizenship, scholars have insisted on the need to avoid essentialising the category women. That is to look at the question of women's citizenship not only in relation to that of men, but also in terms of women's affiliation to dominant or subordinate groups, to their ethnicity, 'race', class, religion and other social divisions (Yuval-Davis 1997a: 4). In other words these specific affiliations mediate access to citizenship, as well as entitlements in different collectivities. This is clearly illustrated today by women wearing headscarves in several contexts, who see their presence and participation in different areas of public life as being con-

---

4   The Turkish case is a good example, where 'modern' women (e.g. not wearing headscarves) were identified as the symbol of morality for the new Republic when it was first established, and where their bodies have continued since then to occupy a central place in the ideology of secular and Islamist elites alike (see, Cinar 2005). The Iranian Revolution is another case in point, in which women's bodies and performances were used as "sites of interventions" to indicate the change in ideology, and the new rules and regulations that structured the Islamic regime.

ditioned or facilitated by whether or not they wear headdress. In these cases access to full citizenship rights is mediated by both gender and religion[5].

Understanding membership as being mediated by different types of affiliations also sheds light on how women might be considered to be border-guards of more than one community at once. Migrant women are in many instances the first to be targeted by policies inciting them to assimilate in their host country so that they become border-guards of this collectivity's culture, while being at the same time responsible for (re)producing the customs of their ethnic or religious groups – finding themselves in the difficult position of facing restrictions in their entitlements in one collectivity if they abide to the regulations of the other and vis-versa (Yuval-Davis/Anthias/Kofman 2005). Salih sums up this reality quite nicely in her study of Moroccan migrant women in Italy: "Moroccan migrant women, in fact, face opposing pressures which pull them in different directions by making their bodies become symbols of the purity of culture, on the one hand, and of the success of assimilation on the other hand" (2000: 332). In other words, women frequently end-up being the target of multiple and contradictory rules because of their multiple affiliations, which can incite them, in order to cope with this reality, to develop strategies and discourses that highlight and attempt to transcend these exclusive dimensions of belonging (e.g. Fadil 2009; Jouili 2009; Salih 2009; Barras 2012).

EMPIRICAL ILLUSTRATION: A DISCUSSION OF THE CONTEMPORARY OBSESSION WITH 'REFORMING' MUSLIM WOMEN'S BODIES

Over the last decade dozens of states in and outside Europe have been busy discussing how to effectively 'manage' and 'contain' the presence of visible religious 'symbols' in their public spaces[6] – visible religious symbols, which have

---

5   I understand full citizenship rights in line with the definition provided by Salih and
    Moors: that is not only as formal rights in a polity but also in terms of 'practical' na-
    tional belonging, which implies an "acceptance in everyday life as part of the national
    community by dominant groups" (2007: 2).

6   Symbol is put in quotations in reference to the work of Saba Mahmood who argues
    that we need to be aware of the power that the usage of the term 'symbol' or 'sign'
    produces. Through the usage of this term the headscarf is considered to be an arbitrary
    representation of the sacred – located outside the subject and her sovereign con-
    science. This interpretation erases other readings, including the fact that the headscarf

in public debates almost always been conflated with symbols belonging to the Islamic faith. The most virulent concerns have been around the wearing of full-face veils (i.e. *niqāb*, a veil where all the face except for the eyes of the wearer is covered, and *burqa*, a veil that covers the entire face of its wearer) – a concern which many European states have chosen to deal with by implementing either a partial or entire ban in the public realm[7]. Concerns have also been expressed with regards to the wearing of headscarves (veils that generally cover the hair and ears of the wearer), which have become the target of restrictions in different areas of public life or/and affecting citizens involved in particular activities (e.g. students in schools, public servants, and so on)[8].

Uneasiness over these symbols is well summarised in a resolution passed by the EU Assembly in 2010 on Islam, Islamism and Islamophobia:

> [...] the veiling of women, especially full veiling through the *burqa* or the *niqab*, is often perceived as a symbol of the subjugation of women to men, restricting the role of women within society, limiting their professional life and impeding their social and economic activities. Neither the full veiling of women, nor even the headscarf, are recognised by all Muslims as a religious obligation of Islam, but they are seen by many as a social and cultural tradition [...] *The Assembly considers that this tradition could be a threat to women's dignity and freedom* [...] The Assembly calls on member states to develop targeted policies intended to *raise Muslim women's awareness of their rights, help them to take part in public life and offer them equal opportunities to pursue a professional life and gain social and economic independence. In this respect, the education of young Muslim women as well as of their parents and families is crucial.*
>
> (Council of Europe, Parliamentary Assembly,
> Resolution 1743, 2010, my emphasis)

---

could be considered a divine duty, a religious prescription that is part and parcel of ones ethical practice and subjectivity (Mahmood 2006: 343).

7   France (2010), Italy (2011), Belgium (2010) and the Netherlands (2013) have or plan to pass laws banning the wearing of the full-face veil. Debates on whether and where to ban it have also been taking place in other countries such as Canada, Switzerland, Germany and Australia (for a more detail discussion of these bans see Nussbaum 2012: 3-6).

8   Teachers and/or students have for instance been prohibited to wear a headscarf in public schools in Bulgaria (2009), France (2004), Turkey (ongoing since the 1990s), Kosovo (2010) as well as in certain regions of Germany, Belgium, the Netherlands, Spain and Switzerland (for a more detail discussion of these bans see Nussbaum 2012: 3-6).

This excerpt is interesting inasmuch as it allows us to see how Muslim women are depicted as being in 'need' of saving, echoing the 'traditional' passive role given to women in nation-building projects. As such, particular stress is put on the fact that the wearing of this symbol is not considered by everyone to be a religious requirement but actually in many instances a "cultural tradition". Voiding this "tradition" of its religious character is not trivial, as it facilitates the justification to 'reform' and 'contain' it – to reform an 'archaic' and 'gender discriminatory' "tradition" that does not coalesce with the modernity of the European project[9]; that exists 'outside' European time. This process of reform is achieved through education, ensuring in a sense that Muslim women become fluent in the rules and regulations of the polity they are living in. This resonates with Yuval-Davis's argument that women are the border-guards and markers of the ideology of a community. Thus, women wearing headdress find themselves affected by policies that seek to ensure that they become loyal to a specific 'national' project, while at the same time relinquishing 'traditions' narrated as binding them to an alternative project. However, when they fail to forsake them, they are often perceived as a threat to the polity as they then carry the risk of transmitting 'dangerous' ethical standards to future generations.

This ambivalence finds itself at the heart of many discursive and visual representations of women wearing headdress today. The main poster of the far right Schweizerische Volkspartei (SVP, Swiss People's Party) inciting Swiss citizens to vote for the banning of minarets in the 2009 national referendum is a case in point. This poster (cf. this volume p. 300) showcased a woman wearing a dark *niqāb* standing in the front left-side of a Swiss flag being perforated by minarets[10]. What does the presence of this woman on a poster campaign for the ban on minarets produce? It seeks, one could argue, to render the existence of another moral project tangible: symbolising what could happen to Switzerland if min-

---

9   This distinction between 'religion' and 'tradition' is recurrent in many debates on Islam, where policy makers and commentators end-up deciding what is 'religious' and what is not. For instance, former French President Nicolas Sarkozy in his justification for banning the wearing of the full-face veil in France had argued that this veil was not a "religious" problem but a problem of "women's dignity" (2009). This is interesting as locating this practice outside the realm of the religious (or the religiously acceptable) could be understood as a way of avoiding discussion as to whether bans infringe on the right to freedom of religion and conscience.

10   The fact that this woman is located in the front left side of the ad campaign is not insignificant. Swiss readers, well versed in German, French or Italian, read from left to right, and thus this woman will most likely be one of the first things they see on the ad.

arets were not banned, i.e. it could be invaded by non-democratic and patriarchal values – values that would perforate the Swiss polity from within[11]. This woman therefore represents a potential threat to the stability of the Swiss polity that needs to be tamed through laws that will 'save' her from the 'dangerous culture' to which she is subjugated (e.g. in this case the law banning minarets was portrayed as a necessary measure to limit the progression of political Islam in Switzerland). As such, this 'veiled' woman remains a passive actor – a marker – whose faith can only change if she is 'saved' by an active Swiss citizenry (Guillaume/Barras 2013: 321).

While this western obsession has reached an unprecedented peak over the past decade in several Europeans countries, the French state, and its multiple laws and regulations restricting the wearing of the headgear in different spaces, remains at the forefront of this trend. After banning visible religious symbols in public schools in 2004 and banning the full-face veil in 2010, French politicians have recently been trying to pass two new sets of regulations. The first, which received the support of the French Ministry of Education in March 2012, aims at regulating the presence of mothers wearing headscarves in public schools. It seeks to restrict their participation to school activities, such as accompanying their children on school outings on the grounds that like public servants they are responsible for embodying the 'neutrality' of public services[12], which is set as a

---

11 It is relevant to note that while the far right SVP party in Switzerland has generally been quite conservative with respect to the role of women in society, when it discusses Islam and the predicaments of Muslim women it becomes a defender of gender equality. This resonates with the argument developed by Salih with respect to the Catholic Church in Italy and the way it has mobilised the image of a Muslim woman to portray the Christian faith as a religion favoring women's liberation in opposition to Islam (Salih 2009: 413). For a more detailed discussion of the SVP anti-minaret campaign see Mayer 2011.

12 This concept of 'neutrality' has been challenged by several scholars. Danchin (2011) argues that this neutrality is based on a Christian reading of religion, where 'modern' religion is understood as being located in one's private conscience. Other scholars informed by a feminist perspective have argued that the baseline around which this neutrality has been articulated is a white, bourgeois male (Salih 2009: 421; Scott 2007: 169), which explains why women who have for a long time been depicted as being unable to abstract themselves from their sex, and thus become neutral, have and continue to pose a deep challenge to this concept (see Scott ibid; Hurd Shakman forthcoming).

pre-requisite of French secularism *(laïcité)*[13] (Ministère de l'Education nationale 2012). The second law proposal, drafted by a leftist member of parliament and approved by the French Senate in January 2012[14], requires that child-carers responsible for children under the age of three working in nurseries or at home be subject to the same principle of neutrality (Assemblée Nationale, 2012). That is: either they choose not to manifest their religion when they work or they clearly stipulate their inability to respect this neutrality requirement in their work contract with their employer (e.g. parents; Merckx 2012)[15].

Until that point formal or ad-hoc bans on headscarves, and thus women's bodies and their performance, participated in identifying the boundaries of 'public' spaces (public schools, city halls, senate and so on) that were to conform to the 'neutrality' principle (Barras 2010)[16]. With this law this process is now ex-

---

13 This recommendation extends the principle of neutrality which was applicable to public servants (e.g. teachers and school staff) and students (since the passing of the 2004 law) to parents of students who are now considered to be 'temporary' public servants. While this recommendation limits the manifestation of religious, political and philosophical beliefs, in a similar vein than in 2004 public debates have almost entirely focused around women wearing headscarves. It is important to note that this recommendation inscribes itself in a climate where over the last decade devout Muslim mothers have seen their ability to participate in the activities of some public schools heavily restricted. Yet, until now these exclusions were characterised by their ad-hoc dimension (e.g. depending of teachers or headmasters).

14 Before being implemented, this law needs to be approved by the French Assembly. It is noteworthy that both the French right and left have supported the passing of these laws and regulations. For instance, the MP Francoise Laborde (2012) who initiated the law targeting child-carers was a member of the Radical Left Party. For a discussion on how concerns over the headscarf cross party lines in France, see Kuru 2008: 14.

15 Commentators have highlighted that what is meant by the term 'manifestation' remains unclear (Le Bars 2012), i.e. is it only applicable to the wearing of the headscarf or does it also include the presence of a Qur'an in a household or the serving of *halāl* food. Although here again all religions are targeted in the articulation of the law, societal debates have focused almost entirely on Islam.

16 In fact who (e.g. public servants, users of public services) and which spaces have been affected by these bans have varied greatly in terms of the political climate and individuals in 'charge' of particular spaces (e.g. mayors, teachers, professors). It is important to note, as Gökariksel and others have underlined, that delimiting private and public spaces is intimately linked to how secular states maintain and (re)produce their power (Gökariksel 2007: 63).

tended to a new space traditionally narrated as 'private' – the household. In a sense, it is almost as if religious practices of particular citizens that used to be considered 'private' matters if practiced in their homes[17], are now constructed as 'public' and become subject to wide scrutiny[18]. This shift, justified because of the profession exercised by these individuals, points to the deeply constructed character of the private/public distinction that varies by time, political climates and the positionality of individuals (e.g. Kandiyoti 1991: 430; Scott/Keates 2004; Gal 2004; Gökariksel 2007: 63). Also noteworthy in this case is how the state and its public servants are not identified as the sole actors responsible for scrutinising the performance of child-carers, but parents also become in charge of ensuring that nannies conform to these rules. This reality echoes Kandiyoti's remarks on state sponsored religious fundamentalism: "the exercise of patriarchal authority may be extended to [...] *'concerned' citizens who are given a free hand in monitoring women's dress and conduct in public places*" (Kandiyoti 1991: 440; my emphasis). The bodies and predicaments of Muslim women are thus used to facilitate the surveillance of 'Muslim' communities (Razack 2008b: 144) – a surveillance that extends its tentacles to the intimate sphere of the 'Muslim' family.

Going back to Yuval-Davis's point that women are "often constructed [...] as its [sc. the collectivity's] intergenerational reproducers of cultures" (cf. p. 83 supra) is helpful to better comprehend why French policy makers are now considering passing regulations that specifically affect mothers and child-carers. Indeed, given that several devout Muslim women exercise the profession of nanny and that several of them seem as well to be quite invested in school activities[19],

---

17 The neutrality of public spaces (schools, city halls, and so on) had been until that point discursively constructed by policy makers in contrast with the private sphere of the family in which religious and ethnic particularities could prevail.

18 This is a good example of how religious freedom is becoming less about practices and more about 'private' beliefs, i.e. beliefs that are protected as long as they belong in one's conscience. For further discussion on this emphasis on belief see: Danchin 2011 and Mahmood 2009.

19 No statistics are available to support these claims; however observers and interviews have indicated that devout Muslim women wearing a headscarf are generally faced with a limited access to the job market. Caring for toddlers in one's home was until that point considered to be an accessible profession (Jasmine, 2011a and b, and author's interviews with devout women activists, April 14 and 16 2012, Paris, France). This reality could also explain partly why these women have time to invest themselves in their children's school activities.

their positionality as "intergenerational reproducers of cultures" becomes ever more visible. While one can understand the 2004 law banning visible religious symbols in public schools as seeking to fashion future 'border-guards' who will (re)produce the 'rules and regulations' of citizenship, these new regulations are conceived this time to discipline women in charge of transmitting the values of the Republic to future citizens.

This understanding of the role played by child-carers and mothers along with the need to educate them is not novel, but has been a theme frequently raised in debates on secularism and Islam over the last decade. Ms. Michèle Vianès' contribution to the Gerin commission is a good illustration of some of the concerns that have run through these debates[20]:

> Si la femme voilée est le modèle, comment s'étonner de leur multiplication? [...]
> Nous savons désormais que les difficultés rencontrées par les femmes se trans-
> mettent aux générations qui suivent: c'est ainsi que perdurent les violences, les
> mariages sous contrainte, les crimes d'honneur.
>
> (Michèle Vianès, présidente de l'association Regards de femmes,
> Assemblée Nationale 2010: 301)[21]

These anxieties, in fact, echo those of the colonial government in Algeria in the 1940s and 1950s that had chosen to address them with very similar remedies structured around reforming Muslim mothers and their daughters: "[...] *Des écoles de 'jeunes filles musulmanes' se multiplient*. Les institutrices ou les religieuses, à l'approche de la puberté de leurs élèves, déploient une activité véritablement exceptionnelle. *Les mères sont d'abord touchées, assiégées* et on leur confie la mission d'ébranler et de convaincre le père" (Fanon 1959: 21, my emphasis)[22].

---

20 The Gerin commission was put in place in 2009 to evaluate whether the full-face veil should be banned.

21 "If a woman wearing a headscarf is the model, how can we be surprised by their multiplication? [...] We now know that the difficulties encountered by women are transmitted to following generations: this is how violence, forced marriages and honour killings are perpetuated" (my translation).

22 "[...] Schools for 'young Muslim girls' are multiplying. Teachers and nuns, when their students approach puberty, deploy a really exceptional energy. Mothers are first targeted, besieged and are given the mission to shake and convince the father" (my translation).

Thus, looking at current debates on Islam with the lenses provided by the literature on gender and nationalism is particularly insightful. First, it helps better comprehend why tropes and policies on Islam are often articulated around the bodies and predicaments of Muslim women. Their bodies and performances are constructed as delimiting the boundaries of different spaces. That is, by marking spaces as 'public', 'national' and so on. In fact their headscarf is often discursively understood as symbolising what a particular space is not, as carrying a set of values that are not endorsed by this space – participating in so doing to the production of a cohesive and stable 'us' defined less in terms of what it is than what it is not. This literature also makes us aware of the importance of considering the positionality of women to better understand why some of them are more affected than others; a positionality not only defined in terms of ones affiliation to a particular 'ethnic', class or religious group, but also in terms of ones membership into a particular age group (e.g. student)[23], profession (e.g. public servant, child-carer) and familial bonds (e.g. mother, daughter, sister). This focus on positionality should be valuable in efforts to deconstruct debates on the Muslim 'other' – shedding light on the multiple layers that constitute this 'other'. Ultimately these lenses point to the very intimate relation that exists between the (re)production and stability of European polities and the figure of the Muslim woman.

CONCLUDING THOUGHTS

This chapter has sought to remind the reader of the importance of critically assessing *why* Muslim women find themselves at the center of debates, policies and programmes on Islam. By looking more generally at the gendered dimension of community building processes, and the pivotal role women are given in those projects, one realises that this 'obsession' on 'saving' and 'reforming' Muslim women is far from being trivial. It seems, in fact, to be essential to the (re)production and stability of many European political formations. One central question we should therefore be asking ourselves when analyzing discourses on Islam in Europe and elsewhere is what does this 'obsession' with Muslim women bodies and predicaments "produce" and what does it "erase" (Razack 2008a: 86)?

While this chapter has focused on exploring the European obsession with headscarves, the above mentioned question should invite us to examine the gendered dimension of other discourses and policies that seek to 'save' Muslim women. For instance, Beaman (2012), Razack (2008b), Jiwani and Hoodfar

---

23 Yuval-Davis speaks of "stage in the life cycle" as an axis of difference (2006: 200).

(2012) and others have critically assessed the usage of the term 'honour killings' frequently mentioned to characterise crimes against Muslim women perpetuated by members of 'Muslim communities'. They have highlighted how differentiating this type of violence from other violence against women "produces" a divide between "civilized" collectivities that do not practice such heinous crimes and "uncivilized" ones (Beaman 2012: 231). At the same time it "erases" the fact that 'non-Muslim' women in European and North-American societies suffer similar ills - erasing patriarchal tendencies and violence affecting women and girls born in 'modern' societies:

> Calling the murders 'honour killings' accomplishes two goals. First, it makes it seem as if femicide is a highly unusual event. Second, it makes it seem as if femicide is confined to specific populations within Canada and specific national cultures or religions in the world at large [...]. According to StatsCan figures, from 2000 to 2009 an average of 58 women a year were killed in this country as a result of spousal violence [...]. In contrast, recent estimates tell us that there have been 12 or 13 so-called honour killings in Canada in the last decade.
>
> (Jiwani/Hoodfar 2012: 2-3)[24]

For Scott the French ban on the headscarf produces similar effects as it creates the illusion that gender inequality exists only in 'other' [Muslim] communities, while erasing pervading patriarchal tendencies that run through French society, where laws condemning domestic violence or sexual harassment, unlike laws restricting headscarves, have been approved with much difficulty (Scott 2010).

Pushing our reflection further one could wonder whether this heightened obsession with the bodies of Muslim women and their predicaments during the past decade does not share similarities with the dynamic described by Wendy Brown in her study of why modern nation-states are obsessed with the constructions of walls to 'protect' their borders. In a similar way, it may be a sign indicating the deep crisis of sovereignty and identity that contemporary political formations,

---

24 These authors are commenting on a Canadian case, where Mohammad Shafia was found guilty of first degree murder of his three daughters and his second wife, who were all found dead inside a car discovered in a river in Ontario. His first wife and son were also incriminated in the verdict released in January 2012. Beaman (2012) offers a similar argumentation than Hoodfar and Jiwani.

such as nation-states or the European Union are facing today[25]. In an era where the borders of nation-states are being eroded due to the impact of late modern processes and where states are disinvesting themselves from several of their functions, this focus on the 'other' may be a way for these political formations to symbolically assert their power and create the illusion of undisrupted borders (Brown, 2010: 24). As such, banning headdress from different public institutions could symbolise efforts by political formations to maintain the fantasy that they remain "progressive agent of national modernity" (McClintock 1996: 359). Thus, it is possible that this discursive focus on 'reforming' Muslim women produces the illusion of an 'active' and 'invested' polity. At the same time, this effect erases the social, economic and political conditions that might "push immigrant communities to adopt more patriarchal and conservative practices" (Razack 2008b: 135), the different forms of violence devout Muslim women might be confronted to in their daily encounters with 'modern' societies (id., 144), and finally the similarities and blurrinesses that exist between the 'us' and 'them'. Not unlike walls, Muslim women's predicaments today seem to "produce not the future of an illusion, but the illusion of a future aligned with an idealized past" (Brown 2010: 133).

Being aware of how their bodies and predicaments participate to this illusion of stability seems to be a first step in understanding power relations that run through debates on the Muslim 'other'. A second step - the importance of which has already been highlighted by several scholars (e.g. Razack 2008b: 168; Beaman 2012; Barras 2012; Salih/Moors 2007) - lies in an effort to document the experiences and narratives of devout Muslim women. So doing might not only contribute to deconstructing the category 'Muslim women' by highlighting the diversity of experiences and contextualising them, but also to blurring and complexifying the 'us' versus 'them' divide - a path that some might find risky however, as it will inevitably further interrogate the stability, comfort and universality of the 'us'.

ACKNOWLEDGEMENT

Research for this paper was supported by a generous Swiss National Science Foundation post-doctoral fellowship.

---

25 The parallel with colonial Algeria is interesting here, as one could argue that in the 1950s the French government in Algeria was also faced with a deep crisis of legitimacy.

REFERENCES

Abu-Lughod, Lila (2002): "Do Muslim women really need saving? Anthropological reflections on cultural relativism and its others", in: *American Anthropologist* 104:3, pp. 783-790.

Assemblée Nationale (2010): Rapport d'Information – Au nom de la mission d'information sur les pratiques du voile intégral sur le territoire national (No 2262) [online]: Assemblée Nationale. [online] Available at: http://www.assemblee-nationale.fr/13/rap-info/i2262.asp (accessed 5 December 2012).

— (2012): Proposition de loi visant à étendre l'obligation de neutralité à certaines personnes ou structures privées accueillant des mineurs et à assurer le respect du principe de laïcité. Proposition de loi no 4182. Paris: Assemblée Nationale. [online] Available at: http://www.assemblee-nationale.fr/13/propositions/pion4182.asp (accessed 6 November 2012).

Barras, Amélie (2010): "Contemporary laïcité: setting the terms of a new social contract? The slow exclusion of devout Muslim women", in: *Totalitarian Movement and Political Religions*, 11:2, pp. 229-247.

— (2012): "The struggle of devout Turkish women for full citizenship", in: *MERIP*, 262, pp. 32-35.

Beaman, Lori (2012): "The status of women: The report from a civilized society", in: *Canadian Criminal Law Review*, 16:2, pp. 223-246.

Brown, Wendy (2010): *Walled states, waning sovereignty*, London: MIT Press.

Cinar, Alev (2005): *Modernity, Islam and secularism in Turkey: Bodies, places and time*, Minneapolis: University of Minnesota Press.

Council of Europe, Parliamentary Assembly (2010): Islam, Islamism and Islamophobia in Europe. (Resolution 1743) [online] Available at: http://assembly.coe.int/Mainf.asp?link=/Documents/AdoptedText/ta10/ERES 1743.htm (accessed 24 May 2012).

Danchin, Peter (2011): "Islam in the secular nomos of the European Court of Human Rights", in: *Michigan Journal of International Law*, 32, pp. 663-2011.

Fadil, Nadia (2009): "Managing affects and sensibilities: The case of not-handshaking and not-fasting", in: *Social Anthropology*, 17:4, pp. 439-454.

Fanon, Frantz (2011 [1959]): *L'an V de la révolution algérienne*, Paris: La Découverte.

Fassin, Eric (2010): "National identities and transnational intimacies: sexual democracy and the politics of immigration in Europe", in: *Public Culture*, 22:3, pp. 507-529.

Gal, Susan (2004): "A semiotics of the public/private distinction", in: Scott, Joan W. / Keates, Debra (eds), *Going public: Feminism and the shifting bounda-*

ries of the private sphere, Urbana/Champaign: University of Illinois Press, pp. 261-278.

Gökariksel, Banu (2007): "A feminist geography of veiling. Gender, class, and religion in the making of modern subjects and public spaces in Istanbul", in: Morin, Karen M. / Guelke, Jeanne-Kay (eds), *Women, religion, and space: Global perspectives on gender and faith,* Syracuse/New York: Syracuse University Press, pp. 61-81.

Guillaume, Xavier / Barras, Amélie (2013): "The safety of authenticity: Ali Kebap or an exploration in the contemporaneity of foreignness and the self's post-colonial imaginary", in: *European Journal of Cultural Studies,* 16:3, pp. 310-328.

Hurd Shakman, Elizabeth (forthcoming): "Rescued by law? Gender and the global politics of secularism", in: Cady, Linell / Fessenden, Tracy (eds), *Gendering the divide,* New York: Columbia University Press.

Jackobsen, Janet (2010): "Ethics after pluralism", in: Bender, Courtney / Klassen, Pamela (eds), *After pluralism: Reimagining religious engagement,* New York: Columbia University Press, pp. 31-59.

Jasmine (2011a): "Assistante maternelle, voile et laïcité", in: *Blog Jasmine and co,* [blog] 29 November, available at: http://blog.jasmineandco.fr/assistante-maternelle-voile-laicite (accessed 7 November 2012).

— (2011b): "Une loi contre les nounous?", in: *Blog Jasmine and co,* [blog] 5 December, available at: http://blog.jasmineandco.fr/loi-contre-nounous-voile (accessed 7 November 2012).

Jiwani, Yasmin / Hoodfar, Homa (2012): "Should we call it 'honour killing'? No. It's a false distancing of ourselves from a too-common crime: the murder of females", in: *The Gazette,* 31 January. [online] Available at: http://mrcssi.com/wp-content/uploads/2011/10/The-Gazette.pdf (accessed 24 August 2013).

Jouili, Jeanette (2009): "Negotiating secular boundaries: Pious micro-practices of Muslim women in French and German public spheres", in: *Social Anthropology,* 17:4, pp. 455-470.

Kandiyoti, Deniz (1991): "Identity and its Discontents: Women and the Nation", in: *Millenium-Journal of International Studies,* 20, pp. 429-443.

— (1997): "Gendering the modern: On missing dimensions in the study of Turkish modernity", in: Bozdogan, Sibel / Kasaba, Reşat (eds), *Rethinking modernity and national identity in Turkey,* Seattle/London: University of Washington Press, pp. 113-133.

Kuru, Ahmet (2008): "Secularism, state policies and Muslims in Europe: Analysing French exceptionalism", in: *Comparative Politics,* 41:1, pp. 1-19.

Le Bars, Stéphanie (2012): "Le Sénat vote l'extension de la neutralité religieuse pour les 'nounous' à domicile", in: *Monde Blogs,* [blog] 18 January, available

at: http://religion.blog.lemonde.fr/2012/01/18/le-senat-vote-l%E2%80%99extens
ion-de-la-neutralite-religieuse-pour-les-nounous-a-domicile (accessed 6 November 2012).

Mahmood, Saba (2006): "Secularism, hermeneutics, and empire: The politics of
Islamic reformation", in: *Public Culture,* 18:2, pp. 323-347.

— (2009): "Religious reason and secular affect: An incommensurable divide?,
in: Asad, Talal et al., *Is critique secular? Blasphemy, injury and free
speech",* pp. 64-100 (The Townsend Papers in the Humanities, 2).

Mayer, Jean-François (2011): "A country without minarets: analysis of the background and meaning of the Swiss vote of 29 November 2009", in: *Religion,*
41:1, pp. 11-28.

McClintock, Anne (1996): "No longer in a future heaven': Gender, race and nationalism", in: Eley, Geoff / Suny, Ronald Grigor (eds), *Becoming national.
A Reader,* Oxford: Oxford University Press, pp. 260-286.

Merckx, Ingrid (2012): "Pas laïque ma nounou?", in: *Politis,* 2 February.

Ministère de l'Education nationale (2012): *Orientations et instructions pour la
préparation de la rentrée 2012,* circulaire no 2012-056. [online] Available at:
http://www.education.gouv.fr/pid25535/bulletin_officiel.html?cid_bo=59726
(accessed 24 May 2012).

Moghadam, Valentine (1999): "Gender, national identity and citizenship: Reflections on the Middle East and North Africa", in: *Comparative Studies of
South Asia, Africa and the Middle East,* 19:1, pp. 137-156.

Nussbaum, Marta (2012): *The new religious intolerance. Overcoming the politics of fear in an anxious age,* Cambridge MA/London: The Belknap Press of
Harvard University Press.

Razack, Sherene (2008a): "Between a rock and a hard place: Canadian Muslim
women's responses to faith-based arbitration", in: Mehdi, Rubya et al. (eds),
Law and Religion in Multicultural Societies, Copenhagen: DJØF, pp. 83-95.

— (2008b): *Casting out: The eviction of Muslim from Western law and politics,*
Toronto: University of Toronto Press.

Salih, Ruba (2000): "bhifting Boundaries of self and other: Moroccan migrant
women in Italy", in: *European Journal of Women's Studies,* 7:3, pp. 321-
332.

— (2009): "Muslim women, fragmented secularism and the construction of in-
terconnected 'publics' in Italy", in: *Social Anthropology,* 17:4, pp. 409-423.

Salih, Ruba / Moors, Annelies (2007): "'Muslim women' in Europe: Bodily
performance, multiple belongings and the public sphere", in: Workshop
Description: 8th Mediterranean Research Meeting, European University Institute, Florence/Montecatini Terme, 21-25 March. [online] Available at:
http://www.eui.eu/Documents/RSCAS/Research/Mediterranean/WS10MRM

2007.pdfhttp://eui.eu/Documents/RSCAS/Research/Mediterranean/WS10M RM2007.pdf%20 (accessed 6 November 2012).

Sarkozy, Nicolas (2009): *Déclaration du Président de la République devant le Parlement réuni en Congrès.* 22 June. [online] Available at: http//www.assemblee-nationale.fr/histoire/messages-et-declarations-du-president-de-la-republique/sarkozy-declaration-22juin2009.asp (accessed 6 November 2012).

Scott, Joan (2010): "France's ban on the Islamic veil has little to do with female emancipation", in: *The Guardian,* 26 August 2010. [online] Available at: http://www.guardian.co.uk/law/2010/aug/26/france-ban-islamic-veil (accessed 6 November 2012).

— (2007): *The Politics of the veil,* Princeton: Princeton University Press.

Spivak, Gayatri (1988): "Can the subaltern speak?", in: Nelson, Cary / Grossberg, Lawrence (eds), *Marxism and the interpretation of culture,* Hampshire, Basingstoke: Macmillan Education, pp. 271-317.

Yuval-Davis, Nira (1997a): "Women, citizenship and difference", in: *Feminist Review,* 57, pp. 4-27.

— (1997b): *Gender and nation,* London: Sage.

— (2006): "Belonging and the politics of belonging", in: *Patterns of Prejudice,* 40:3, pp. 197-214.

Yuval-Davis, Nira / Anthias, Floya / Kofman, Eleonore (2005): "Secure borders and safe haven and the gendered politics of belonging: Beyond social cohesion", in: *Ethnic and Racial Studies,* 28:3, pp. 513-535.

Yuval-Davis, Nira / Werbner, Pnina (1999): "Introduction", in: id. (eds), *Women, citizenship and difference,* London/New York: Z Books, pp. 1-39.

Formatting Islam versus mobilising Islam in prison: Evidence from the Swiss case

MALLORY SCHNEUWLY PURDIE

INTRODUCTION

Contemporary religion evolves in a paradox: while some studies show that Occidental societies are secularising and that religion is losing its historical influence on defining norms (Bruce 2002; Davie/Woodhead/Heelas 2003; Voas 2009; Storm 2009), we notice that religion nevertheless remains an important topic in public debates. While on one hand, people tend to develop distanced forms of religiosity (Stolz et al. 2013); on the other hand, we note a publicisation of elements that are connected to religion without being essentially religious (Parini/Gianni/Clavien 2012; Clavien 2009; Lüddeckens/Uehlinger/Walthert 2010). In other words, it is not religion as such that is discussed in the public sphere, but it is used as an interpretative category in order to discuss political and social issues. One way to understand this paradox lies in the need for a community to define itself in relation to others in order to secure social cohesion and internal consistency. Collectivities, more or less consciously, build symbolic boundaries between an 'us' and an 'other' that allows individuals to define themselves and belong to one or another subgroup (Lamont/Molnar 2002; Wimmer 2008). At a time when secularity and *laïcité* function as socially admitted norms, the social construction of the 'other' (again) goes through its religious identification. Although one may patronise (or even mock) the Christian who publically claims his devotion to God, the Muslim declaring his faith will be considered with suspicion, fear, even hostility. One can witness the development of a public discourse on Islam that describes it as a tremendous factor in social disintegration, as a religion that challenges shared social codes (Poole 2002; Poole/Richardson

2006; Ettinger/Udris 2009). More than a religious belonging, Islam becomes a marker of social differentiation conditioning the process of inclusion and exclusion (Dahinden/Duemmler/Moret 2010; Schneuwly Purdie/Salzbrunn 2011).

Correctional facilities in Switzerland are characterised by cultural and religious diversity. In 2009, the Federal Statistical Office published a report showing that foreign infractors form 70.2 per cent of the prison population. The Swiss Federal Census 2000 indicated that Muslim and Christian-Orthodox inmates were overrepresented: according to these statistics, a quarter of the detainees were Muslim (23.6%), whereas the Muslim population only represented 4.3 per cent of the Swiss population (Broquet 2007).[1] Beside federal data, some prisons have published socio-demographical data concerning inmates: in 2011, a Geneva prison announced that 57 per cent of inmates recorded were Muslims and a Zurich prison recorded Muslim detainees at 28 per cent.[2] These numbers were widely echoed in the regional press and feed the mediatic and political debates on immigration, integration and social dangerousness of 'Muslims'.[3] In a context of publicisation of Islam, a context dominated by a "total discourse" on Islam and

---

1   It is imperative to interpret these numbers with extreme care. Indeed, the data concerning correctional facilities is incomplete. The percentages concern 2968 defendants and convicted inmates out of 5666 people incarcerated in 2000. Moreover, this analysis shows that 29.7% of the inmates did not provide any information at all about their confessional affiliation, which could be due to problems understanding the languages or questionnaires used. One should also note that due to a methodological modification of the Federal census in 2010, confessional affiliation of the penal population is no longer collected. The 2000 data is thus the most recent upon which our analysis can be based.

2   See the activity reports 2011 of Champ-Dollon and Pöschwies (Département de la sécurité, de la police et de l'environnement 2011; Direktion der Justiz und des Innern 2011). I emphasise that this overpopulation is not the norm in all Swiss correctional facilities. Interviews with chief security officers suggest smaller numbers. Indeed, small to mid-size prisons often do not have any Muslim inmates, whereas big prisons (over 100 beds) often exceed the year 2000 national average.

3   Religious affiliation should not be taken as an explainable criterion in criminal trajectories. As Montero-Perez-De-Tudela (2009) shows, the conjunction of three factors: sex (male), age (18-25) and socio-economic status has a direct influence on deviance. Indeed, from the Muslim prison population questioned in 2000, 98.1% were male, 49.2% were aged between 20 and 29 years old and 72% had a low level of education. Since social determinants are the same for Muslim affiliations as for other confessional affiliations, we will avoid making assimilations between religious affiliation and criminal behaviour.

Muslims (Behloul 2009), religious affiliation of the prison population is (regularly) used in order to justify alarmist discourses.

In a research conducted in Swiss prisons between 2007 and 2010 (Becci et al. 2011), I studied 'Muslim inmates'. This section of the prison population is the object of a double discourse: on the one hand, because of its infractor status (guilty of having committed crimes they are considered – by extension – guilty of contributing to social disintegration); on the other hand because their religious affiliation is represented as an additional source of social dangerousness. This double postulate contributes to a construction of the 'Muslim inmate' not only as 'the other' from the point of view of the 'free' civil society, but also from the point of view of the prison community.

In this contribution, I will demonstrate how a social and political category imposes itself in the (apparently) closed world of prisons. I will also describe how the 'total discourse' on Islam and Muslim influences the Islamic mobilisations of some 'Muslim inmates'. Firstly, I will show how, in the context of a total institution, the 'Muslim' social category influences the ways that non-Muslims (wardens and inmates) perceive Islam and Muslim inmates. Secondly, I will describe the variegated ways that 'Muslim inmates' refer to Islam and how they react to the categorisation. Finally, I will also comment on the role of detention in respect to the (eventual) mobilisations of Islamic references in the construction of their identities.

METHODOLOGY

Our research on religious plurality in Swiss prisons combined different methodological approaches: legal frameworks were analysed, quantitative data on the variegated offer in terms of religious and spiritual care in prison was collected, observation and semi-structured interviews were conducted ethnographically (Spradley 1979). The results presented in this article concern the ethnographical data; I shall thus not describe the methodology of the whole project but will concentrate on the interviews with inmates, prison wardens, as well as on the field notes[4]. The ethnographical journal recalls material as well as immaterial obser-

---

4   Fieldwork was conducted in four correctional facilities, but the data analysed in this contribution only concerns two institutions: prison A and prison D. Prison A is a penal institution situated in a Catholic region. With a capacity of 200 places, prison A essentially accommodates detainees in semi-open incarceration (allowing for some detainees to work outside the walls, for instance in the institution's fields or orchards). Prison D is a correctional facility situated in an Evangelical Reformed area. It accommodates 270

vations: descriptions of the prisons environment, of the divisions of cells, of the rooms where the religious services take place and of the rooms where we interviewed the inmates, as well as notes on the relationships between the guardians and the inmates, and inmates with each other.

Between 2009 and 2010, the research team[5] conducted 25 semi-structured interviews with male inmates living in two different prisons (prison D and prison A). Recruited on a voluntary basis, informants were told that sociologists were conducting a research on religious pluralism in Swiss prisons. In prison D, with the assistance of two chaplains, we posted short notices and registration forms on the billboards. After ten days, the chaplains gave us a list of inmates interested in having a conversation with us. We interviewed every inmate who volunteered, no matter his age, crime or confession. In prison A, however, we specifically requested permission to interview Muslim inmates. With the assistance of the social services, we organised 13 interviews with Muslim detainees. All interviews were digitally recorded, transcribed verbatim and analysed taking into account the premises of the grounded theory (Glaser/Strauss 1967). We privileged an inductive approach, developing a codebook interview after interview. Firstly, we analysed each interview alone and then we systematically compared them. In total, we interviewed 25 male inmates aged between 20 and 63 years old. They were all serving long sentences, from 21 months to 20 years. They came from different parts of the world, including Switzerland (9), France (2), South America (2), Maghreb (3), the Middle East (3) and Sub-Saharan Africa (6). Two were agnostics, five were Catholics, two were Protestants, one mixed Protestantism and Hinduism together and fifteen were Muslims[6].

To complete our data, we also conducted a group interview with three prison wardens. This group interview was digitally recorded as well, transcribed verbatim and triangulated with the other discourses on religion in prison. Two of the wardens were Swiss and one was Spanish, one was a declared atheist, one was Catholic and the other was Buddhist. They were aged between 35 and 43 years old.

---

inmates who execute long sentences (up to life in prison). Highly secured, the perimeter is divided in two sections: one building hosts inmates in total detention while in the second building, inmates can work in the fields surrounding the facility. – All field sources are in French, all translations for this chapter are mine.

5   The interviews in prison A were gathered by me and my students at the University of Fribourg (fall 2010) and the interviews in prison D were conducted by Brigitte Knobel, Delphine Gex-Collet and myself (spring 2009).

6   Out of the 25 inmates, 12 were interviewed in prison D and 13 in prison A.

PRISON AS TOTAL INSTITUTION

The concept of total institution developed by Erving Goffman (1961) in the 1960s still influences the ways in which researchers study prisons. Goffman defines a total institution as an institution that exercises an authority and defines the normativity of all aspects of the lives of the residents. A total institution applies a unique collective regulation to all of its residents and takes responsibility for all their needs (physical, psychological, spiritual, etc.). Prison institutions constitute a perfect example of total institutions, since they support, regulate and control all aspects of the individuals' life: Meals, clothing, movements, neighbourhood relations, relations with the outside, leisure, work activities and sexuality are domains of one's identity that are strongly determined by the institution. Prisons interfere in all aspects of the individual's life; its main purpose is the "caretaking of men and the control of their ways of living" (Rostaing 1997) Incarceration inevitably leads to prisonisation (Clemmer 1958 [1940]; Sykes 1958). Prisonisation is a process designating the incorporation in one's social identity of the prison norms. From the detainee's point of view, entering the penal institution constitutes a drastic break from his preceding life, establishing a rupture with one's habits and a loss of social status.

However, penal sociology shows that today's prisons do not resemble the total institutions described by Goffman on all points. It is necessary to go over the conception of the prison as an institution withdrawn into itself and to take into consideration the fact that it is also opened to the surrounding world, be it only through the daily relations that it maintains with the outside (Rostaing 1997; Chatraine 2006; Chauvenet/Rostaing/Orlic 2005). Of course, the personality mortification process (Rostaing 1997) through admission procedures is still at work, but the instauration of rights to detainees contributes to dismantling the wall between the world of the inmates and the outside world. As Corinne Rostaing underlines, "the most striking signs of the depersonalization of the inmates are disappearing" (1997: 6): in this way, in most prisons around the world, prison uniforms are no longer mandatory and personal outfits (such as sport cloths) are legion. Cells are often personally decorated, inmates can follow special diets, cook for themselves, receive visits and they also have access to the media (paper, radio and television). Penal institutions also allow a right to education and organise leisure activities to occupy the inmates: football or table-football tournaments, theatres and concerts are organised. Nevertheless, this permeability between the world of the cloistered and the outside world does not singifiy the end of the total institution: access to all activities, to the media, to mail and to visits is largely controlled and supervised by the administration.

In this chapter, given the power the prison has over the life of the detainees, I consider the Swiss prisons as total institutions. I take into consideration, however, the fact that it maintains daily relations with the outside world, that those frequent contacts reciprocally influence the relations and interactions that take place within its walls.

ISLAM AND MUSLIMS AS SOCIAL CONSTRUCTS

For over a decade, researches have acknowledged that Muslims are considered as a cultural and religious group which is difficult to integrate (European Monitoring Center on Racism and Xenophobia 2006; Angst/Kreienbühl/Naguib 2006; Commission fédérale contre le racisme 2010). In the public sphere, notably in the media, Islam is described as a coercive religion that contests social manners and norms of democratic societies (such as freedom of religion, expression, sexual orientation, marriage, clothing, etc.). Often reduced to notions of underdevelopment, barbaric civilisation (e.g. corporal punishments), fundamentalism and political instability, Islam is also depicted as a religion that favours the collective over the individual, a religion that discriminates against women and that calls upon violence and terrorism (Poole 2002; Poole/Richardson 2006). In *Covering Islam* (1981), Said identifies the 1979 Iran Revolution as the starting point of the publicisation of Islam as a threat. From that point on, Muslims have tended to be pictured as militant, dangerous and anti-Western. Saïd argues that in the media, Islam is simply 'covered up' and not problematised; ignorance and cultural hostility have largely conditioned the ways the press reports on Islam and Muslim affairs. As Poole (2002) points out in regards with British society, Muslims are rarely treated as part of society and they rarely appear in everyday stories. Coverage of Muslim stories is limited to sensational events, reaffirming on one hand the common stereotypes and on the other hand following a political agenda. Richardson (2006) notes that the media is constantly tying Islam and negativity together, including when Muslim experts are given the chance to speak. He explains that such experts are only invited to discuss critical situations in Muslim countries or to comment on Islamic deviation. The fact that they are extremely rarely invited to comment on non-Islamic or non-Muslim topics contributes to creating a symbolic and ideological distance between Muslims and non-Muslims, by stating the fact that Muslim experts only are qualified to talk about negative subjects.

Research on representations of Islam in the Swiss media show similar results. Triangulating qualitative interviews with religious leaders and journalists with content analysis of press articles, Urs Dahinden (2009) shows that Muslims tend to be represented as 'the guilty' and 'the bad guys', whereas Christians tend to be seen as 'the good mothers', Buddhists as 'the heros' and Jews as 'the victims'. Based on an analysis of various media (talk shows, tabloids, specialised press), researchers observed "a discontinuing but intensifying problematisation of foreigners and ethnic minorities" (Ettinger/Udris 2009: 93) and they showed that semantics used by the media tends to link immigration with criminality. In the contemporary context of social insecurity, Ettinger and Udris underline that what is true for foreigners in general is particularly salient for Muslims. Focusing on the transversality of gender in the reporting of Islam in the media, Parini, Gianni and Claiven show to what extent gender issues are mobilised in order the construct 'the Muslims' as *the* figure of otherness. They also show that Muslims are most often mentioned in topics relating to national security, cultural difference (e.g. caricatures), community leaders (Parini/Gianni/Clavien 2012; Gianni/Clavien 2012) or to politics and laws (Eugster et al. 2010). Representing the Muslim as the figure of otherness, this varied research illustrates the process of boundary-making at work in society. Indeed, the Muslim as 'the other' not only exists in the media but it is an emanation of a political agenda that determines to a large extent public opinion.

Returning to our subject with these findings in mind, the following questions arise: Is the social construction of the Muslim category also present in Swiss prisons? Does it influence relations between staff and Muslim inmates as well as between inmates, independently of their respective religious affiliations? Does the 'Muslim' category work as a frontier between the inmates; and between inmates and wardens? Are the semantics regarding Islam and Muslims in prison similar to those outside the prison walls? Are criminality and violence also mobilised to define 'Muslim' inmates as a social category within the prison?

DEFINING ISLAM AND MUSLIMS IN PRISON

Before going any further, I would like to point out that in the interview grid, we never specifically asked questions about Islam and Muslims. Throughout the interviews, we were careful to use non-confessional vocabulary such as 'religion', 'practices', 'faiths', 'plurality' or 'diversity'. Nevertheless, a large majority of informants (chaplains, security officers, inmates) spontaneously shared with us their thoughts about Islam and Muslims; they all expressed clear negative opinions. The dominant opinion pictures Islam as a religion that encourages violence, as a dogma which crushes and manipulates. It is critical towards food prescriptions, prayer and the Qur'an. The account of Carlos[7] is symptomatic of the dominant opinion:

Carlos: There are religions that don't help.
Interviewer: For example?
Carlos: The Muslims, Islam. No, it doesn't help, because there are people who use it and one can say they are terrorists. Because many things that are said in the Bible, no, how do we call that already…
Interviewer: The Qur'an.
Carlos: The Qur'an and I don't agree with it. They treat women like dogs. I don't think it is written that way. I saw a TV show about men that didn't even know for sure but who said that their wives had betrayed them and then they would take them in the garden and shoot them in the head and then just offer a cow to the police officer. Or they would bring her to the football stadium and cut her throat off in front of everyone. She hasn't done anything! Killing people, exploding kids in the bus, for nothing. And then say that 40 virgins are waiting for them beside God and that they are going to make love to them forever. Me, when they tell me that, I tell myself: "There are forty devils that will sting you for eternity." Me, I don't have anything against religions, but as soon as one touches children, it puts me in a rage.

The spontaneity with which informants talked about Islam is an interesting result. It shows to what extent, when we talk about religion and pluralism, Islam tends to impose itself as *the* figure of diversity and otherness.

Taking a closer look at the discourses on Muslim, we can distinguish the following trends:

- an overrepresentation of the number of Muslim inmates in the prison,
- an amalgam between religion, ethnicity, race and nationality,
- a tendency to consider Muslim inmates as source of social disorder within the prison.

Firstly, it appears that the Muslim presence tends to be overrepresented by both the security officers and the inmates. Even though at the time of the research, 33

---

7   In order to guarantee confidentiality to informants (inmates as well as wardens), all names have been changed.

per cent of the inmates in Prison D were Muslim, the guards and inmates interviewed thought they represented a large majority. The following sequences shall offer a short illustration. Questioned about the reality of diversity in prison D, the guards answered:

Hervé:	Not far from three quarters are Muslims. Yes, I think not far from three quarters. Therefore, we cannot really talk about diversity.
Interviewer:	And the rest?
Jacques:	Christians and atheists.
José:	Yes, there really are the Muslims, Catholics, Protestants and then yes, atheists or Buddhists. Well, me, I would say that, yes, Muslims dominate, with Christians, especially those from South America that are mostly Catholic.

Interviews with inmates show the same trend: Bruno says that the only religion that one can see in prison is Islam; Konstantin thinks that most inmates are Muslim and according to Quentin "One should do statistics, but I think there are 80 per cent of Muslims in here".

How can we explain how individuals who mix with inmates on a daily basis can be so wrong about the actual numbers? The total discourse on Islam and Muslims cannot be enough to explain the gap between their perceptions and the reality. One path to understanding this result lies in the importance of arrangements implemented for the attention of Muslim prisoners. Indeed, 'Muslims' are the ethno-religious group to which the greatest number of arrangements are organised: prison A as well as prison D plan the regular presence of Muslim representatives for Friday prayers; on registration, both accommodate (to some extent) the requirements of inmates during Ramadan; both give special instructions to wardens in order to respect the prayers in cells; both provide meals without pork and/or vegetarian meals and allow the possession of prayer rugs in cells (cf. Schneuwly Purdie/Vuille 2010).

Another path to understanding this overrepresentation lies in the amalgam made by the informants between religious, ethnic, cultural and national belongings. For security officers as well as for inmates, those four belongings tend to designate a single reality: being a Muslim. The following quotation offers a good picture of this blending together:

Hervé:	There are more Muslims.
Jacques:	Yes, more Muslims. Well, it is because of the Balkan countries, there was an increase of Balkan inmates.
José:	In general, the thing is that there are Arabs and we say Muslims.

Jacques: No, no.

José: No, but there are many that I see that do not practice their religion at all. But we talk about Muslims, but yes, it is us that often make the amalgam and we say: "He is an Arab, so a Muslim." Me, I often make the entries, I register the new comers. So it is true that some of them, when we ask them about their religion they are often Muslims. But it is true that Arabs are often Muslims, but it is also us that... However they do not practice their religion anymore than me or anyone else. But, they say they are Muslims as one could say he is Catholic or Protestant.

Hervé: And if it is a person that comes from one of these countries and that cares about his religion, I don't know, they are a really small minority. Maghreb, there are few. But from Yugoslavia they are quite a few, the Serbs Christian-Orthodox.

Jacques: But I think that with the Muslims, the barrier between education and the Church is really small. So, the ways they behave in life, everything is related. Me, I feel it this way, it is much stronger than with a Catholic or a Protestant.

Interviewer: What you want to say is that religion is less a private affair for Muslims than for others?

Hervé: Yeah.

Jacques: More their ways of living, of behaving, their ways of...

Hervé: You mean education?

Jacques: All their education is much closer to religion than in any other religion.

Hervé: Because, me, I am polite. I have been educated the old way by my parents, but...

José: I don't see the point.

Jacques: Very often, it is all about religion. There are certain things that they will do, ways they will behave. Let's take again the example of women! It is coming from religion. Such things are not about education.

José: Yeah... but no.

Jacques: Yes, in this case, it is about religion.

José: Me, I don't agree, because I think that it is more about education than religion because they agree to touch our women. But, we, on the contrary, are not allowed to touch theirs. And that, according to me is not a question of religion.

Hervé: They don't share (laughs).

This sequence illustrates the ways the security officers mingle religious affiliation (Islam), cultural origin (Maghreb/Balkan) and ethnicity (Arab). One can also read that they mix religious belonging together with the strength of the religious convictions. It appears to them that being Muslim goes along with the practice of their religion.

A third path to understanding this overrepresentation lies in the social representation of the Muslim inmates in prison. Both inmates and staff defined them as scrappers, grumblers, liars, or as 'pains in the neck'. Talking about the way the administration handles pluralism, Karl-Alex says:

> I find them really cool with the Muslims. They are pains in the neck! Because they don't want to eat what's on the menu, because they are always grumbling about the food. They are complainers because they want to push their religion so bad. Me, I had fights, moral fights with inmates because I did not have enough Qur'ans in the prison library! Or I had the Qur'an, but not in the right language, because they wanted it in German/Arab or English/Arab. I had all those languages, but from time to time, it was missing. And every Muslim has to have a Qur'an in his cell, even if he doesn't open it because he can't read. Because often, they can't read! But they have to have it. They have to have this book, it has to be in their cell. It is a constant record. I tried to make them read, because reading in prison is extremely important, because you don't have anything else to do. But all they wanted was the Qur'an. (Karl-Alex)

Theo and Karl-Alex criticise what they see as hypocritical practices:

> All the Arabs are the same. Well, some pray, yes, some do. But they pray and they steal right after! I don't know, but what's the point! (Theo)

> There are many Muslims here. In prison C, it was even the majority or almost. And Muslims, they practice their religion a lot. Even in the middle of work! They stop working to pray. It's quite funny, I have to say. It's very special, it's a thing that questions a lot, seeing that is weird. So, they are really tough guys, scrappers, thugs but when it is time to pray, it is time to pray. Paf, we stop everything, we get on our knees and we pray. This is funny. Honestly, I am not sure that they are really sincere. I am not convinced. I don't really understand. I find it very good if it makes them feel good, but once they are finished with their prayers, they start the fights again! Something doesn't sit right. (Karl-Alex)

Using the Islamic concept of the *jihād*, Konstantin describes the Muslim inmates as angry men, always dissenting:

Konstantin: In prison, it is really better to be Christian than Muslim. Yes, yes. Christianity never institutes the *jihād* for example. And here, it is *jihād* all the time, we can see it in here. This is why I have the feeling that there are so many Muslims here because we are always in *jihād*.

Interviewer: What do you mean by *jihād*?

Konstantin: In Arabic it is… How can I explain that? Permanent rebellion, there it is, permanent rebellion. This is how I would describe it. It is not a Holy War or I don't know what, no. It is a derivation, no, *jihād* is to manifest loud and clear when one doesn't agree. Christians are not at all like this.

The same remarks are present in the discourses of the prison guards. Talking about an incident that happened a year before, the wardens interpreted it in terms of Muslim deviance. On a July afternoon, a Swiss/Tunisian inmate sentenced to 20 months in prison, but incarcerated for over ten years (and for an undetermined duration because of his psychological condition) climbed on the prison's roof, refused to return to his cell and threatened to kill himself if he was not allowed to speak to the media. The security finally managed to control him after 30 hours:

Hervé: And it was a Muslim. And the whole time, there were inmates watching through the windows. Because what happened was that some inmates went to work and the riot exploded when the inmates were off to work. Then, they didn't want to go to work either nor back to the cells. Some stayed in their cells and put their tape player on the windows and listened to incantations, things for future martyrs and all the mess. It's extreme! It's a bit like pushing him to make trouble! Somehow, I think they were pushing him to jump.

Jacques: Well, at the end he looked stupid because he didn't know what to do anymore.

Hervé: Yes, he looked stupid. But how many inmates did we have to move after that episode? Approximately nineteen. And again, three quarters were Muslims. And the ones who yelled the loudest and were the most aggressive with us, they were Muslims too. There is a mass effect for sure: "He is a martyr! Let's help him." This is why I say that we need a balance. And at the moment, it is unbalanced in favour of Muslims. When you hear those stories about incantations, chanting, martyrs etc. This inmate told me it was about martyrs, but I don't understand anything about what they were saying (laughs).

Jacques: I didn't study Arab as a third language.

This incident had absolutely nothing to do with religion. Nevertheless, it is told as an episode that one can explain about the Muslim potential to challenge social order and create instability.

As these various excerpts show, the dominant representation of Islam and Muslims in the prison very much resembles its outside social representation: Muslim inmates are seen as a monolithic category, potentially dangerous to social order. All their attitudes and practices tend to be solely explained with their (supposed) religious affiliation, no matter if the inmate himself cares about his religion or not.

MOBILISING ISLAM IN PRISON

After having described the ways that non-Muslim penal actors consider Islam and Muslim inmates, we will now analyse how Muslim inmates mobilise (or not) Islamic references. Our research shows that, in the Swiss prisons, inmates mobilise Islam through five main practices: daily prayers, Friday prayer, food prescriptions (*halāl* consumption and the Ramadan fast), readings and conversations. Some inmates pray on a daily basis, but never attend Friday ceremonies. Others never formally pray, but make a point of eating *halāl* and watching preachers broadcasted on television.

Looking at the signification given by the detainees, those mobilisations are plural; each inmate resorts to religion subjectively and contextually. The following three portraits evidence the variety of these individual mobilisations.

Ezzeddine

Aged 22, Ezzeddine is French and Tunisian. Sentenced to 48 months for drug dealing, he has no proper professional education. Ezzeddine prays regularly. He uses prayer beads "as a support for meditation". He considers prayer and meditation as two different things: "prayer is just for God", it does not bring him anything, whereas meditation cools him down. He owns a prayer rug and says that he prays on his jacket when he is at work. He talks to God when he feels bad or when he is sick. Ezzeddine does not attend Friday prayer. He does not like it when there are many people, because it gives him a headache. He started the Ramadan fast, but he stopped once they sent him "to the dump" (isolation cell). Concerning food, he is careful what he eats and chooses the vegetarian menu. Ezzeddine reads the Qur'an; he finds that important. He thinks that Muslim inmates are not really practicing their religion, including himself since he does stupidities. He says that he will see that directly with God later. Religion has cooled him down. Since he began practicing Islam, he argues and fights less, he also swears less. However, he specified that he would not hesitate to kill somebody if they insulted the Prophet or his God.

Habib

Aged 23, Habib is from Guinea, where he worked as a bookbinder. Sentenced to five years for drug dealing, Habib prays every day: on a prayer rug in his cell and on cardboard at work. He attends Friday prayer and volunteers to perform the *ādhān*. He says that praying allows him to escape, "to feel somewhere else". He regrets that prayers do not take place every week, "it would be the jackpot", because the imam's visit gives him "100 per cent courage". Habib fasts and does not eat pork. He often reads the Qur'an, particularly when he "think[s] about negative things such as suicide". He justifies his incarceration because he did not respect the deals he made with God. Thus, God sent him to prison in order to make him think about his behaviour. Before going to prison, Habib did not pray. Religion as such has not become more important to him, he simply has more time to pray.

Slimane

Aged 37, Slimane is Moroccan and was sentenced to 56 months for drug dealing. He works (in prison) as an electrician (his profession). Since Slimane does not like to wake up, he never prays in the morning, but only prays when he "feels like it", when he does not feel good, when he gets bad news or when he has time and nothing else to do. Depending on his mood, he sometimes attends religious services: Friday prayer or the Catholic Mass. He does his best to fast during Ramadan and he tries hard to also fast with his hands, eyes and spirit (i.e. not get into any fights, not look at improper images on television, not think about improper subjects). Slimane does not eat pork, he reads the Qur'an and the Bible and he sometimes watches prayers and lectures on Al Jazeera. He explains that religion is really the last topic inmates would talk about because it inevitably leads to conflict. According to him there is absolutely no solidarity between detainees of the same religion.

Among the practices of Islam, prayers and food prescriptions are the most mobilised. However, it would be erroneous to consider that this fragmented practice reveals structural difficulties to actively practicing one's religion. As mentioned above, correctional facilities organise settings that allow the detainees to practice their faith. However, this result shows that Muslim inmates do not give particular relevance to religious orthopraxy and that they have situational recourses to religion: they pray because they have time to do so, they attend Friday prayer in order to meet people, they try not to eat any pork and/or to avoid all meat "because we [Muslims], we eat *halāl*".

In the various discourses, one can notice that religious belonging functions as a marker of a boundary between Muslim inmates, the other inmates and the staff. In the same way that non-Muslims define them by their religious belonging, Muslim inmates mobilise Islamic references in order to distinguish themselves from the non-Muslims. While the majority of them did not see any particular relevance in their religious belonging before their incarceration, references to Islam now partly defines their individual identities. There are four potential explanations to this phenomenon.

Firstly, religion is one of the rare belongings that an inmate 'can take with him' to prison. As previously mentioned, incarceration goes together with depersonalisation: the majority of the inmate's belongings are left behind (member of a sport club, a family, a social class, etc.) along with his social roles (a worker, a father, a neighbour, etc.). From that point on, he is reduced to a person of a certain sex and age, and a crime. Religion is a portable belonging that inmates can keep despite depersonalisation. It becomes a tool that can help them to (re)construct an alternative identity for themselves than the one assigned to them by prison and society (criminal, deviant, marginal).

Secondly, prisons are spaces of deprivation (Sykes 1958) where religion can fill some needs[8]. Religious mobilisation and, to a certain extent, religious involvement can become a means to avoid the prisonisation process and to partially answer the deprivation endured. Indeed, being religious can offer moments and places of freedom as well as special meals. It can return some pride by doing something positive (not violent, not degrading). As Dammer (2002) showed in his study on religious involvement in American prisons, being a Muslim can also fill the lack of security. Since the 'Muslims' are seen as potentially dangerous inmates, being one of them offers protection.

Thirdly, prisons can be considered (among other things) as places of religious socialisation (Beckford 1997; 2003). They constitute spaces where religious matters are present through the institutional chaplaincy, the various religious ministers or visitors, and the religious diversity of the staff and inmates. Correctional facilities authorise the detainees not only to practice their religion, but also to meet with a representative of their religion. Thus, inmates do not have

---

8   Sykes distinguished five types of deprivation in prison: deprivation of freedom, goods and services, autonomy, security and heterosexual activities.

to look for a representative of their confession, they just have to put their name on a list and wait for his visit or attend the service. Concerning Islam in Swiss prisons, Muslim representatives[9] do not belong to the prison chaplaincy. The large majority of them only enter the prison for Friday prayer. Nevertheless, the ways in which Muslim representatives talk about Islam, about guilt, forgiveness or destiny also has its influence on the ways that Muslim inmates mobilise (or not) Islamic references.

Fourthly, one can see that the social representation reducing the 'Muslim' to his religious belonging prevails in the prison and that it influences Muslims' mobilisations of Islam. Some detainees try to answer to an implicit norm[10] and to practice their religion as one thinks they should do. In this way, it is frequent to hear that those situational believers (the large majority) constantly justify their practices, their 'bricolages' and their deviations. Ahmed does not pray "because it is not good to pray one day and make shit the other day". Ezzeddine does not attend Friday prayer, because "it gives him a headache" to be with people and he stopped the Ramadan fast "when they put me in isolation". Bilal eats pork meat because "anyway, nothing is *halāl* in here". To assume the symbolic weight associated to the Muslim category pushes a number of Muslim inmates to adhere to practices and discourses that they did not follow before the incarceration and pushes them to justify any failures to the implicit norm.

CONCLUSIVE ELEMENTS

Most of the Muslim inmates we interviewed can be qualified as 'situational religious players', that is to say that they do not refer to religion on a regular and normative basis, but they mobilise the religious component situationally when they need to, when they feel like it, when they have time, or when it is useful.

There is a strong discrepancy between the ways that non-Muslims picture 'Muslim inmates' and the ways that 'Muslim inmates' describe their relations to Islam. For the first ones, Islam equates to

---

9   In a previous paper, I explained why I rather talk about Muslim representative as about imam. In order to complexify the roles and functions of the commonly designated imam, I distinguish five types of Muslim representatives acting in Swiss prisons: Friday imam, the counsellor, the big brother, the mediator and the visitor (Schneuwly Purdie 2011).

10 This implicit norm designates the regular practice of the five daily prayers, attendance to Friday prayer, ban on pork and alcohol and the Ramadan fast.

- a marker to identify an ethno-cultural group under one single label;
- a religion that, in many cases, leads to social disorder and violence;

whereas for the second, Islam is understood as:

- a "structuring norm" (Khosrokhavar 2004) that can help to temper anger; protect from suicide; teach patience, respect and forgiveness;
- a "therapy" (Sarg/Lamine 2011) that can comfort, give hope, strength and confidence: prayers work as anxiolytics; fasting purifies the body and the mind; Muslim representatives can replace psychologists, etc.;
- social ties: it can bring solidarity among inmates or be a link to the outside world and their families;
- a prison strategy in order to occupy the time, to improve living conditions, and to get protection;
- a marker in order to differentiate them from the other inmates as well as from the institution staff;
- a means by which to contest of the prison order and authority; or challenge other detainees on their religious affiliation or the correctness of their practices and discourses, etc.

As "total institutions", prisons try to supervise all religious matters within their walls. In this sense, religious experiences are strongly determined by the institution (Becci 2010; 2011), but not only by the institution. The social category of 'the Muslim' also has an impact on the way in which Muslim inmates mobilise (or not) their religious belonging. Finally, one should not underestimate the individual strategies used by inmates to preserve privacy. Mobilising religion, Islam in this case, can provide inmates with times and places when and where they can feel free.

REFERENCES

Research reports of all projects in the Swiss National Research Programme NRP 58 on "Religions, the State, and Society" are available online at http://www.nfp58.ch.

Angst, Doris / Kreienbühl, Sabine / Naguib, Tarek (2006): *Les relations avec la minorité musulmane en Suisse,* Research report, Bern: Commission fédérale contre le racisme. [online] Available at : http://www.ekr.admin.ch/shop/00007/00032/index.html?lang=fr (accessed 2 August 2013).

Becci, Irene (2010): "Tactiques religieuses dans les espaces carcéraux d'Allemagne de l'Est", in: *Revue d'Histoire des Sciences Humaines*, 23, pp. 141-156.

— (2011): "Religion's Multiple Locations in Prison. Germany, Italy, Switzerland", in: *Archives de sciences sociales des religions*, 153:1, pp. 65-84.

Becci, Irene et al. (2011): *Enjeux sociologiques de la pluralité religieuse en prison*, Lausanne: Ecole d'études sociales et pédagogiques, Research report NRP 58.

Beckford, James A. (1997): "The transmission of religion in prison / La transmission de la religion en prison", in: *Recherches Sociologiques*, 28:3, pp. 101-112.

— (2003): "Sans l'Etat pas de transmission de la religion? Le cas de l'Angleterre", in: *Archives de sciences sociales des religions*, 121:1, pp. 57-68.

Behloul, Samuel M. (2009): "Discours total! Le débat sur l'islam en Suisse et le positionnement de l'islam comme religion publique", in: Schneuwly Purdie, Mallory / Gianni, Matteo / Jenny, Magali (eds), *Musulmans d'aujourd'hui: Identités plurielles en Suisse*, Genève: Labor et Fides, pp. 53-72.

Broquet Raphaël (2007): La population carcérale du recensement 2000: Internal document, written within the research project "Enjeux sociologiques de la pluralité religieuse en prison", Research report.

Bruce, Steve (2002): "Praying alone? Church-going in Britain and the Putnam thesis", in: *Journal of Contemporary Religion*, 17, pp. 317-328.

Chantraine, Gilles (2006): "La prison post-disciplinaire", in: *Déviance et Société*, 30:3, pp. 273-288.

Chauvenet, Antoinette / Rostaing, Corinne / Orlic, Françoise (2005): *La violence carcérale*, Paris: Presses Universitaires de France.

Clavien, Gaëtan (2009): "Médias et discours islamophobe: au croisement du dicible et du recevable", in: Schneuwly Purdie, Mallory / Gianni, Matteo / Jenny, Magali (eds), *Musulmans d'aujourd'hui: Identités plurielles en Suisse*, Genève: Labor et Fides, pp. 95-109.

Clemmer, Donald (1958 [1940]): *The prison community*, New York/London: Holt, Rinehart and Winston.

Commission fédérale contre le racisme (ed.) (2010): *Muslimfeindlichkeit = Hostilité envers les musulmans = Ostilità verso i musulmani*, Tangram, 25, Bern: Commission fédérale contre le racisme.

Dahinden, Janine / Duemmler, Kerstin / Moret, Joëlle (2010): *Religion und Ethnizität: Welche Praktiken, Identität und Grenzziehungen? Eine Untersuchung mit jungen Erwachsenen*, Neuchâtel: Université de Neuchâtel, Research report NRP 58.

Dahinden, Urs (2009): *Die Darstellung von Religionen in Schweizer Massenmedien: Zusammenprall der Kulturen oder Förderung des Dialogs?*, Chur: Hochschule für Technik und Wirtschaft. Research report NRP 58.

Dammer, Harry R. (2002): "The reasons for religious involvement in the correctional Environment", in: *Journal of Offender Rehabilitation*, 35:3/4, pp. 35-58.

Davie, Grace / Woodhead, Linda / Heelas, Paul (eds): *Predicting religion. Christian, secular and alternative futures*, Hampshire: Ashgate.

Département de la sécurité, de la police et de l'environnement, Prison de Champ-Dollon (2011): Rapport d'activités 2011, Geneva. [online] Available at: http://www.ge.ch/champ-dollon/doc/rapport-d-activites-2011.pdf (accessed 5 January 2013).

Direktion der Justiz und des Innern, Amt für Justizvollzug, Kanton Zürich, Justizvollzugsanstalt Pöschwies (2011): Jahresbericht 2011, Zürich. [online] Available at: http://www.justizvollzug.zh.ch/internet/justiz_inneres/juv/de/ueber_uns/veroeffentlichungen/jahresberichte.html, (accessed 5 January 2013).

Ettinger, Patrik / Udris, Linards (2009): "Islam as a threat? Problematisation of Muslims in the mass media and effects on the political system", in: Marsden, Lee / Savigny, Heather (eds), *Media, religion and conflict*, Surrey: Ashgate, pp. 59-79.

Eugster, Veronika et al. (2010): *Religion im Fernsehen*, Freiburg: Universität Freiburg. Research report NRP 58.

European Monitoring Center on Racism and Xenophobia (2006): Les musulmans au sein de l'Union européenne: Discriminations et islamophobie, Research report, Vienna.

Gianni, Matteo / Clavien, Gaëtan (2012): "Representing gender, defining Muslims? Gender and figures of otherness in public discourse in Switzerland", in: Flood, Christopher et al. (eds), *Political and cultural representations of Muslims: Islam in the Plural*, Leiden: Brill.

Glaser, Barney / Strauss, Anselm (1967): *The discovery of the grounded theory: Strategies for qualitative research*, Chicago: Aldine.

Goffman, Erving (1961): *Asylums: Essays on the social situation of mental patients and other inmates*, New York: Anchor Books.

Khosrokhavar, Farhad (2004): *L'Islam dans les prisons: Voix et regards*, Paris: Balland.

Lamont, Michele / Molnar, Virag (2002): "The study of boundaries in the social sciences", in: *Annual Review of Sociology*, 24, pp. 167-195.

Lüddeckens, Dorothea / Uehlinger, Christoph / Walthert, Rafael (2010): *Sichtbar gemachte religiöse Identität, Differenzwahrnehmung und Konflikt*, Zürich: Universität Zürich. Research report NRP 58.

Montero Perez de Tudela, Esther (2009): "L'expulsion des étrangers: Une étude des facteurs influençant l'expulsion judiciaire hors de Suisse", in: *Revue Internationale de Criminologie et de Police Technique et Scientifique*, 62:1, pp. 63-78.

Parini, Laura / Gianni, Matteo / Clavien, Gaëtan (2012): "La transversalité du genre: l'islam et les musulmans dans la presse suisse francophone", in: *Recherches féministes*, 25:1, pp. 163-181.

Poole, Elizabeth (2002): *Reporting Islam: Media representation of British Muslims*, London: I. B. Tauris.

Poole, Elizabeth / Richardson, John E. (eds) (2006): *Muslims and the news media*, London: I. B. Tauris.

Richardson, John E. (2006): "Who gets to speak? A study of sources in the Broadsheet Press", in: Poole, Elizabeth / Richardson, John E. (eds), *Muslims and the news media*, London: I. B. Tauris, pp. 103-112.

Rostaing, Corinne (1997): *La relation carcérale: Identités et rapports sociaux dans les prisons de femmes*, Paris: Presses Universitaires de France.

Said, Edward (1981): *Covering Islam. How the media and the experts determine how we see the world*, New York: Vintage.

Sarg, Rachel / Lamine, Anne-Sophie (2011): "La religion en prison: norme structurante, réhabilitation de soi, stratégie de résistance", in: *Archives de sciences sociales des religions*, 153:1, pp. 85-104.

Schneuwly Purdie, Mallory (2011): "'Silence... Nous sommes en direct avec Allah': L'émergence d'intervenants musulmans en contexte carcéral", in: *Archives de sciences sociales des religions*, 153:1, pp. 105-121.

Schneuwly Purdie, Mallory / Vuille, Joëlle (2010): "Egalitaire ou discriminatoire? Regards croisés sur l'exercice de la liberté religieuse dans les prisons suisses", in: *Revue internationale de criminologie et de police scientifique et technique*, 63:4, pp. 469-490.

Schneuwly Purdie, Mallory / Salzbrunn, Monika (2011): "De l'événement en religion: Manifestations de l'islam dans les espaces urbains", in: *Bulletin de la Société suisse Moyen Orient et Civilisation islamique*, 32, pp. 9-12.

Spradley, James P. (1979): *The ethnographic interview*, New York: Holt, Reinhart and Winston.

Stolz, Jörg et al. (2013): *Religion und Spiritualität in der Ich-Gesellschaft: Die vier Gestalten des (Un)glaubens*, Zürich: Theologischer Verlag Zürich.

Storm, Ingrid (2009): "Halfway to heaven: Four types of fuzzy fidelity in Europe", in: *Journal for the Scientific Study of Religion*, 48, pp. 702-718.

Sykes, Gresham (1958): *The society of captives: A study of a maximum security prison*, Princeton: Princeton University Press.

Voas, David (2009): "The rise and fall of fuzzy fidelity in Europe", in: *European Sociological Review*, 25, pp. 155-168.

Wimmer, Andreas (2008): "Elementary strategies of ethnic boundary making", in: *Ethnic and Racial Studies*, 31:6, pp. 1025-1055.

The politics of Sikh Islamophobia

KATY P. SIAN

> The worldly context remains both perplexingly stirred up
> and ideologically fraught, volatile, tense, changeable and
> even murderous.   (Said 2003: 348)

INTRODUCTION

The emergence of a Muslim public identity in Britain in the context of the war
on terror, as well as the proliferation of ethnically marked populations and the
introduction of categories such as asylum seeker, economic refugees and eastern
European immigrants are key factors which have come together to produce a situation in which Britain's ethnoscape has been dramatically transformed. In this
transformation, Muslims have come to occupy a complex position linking older
commonwealth immigration of the 1960s and 1970s with more contemporary
manifestations. To investigate this linkage, this chapter will examine the articulation of a hegemonic Sikh diasporic identity that increasingly positions itself in
contrast to Muslims. This inter-ethnic focus shifts attention away from studies on
relations between the Anglo-British national majority and ethnic minorities, to
an understanding of inter-ethnic relations in the postcolonial context.

This chapter will provide a critical conceptualisation of Islamophobia as
means of addressing the reconfiguration of the British ethnoscape. In particular it
will provide an examination of the various ways in which Sikhs in the diaspora
have sought to differentiate themselves, in primarily conflictual terms, from
Muslims. I will analyze the extent to which such structures of differentiation can
be read as being Islamophobic. In doing so the account will investigate how cen-

tral the role of Islamophobia becomes in articulations of Sikhness against the backdrop of contemporary Britain.[1]

CONCEPTUALISING ISLAMOPHOBIA[2]

The concept of Islamophobia gained prominence in the British context following the publication of a report by the Runnymede Trust entitled, *Islamophobia: A challenge for us all* (Runnymede Trust 1997). The notion that Muslims and Islam have been subject to prejudice and discrimination is itself not new.[3] Many commentators have examined the aversion felt in western circles towards Islam in various forms from its inception. For example, in his critique of Orientalism, Edward Said points to the way in which constructs of the Arab, the Moor and the Turk have been iconic representations of both a hostile and baneful Islam (Said 2003).

The term 'Islamophobia' made its first published appearance in French, in 1918. It was only in 1976 that it appeared in a published form in English (Vakil

---

1   It is important to stress that the Sikh Islamophobic discourse drawn upon throughout this paper does not serve as a representation of all Sikhs in the diaspora, as such I do not intend to discount or dismiss other (more positive) accounts of Sikhs in the UK, however, for the purpose of this paper I am more concerned with the dominant forms of articulation. For alternative readings of Sikhs, see Singh/Tatla 2006 and also, Ali/Kalra/Sayyid 2006.

2   For more details see Sian 2009, pp. 209-232, and Sian 2013.

3   There is a debate as to whether Islamophobia is the correct term to describe discrimination towards Muslims. For example Fred Halliday prefers to use 'anti-Muslimism', arguing that the discrimination is directed against actual Muslims rather than a body of religious ideas, thus, the use of Islamophobia prevents legitimate criticism of Islam making it difficult for secular voices to be heard. In this paper however, I will continue to use the term 'Islamophobia' for a number of reasons. Firstly it is not possible to make the distinction between Islam and Muslims in such a neat way. For example one could question whether the throwing of a pig's head at a mosque is directed at Islam or Muslims? Similarly is the throwing of a pig's head at a Muslim business directed at Muslims or Islam? Furthermore, there has been a considerable investment in the term, as such it has a certain strategic use, therefore by speaking about Islamophobia this paper aligns itself with those debates, some of which are global in nature regarding the critique of the term, see Halliday 1999.

2010: 40).[4] In its English incarnation AbdoolKarim Vakil points out that Islamophobia is applied not to describe racism experienced by Muslim settlers in the west, but rather, as a term of censorship by which Muslims hinder discussion and criticism of Islam. The argument being that by charging the critics of Islam as Islamophobes, Muslims stifle free expression and study (ibid.).[5] This idea that Islamophobia is an illegitimate category with polemical pro-Muslim motivations is well established.[6] Many commentators argue that Islamophobia is deployed by 'extremist' Muslims to silence criticism of Islam and Muslim practices, and thus does not reflect the discrimination against Muslims in British public life.[7]

Regardless of the complexities surrounding the initial coinage, the Runnymede report "(re)introduced" the term 'Islamophobia' and its contemporary usage can be traced back to the influence of that report (Sayyid 2010: 7). *Islamophobia: A challenge for us all*, emerged out of deliberations around an earlier report on anti-Semitism by the Runnymede Trust entitled, *A Very Light Sleeper* (1994), such an account sought to document the continuation of anti-Semitism in British society (ibid.). It was felt by the writers of the 1994 report that many of the issues confronting the Jewish community in relation to anti-Semitism, had a certain kind of homology with the discrimination faced by the Muslim community (ibid.). The term 'Islamophobia' was then coined (or re-coined) to address the sense of discrimination experienced by Muslims who were not, and are still not, recognised by the British *Race Relations Act* (1976). The reason for this was that discrimination on the basis of religion was not illegal; as such Muslims could be discriminated against as long as the discrimination was not 'racial' in character

---

4　For a detailed genealogy of the term 'Islamophobia' and its circulation in different languages, see Vakil 2010.

5　Contrast this with the claim made by Rana that the category was used to explain the vestiges of a pre-existing racism felt by many Muslim communities living within Western societies (Rana 2007: 148). Apart from the empirical problems with such a claim, it is also difficult to see how there could be an Islamophobia before there were Muslims. Muslims as a distinct public identity only appear in the late 1980s.

6　Critics of the term 'Islamophobia' include Polly Toynbee the liberal Guardian columnist (Toynbee 2004) and Michael Gove, Conservative parliamentarian (Gove 2007). One of the most influential academic criticisms of the concept of Islamophobia has been advanced by Kenan Malik (Malik 2005).

7　For an excellent example of the idea that Islamophobia is used to silence criticism of Muslim extremists see right wing Daily Mail commentator Melanie Philips' article "The Truth Phobia" (Philips 2008).

(Sayyid 2010). Its very British context however, has not prevented the term from gaining a wider currency in very different national settings (Vakil 2010: 33-40).

The widespread use of the term in the contemporary context, especially in the wake of the war on terror, has not necessarily meant that its meaning has become any clearer. According to the report, Islamophobia is defined as:

> [...] unfounded hostility towards Islam. It refers also to the practical consequences of such hostility in unfair discrimination against Muslim individuals and communities, and to the exclusion of Muslims from mainstream political and social affairs. (Runnymede Trust 1997: 4)

This conceptualisation seems to imply that hostility that is 'founded' and exclusions based on it, would be legitimate. The difficulty of course, is that very few Islamophobes would actually argue that their hostility towards Islam is unfounded. The concept of Islamophobia has thus come to encapsulate a plethora of interpretations across the globe. Islamophobia is widely circulated and intensely challenged, but it is rarely deployed in public policy contexts where it could be useful (Sayyid 2010: 6). As such it remains a concept that is neither consistently defined or understood and, as a consequence, it makes it difficult for the category to be taken seriously beyond its polemical usage to silence criticism of Muslims and Islam (Sayyid 2010).

The limits of the term 'Islamophobia' are largely due to the initial conceptualisation by the Runnymede report which distinguished between 'closed' and 'open' views of Islam. The formulation of the 'closed and open views' of Islam were central to the report in which eight distinctive features, whereby so-called 'Islamophobic' actions could be experienced, were developed (see table).

The general impression given by the report, as Chris Allen points out, was that the 'closed' views could be simply interpreted as discriminatory or prejudiced (Allen 2010: 53), whereas the 'open' views could not, which meant that the category of Islamophobia was restricted to those instances in which it was argued that people held 'closed' views of Islam. Allen goes on to criticise the Runnymede report for its focus on 'closed/open views of Islam' pointing out that,

> [...] those who wanted to detract from, or dismiss, Islamophobia could easily do so by merely suggesting that if 'closed views' equalled Islamophobia, one must presume that 'open views' equalled 'Islamophilia'. Those who wanted to argue against Islamophobia therefore suggested that the only solution being put forward by the Commission was an abnormal liking or love of Islam and Muslims (philia). (Allen 2010: 53)

Table 1: Closed and open views of Islam

Distinctions	Closed views of Islam (Islamophobia)	Open views of Islam
Monolithic / diverse	Islam seen as a single monolithic bloc, static, and unresponsive to new realities.	Islam seen as diverse and progressive, with internal differences, debates and development.
Separate / interacting	Islam seen as separate and other – (a) not having any aims or values in common with other cultures (b) not affected by them (c) not influencing them.	Islam seen as interdependent with other faiths and cultures – (a) having certain shared values and aims (b) affected by them (c) enriching them.
Inferior / different	Islam seen as inferior to the West – barbaric, irrational, primitive, sexist.	Islam seen as distinctively different, but not deficient, and as equally worthy of respect.
Enemy / partner	Islam seen as violent, aggressive, threatening, supportive of terrorism, engaged in 'a clash of civilisations'.	Islam seen as an actual or potential partner in joint cooperative enterprises and in the solution of shared problems.
Manipulative / sincere	Islam seen as a political ideology, used for political or military advantage.	Islam seen as a genuine religious faith, practised sincerely by its adherents.
Criticism of West rejected / considered	Criticisms made by Islam of 'the West' rejected out of hand	Criticisms of 'the West' and other cultures are considered and debated.
Discrimination defended / criticised	Hostility towards Islam used to justify discriminatory practices towards Muslims and exclusion of Muslims from mainstream society.	Debates and disagreements with Islam do not diminish efforts to combat discrimination and exclusion.
Islamophobia seen as natural / problematic	Anti-Muslim hostility accepted as natural and 'normal'.	Critical views of Islam are themselves subjected to critique, lest they be inaccurate and unfair.

Source: Runnymede Trust 1997: 5.

Therefore Allen suggests that the report unintentionally reinforced a duality of the love/hate of Muslims and ignored all intermediate positions, thus giving the 'grey' opinions the opportunity to gain momentum and form the basis of indirect forms of Islamophobia, which are not detected as 'racist' (ibid.). Not only however, was the Runnymede's formulation restrictive, it was also descriptive, offering very little analytical purchase. Such a conceptualisation of Islamophobia saw it as a set of distinct attitudes and reducible to individuals holding 'closed' views of Islam. As such, the Runnymede report's version of Islamophobia remains within what has been described as Anti-Orientalism rather than Post-Orientalism (Sayyid 2003: 31-51).

A more compelling account of Islamophobia which focuses on its constitutive role is provided by Madina Tlostanova (2010). In her analysis of Russian Islamophobia, Tlostanova demonstrates how the concept emerges as Russia begins to describe itself as being 'western' from the seventeenth century onwards. Islamophobia in this sense becomes a mechanism of westernisation which involves the distancing of Russia's Islamicate past from its European trajectory (Tlostanova 2010: 165-184). During the early modern period, what became Russia, occupied a complex relationship with Muslims, that is, as Russia culturally turned westwards, the Islamicate period and influence was re-described as a source of Russian 'backwardness' and one of the main reasons for its failure to achieve its western destiny as envisaged by its Enlightenment inspired intellectuals (ibid). The Islamophobia that emerges from Tlostanova's account is not merely the possessing of a 'closed' or 'open' view of Islam, but rather the depiction of Islam as the antithesis of a western trajectory.

This form of what can be described as a Russian Islamophobia has a number of common features with British-Sikh Islamophobia. These commonalities are not necessarily coincidental, the Russian case can as such be seen to reflect in many ways the Sikh case. In both contexts the appearance of Islam coincides with the formation of these entities, in other words, Islam was the 'other' against which early modern Russia and Sikhism constituted themselves.[1] Secondly in both cases, the prime antagonism between Islamicate polities and the new emerging Russian and Sikh orders are often recycled at moments of tension and constantly reiterated as part of the 'sacred' myths of these communities. Thirdly, both these contexts demonstrate what could be expressed as an Orientalist reading of their own history

---

1   Coincidentally the formation of both Sikhism and Russia occur at a similar time around the fifteenth century. Hodgson (1974) describes this time as a period when the Eastern hemisphere was dominated by Islamicate polities including Ottoman, Timurid and Safavid empires (see Hodgson 1974 and McNeil 1963 for more details).

and world history,[2] in which the west was constituted by its opposition to the Orient and therefore westernisation implied a de-orientalisation. Islam then, was marked out as the exemplar of the Orient, so in both communities (Sikh and Russian), Islamophobia is a marker of westernisation.

Islamophobia in both contexts signifies more than an irrational fear or hatred, rather, it becomes a means of articulating the aspirations of a western identity through their exclusion and dismissal of the 'non-western' that is the Muslim subject. This suggests the need to define Islamophobia other than in terms of 'unfounded hostility'. Here I think it would be useful to draw upon Salman Sayyid's conceptualisation of Islamophobia (2010), which departs from framing Islamophobia as simply a set of reducible individual attitudes, in favour of "the disciplining of Muslims by reference to an antagonistic western horizon" (Sayyid 2010: 15). In other words for Sayyid, Islamophobia is established through, "the maintenance of the violent hierarchy between the idea of the west and Islam" (Sayyid 2010: 15). Sayyid's definition offers a conceptual understanding of Islamophobia and facilitates a critique which accounts for structural operations of power, rather than individual behaviour.

SIKH ISLAMOPHOBIA[3]

It can be argued that Sikhs have an ambiguous position in relation to the west. The pride of many Sikhs serving under the colonialism of the British Empire suggests a community in which decolonisation is still incomplete. The standing of the Sikh community as defenders of British imperial rule in India and as one of 'martial races' helped separate many of them from an anti-colonial, political identity. Thus, Sikhs were both subject to the empire and in many cases enthusiastic in its service. Sikhs and their affiliation with Britain and the British Empire can as such be seen as multifaceted and intimate.

Although the British defeated Sikhs twice in the mid-nineteenth century in the first and second Anglo Sikh wars of 1845-1846 and 1848-1849, commanders were full of praise and admiration for the courage and bravery presented by Sikh

2   Both Sikh and Russian contexts are also similar to the Kemalist transformation of the Ottoman Empire: "To become modern, the Kemalist's believe they have to become Western; one could not be Western and at the same time be Oriental. Islam was represented in Kemalist discourse as the epitome of the0 Orient. Kemalist Turks had to stop being Orientals and start being Europeans; they had to eradicate any association with the Orient, and define themselves as being part of the West" (Sayyid 2003: 68).

3   See Sian 2010 and Sian 2013.

soldiers (Yong 2005: 61). Sikhs were thus seen as a 'warrior' collective with military efficiency and European-like organisation and training, they were as such regarded in high esteem as a 'martial' people (Yong 2005: 61). As the 'martial race theory' became established, recruitment into the colonial army became guided by a series of manuals, textbooks and anthropological studies based entirely upon imperialistic stereotypes and racism in which particular groups were marked out quite literally as possessing inherent qualities such as courage, masculinity, loyalty and bravery etc., which made them more likely to be chosen for the army, as Tan Tai Yong (2005) describes:

> Couched as ethnographical and anthropological studies, these handbooks were often nothing more than observations based on colonial stereotypes and racism that imbibed an extreme form of cultural and environmental determinism. These handbooks justified their choice [of] recruits by attributing to them inherent qualities such as masculinity, fidelity, bravery and loyalty. (Yong 2005: 65)

In such manuals it was often advised that: "[...] in judging the values of tribes which supplied converts to Sikhism in the time of Guru Gobind Singh, who in fact formed the Singh people, [...] those tribes who, though they now supply converts to Sikhism, did not so then, cannot be considered (or it is inadvisable to consider) as true Sikhs" (Yong 2005: 72).

This is quite remarkable and illustrates the dominant role of such colonial discourses in deciding what constituted a 'true' Sikh (rather than Sikhs themselves). Yong (2005) notes that such prejudice did not end there:

> In addition to stressing the importance of being the 'right social and religious type', these handbooks revealed an astonishing adherence to elements of environmental determinism by articulating that the value of Sikh recruits and the characteristics they were likely to show depended more upon the district they came from rather than the caste or clan to which they belonged. (Yong 2005: 72)

Such a system of instrumental, reductive and racialised recruiting meant that a science of classification was prescribed in which specific ethnic groups were deemed more 'martial' than others (Yong 2005: 65). As such, over decades the British were able to carefully cultivate and secure the loyalty and allegiance of many Sikhs through 'special' considerations such as a 'martial race' (Yong 2005: 289).

The incorporation of Sikhs into the British imperialist apparatus facilitated migration to Britain in the wake of the Second World War and associated reconstruction labour shortages. Following the collapse of British colonialism and India's independence of 1947, many Sikhs migrated and settled in the UK. However, the Sikh community were soon to learn that they were not necessarily welcomed with open arms despite their long service and loyalty. In the earlier phases of migration Sikh men often found it easier to find employment if they took off their turbans, but in 1959 when a Sikh was banned from wearing his turban in the workplace the issue became political as the Sikh community launched a number of campaigns and protests to gain the right to wear turbans at work (Brah 2006: 38). This context unravelled an unresolved association with Sikhs and the colonial and anti-colonial, demonstrating that the west is neither totally 'other' to the Sikhs nor are they the same as the west (Sian 2009).

In postcolonial Britain the effort to negotiate this position has seen the development of a Sikh Islamophobia which attempts to write a western character of the Sikh community by differentiating itself in radical ways from the Muslim community. The project to locate Sikh communities around a western pole implies the construction of a new Sikh identity. This construction is currently dependant on a version of Islamophobia, therefore it is important to understand whether this Sikh project is articulating a distinct form of Islamophobia, or simply expressing a generic global Islamophobia heightened by the war on terror (Sian 2009). In order to understand this it is important to examine two major periods of intense Sikh-Muslim hostility including firstly, Mughal confrontation with early Sikhism in fifteenth century India, and secondly violence associated with the Partition of 1947. For the Sikhs these episodes are total and thus affect all of the community, where as for Muslims these conflicts only affected a section of the global Islamicate order. For Muslims these experiences are local and have little effect on Islam itself, in other words Sikh-Mughal conflict and the Partition was not represented as a threat to the entire Muslim community (the *umma*).

For Sikhs however the story takes a different turn. It could be argued that what was at stake in the conflict with the Mughals was the very survival of Sikhism, similarly, the violence of the Partition of India saw the division of the Punjab and as a consequence some of the most important Sikh shrines and temples ended up in Pakistan, and the capital of Punjab, Lahore, also ended up in Pakistan. Thus in different ways the conflict associated with Sikhs and Mughals and the violence of Partition can be seen to have threatened Sikhism to an extent that they did not threaten Islam. This would account for the intensity of Sikh perceptions of a distinct existential Muslim threat; in other words, Muslims could threaten the existence of Sikhs, but Sikhs could not threaten the existence of Islam.[4] It is however important to recall that there were long peri-

---

4   It is worth pointing out that partition violence was not just unique to Sikhs, as both Hindu and Muslim communities were also involved in the communal bloodshed. The

ods in which Sikh-Muslim relations were not necessarily antagonistic. Thus, it becomes significant to account for the reasons as to why Sikh-Muslim relations are increasingly defined in conflictual rather than convivial terms in the postcolonial setting of Britain (Sian 2009).

The historical narratives of Mughal tyranny and Partition violence have been adapted to fit within the landscape of contemporary Britain where a more scandalous and shocking tale emerges in which Sikh girls become the particular targets for Muslim 'predatory' behaviour. Alongside this the global war on terror also created a situation which facilitated further the division of Sikhs from Muslims through the phenomenon of mistaken identity. Although the context has dramatically changed since fifteenth century India, the overall structure of the narrative has not, that is, in such discourses the figure of the Muslim always remains as the principle 'enemy'. The two key discourses in which the antagonism between Sikhs and Muslims can be seen played out in the contemporary context can thus be seen manifested through the 'forced' conversion narrative and mistaken identities.

The 'forced' conversion narrative is embedded in the British Sikh diaspora and continues to circulate despite little evidentiary support (Sian 2011). It is a cautionary tale which describes the threat of Muslim predators lurking on university campuses ready to lure vulnerable Sikh girls into the folds of Islam through disguise and manipulation (ibid.). The tale of 'forced' conversions appears to have emerged around the mid to late 1980s, around the same time when moves were afoot, especially in Hounslow, to introduce a separate 'Asian' category into equal opportunities monitoring schemes alongside Black and White (Modood 1988). This fragmentation of a residual non-white category would have helped open up the space for the further disaggregation of this category, especially in light of campaigns around provisions for *halāl* meat, Muslim faith schools and so on, which began to introduce a distinct Muslim subject position into the public arena. The 'forced' conversion narrative, appears to provide a means by which a discreet Sikh identity can be set off against the nascent Muslim identity in the context of a general contestation of the ways of categorising Britain's ethnically marked populations.[5]

---

way partition has been narrated in the dominant Sikh imaginary is thus interesting as it tends to construct the violence as a specific Muslim attack on Sikhs, rather than seeing the violence as occurring between all three groups.

5   It could also be suggested that the 'forced' conversion narrative arose from the tensions between the Chalvey Boys and the Sheree Punjabs starting in the mid 1980s in Slough, however, it is worth pointing out that the predominantly Sikh and Muslim

The central element of the 'forced' conversion narrative is the idea that Sikh societies are subverted or threatened by Muslim powers to comply with 'predatory' practices of Muslim men. Such a narrative has a phantasmagoric structure which works to reproduce the historical battle between 'good' and 'evil', it is a tale used to rescue the Sikh community from moral decay, and although it may or may not be true, it re-engages, stabilises and regulates the community through the articulation of a fear (Sian 2011). Within the story we see the elaborate production of the Muslim 'enemy' whereby Islamophobic themes of the 'depraved' and 'lecherous' Muslim is prominent, consequently, the Islamophobic vision of the Muslim 'other' threatening the purity of Sikhism is cemented (Sian 2011).

The war on terror also contributed to increasing Sikh Islamophobia, and at the same time saw the heightening of a global Islamophobia. On the ground this meant that there was a marked increase in what the Metropolitan Police described as 'faith related hate crimes', most of these cases involving verbal or physical attacks on perceived Muslim targets (EUMC 2005: 11).[6] Attacks and incidents however, were not confined only to the Muslim population as many Sikhs were often confused or mistaken for being Muslims. Following the attack in London of 7/7 it was reported that a gurdwara in Kent was firebombed, the Sikh Federation (UK) also recorded a total of five further attacks on gurdwaras and two violent assaults on people from the Sikh community, it was suggested that, "the turban-wearing Sikh community is under siege" (Nagarajah 2005). As Kathleen Hall (2002) points out, following 9/11 many Sikhs in the UK and the US became the targets of a discrimination which was "rooted in the racialisation of the global terrorism" (Hall 2002: 206), as such, the war on terror created "its own form of terror in the lives of those, like Sikhs, who have been implicated however mistakenly as 'other'" (Hall 2002: 206).

The war on terror thus created conditions in which Islamophobia flourished. The Sikh community were not immune to this development – but again they were in a complicated relationship as both consumers of the Islamophobic discourse, which would seem to confirm the negative image of the Muslim community, but also as victims of Islamophobia, since many Islamophobes could not tell the difference between a Sikh or a Muslim, for example following 9/11 a turbaned Sikh was shot down in Mesa, Arizona, by a white man who thought he was an Arab – thus mistaken for a terrorist (Sian 2012). Yet

---

gangs of the 1970s named the Holy Smokes and the Billy Boys predate the conflicts in Slough (for more details see Kundnani 2002).

6   See Malik 2005 for a contrary view that there was no significant increase in Islamophobia in the UK.

remarkably the Sikh community failed to find a common cause with Muslims, instead the mistaken identity phenomenon perpetuated the divide between both communities, for example Arun Kundnani (2002) describes a demonstration in which: "Some Sikhs, instead of marching with Muslims and calling for an end to any revenge attacks, marched separately with banners saying 'we are not Muslims', as if American Muslims were any more valid as targets for revenge than they were" (Kundnani 2002).

This illustrates the way in which the hegemonic Sikh discourse sought to articulate a position in which Sikh interests (i.e. not to be confused with Muslims) were seen to be more important than the general principles of racial equality and justice (i.e. the exclusionary and discriminating nature of the disciplining of ethnic minorities). As such it can be argued that the Sikh community naturalised Islamophobia rather than question it (Sian 2012). The absence of irony within this dominant discourse facilitates its absorption within the framework of coloniality. To elaborate, British Sikhs are on the whole regarded as an example *par excellence* of successfully integrated ethnically marked populations, this is confirmed by various socio-economic indicators including high educational achievement, high rates of home ownership and high rates of employment.[7] This contrasts with Muslims who are often constructed in opposite terms, i.e. they exemplify an unassimilated ethnically marked community whose poorer housing conditions, poorer health and poorer educational attainment demonstrates their membership to a 'troublesome underclass'.[8]

This contrast between Sikhs on the one hand and Muslims on the other has opened up the space for the enunciation of a separate Sikh identity which increasingly aligns itself with the majority community. Such a process of ethnic unmarking enables Sikhs to assimilate into the majority community and also facilitates the narration of a western character in the project to locate themselves as an unmarked, westernised community, this is achieved firstly by adopting the various western tropes of 'modernity', 'liberation' and 'agency' and secondly, by continually differentiating themselves with the ethnically marked, non-western community that comes typically through the figure of the Muslim (Sayyid 2003). In other words there is a paradox in play in which attempts to affirm a

---

7   For an analysis of the figures examining South Asian demographics in the UK and patterns of settlement and socio-economic success see Peach 2006 and Thandi 2006.

8   See Tahir Abbas (2005: 10sq.) who examines the disadvantaged socio-economic position of British Muslims by drawing upon 2001 census data, for example education studies have shown that "the Muslim percentage of those with higher educational qualifications was just below the England and Wales average (13.5% versus 14.3%). For Sikhs however it was 17%" (id., 30).

distinct and separate Sikh identity can only be imagined in the context of a westernising gaze which sees no future for Sikhness beyond a naïve and uncritical assimilation into the national majority (Sian 2012). As such, by separating themselves from Muslims, Sikhs are abandoning not only the past of struggles for racial equality but also a present in which racism in its various forms (including Islamophobia) continues to condition the life experiences of all of Britain's ethnically marked populations (including Sikhs themselves).

CONCLUSION

This chapter first set out to provide a detailed conceptualisation of the term 'Islamophobia' by abandoning descriptive accounts as presented by the Runnymede Trust, in favour of an analytical understanding which locates Islamophobia beyond the confinements of a set of reducible individual opinions. By drawing upon the Russian case to explore Islamophobia as the product of the writing and narration of a western character, I examined how this approach could also be seen to account for the rise of a Sikh Islamophobia. I attempted to demonstrate that the current articulation of a distinct Sikh subject position is dominated by a discourse in which Islamophobia plays an increasingly central role, the exploration of historical and contemporary narratives seem to point to a specific Sikh form of Islamophobia yet its contemporary nature also shares a familiarity with the generalised forms of western Islamophobia.

The chapter examined how this is further cemented with the ongoing ambiguity surrounding Sikh identity in relationship to Britain, where we can see in the contemporary landscape even though Sikhs have themselves also been victims of racism and Islamophobia, the western template appears to remain the model for Sikh development. As a consequence, Islamophobia becomes one of the key drivers of achieving an identification with the west. Although historically the distinction between Sikhs and Muslims is not necessarily novel, against the Anglo-British backdrop such an effort to illustrate this difference has been enforced to a much greater extent and has become more prominent within the current climate. As a result Sikhs appear to have adopted the racial pathologies which are widely embedded within western discourse to identify themselves in opposition to Muslims; 'us against them'. The equivalencial logic of this discourse can be seen to organise the hegemonic Sikh discourse in Britain. It is within this oppositional binary that the frontiers have been established to divide the 'friends' from the 'enemies' (Schmitt 1996).

There is often a tendency to assume that ethnically marked populations are significantly influenced by western governments and policies, in other words, they lack what could be described as an interior life of their own. Any social actor has to navigate the environment in which they find themselves, thus it does not follow that such an environment is an exclusive patrimony of a nation state, so for example in the Sikh case, while the Sikh community in Britain are affected by the various legislative, economic and cultural frameworks of British life, their subjectivity is not exhausted by such processes. In particular, as I have attempted to demonstrate, it can be seen that while there is a general, western, global Islamophobia and some Sikhs have articulated their position in relation to that particular form, there is little denying the specificities of the Sikh interpretation and their distinct relationship with what is hegemonically constructed as an oppressive Muslim force, such an interpretation goes hand in hand with the complex history of the formation of the Sikh community.

In other words, central to this chapter has been to demonstrate the argument that Sikh canonical literature which predates the British ethnoscape has been the major influence on Sikhs in providing the resources by which they narrate themselves, as such, British multiculturalist policies are not the cause of Sikh Islamophobia, but rather it is precisely the complex histories and the subsequent diasporic inflections that make the Sikh form of Islamophobia all the more interesting. There is no necessary reason however why a Sikh subject position could not be articulated in which Islamophobia would be absent or at least marginal. That is, the current narrative does not have to be the future of the Sikh community, it is possible to imagine different ways of being Sikh and given the postcolonial condition it is perhaps necessary to do so...

REFERENCES

Abbas, Tahir (2005): *Muslim Britain: Communities under pressure,* London: Zed Books.

Ali, Nasreen / Kalra, Virinder / Sayyid, Salman (eds) (2006): *A postcolonial people: South Asians in Britain,* London: Hurst.

Allen, Christopher (2010): "Islamophobia: from K.I.S.S to R.I.P", in: Sayyid, Salman / Vakil, AbdoolKarim (eds), *Thinking through Islamophobia: Global perspectives*, London: Hurst, pp. 51-64.

Brah, Avtar (2006): "The 'Asian' in Britain", in: Ali, Nasreen / Kalra, Virinder / Sayyid, Salman (eds): *A postcolonial people: South Asians in Britain,* London: Hurst, pp. 35-61.

EUMC [European Monitoring Center on Racism and Xenophobia] (2005): *The Impact of 7 July 2005 London Bomb Attacks on Muslim Communities in the EU,* November 2005. [online] Available at: http://www.eumc.eu.int/eumc/index.php (accessed 25 June 2012).

Gove, Michael (2007): *Celsius 7/7*, London: Phoenix Press.

Hall, Kathleen (2002): *Lives in Translation: Sikh youth as British citizens*, Philadelphia: University of Pennsylvania Press.

Halliday, Fred (1999): "Islamophobia reconsidered", in: *Ethnic and Racial Studies*, 22:5, pp. 892-902.

Hodgson, Marshall (1974): *The venture of Islam*, vol. 3, London: The University of Chicago Press.

Kundnani, Arun (2002): *An unholy alliance? Racism, religion and communalism*, Institute of Race Relations. [online] Available at: http://www.irr.org.uk/2002/july/ak000001.html (accessed 25 June 2012).

Malik, Kenan (2005): *Islamophobia Myth*. February 2005. [online] Available at: http://www.kenanmalik.com/essays/prospect_islamophobia.html (accessed 16 November 2011).

McNeil, William (1963): *The rise of the West: A history of the human community*, London: The University of Chicago Press.

Modood, Tariq (1988): "'Black', racial equality and Asian identity", in: *New Community*, 14, pp. 397-404.

Nagarajah, Shivani (2005): "Mistaken identity", in: *The Guardian*, 5 September. [online] Available at: http://www.guardian.co.uk/world/2005/sep/05/religion.july7 (accessed 22 May 2010).

Peach, Ceri (2006): "Demographics of BrAsian settlement, 1951-2001", in: Ali, Nasreen / Kalra, Virinder / Sayyid, Salman (eds): *A postcolonial people: South Asians in Britain*, London: Hurst, pp. 168-181.

Philips, Melanie (2008): "The truth phobia", in: *The Spectator*, 9 December. [online] Available at: http://images.spectator.co.uk/melaniephillips/3075851/the-truth-phobia.thtml (accessed 22 December 2012).

Race Relations Act 1976. (ch. 74), London: HMSO.

Rana, Junaid (2007): "The story of Islamophobia", in: *Souls*, 9:2, pp. 148-161.

Runnymede Trust (1994): *A very light sleeper: The persistence and dangers of antisemitism*, London: Runnymede Trust.

— (1997): *Islamophobia: A challenge for us all: report of the Runnymede Trust Commission on British Muslims and Islamophobia*, London: Runnymede Trust.

Said, Edward (2003): Orientalism, London: Penguin Books.

Sayyid, Salman (2003): A fundamental fear: Eurocentrism and the emergence of Islamism, London: Zed Books.

— (2010): "Out of the Devil's Dictionary", in: Sayyid, Salman / Vakil, Abdool-Karim (eds), *Thinking through Islamophobia: Global perspectives*, London: Hurst, pp. 5-18.

Sayyid, Salman / Vakil, AbdoolKarim (eds) (2010), *Thinking through Islamophobia: Global perspectives*, London: Hurst.

Schmitt, Carl (1996): *The concept of the political,* London: The University of Chicago Press.

Sian, Katy Pal (2009): *The persistence of Sikh and Muslim conflict in diasporic context: BrAsian Sikh.* Unpublished PhD thesis, University of Leeds.

— (2010): "Don't freak I'm a Sikh", in: Sayyid, Salman / Vakil, AbdoolKarim (eds), *Thinking through Islamophobia: Global perspectives,* London: Hurst, pp. 251-254.

— (2011): "'Forced' conversions in the British Sikh Diaspora", in: *South Asian Popular Culture, 9:2,* pp. 115-130.

— (2012): *The grooming we can't hide from,* June 2012. [online] Available at: http://www.the-platform.org.uk/2012/06/20/the-grooming-we-cant-hide-from (accessed 28 June 2012).

— (2013): *Unsettling Sikh and Muslim conflict: Mistaken identities, forced conversions and postcolonial formations,* Lanham: Lexington Books.

Singh, Gurphal / Tatla, Darshan Singh (2006): *Sikhs in Britain: The making of a community,* London: Zed Books.

Thandi, Shinder (2006): "Brown economy", in: Ali, Nasreen / Kalra, Virinder / Sayyid, Salman (eds): *A postcolonial people: South Asians in Britain,* London: Hurst, pp. 211-229.

Tlostanova, Madina (2010): "A short genealogy of Russian Islamophobia", in: Sayyid, Salman / Vakil, AbdoolKarim (eds), *Thinking through Islamophobia: Global perspectives,* London: Hurst, pp. 165-184.

Toynbee, Polly (2004): "Get off your knees", in: *The Guardian,* 11 June. [online] Available at: http://www.guardian.co.uk/politics/2004/jun/11/religion. world (accessed 27 June 2012).

Vakil, AbdoolKarim (2010): "Is the Islam in Islamophobia the same as the Islam in Anti-Islam; Or, when is it Islamophobia time?", in: Sayyid, Salman / Vakil, AbdoolKarim (eds), *Thinking through Islamophobia: Global perspectives,* London: Hurst, pp. 23-43.

Yong, Tan Tai (2005): *The garrison state: Military, government and society in colonial Punjab, 1849-1947,* London: Sage.

Part II

The one facing the many

The one facing the many

SUSANNE LEUENBERGER

Fuelled by sensational stories about Western converts to Islam involved in terrorism and radicalism, the phenomenon of European citizens embracing Islam and (seemingly) turning away from liberal and secular norms and values has become the focus of public attention in recent years. The medial framing of the convert as a dangerous zealot and cultural renegade prone to be attracted to fundamentalist, at times even violent forms of Islam has dominated the public perception of conversion to Islam in European debates. Pictured as an antagonist figure who performs a 180 degree turnaround from his/her former religious and cultural upbringing, the public image of the convert iterates the trope of a clash of cultures that structures present debates on Islam on a biographical register. This section builds up upon the findings and research questions developed in the opening part of this volume ("Rules and roles"). Rather than understanding present problematisations of Islam as a mere misrepresentation or discrimination of Muslims, the following section aims to work out the constitutive effects of public framings and imaginaries on current processes of Muslim self-formation.

Given the intense news coverage on converts lately, academia has also turned its attention to the phenomenon of conversion to Islam in Europe. Academic discussion mirrors public perception in describing converts as both 'bridge builders' as well as radical 'new borns'. Due to their liminal position of being both 'born European' and Muslim, converts are conceptualised as hybrid figures capable of both affirming and dissolving the 'cultural' difference between 'us and them'. Thus, in the latter case, the convert is discussed as an 'interpreter' and 'bridge builder' able to construct a 'European' Islam adapted to liberal and secular norms and values in terms of religious freedom, gender equality, and democracy. Hence, while in the public perception the convert is more often framed as a 'renegade', qualitative studies have shown that converts mostly understand themselves as taking in the role of 'interpreters'; 'cultural' and 'religious' brokers within their closer social environment, both vis-à-vis the non-Muslim public, as well as within Muslim contexts (see for example Allievi[1], Roald[2], Zebiri[3], Moosavi in this volume). However, while being celebrated as unwitting 'integration agents' by a number of authors, given the growing visibility of 'extreme', 'Salafi' forms of Islam that have proved attractive for 'new borns' and 'reverts', the convert has also come to be described as a dominant actor in "deculturalised", radicalised forms of Islam (Roy[4], see also Thielmann and Leuenberger in this volume). While Islamic fundamentalism has been discussed as an outcome of late modernities' secular condition, fuelled by the process of religious desinstitutionalisation and individualisation, this radical trend is often understood to be at odds with liberal and secular norms and values, notably gender equality as well as religious and sexual freedom.

On a symbolic level, in his/her latter guise as a 'new born zealot', the convert therefore figures as a *locum tenens* for Islam as an antagonist force who structures national debates on immigration, integration, nationalism, secularism and liberalism Europe-wide. Thus, in her comparative analysis of the public debates on religious converts in Turkish society and Germany respectively, sociologist Esra Özyürek discusses how, "religious converts are [perceived as, S.L.] dangerous hybrids, polluting and challenging the cultural superiority and purity of the dominant group"[5], and thus become the mediatised focal point of anxieties and articulations of national unity in the context of Turkey, and European integration in Germany.

Building up upon existing research on conversion to Islam in Europe, the four contributions gathered together in this section all depart from the convert as a symbolic proxy for current negotiations of the social position and possibility of (future) Islams and Muslims in Europe. Nonetheless, the case studies conducted in Switzerland, Germany and Great Britain respectively approach the

---

1   Allievi, Stefano (1998): *Les convertis à l'Islam,* Paris: L'Harmattan.

2   Roald, Anne Sophie (2004): *New Muslims in the European context: The experience of Scandinavian converts to Islam,* Leiden: Brill.

3   Zebiri, Kate (2008): *British Muslim converts: Choosing alternative lives,* Oxford: Oneworld.

4   Roy, Olivier (2004): *Globalised Islam: The search for a new ummah,* London: Hurst.

5   Özyürek, Esra (2009): "Convert alert: German Muslims and Turkish Christians as threats to security in the new Europe", in: *Comparative Studies in Society and History,* 51, pp. 91-116, citation p. 95.

phenomenon of the convert from very different angles, methodologies and theoretical perspectives.

The section "The one facing the many" opens with a focus on individual processes of Muslim self-formation. In their respective contributions, Petra Bleisch Bouzar and Leon Moosavi look at how convert individuals negotiate their Muslim identity. Both case studies show how converts are forced to reconcile intricate and seemingly conflicting notions of 'cultural', 'religious', and 'national' identities and allegiances in their self-construction. Thus, in his case study conducted in the UK, Moosavi departs from the public perception of British converts as 'traitors', as their conversion to Islam is often equaled to a break with their national belonging and loyalty. Basing his analysis on 37 interviews led with male and female converts, Moosavi shows that the public perception of British converts to Islam stands in stark contrast to the converts' own sense of self. Using the concept of 'hybrid identity' as described by Stuart Hall, Moosavi argues that the majority of British converts to Islam are very comfortable with a fluid and anti-essentialist identity, and that their conversion does not involve any affective departure from British society.

While Moosavi discusses the sense of belonging of British converts in terms of national and cultural allegiances, in her Swiss case study, Petra Bleisch Bouzar focuses on the self-formation of an individual female convert to Islam in respect of how she constructs religious authority. Her study is set within the Muslim milieu of Bienne, a former industrial town in the Western part of Switzerland with a high percentage of Muslim 'migrant' population, notorious for being a hotspot of Islamic radicalism. Employing a methodological approach situated in the field of cognitive narratology, cultural psychology and cognitive anthropology, the author unfolds the complex processes of boundary making involved in how convert Amadea constructs her religious self. Bleisch Bouzar employs the concept of "small stories" coined by narratologists Bamberg and Georgakopoulou to analyse narrative sequences; in her study, the author reconstructs the life world and sources of self-construction of the female convert who is married to a Muslim of West African origin, and visits the local Ahbash-mosque. Bleisch Bouzar's narratological approach shows how Amadea's religious self-formation is a fluent and ongoing interactive process that involves the negotiation of a plethora of sources of normativity and strategies of self-positioning.

While Petra Bleisch-Bouzar and Leon Moosavi focus in their respective case studies on individual processes of Muslim self-formation in the face of current problematisations of Islam and Muslims, Thielmann and Leuenberger discuss converts as social actors within specific fields of symbolic and political power.

Presenting an empirical case study in the German context, Joern Thielmann analyses the convert as an idealtypological actor within Islamic communities. His study draws on fieldwork conducted in Muslim communities in the region of Rhineland-Palatinate. Connecting Bourdieu's studies on the religious field to the Foucauldian concept of "technologies of the self", he works out an idealtypological portrait of 'Salafi' converts and 'reverts' with a migrant background as players within a wider Muslim field. He describes the converts as actors in a complex power field competing with other Muslim actors and communities over the recognition of their specific forms of religious and spiritual capital, and the definition of what counts as 'Islamic truth' and 'being a good Muslim'. Nurtured by the public image of Islam as a 'pre-modern', 'extreme', 'strict' religion, Thielmann shows how converts and reverts active in 'Salafi' circles appeal to their strict Islamic practice aimed at imitating the Prophet in all aspects of their daily lives as a creditable symbolic capital to position themselves as 'true Muslims' vis-à-vis other Muslim (migrant) communities.

The dialectic relationship between public perception and Muslim self-construction is also topical in the contribution of Susanne Leuenberger. Her case study is set within the context of the media hype triggered by a number of 'radical converts to Islam' heading the organisation Islamischer Zentralrat Schweiz (ICCS) founded in late 2009, as a reaction to the minaret referendum in Switzerland. The case study reconstructs a Swiss convert's speech held at an early venue of the ICCS. Expanding existing narratological approaches on religious conversion with a poststructurally informed, performative concept of subjectivation, the article shows how the narrative self-construction of convert Gibril is structured by the public gaze on Islam and Muslims.

While varied in terms of the questions raised, the case studies presented in the following section all focus on conversion to Islam as a paradigmatic form of Muslim self-constitution in contemporary European settings. Thereby, the contributions scrutinise the nexus between present forms of debating Islam and the self-formation of convert individuals as religious subjects and citizens in the respective national contexts of Switzerland, Germany and Britain.

Celtic ancestors and Muhammad's legacy: Types of narratives in a convert's construction of religiosity

PETRA BLEISCH BOUZAR

Biel/Bienne is a small, bilingual, and industrial town set between a beautiful lake and the Jura Mountains in Switzerland. Furthermore, Bienne has proportionally one of the highest Muslim populations in the country. According to the Swiss Federal Statistical Office, in 2000 Bienne had 3146 Muslims among its inhabitants, amounting to 6.5 per cent of the population in total, compared to 4.3 per cent in Switzerland (Bundesamt für Statistik 2003, table 3.1 and 3.4; Bovay 2004: 11). Today's estimations for Bienne go up to 10 per cent (Daum 2010).[1] As elsewhere in Switzerland, the Islamic landscape in Bienne is highly plural, with most of the diverse currents present. Furthermore, Bienne's Muslim population is composed of a variety of origins: Turkey, the Balkans, North Africa, West Africa, Switzerland, Afghanistan, and Pakistan, just to name the most common.

The Muslims in Bienne most prominent in the media are members of the Islamischer Zentralrat Schweiz (IZRS),[2] founded in October 2009 by Swiss converts and established in reaction to the minaret ban approved by the Swiss voters on 29 November 2009. Dressed in Arab desert style with long dyed beards for men, or the *niqāb* for women, and demanding legal recognition and other concessions, the IZRS converts quickly became, in Swiss public discourse, a symbol of the non-integrability of Islam within Swiss society (Bleisch/Leuenberger 2012: 245; Leuenberger this volume).

---

1 The national average rose to 4.5% for those aged 15 years and over (Bundesamt für Statistik 2012). It can be estimated at ca. 5.5% if those under 15 are included.

2 Islamic Central Council Switzerland, see their homepage: http://izrs.ch.

It was just a few months before the minaret ban, in the summer of 2009, that Amadea[3], living in Bienne and married to a West-African Muslim, converted to Islam at the Centre Islamique de Bienne, a mosque attached to the Ahbash movement. A deeper look into this case would be worthwhile, as Amadea faced many different dominant and marginalised discourses in Switzerland during her conversion process, a time when converts tend to absorb as much information about Islam and Muslims as possible (Roald 2006: 49). As Esra Ösyürek argues, in the context of a dominant Islamophobic discourse in Germany, ethnic German converts tend to strengthen the supposed distinction between *Islam* and *Culture* and "to distance themselves and Islam itself from born Muslims in Germany and the Middle East" (Özyürek 2010: 174). If this is true for the IZRS converts, Sheikh Muhammad Osman, who leads the Centre Islamique de Bienne, and whose teachings Amadea frequently follows, doesn't share this idea at all. Therefore, studying how Amadea deals with these opposed discourses will also give us insights into her attribution of authority.

To tackle this question, an approach situated in the field of cultural psychology, cognitive anthropology, and cognitive narratology is proposed here. It is argued that narrations not only render identity constructions visible, but are constitutive for identity formation.[4] Therefore, the analytical frame draws extensively on the concept of 'small stories', developed by Michael Bamberg and Alexandra Georgakopoulou in the course of their investigation of identity construction in adolescents' conversations (Georgakopoulou 2007a: 60; 2007b; Bamberg 2007b; Bamberg/Georgakopoulou 2008), and completes the toolset they proposed with other instruments developed by cognitive narratologists. This approach will be outlined in the next section.

NARRATIVES, IDENTITY, AND CONVERSION

According to Jérôme Bruner, one of the founders of cultural psychology, narratives are seen as a "mode of thought" (Bruner 1990: 13) that allows people to understand both the intentions of other people and one's own life. Narratives are the fundamental way through which people apprehend the world and attribute meaning to it (Bruner 1986: 17; Read/Miller 1995; Ochs/Capps 2001: 15). From

---

3   With the exception of the imam, Sheikh Muhammad Osman, all names of interviewees have been changed.

4   On the link between narration and identity, see Bruner 1986/1990; Somers 1994: 606; Georgakopoulou 2007a: 14; for a critical discussion, see Herman 2009: 155-159.

the perspectives of cognitive psychology and cognitive narratology, this process can be described as a complex interplay of "bottom-up" and "top-down" processes: information derived from the surrounding world (e.g. the ongoing conversation or the text one is reading) and the individual's memory (e.g. previous experiences or narrative templates) are simultaneously processed (Speer et al. 2009: 989; Martinez/Scheffel 2009: 150). A group of people who form a "community of discourse", or an *Erzählgemeinschaft* (Dégh 1962), share and transmit "meaningful templates that carry social, cultural, and communal currency for the process of identity formation" (Bamberg 2007a: 3) in the form of plotlines, master narratives, or dominant stories (Bamberg 2007a: 2-3).

At the turn of the twenty-first century, heated discussions started in the field of narrative psychology concerning the optimal data for identity studies. On the one hand, Alexandra Georgakopoulou and Michael Bamberg, two sociolinguistic-oriented researchers simultaneously directed their attention toward the everyday conversation of young people. In their work, they both argue that the analysis of short narratives, or narrative fragments, for which Bamberg coined the term 'small stories'[5], not only enrich narrative studies but also bring an important contribution to the understanding of how identities are negotiated and enacted (Georgakopoulou 2007a: 60; 2007b; Bamberg 2007b; Bamberg/Georgakopoulou 2008). As Georgakopoulou puts it, the shift from biographies to 'small stories' as privileged data is

> [...] one that does not prioritise a unified, coherent, autonomous, reflected upon and rehearsed self within a restrictive view of narrative as [...] a version of life given at a particular moment as expressing the given story as consistent and sequencing experience as lived [...]. Instead, one that allows for, and indeed sees the need for a scrutiny of fleeting, contingent fragmented and multiple selves, [...] deriving their definition through relations with others, [...] becoming on the boundaries of self and other [...] in narrative tellings in situ.
>
> (Georgakopoulou 2007a: 152)

From this perspective, a narrative is seen more as a talk-in-interaction and a social practice. Accordingly, narratives should always be analyzed in their interactional context (Georgakopoulou 2007a: 3-6). On the other hand has Mark Freeman de-

---

5   Bamberg 2004. Following Georgakopoulou, 'small stories' cover "a gamut of under-represented narrative activities, such as tellings of ongoing events, future or hypothetical events, shared (known) events, but also allusions to tellings, deferrals of tellings, and refusals to tell" (Georgakopoulou 2007b: 146).

fended the life-story analysts. He agreed that identity is produced and re-produced in specific discursive situations and that biographies perpetuate an image of identity that is much more stable than the 'small stories' in conversations would suggest. "But", he argues, "we are not only the selves that issue from 'small stories'. Whether we like it or not, we are also – at this moment in history, in the context of contemporary Western culture – big story selves" (Freeman 2007: 159).

Several points are especially worth noting. What the aforementioned authors have in common is that both perspectives are guided by the assumption that identity construction as a meaning-making process is framed in narratives – be they 'big' or 'small'. The object of their disagreement is the data that should be privileged in the analysis of identity and their research agendas: while Freeman and other life story analysts study experiences as texts, Bamberg and Georgakopoulou focus on people as interactive agents (Bamberg 2007b: 168). Therefore, regarding the question of proximity to 'real' life, 'small stories' are claimed by Georgakopoulou and Bamberg to be linked to experience much closer than life stories are (Georgakopoulou 2007a: 32), emphasising the "dialogical/discursive origins of our interiors" (Bamberg 2007b: 170), while biographic analysts assume an individual who seeks coherence and authenticity as the organising forces of his/her life story.

It is argued here that since identity formation is, as Jean-Claude Kaufmann puts it, at the same time "stable et provisoire" (Kaufmann 2004: 113), it is "stable dans le sens où elle assure une cohérence à l'individu dans son histoire personnelle et dans le temps, mais elle est aussi provisoire car elle est une construction individuelle répondant aux impératifs d'une situation donnée" (Schneuwly Purdie 2009: 157). Therefore, this article attempts to provide both, a rendering of Amadea's life story in order to detect the more stable and coherent aspects of her identity formation, and a deeper analysis of her 'small stories', in order to catch the dialogical/discursive aspects of her identity formation at the time of the interview.

Current research on conversion to Islam still focuses almost exclusively on biographies.[6] This tradition has recently been challenged by a psychological-anthropological approach (Mansson McGinty 2006) and discourse analysis.[7] To my knowledge, the concept of 'small stories' has not yet been applied to conversion. Thus, this chapter also proposes the use of an enlarged data corpus and new, fruitful analytical tools in this field.

---

6   See, for example, van Niewkerk 2006; Wohlrab-Sahr 1999; Allievi 1998; Poston 1992.
7   See Leman/Stallaert/Lechkar 2010, Leuenberger (this volume).

THE SETTING: THE CENTRE ISLAMIQUE DE BIENNE

The present study is based on fieldwork I conducted between March 2010 and June 2011 at the Centre Islamique de Bienne. This is the first time that the centre has been studied, and the data has not yet been presented. The material consists of an observation protocol and six narrative and episodic interviews.[8] The protocol comprises several informal talks during eight evenings at the Centre, as well as the notes that I took during nine lessons, which were given by the Centres imam, Sheikh Muhammad Osman, either to the women (six) in the women's premises or the men (three) in the main prayer room. The lessons to the men were broadcasted in the women's rooms. Amadea attended eight of the nine observed lessons. At four of the lessons, she served Sheikh Osman as a translator from German into French. The interviews with Sheikh Osman, as well as with other converts, were conducted in the Centre's premises; the one with Amadea took place at her apartment.

Because of the lack of official documents, the centre's early years have to be reconstructed through interviews and informal talks. As one convert informed me, it started in the 1980s as a small group of people around a couple of Algerian origin who "came from Lausanne". After a few years of meeting in a private house, they moved to an old building and, later on in the 1990s, to a flat near the central station of Bienne.[9] In 2008, a new location at the *Zukunftsstrasse* was opened. It was comprised of a bigger prayer room for men, two connected small rooms for women, an office, a store, a very small space for the Sheikh's bed, and a kitchen. According to Barbara Hussein, the president of the Centre's women's association founded in 2010, 15-20 families are regular visitors. They originate from Switzerland, Somalia, Ethiopia, Algeria, Morocco, Bosnia, and Afghanistan. Religious education classes and prayers from Thursday evening to Saturday evening are provided by Sheikh Muhammad Osman, a Swiss with Lebanese ori-

---

8   See Flick 2000; Schütze 1983; 1987. Transcription symbols: for the transcription, the following notation system has been used: normal voice, **loud voice,** *low voice,* <u>emphasis</u>, exte:::nsion, - → short pause, - - → longer pause, . → fall in tone, (non-verbal expressions, such as gestures or laughter), [editorial comments]. The original language of the interview is Swiss German – all translations are mine. Numbers given in brackets refer to the line of the transcript. The interview is slightly edited, in order to increase coherence.

9   The founding couple moved back to Algeria and was, therefore, not available for an interview.

gins who lives in Zurich and also works in the Centre Islamique de Lausanne.[10] During an interview I had with him, Sheikh Osman confirmed that he was part of the Ahbash movement.[11]

The founder of the Ahbash movement is Sheikh Abdallah ibn Muhammad ibn Yusuf al-Shaibi al-Abdari al-Harari (b. 1910 or 1920 in Harar/Ethiopia), also known later on in Lebanon by the name of al-Habashi, 'the Ethiopian'. The founder's origin is the reason behind the movement's appellation (Hamzeh/Dekmejian 1996: 219).[12] In 1947 he was expelled from Ethiopia due to struggles with both the *'ulamā'* of the Wahhabiyya[13] and the political authorities (Kabha/Erlich 2006: 522; Erlich 2007: 81-87; Avon 2008: 3). After travelling to Medina, Jerusalem, and Damascus, Abdallah al-Harari settled in 1950 in Beirut – where he resides to this day – "and was licensed as a shaykh by al-Azhar University's branch in Lebanon" (Hamzeh/Dekmejian 1996: 219). In his first 30 years in Beirut, al-Harari gained fame as "a thinker, an author [...], a mufti, and a preacher" (Kabha/Erlich 2006: 523). In 1983, when the previous president died, he was declared the leader of the association called *jam'īyat al-mashārī' al-khairīyya al-islamīyya* (Association of Islamic Charitable Projects, AICP; Kabha/Erlich 2006: 523)[14]. This can be considered to be the starting point of the political activities of the association and the Ahbash movement in Lebanon.

From the 1980s on, thanks to the Lebanese diaspora, al-Ahbash became a transnational movement with branches in South Asia, Western Europe, North America (Kabha/Erlich 2006: 523sq.), and Australia (Avon 2008: 8). As far as Europe is concerned, most of the associations were founded by Lebanese students (Boubekeur 2007: 29).[15] Germany (Kabha/Erlich 2006: 523) or Paris

---

10 Informal talk with Barbara Hussein, 30 April 2010.

11 Interview with Sheikh Muhammad Osman, 12 June 2010, 1042-1060.

12 For a comprehensive discussion of the roots and meanings of the designations *al-ahbash* and *al-habasha,* see Kabha/Erlich 2006.

13 "Wahhabiyya" is subsequently used as an emic designation in the Ahbash sense for people referring to a political Islam based on the writings of Ibn Taymiyya and Ibn 'Abd al-Wahhab (Kabha/Erlich 2006: 520, 524).

14 However, the researchers have different interpretations of this incident. Some describe al-Harari as being supported by the former president (Kabha/Erlich 2006, 523), others speak of a "take over" (Hamzeh/Dekmejian 1996: 219) or even an infiltration, a "tactique de coucou" (Avon 2008, 3) by the Ahbash movement.

15 As far as I know, there are no critical studies about the historical development of al-Ahbash in Europe, and our knowledge is limited to their self-representation.

(Boubekeur 2007: 29) are mentioned as the European headquarters. In Switzerland, the first activities began in Lausanne at the end of the 1970s where, according to Amel Boubekeur, Lebanese students founded the still existing association called the Centre Islamique de Lausanne. However, the homepage of the association informs us that the Centre "fut fondé en 1979 sur l'initiative d'un groupe d'étudiants et de travailleurs musulmans venus de divers pays" (Centre Islamique de Lausanne [n. d.]), hiding their link to Lebanon. "In just a few years", Boubekeur stated, "the movement became the official representative body for Muslims of that region" (Boubekeur 2007: 29). Besides Biel/Bienne and Lausanne, a third centre exists in Zurich.[16]

AMADEA AS AN AUTONOMOUS BELIEVER

I met Amadea in summer 2010 at the women's rooms in the Centre Islamique de Bienne, about one year after her conversion to Islam. She is about 30 years old and has been married for several years to a West-African man. The interview took place in March 2011 at her apartment in the suburbs of Bienne and lasted about three hours. It started with the invitation to narrate her life story.

At the very beginning of her life-story narrative, Amadea states that it has always been clear to her that God exists, thereby positioning herself as a religious believer. The story of her socialisation in a Protestant family starts with her memory of saying children's prayers with her grandmother, celebrating Easter and Christmas more as a "cultural celebration" (10) during childhood, and attending boring religious education classes in the house of the Protestant pastor. This led, as she explains, to an absence of religiosity during her adolescence. After the 9/11 attacks she felt the need to pray for all of the victims but failed to connect to God – "the lines went dead" (30sq.). Subsequent attempts to connect to God in "a Christian way" (33) failed as well.

During her adolescence, Amadea discovered a passion for the Celts and Native Americans, as well as (other) nature religions ("Naturreligionen"); she struggled and failed in following her best friend Laura in "going this way"(57) – stating that "I felt in my heart that it was not mine, that it was not your thing" (61sq.). Nevertheless, she (still) feels a spiritual and "almost blood relation" with the Celts, because the grandmother of her English grandfather was Irish. A small story narrated later on in the interview analyzed below, will strengthen this point.

---

16 See Martens 2007.

During her struggle with adhering, or not, to nature religion or neo-paganism as practiced by her friend Laura, she fell in love with her future (Muslim) husband. She states that she had the same opinion about Islam that the (Swiss) media transmitted to her: "Islam [is] evil, Islam [is] oppression of women, Islam [is] a no-go" (68sq.). However, for her it was also a "no-go" to be with someone without having knowledge about his religious and cultural background. Therefore, she started to read books about Islam and Africa: its history, culture and religion. Through her study, she slowly revised her prejudices and adopted the opinion that "in theory it is – it seems that the religion is ok but in practice it's a no-go" (81sq.), pointing out that in Arab countries women have to wear the headscarf, and a lot of things are prohibited for them. At Ramadan 2007[17] she had an emotionally touching experience while reading the *ayat* 30:21 in a German translation of the Qur'an. She explains in the interview that she was affected by the Qur'an's statement that the basic idea of a relationship is love and respect: "[...] then my heart opened up and then my heart already decided that, yes, I will become Muslim one day" (95sqq.).

At the beginning of 2009, she started to be concerned with theories about the end of the world in 2012, which made her pretty nervous. She explained in the interview that she was convinced that she must absolutely become Muslim before December 2012, "[...] just to be sure" (145). The pronouncing of the *shahāda* took place during the first week of Ramadan in 2009 in the Centre Islamique de Bienne. Unlike other conversion narratives collected during research, the narration of this event is rich with details (dialogue, feelings, people involved), and includes many references to time and place, indicating a personal experience that made a deep impression. At the beginning of Ramadan, Amadea tells us, she had decided to do a "real Ramadan" and requested that her husband teach her how to pray. Her husband explained that an imam would be the right person to do this, and he promised that he would arrange a meeting in the mosque, which happened a week later. At the meeting, Sheikh Osman explained the basics of Islam to Amadea and asked her if she wanted to convert. Amadea narrates that she was very surprised by this question, but finally agreed. The same night she also got Islamically married to her husband and started to get to know the other members of the women's group. She got particularly close to Lubna, a girl in her early twenties, born in Switzerland of Lebanese origin. It was Lubna who "adopted [me], she said you are now my sister" (253), and who took care of her religious education by teaching her the basic rituals, such as prayer or ritual ablution. At the same time, Amadea started to follow the teach-

---

17 This is the first moment in her life story narration where she refers to a specific time.

ings of Sheikh Osman, and read Kristiane Backer's (2009) conversion story, who became, as Amadea argues later on in the interview, her model, "because she wants to live a European – Islam [...] – that is my opinion as well" (337sqq.).

While the vast majority of her family and friends, as she tells us, reacted in a negative way to her conversion, her husband's friends – all African Muslims – were delighted. Amadea insists in the interview that her husband never urged her to become Muslim, and would only respond to questions about Islam but never speak about religion of his own accord. In a lengthy section of the interview, she narrates her decreasing interest in hanging out with her friends in bars and discos. Her neo-pagan friend Laura was the only exception among her friends; after a long process, she was able to accept Amadea's conversion.

Analyzing Amadea's live-story narrative, we get the following general plotline of her religious biography: Amadea was born as a believer; experienced a Christian childhood, which felt wrong; searched unsuccessfully for a connection to God; was attracted to neo-paganism; met her future Muslim husband; and finally converted to Islam after a long period of struggle and doubts. This plot corresponds with a lot of other conversion-to-Islam narratives where the encounter with a (male or female) Muslim is one of the most common triggering factors (Roald 2004: 99).[18] As noted above, Amadea narrated her personal experience of her pronouncement of the *shahāda* in a quite long and intense 'small story'. If we read this 'small story', as Jerome Bruner proposes, as the breach of an implicit canonical script (Bruner 1990: 11), we may sketch the following 'canonical' plotline: a Swiss (or European) woman gets in touch with Islam, mainly through an acquaintance with a Muslim man; then informs herself and reflects (a lot); then, when she is ready, she decides to convert, choosing the place and witnesses.[19] The breach in Amadea's narrative occurs during the last event of the 'canonical script': she was ready to learn prayer, but not to convert, and she didn't control the time, place and witnesses of her conversion. In this sense, the 'small story' implicitly affirms the general aim of conversion-to-Islam narratives in representing the convert as a reflected, rational and self-determined believer,

---

18 See also Allievi 2006: 122-123. Amadea's story further confirms Roald's observations that crises are not part of the 'canonical' conversion narrative to Islam as a cause for conversion (Roald 2004: 94sq.).

19 See, for example, Kristiane Backer 2009, Amadea's favourite biography of a convert; for the recurrent motive of conversion to Islam as a 'rational choice', see also Poston 1992: 171; Wohlrab-Sahr 1999: 159.

thereby contradicting the general public discourse of fanatic Muslim subjects.[20] Following Beckford, conversion narratives always include elements of the religion's ideological rationale (Beckford 1978). Amadea's statement at the very beginning of her life story narration that she has always been a believer integrates and reaffirms the concept of *fitra* as the idea of believing in a one and only God as the natural religion of humankind (Roald 2004: 87).

NARRATING INNER CONFLICTS IN 'SMALL STORIES'

Most of the conversion narratives I collected during my fieldwork include an account of a period of struggle over whether or not the women will become Muslim. Amadea rendered this period of being torn between paganism and Islam in the following 'inner-conflict' 'small story':

> [that happened] in October during Ramadan [...] in 2007 and then I read the Qur'an in German, the translation of the Reclam Edition – I read *sūra* 30 verse 21 – and it has to do with – that God created men and women out of one substance [Wesen], and that he created them to be together, and that (High German) love and respect be among them (continuing in Swiss German) just this – [explanation about love and respect] then my heart opened up and then my heart already decided that yes one day I will become Muslim. My head **didn't agree** with that yet [...], during two months [I had] really, (High German) an emotional roller-coaster [Sturm der Gefühle], (continuing in Swiss German) – *yes* – (fast) you're nuts [geht es eigentlich noch] do you want to become Muslim are you sure – (normal) yes I want to – ok, but have you given a thought here and there and afterwards, it has been a discussion if I want more in the nature religious sense – (hesitating) ye::::s – or better Islam – or maybe one can merge this somehow – *no I can't ok, all right*, and then I tried afterwards – to make my choice in one direction – and – [...] afterwards I realized that the Celtic, the nature religions, attract me strongly, but that it isn't my thing. – And that I feel attracted to Islam, and simply my rationale [meine Ratio] still having a problem with that, it is not ok – ok then, we will just have a look now [wir luegen jetzt mal] afterwards, to start with, I decided for the moment for the direction Islam.   (85-112)

---

20 See van Nieuwkerk 2006: 102. For the public discourse on Muslims in Switzerland, see, for example, Clavien 2009; Behloul 2009; for the media discourse in Switzerland see, for example, Koch 2011.

The episode in which she read the *sūra* led to her subsequent narration about a split between her heart which opened up and decided that it wanted to be Muslim and her mind which didn't agree and started to argue with her heart. Amadea attributes independent agencies to both of them, identifying the 'me' with her heart while her mind, her rationality, addresses the heart as 'you'. At a specific moment, her mind asks the crucial question about whether it would be possible to merge paganism and Islam. It gets and accepts the (very soft-spoken) answer that it's not possible – and the author of the answer remains unidentifiable. Subsequently, Amadea/her heart decided that she was more attracted to Islam, while her mind *("meine Ratio")* still had a problem with that. In the evaluation part[21] of this 'small story', Amadea reunites her 'heart' and her 'mind' (while the heart understands the mind's reservations) in a 'we' and decides as the 'I' that one day she will convert.

Later on in the interview, two other 'inner-conflict-stories' occur. They are embedded in an argumentative part where Amadea talked about her involvement with Pierre Vogel:

> [...] somehow I also have been very enthusiastic about Pierre Vogel, and then – Laura already started to worry about (laugh) me and then later on my rational mind has again – and then – so – so (clearing her throat) hmhm – hello – ah have you seen how people behave, how they isolate themselves – that everything that doesn't fit in their value-system is just basically wrong, do you really want to end up like them. Then I had to say – *hmm no not really*. This was then, in fact, I can always, [when] an idealistical ideal takes hold in my head, I can count on my mind getting in touch with [me] at least after three months saying ye::s. Did you calm down? Yes. It's ok.   (1077-1088)

As in the 'inner-conflict' 'small story' mentioned above, she renders her involvement with Vogel's interpretation of Islam in an inner dialogue attributing independent agency to both, the 'me' and the 'mind'. While the 'me' gets enthusiastic about Vogel, her nature-religious friend Laura starts to get worried. On the level of the narrative structure, Amadea first supersedes Laura with her 'mind' and then merges her 'mind' and Laura as her vigilant and critical counterpart. After a long argumentative part in which she emphasises and argues her rejection of Vogel's interpretations of 'true Islam', which are judged by her as intolerant, she concludes

---

21 The structure of 'small stories' usually consists of a plotline and an evaluation (Georgakopoulou 2007a: 92). Plot is defined here as the motivated composition of events (Martinez/Scheffel 2009: 109; Fludernik 2008: 40).

with a metaphorical 'small story', comparing her initial enthusiasm with Vogel's ideas with swimming in a river. At a specific moment, facing the danger of a waterfall or a floodgate, her mind becomes active and saves her (1109-1114).

In all of the three 'small stories', Amadea creates an inner dialogue as a narrative technique through the split of her heart and her mind to give access to her inner thoughts and struggles. In the first of the three mentioned 'small stories', her heart convinces her mind to convert to Islam (while rejecting paganism), thereby legitimating this choice through emotion (Bleisch Bouzar 2012: 292). The priority she gives to her heart can be explained in two ways. One possible explanation is to see this as the inclusion of a Sufi-oriented conversion narrative pattern. Another possibility is to read this as a reaction to "the public", which is often puzzled that people choose, as Jawad puts it, "Islam against all the odds" (Jawad 2006: 156). As holding a rational argumentation in favor of Islam is costly, time-consuming, and probably unsuccessful, the emotional legitimation can hardly be put into question. However, the mind has to be convinced in order to make a decision. In the other two 'small stories', it is her mind that saves her heart from choosing the "wrong" interpretation of Islam, starting to think, to read, and, thereby, creating coherence. The priority Amadea attributes to her mind is in line with the self-representation she gave in her life story account. In these 'small stories', the choice of the "right" interpretation of Islam is thematised, thereby, her mind is choosing the more accepted one in the eyes of the society. The narrative technique of inner dialogue (splitting herself into a heart and a mind) allows her to explain her navigation between the different discourses and to make her choices understandable to the interviewer.

NARRATING BOUNDARIES IN 'SMALL STORIES'

Christianity and Neo-Paganism

As we have seen in Amadea's *small story* about her choosing between Neo-Paganism and Islam, she agreed with an unknown author that the two cannot be combined. However, in a long part in which Amadea discussed evolution, she came back to her family background, proposing the following 'hypothetic-general-law-story':

Why do I now have such a penchant for Celts and Indians? As a child, I always wanted to migrate to Canada – why [...] and afterwards I considered it as follow[:] ye::::s – well some people explain it with reincarnation, because in a previous life you have been an Indian, that's why you want to go back. I considered – because –

the <u>body</u> of the child emerges out of the parts of [its] <u>mother</u> and <u>father</u>. – And what if a <u>part</u> of the <u>soul</u> – from the <u>parents</u> – because for me it is always that the child has a new soul – I rather believe that God, that every <u>soul</u> - simply exists <u>once</u> – **but** – maybe a part of the parent's souls or of previous ancestors merges into the child's soul and that this, […] as for example, longing for Canada, maybe I had an ancestor 200 years ago who absolutely wanted to go there because – in Ireland there was a <u>famine,</u> because I have Irish people in my family.   (958-972)

The plotline here is embedded in an explication and can be traced as follows: an Irish ancestor lived in Ireland 200 years ago during the famine and may have longed for Canada. This desire became enclosed somehow in his soul. Then he/she had a child and a part of his/her soul (still containing the longing for Canada) somehow merged with the soul of his/her child and so on until this (same?) part of the soul merged with her own soul when she was created. God is introduced in the narrative as a character, but it remains unclear what part he takes or action he performs. It is interesting to note that unlike other 'small stories', this story is narrated anachronistically.[22] One may take this as an example of an ongoing emplotment. The story's structure is created while narrating, rather than reproduced. Through this she merges the Islamic representation of an undividable unique soul with a specific template of reincarnation – presumably the concept of 'hereditary memory' (*Erberinnerungen*[23]). The story in itself – even if presented as hypothetical – functions as an attempt to explain and solve her puzzling question (why she has this longing for Canada), which canonical Islamic view cannot solve.

It is worthwhile to note here that unlike her attempts to merge the pagan ideas with Islam, her demarcation of Christianity is very strong, as the following 'small story' shows:

Ok I generally struggled with Christianity, I couldn't set up a connection – in fact me and Christianity, an appropriate image is if you want to put a cat into a bathtub

---

22 See Martinez/Scheffel 2009: 33-34.

23 The German writer Carl Friedrich Wilhelm Jordan (1819-1904), who used *Erberinnerungen* to describe the idea that we have "eingeborene Empfindungen" (Jordan 1886: 195), innate perceptions that have been transmitted from generation to generation (see Martini 1981: 387). Later on, the *völkisch* esoteric movement used *Erberinnerung* as a method to enter into contact with the hidden world of the pagan Germanic ancestors (Wiedemann 2007: 140-141). Nowadays, it is reported that, at least in neo-pagan groups, the concept regained popularity, although it remains contested (Gründer 2010: 26).

full of water, that is the same inborn reaction pattern. – I would have wanted to – but as soon as I tried it is like to [push] a cat into a bathtub. – (she pushes her palms forward) away. – **go away stop it** (fast voice) let it be.   (34-40)

It is interesting to note that the boundary of the Christian faith is not drawn by the rejection of the Trinity as in many other cases,[24] but through the emplotment of a kind of instinctive and genuine reaction by means of a metaphorical 'small story'. The rejection of Christian faith is not only narrated, but properly enacted with vivid gestures and voice. The same metaphorical story is used when she informs me about her best friend Laura rejecting all monotheistic and patriarchal religions.[25]

In both 'small stories', Amadea doesn't make use of rational arguments to draw boundaries, but rather advocates in the "cat" story an innate 'decision-maker' that preserves the *fitra* and is coded against Christianity. However, in another part of the interview she positions herself as an open-minded and tolerant person who accepts all religions, in order to dissociate herself from, as she states, the many Muslims who despise Christians, Jews, and the even worse pagan people (353sq.).

Arab Islam and Wahhabi converts

In a long explanation following the life story narration, Amadea advocated her preference of a "good African" and a "good European Islam" over a "bad Arab Islam". In her eyes, Arabs are narrow-minded, blinkered and hostile to critical thinking, whereas Africans are likeable and open-minded. Contrary to their Arab sisters, African women are allowed to move about freely, to trade and to entertain informal relationships with men. Amadea takes the IZRS converts with their beards and dress codes as a proof for the Arabs aim to impose their culture on all Muslims. However, taking a closer look at the 'small stories' that occurred during the whole interview, her rejection of "Arab Islam" must be nuanced. She rejects the "Saudi Arabian" and, as noted above, the "Pierre Vogel" interpretations of Islam – thereby following her Lebanese teacher, Sheikh Osman. These stories will be analyzed in this section. In the next section, we will take a closer look at her ambivalence when dealing with Sheikh Osman's 'Arabicity'.

In a passage where Amadea talked about the importance of the Centre to her religious life, she illustrated her approval of the way gender separation is practiced in the Centre with the following 'hypothetical general law' story:

---

24 See, for example, Roald 2004: 103sqq.

25 Laura, by the way, remained her preferred interlocutor at least until the interview took place.

I must say that I'm not a supporter of gender separation, and in my view it is a disaster when boys and girls are separated at an early age and then do not meet each other until the bridal night, as, for example, in Saudi Arabia – that is a shock, that is an absolute disaster – then it is expected as well – then you are, for the first time in your life, you have been kept away from men during your whole life, then you are locked up with one of them, and then it is expected of him that he has sex with you because the virginity has to be proven, and this is an absolute disaster, this is – this is extremely traumatic, and I'm not a supporter of gender separation at all.   (657-667)

Her evaluation in this 'small story' is given at the beginning, in the middle, and at the end of it: that gender separation as practiced in Saudi Arabia is a disaster. In a hypothetical story, she constructs the following plotline: you have been separated from men your whole life – then you are together with one of them for the first time, and locked up with him in a room – and then it is expected that he has sex with you. Therein, she pictures two characters, a man and a woman who are strangers. By using the second person singular, "you", she invites the interviewer to identify with the woman. Thus, Amadea, as the teller, seeks to enhance the listener's empathy. If we read this narration as the breach of an implicit canonical script (Bruner 1990: 11), one may sketch the following "European" plotline: a man and a woman meet, get to know each other, then they fall in love with each other, and then they have sex together. The breach of this canonical script is twofold: first, the "Arab" story omits the initial events and jumps to the abrupt sexual intercourse, and second, the sexual relationship is not the outcome of a common decision but a unilateral action undertaken by the man on the woman. According to this story line, "it" is expected that the man does sex to the woman. "It" functions here as a blank (*Leerstelle*[26]) to be filled in by the listener (maybe with "tradition" or "their families"); the man and woman are portrayed as having been conditioned by "it", and the woman is more passive than the man. While in Amadea's statement, she advocates relaxed relationships between men and women, in the 'small story' she creates a situation of potential sexual violence. She directly addresses the listener and claims his or her empathy. As the listener unavoidably imagines the scene (being locked up with a stranger who is expected to have sex with you), experientiality is created, conferring plausibility to her initial statement that gender separation "is a disaster".

Besides Pierre Vogel, it is Nicolas Blancho "and his gang" (633sq.) who are the incarnation of her "Swiss convert but living as an Arab" counterpart.

---

26 In narratology, *Leerstellen* or "Unbestimmtheitsstellen" (Iser 1984: 284) are blanks or vague passages that have to be completed or filled in by the reader.

Blancho, president of the aforementioned IZRS, frequents the nearby 'Arab speaking' Al-Rahman mosque described by other members of the Centre Islamique de Bienne as extremist.[27] In order to illustrate their standpoint, Amadea narrates a secondhand about her friend Lubna visiting the mosque for the purpose of a paper Lubna had to write for school:

> For example, behind the Islamic Centre there is the Al-Rahman mosque. Nicolas Blancho and his gang are hanging around, because – once Lubna had – visited different mosques for a task and she had also been there – and she always wore a headscarf but she put on colorful clothes and also European clothes and not Arab clothes, simply longer at the back [...] – then she had a sweater on and a long spaghetti strap dress reaching down to the knees or in the middle of the upper legs, simply nothing slinky, simply European clothes that can be combined [...] – yes she is dressed up normally with local clothes – that conform to the prescriptions but they are not too saucy - - but what she wore wasn't welcomed at all, so they [...] frowned at her. (633-649)

The plotline is cut in two and, in between, Amadea provides an extended and detailed description omitted in the citation of the clothes that – one assumes – Lubna was wearing that day. In summation, the clothes are labelled as European but respecting Islamic prescriptions. Amadea does not dress in as sophisticated a way as Lubna, who has, as I observed in the Centre, a very artful and thoughtful way of styling herself. Amadea dresses most often in jeans, a men's hemp shirt, and a simple headscarf. Amadea interprets the reaction of the mosque's visitors as a critique of the non-Arab, European dress style. As this 'small story' is embedded in a paragraph about the Centre itself, it serves as a background against which the Centre is portrayed as tolerant. However, the Center's imam, Sheikh Osman, whose teaching Amadea follows frequently, is an Arab as well. One may wonder how she deals with his "Arabicity".

Sheikh Osman's "Arabicity"

In her rejection of the "bad Arab Islam" as personified by Nicolas Blancho and Pierre Vogel, Amadea follows the Centre's imam, Sheikh Osman. In short, in his teachings, Sheikh Osman perpetuates the Ahbash's initial opposition towards the Wahhabiyya (Kabha/Erlich 2006: 522; Erlich 2007: 81-87).[28] He also upholds

---

27 Field protocol Centre Islamique de Bienne 1.
28 Interview with Sheikh Osman, 12 June 2010, 1097-1103; 1125sq.

Sheikh 'Abdallah al-Harari's main messages (brought from Ethiopia to Lebanon) of peaceful Islamic-Christian coexistence,[29] which he transformed into amicable Islamic-Swiss cohabitation. Furthermore, Sheikh Osman's lessons aim to protect the Islamic community from terrorism and extremism.[30] However, a very strong boundary is drawn between believers and unbelievers.[31]

Amadea attends as many of his lessons as possible and describes him as a very friendly and open person, a good teacher with a great capacity to explain things (280-284). Moreover, whenever she manages to arrive sufficiently early in the Centre, she discusses the lesson with Sheikh Osman, in order to prepare for the (simultaneous) translation into French. However, as she explains, her (African) husband recommended that she ought to respect Sheikh Osman, but not always listen to him, because – she says imitating her husband's voice – "he is an Arab, you know" (892). She renders one of Sheikh Osman's lessons in a very long and detailed narrative, which, unfortunately, can only be partially presented here:

[...] that was before Mawlid, before the – ah the celebration of the Prophet's birthday, because it is also prohibited by the Wahhabis. - The sheikh explained it to us ye::::s, because that is nothing bad, because what is bad in remembering our Prophet and – praying prayers together and singing religious songs together, what could be bad about it, there is nothing bad about it because we don't do anything – nothing that impinges on the religion. - And then we came to [darauf gekommen] the issue of normal birthdays and the sheikh said, normal birthdays never [niet]. Afterwards I asked him – why not – he simply said because it is – not – the tradition of celebrating birthdays doesn't come out of Islam. So he has a little bit like the attitude that – everything that doesn't come out of Islam, and this is true for a lot of people, – that doesn't originate in Islam isn't good. And here we are back to what we discussed previously [in the interview] – culture – to put your culture on someone else. Who is coming from a completely different culture. [...] – And then afterwards I said to her [Rahel], I said that I simply translated the sheikh's words one-to-one and afterwards when the lesson was over I said please come here [du komm schnell]. - Then I said – I am here – the sheikh asked me to translate - - and then I do this here and I translate

---

29 Kabha/Erlich 2006: 523; field protocol Centre Islamique de Bienne 2.

30 Interview with Sheikh Osman, 12 June 2010, 467-505; field protocol Centre Islamique de Bienne 2. Already in Lebanon during Lebanon's civil war, the Ahbash movement positioned itself "as a non-militant alternative to the Islamists, [...] call[ing] for religious moderation, political civility, and peace" (Hamzeh/Dekmejian 1996: 224).

31 Field protocol Centre Islamique de Bienne 2.

his words exactly how he said them – and now I give you my opinion [...] I said, what is bad in celebrating birthdays? If you invite people to eat cake together and they offer you something that is not – a **glorification of your personality** [...] - [Lubna] would tell you now – yes, when you are celebrating your birthday but not on the same day that you have your birthday, you know like this – *but this is then again so - - that is* – it's **pointless,** that is then just so, so behind the back, sort of a handycraft-mentality [*das ist dann nachher nur so wieder so ein hinten durä irgend öppis Bastelmentalität*], for me that is not ok, that is silly. For me it's silly (laughing) – said shortly it's silly [*kurz gesagt ich finde das jetzt doof*].   (1529-1574)

In this 'small story' of personal experience, Amadea introduces four figures: (1) Sheikh Osman teaching the lesson; (2) herself translating the lesson to the women among them; (3) Rahel, a convert living in her neighborhood; and (4) Lubna, who is introduced as a virtual interlocutor, but it is not clear whether she was present at this specific lesson. Concerning the celebration of *mawlid*, all actors seem to agree that it is permitted – thereby drawing a boundary to the Wahhabiyya. Concerning the celebration of one's own birthday, Amadea renders three different opinions: Sheikh Osman seems to be opposed, arguing that it is not an Islamic tradition and therefore bad; Amadea herself doesn't see it as a problem at all as long as the person is not venerated; Lubna is said to hold that one should just not celebrate one's birthday on the day of the birthday. Amadea transmits all three of the opinions to Rahel – the Sheikh's view as the translation during the lesson – and Lubna's and her own after the lesson in a more intimate talk with Rahel. As noted elsewhere, translators in these kinds of settings are more than simple transmitters of knowledge, but more like 'adjusters' of the knowledge to the cultural context, becoming authoritative figures on their own (see Bleisch Bouzar 2012; Kuppinger 2012).

Amadea narrates her opposition to the Sheikh at two moments. First, she responds to the Sheikh's lesson during the lesson with "why not", implying that she doesn't agree, but seemingly, she doesn't argue with him in front of the other women. As I observed in the lessons I attended, Amadea is one of the most critical of Sheikh Osman's students, often seeking further explanation and confronting him with other interpretations. In return, she is the woman Sheikh Osman addresses most during the lessons when he asks questions to check if the women had understood his teachings. Therefore, we can describe their relationship as privileged. Second, Amadea opposes the Sheikh by transmitting her own point of view to Rahel. Here, again, she doesn't confront him openly or put his authority fundamentally into question, but presents herself as a critical seeker of a sound interpretation of Islam, which can be integrated into Swiss society.

One further point should be mentioned here. In the omitted part of the above 'small story', Amadea argued against Sheikh Osman's imposition of Arab culture (by not allowing the celebration of one's own birthday). She stated that we do not know if the *ahādīth*, which are not of divine origin but were transmitted by people, are authentic or not. After the interview, she told me that one evening, while chatting online in a forum that has nothing to do with religion, she talked to an Alevi girl in a discussion about *ahādīth*. This girl recommended a website that deals critically with this issue.[32] Since then, Amadea has had serious doubts about all *ahādīth*. In her critiques of Nicolas Blancho, as well as different rulings from the Sheikh, she casts doubts on the authenticity of *ahādīth* as a discursive strategy to reject "Arab Islam".

CONCLUSION

In this article, I tried to show how a particular convert deals with different discourses she faces and that an approach within narrative theory using the concept of 'small stories' is particularly fruitful.

As we have seen, Amadea, in her life story narration, distances herself from nature religion stating that she clearly chose Islam. However, the detailed analysis of a 'small story' reveals that she integrates nature religious ideas creating an original conceptualisation of the soul. Moreover, Amadea presents herself in her life-story narration as an autonomous and reflective believer, rejecting, yet at the same time affirming the existence of the public stereotype of oppressed Muslim women. Thus, the analysis of her 'small stories' shows that she is, or has been, at that time searching for an interpretation of Islam that is in line with the public discourses – thereby rejecting the "bad Arab Wahhabiyya". She found the solution in both a "European" and an "African" Islam. It is interesting to note that she doesn't make any differentiation between them. Similar to Roald's and Özyürek's observations (Roald 2004: 114; Özyürek 2010: 174),[33] Amadea, at one point in the interview, evokes a strong gap between "culture" and "religion", while reducing religion to the basic obligations of prayer, fasting, and pilgrimage, allowing her to implement "Islam" in every "culture". However, her husband's "African Islam" is never questioned, and nowhere in the interview does she distance herself from her Muslim-

---

32 See http://islam.alrahman.de (accessed 4 July 2012).

33 For the prominence of the "culture-religion" distinction in European-Muslim discourses, see also Jouili/Amir-Moazami 2006, Peter 2006.

born husband's interpretation of Islam. On the contrary, as shown above, "African Islam" is presented as valuable as "European Islam".

As Amadea faces many discourses about Islam and Muslims in Switzerland, this analysis gives us insights into her authority attribution processes. We may describe the ensemble of authority figures and other instances as a kind of network (Bleisch Bouzar 2010), whereby authority figures can function as experts (Sheikh Osman, Lubna) and role models (Lubna, Christiane Backer) (Bleisch Bouzar 2012), depending on Amadea's purpose. Her relationship with Sheikh Osman can be described as ambivalent. On the one hand, she needs his expertise and religious knowledge. On the other hand, she is very critical regarding the supposed "cultural" aspects in his teachings. However, she never contests him openly.[34] Laura's role is particularly interesting in this setting. Although Laura is neither an expert in Islam nor a role model in living as a convert in Switzerland, she can be depicted as a role model in living, if not as a feminist, then at least as a religious woman aware of 'women's issues', and maybe also as a follower of a minority religious tradition in an increasingly secular society.

If we interpret Amadea's life story narrative as a means for her to construct a coherent story of herself, Laura gains another function. As she is the only friend left from her time before her conversion, Laura, along with Amadea's hereditary Celtic part of her soul and the concept of *fitra*, ensures a self which didn't suddenly change her (religious) identity one day to another, but has always believed and is, in a way, faithful to herself. In this way, Amadea constructs continuity and coherence in her life story narrative as. This is in line with the function Mark Freeman attributes to life-story narratives (Freeman 2007: 159). However, at the same time, as we have seen in the analysis of the small stories, she enacts struggles, difficult decisions, and breaches of canonical scripts, which not only allows us to discern how she is navigating between the different religious or Islamic discourses but also to perceive the impact of the public discourse on her identity formation.

REFERENCES

Allievi, Stefano (1998): *Les convertis à l'Islam*, Paris: L'Harmattan.
— (2006): "The shifting significance of the halal/haram frontier: Narratives on the hijab and other issues", in: van Nieuwkerk, Karin (ed.), *Women embracing Islam: Gender and conversion in the West*, Texas: University of Texas Press, pp. 120-149.

---

34 This ambivalence was first described by Jouili/Amir-Moazami 2006: 619sq., 638.

Avon, Dominique (2008): *Les Ahbaches: Un mouvement libanais sunnite contesté dans un monde globalisé*. [online] Cahiers d'études du religieux. Recherches interdisciplinaires 2. Available at: http://cerri.revues.org/331 (accessed 2 July 2011), pp. 2-15.

Backer, Kristiane (2009): *Von MTV nach Mekka: Wie der Islam mein Leben veränderte*, Berlin: List.

Bamberg, Michael (2004): "Talk, small stories, and adolescent identities", in: *Human Development* 47, pp. 366-369.

— (2007a): "Introductory remarks", in: Bamberg, Michael (ed.), *Narrative – state of the art*, Amsterdam: John Benjamins, pp. 1-5.

— (2007b): "Stories: Big or small: Why do we care?", in: Bamberg, Michael (ed.), *Narrative – state of the art*, Amsterdam: John Benjamins, pp. 165-174.

Bamberg, Michael / Georgakopoulou, Alexandra (2008): "Small stories as a new perspective in narrative and identity analysis", in: *Text & Talk*, 28:3, pp. 377-396.

Beckford, James A. (1978): "Accounting for conversion", in: *British Journal of Sociology*, 29:2, pp. 249-263.

Behloul, Samuel M. (2009): "Discours total! Le débat sur l'islam en Suisse et le positionnement de l'islam comme religion publique", in: Schneuwly Purdie, Mallory / Gianni, Matteo / Jenny, Magali (eds), *Musulmans d'aujourd'hui: Identités plurielles en Suisse*, Genève: Labor et Fides, pp. 53-72.

Bleisch Bouzar, Petra (2010): "Es kommt darauf an, wie du dich wohl fühlst." – Gestaltung und Legitimation islamischer Religiosität in der Schweiz", in: Allenbach, Brigit / Sökefeld, Martin (eds), *Zwischen Minarettinitiative und Scharia: Muslime in der Schweiz*, Zürich: Seismo, pp. 241-265.

— (2012): ""She is simply present": Female leadership and informal authority in a Swiss Muslim women's association", in: Kalmbach, Hilary / Bano, Masooda (eds), *Women, leadership, and mosques: Changes in contemporary Islamic authority*, Leiden: Brill, pp. 279-300.

Bleisch Bouzar, Petra / Leuenberger, Susanne (2012): "Doing Islam – undoing Swissness: Konversion zum Islam im 21. Jahrhundert im Kontext von Geschlecht, Kultur und Körper", in: Luginbühl, David et al. (eds), *Religiöse Grenzziehungen im öffentlichen Raum*, Stuttgart: Kohlhammer, pp. 245-259.

Boubekeur, Amel (2007): "Political Islam in Europe", in: Amghar, Samir / Boubekeur, Amel / Emerson, Michaël (eds), *European Islam: Challenges for public policy and society*, Brussels: Centre for European Political Studies, pp. 14-37.

Bovay, Claude (2004): *Eidgenössische Volkszählung 2000: Religionslandschaft in der Schweiz*, Neuenburg: Bundesamt für Statistik.

Bruner, Jerome (1986): *Actual minds, possible worlds*, Cambridge MA: Harvard University Press.

— (1990): *Acts of meaning*, Cambridge MA: Harvard University Press.

Bundesamt für Statistik [Swiss Federal Statistical Office] (2003): Eidgenössische Volkszählung 2000: Bevölkerungsstruktur, Hauptsprache und Religion. [online] Available at: http://www.bfs.admin.ch/bfs/portal/de/index/news/publikationen.Document.69601.pdf (accessed 10 May 2012).

— (2012): Strukturerhebung 2010: Erste Resultate. [online], Available at: http://www.bfs.admin.ch/bfs/portal/de/index/news/04/01.html (accessed 15 July 2012).

Centre Islamique de Lausanne (n. d.): Historique. [online] Available at http://www.al-islam.ch/presentation_historique.html (accessed 26 July 2011).

Clavien, Gaëtan (2009): "Médias et discours islamophobe: au croisement du dicible et du recevable", in: Schneuwly Purdie, Mallory / Gianni, Matteo / Jenny, Magali (eds), *Musulmans d'aujourd'hui: Identités plurielles en Suisse*, Genève: Labor et Fides, pp. 95-109.

Daum, Matthias (2010): Biel, eine Stadt und ihre Muslime. *NZZ*, [online] 4 September. Available at: http://www.nzz.ch/nachrichten/politik/schweiz/biel_eine_stadt_und_ihre_muslime_1.7439541.html (accessed 10 May 2012).

Dégh, Linda (1962): *Märchen, Erzähler und Erzählgemeinschaft: Dargestellt an der ungarischen Volksüberlieferung*, Berlin/Ost: Akademia.

Erlich, Haggai (2007): *Saudi Arabia and Ethiopia: Islam, Christianity, and politics entwined*, London: Lynne Rienner.

Flick, Uwe (2000): "Episodic interviewing", in: Bauer, Martin W. / Gaskell, George (eds), *Qualitative researching with text, image and sound: A practical handbook*, London: Sage, pp. 75-92.

Fludernik, Monika (2008): *Erzähltheorie: Eine Einführung*, Darmstadt: Wissenschaftliche Buchgesellschaft.

Freeman, Mark (2007 [2006]): "Life 'on holiday'? In defence of big stories", in: Bamberg, Michael (ed.), *Narrative – state of the art*, Amsterdam: John Benjamins, pp. 155-163. [2006 in: *Narrative Inquiry*, 16, pp. 131-138].

Georgakopoulou, Alexandra (2007a): *Small stories, interaction and identities*, Amsterdam: John Benjamins.

— (2007b): "Thinking big with small stories in narrative and identity analysis", in: Bamberg, Michael (ed.), *Narrative – state of the art*, Amsterdam: John Benjamins, pp. 145-154.

Gründer, René (2010): "Zur Rezeption germanischgläubigen Neuheidentums im Deutschland der Gegenwart", in: *Heidnisches Jahrbuch 2007*, Rudolstadt: Edition Roter Drache, pp. 11-33.

Hamzeh, A. Nizar / Dekmejian, R. Hrair (1996): "A Sufi response to political Islamism: Al-Ahbash of Lebanon", in: *International Journal of Middle East Studies*, 28:2, pp. 217-229.

Herman, David (2009): *Basic elements of narrative*, Oxford: Wiley-Blackwell.

Iser, Wolfgang (1984): *Der Akt des Lesens*, München: Fink.

Jawad, Haifaa (2006): "Female conversion to Islam: The Sufi paradigm", in: van Nieuwkerk, Karin (ed.), *Women embracing Islam: Gender and conversion in the West*, Texas: University of Texas Press, pp. 153-171.

Jordan, Wilhelm (1886): *Die Sebalds: Roman aus der Gegenwart, Bd 1*, Stuttgart/Leipzig: Deutsche Verlags-Anstalt.

Jouili, Jeanette S. / Schirin Amir-Moazami (2006): "Knowledge, empowerment and religious authority among pious Muslim women in France and Germany", in: *The Muslim World*, 96, pp. 617–642.

Kabha, Mustafa / Erlich, Haggai (2006): "Al-Ahbash and Wahhabiyya: Interpretations of Islam", in: *International Journal of Middle Eastern Studies*, 38, pp. 519-538.

Kaufmann, Jean-Claude (2004): *L'invention de Soi: Une théorie de l'identité*, Paris: Armand Colin.

Koch, Carmen (2011): *Religion in den Medien: Eine quantitative Inhaltsanalyse von Medien in der Schweiz*, Konstanz: UVK.

Kuppinger, Petra (2012): "Women, leadership, and participation in mosques and beyond: Notes from Stuttgart, Germany", in: Kalmbach, Hilary / Masooda, Bano (eds), *Women, leadership, and mosques: Changes in contemporary Islamic authority*, Leiden: Brill, pp. 323- 344.

Leman, Johan / Stallaert, Christiane / Lechkar, Iman (2010): "Ethnic dimensions in the discourse and identity strategies of European converts to Islam in Andalusia and Flanders", in: *Journal of Ethnic and Migration Studies*, 36:9, pp. 1483-1497.

Mansson McGinty, Anna (2006): *Becoming Muslim: Western women's conversions to Islam*, New York: Palgrave Macmillan.

Martens, Silvia (2007): *Al-Ahbash: Origin and development of a contemporary Islamic movement: History, theological and political issues, and the conflict with other Sunni groups*, unpublished MA thesis, University of Erfurt.

Martinez, Matias / Scheffel, Michael (2009): *Einführung in die Erzähltheorie*, München: Beck.

Martini, Fritz (1981): *Deutsche Literatur im bürgerlichen Realismus 1848-1898*, Stuttgart: Metzler.

Ochs, Ellinor and Lisa Capps (2001): *Living narrative, creating lives in everyday storytelling*, London: Harvard University Press.

Özyürek, Esra (2010): "German converts to Islam and their ambivalent relations with immigrant Muslims", in: Shryock, Andrew (ed.), *Islamophobia / Islamophilia, beyond the politics of enemies and friends*, Bloomington: Indiana University Press, pp. 172-192.

Peter, Frank (2006): "Islamic sermons, religious authority and the individualization of Islam in France", in: Franzmann, Manuel / Gärtner, Christel / Köck, Nicole (eds), *Religiosität in der säkularisierten Welt: Theoretische und empirische Beiträge zur Säkularisierungsdebatte in der Religionssoziologie*, Wiesbaden: VS, pp. 303–319.

Poston, Larry (1992): *Islamic da'wah in the West: Muslim missionary activity and the dynamics of conversion to Islam*, Oxford: Oxford University Press.

Read, Stephen J. / Miller, Lynn Carol (1995): "Stories are fundamental to meaning and memory: For social creatures, could it be otherwise?", in: Wyer, Robert S. (ed.), *Knowledge and memory: The real story*, Hillsdale: Lawrence Erlbaum Associates, pp. 139-152.

Roald, Anne Sophie (2004): *New Muslims in the European context: The experience of Scandinavian Converts*, Leiden: Brill.

— (2006): "The shaping of a Scandinavian 'Islam': Converts and gender equal opportunity", in: van Nieuwkerk, Karin (ed.), *Women embracing Islam: Gender and conversion in the West*, Texas: University of Texas Press, pp. 48-70.

Schneuwly Purdie, Mallory (2009): "Identité cocktail ou double vie: trajectoires identitaires de deux adolescentes musulmanes en Suisse", in: Schneuwly Purdie, Mallory / Gianni, Matteo / Jenny, Magali (eds), *Musulmans d'aujourd'hui: Identités plurielles en Suisse*, Genève: Labor et Fides, pp. 155-176.

Schütze, Fritz (1983): "Biographieforschung und narratives Interview", in: *Neue Praxis: Kritische Zeitschrift für Sozialarbeit und Sozialpädagogik*, 13, pp. 283-293.

— (1987): *Das narrative Interview in Interaktionsfeldstudien I*, Hagen: Fernuniversität Hagen.

Somers, Margaret (1994): "The narrative constitution of identity", in: *Theory and Society*, 23:5, pp. 605-649.

Speer, Nicole K. et al. (2009): Reading stories activates neural representations of visual and motor experiences, in: *Psychological Science,* 20:8, pp. 989-999.

Wiedemann, Felix (2007): *Rassenmutter und Rebellin: Hexenbilder in Romantik, völkischer Bewegung, Neuheidentum und Feminismus,* Würzburg: Könighausen & Neumann.

van Nieuwkerk, Karin (2006): "Gender, conversion, and Islam: A comparison of online and offline conversion narratives", in: id. (ed.), *Women embracing Islam: Gender and conversion in the West,* Texas: University of Texas Press, pp. 75-119.

Wohlrab-Sahr, Monika (1999): *Konversion zum Islam in Deutschland und den USA*, Frankfurt a. M.: Campus.

The imagining of Muslim converts in Britain by themselves and others

Leon Moosavi

INTRODUCTION

The presence of Islam in Europe has led to a range of provocative interactions. On one end of the spectrum, interactions have been hostile and violence has sparked. On the other end of the spectrum, interactions have been so cordial that some non-Muslims have decided that they would like to embrace Islam and become Muslim. The experiences of these Muslim converts can teach us two important lessons about Islam in Europe: Firstly, that Muslims are imagined as threatening to Europe and secondly, that Muslims do not imagine themselves in the same way. This chapter explores the disconnect that exists between how Muslim converts are commonly imagined and how they understand their own sense of self. It is important to remember that the observations made about Muslim converts are indicative of a wider context that can just as likely apply to life-long Muslims as to converts. Based on empirical research that has been conducted with Muslim converts in Britain between 2008 and 2009, I will argue that even though Muslim converts are imagined as threatening, they are more often than not comfortable identifying as British Muslims who belong in a majority non-Muslim society. Despite pervasive perceptions, they are actually comfortable with a hybrid identity that allows them to feel both British and Muslim. For this research, I conducted in-depth interviews with 37 Muslim converts but it is also inspired by countless informal conversations with many more converts. While Muslim converts are a diverse group of individuals with different backgrounds, there are some generalisations that can be made about them because of the commonality that exists between their experiences.

THE IMAGINING OF MUSLIM CONVERTS BY OTHERS

There is a distinct concern across Europe that Muslims residing in Europe are potentially disloyal, a so-called fifth column, or 'enemy-within'. Modern nation states are widely accepted as the currency in which we think about society on a macro scale and there is therefore eagerness to protect the nation, which may also be referred to as the country or the society. In Britain, fears of a lack of loyalty to the nation by Muslims solidified during the era when Muslims were becoming increasingly settled in Britain. These fears were most pronounced during the *Satanic Verses* episode in 1989, continued with the First Gulf War in 1990-91 and were reignited at various points such as during the 2001 riots that involved Muslims in Bradford, Burnley and Oldham, as well as after 9/11 and 7/7 (Allen 2010: 43sq.; Bagguley/Hussain 2005: 209sq.; McGhee 2008: 8, 29sq., 82-85; Weller 2008: 155-165, 194sqq.). Yet, these concerns about Muslims as a threat to the nation can be traced back much further to a Medieval perception of Islam as a threat to Europe in general which developed when Muslims began conquering lands close to and within European territory (Matar 2009: 214sq.). This legacy has resulted today in widespread suspicion about the loyalty of Muslims in European nations, so much so that a British poll found that only 36 per cent of the British public regard Muslims as loyal to Britain (Gallup 2009: 20; Gardham 2009; Green 2009) while another poll found that only 28 per cent of the British public believe Muslims in Britain want to integrate into British society (PEW 2011: 55). The concern that Muslims do not have loyalty to Britain has led to a climate whereby Muslims are often called upon to integrate (meaning assimilate, according to many commentators) into European nations, adopt supposed European values such as liberalism and secularism and pledge their allegiance to the nation (Archer 2009: 74; Kundnani 2007; McGhee 2008: 134sq.; Modood 2005: ix).

The perception of Muslims as disloyal is also held about Muslim converts who have equally been viewed as having inadequate allegiance to the European nations they live in. This view of converts has been well explained with regards to several European countries including Denmark (Jensen 2008), Germany (Özyürek 2009) and Sweden (McGinty 2007: 475sq.). The research I conducted also discovered that British Muslim converts are familiar with a trope that insinuates that they are disloyal to the nation. For instance, they explained that they were regularly told that they were 'traitors' for converting to Islam. They encountered this hostility which doubted their commitment to Britain from strangers who verbally abused them, but also from relatives and friends who were less aggressive, but still comprehended their conversion to Islam in terms of a betrayal. Laura, a 35-year-old mental health nurse, explained how she believes people see her as a traitor:

[Muslim converts] might be seen as almost being a traitor against your own country, you know because there's so many people who have a problem with Muslims
and then you're there being English and you're going over to the 'dark side' if
you like! ... So many people don't like Muslims, hate Muslims, and then there's
me, obviously English, and I've [supposedly] gone away from my own culture or
whatever.   (Laura)

Converts to Islam may therefore be imagined as having abandoned the nation by
converting to Islam and relinquished any loyalty they had towards the nation because in the current era, Islam is viewed as distinctly Other and not part of 'us'.
There is a long history behind such feelings towards Muslim converts as traitors.
Indeed, during the colonial era, Britons who converted to Islam were seen as
'renegades' who undermined the Empire and effectively committed treason
(Dalrymple 2002: 17-20; Gilliat-Ray 2010: 17sq.; Zebiri 2008: 32sq.). Today,
they are still seen as renegades but are now labelled as traitors.

This perception within Europe of Muslim converts as a threat to the nation
has been reinforced by high-profile politicians who have suggested that Muslim
converts are likely to engage in terrorism against the nation. For instance Lord
Carlile, the independent reviewer of British anti-terror laws (Elias 2008), Alard
du Bois-Reymond, the Director of the Swiss Federal Office for Migration (Slater
2010), and Wolfgang Bosbach and Günther Beckstein, two senior members of
Angela Merkel's political party in Germany (Özyürek 2009: 91), have all singled
out Muslim converts and warned of the specific danger they pose to their respective nations. Muslim converts have also been explicitly understood in this manner in the British government's counter-terrorism policy (Home Office 2011: 87)
and a key European report on "radicalisation in European's Muslim communities" (Roy 2009: 16), both of which contain specific references to Muslim converts' supposed susceptibility to engaging in extremism and/or terrorism. The
news media and entertainment media have also played a role in encouraging this
perception of Muslim converts as it is common for converts to be depicted as
threatening, traitorous and extreme. Indeed, Kevin Brice found that 76 per cent
of news stories about Muslim converts between 2001 and 2010 related converts
to terrorism and/or fundamentalism (Brice 2010: 14). Some examples of headlines in news media include "Al-Qaeda's White Army of Terror" (Elias 2008),
"Pakistan Discovers 'Village' of White German al-Qaeda Insurgents" (Nel-
son/Hall 2009), "West Fears Converts Who Become Bombers" (UPI 2010),
"White Britons 'Called Steve and Gerry Killed Fighting for Al Qaeda in Pakistan' by U.S. Drone Missile" (Gardner/Faulkner 2010) and "Osama Bin Laden's
Anti-U.S. Strategy: Exploit Minority Converts" (Thomas 2011). In fictional
works, there are characters like Barry in the British film *Four lions* (Morris

2010), a comedy which mocks an amateur terrorist cell's attempts to conduct a terrorist attack in Britain. As one of the main characters in the film, Barry is portrayed as the most dangerous of the terrorist cell and has an obsession with violence, providing another example of an extremist convert for the viewer's imagination. As well as the politicians and media which encourage converts to be seen as disloyal to the nation, there are some fringe Muslim groups such as al-Qa'ida, al-Muhajirun and Hizb at-Tahrir who encourage Muslims and non-Muslims to think of Muslims as at odds with 'Western civilisation'. Thus, there are various efforts to portray Muslims in general, and specifically converts, as having become Other.

THE IMAGINING OF MUSLIM CONVERTS BY THEMSELVES

My own findings are in sharp contrast to the popular imagining of Muslim converts as traitors to the nation. All of the Muslim converts I interviewed showed signs of being decent citizens of the nation who respected others, helped others, worked hard, educated themselves, raised families, paid taxes, obeyed the law, and so on. Their interpretation of Islam was typically a mainstream and accomodating one, whereby they were content to live alongside people of other faiths and appreciate that they did not have a monopoly on Truth. Furthermore, the majority of the interviewees told me explicitly that since converting to Islam, they had not become hostile to the nation or felt that becoming Muslim meant they had to abandon any attachment to Britain. Their sense of belonging remained intact and in some instances, had even been enhanced by converting to Islam, as was the case for Sumayyah, a 24 year old A-level student:

> Well I suppose I'm very proud to be British now that I'm Muslim. Before I didn't really think of it. Before I was Muslim, I just thought about myself but now I'm Muslim I'm very proud to be a British Muslim because... I just am! [Since converting to Islam, people have asked me:] 'Why are you so British?', and things like this. Yeah, it's like they don't want you to be so English and I'm like: 'Well you know, I am very English and I'm very happy to be English' and they kind of look at it as if it's a bad thing because I'm so British... It's like sometimes, I'll invite some Muslim woman to my house and I'll make them fish and chips or something just to show them... But yeah, I like to think of myself as British but you know... I'm gonna keep my culture...   (Sumayyah)

Sumayyah's comments convey the way in which some consider conversion to Islam as entailing a departing from the nation. Sumayyah is quite clearly comfortable in reconciling her Muslim identity with her British identity. She does not do this indifferently or ambivalently, but actively contests those who challenge her attachment to the nation in order that she may retain her sense of Britishness. One way in which she does this is by appropriating the stereotypically British food of fish and chips. Significantly, she even cooks it at home for her friends even though it is a dish which is most commonly associated with being bought pre-prepared from chip shops. Sumayyah's feelings about where she belongs do not give credence to those who believe converts should be seen as traitors who wish to abandon the nation after converting to Islam. The same can be said about Sofia, a 22-year-old office worker, who seemed to hold similar views to Sumayyah in that she also seemed to not only be proud of being British, but actively asserted this aspect of her identity after converting to Islam:

> I'm kind of more protective of [being British since I converted to Islam]... So I'll be sitting there and someone will be saying something about food and I'll say: 'Yeah, but it's all about the roast dinner and you guys have got to catch up!'. In that sense it makes me think it's special what I've got being Muslim and having another part of my background. So it's reinforced it in that way.   (Sofia)

Like Sumayyah, Sofia also mentions food whilst explaining that becoming Muslim made her more likely to identify as British. For Sofia, it is not fish and chips that represent Britishness, but another stereotypical British meal of roast dinner, which she celebrates as a way of illustrating to her lifelong Muslim friends that she still considers herself as British and is not ashamed about that. In both examples, food operates as a marker of banal nationalism that allows each interviewee to assert how they position themselves in relation to national membership. Through their choices of fish and chips and roast dinner rather than curry and samosas, they label themselves as having more affiliation to Britain than say, to Pakistan or anywhere else. It is their cultural knowledge of what is the appropriate food to consume for one who belongs in the nation, and their proud declaration that they abide by this knowledge, that they display in order to make their allegiance to the nation clear. Sumayyah and Sofia both offer unambiguous and typical examples that show how it is not only possible for Muslim converts to remain attached to the nation after converting to Islam, but even to become more conscious and dedicated to reinforcing their belonging within the nation.

The Muslim converts I interviewed also expressed their affinity with the nation in other ways. For instance, they praised Britain for accommodating Muslims and permitting freedom of religion, in contrast to other countries where there is religious authoritarianism, which would have hindered their ability to change their religion and practice it. For example, Dean, a 41-year-old unemployed electrician, remarked: "We've got freedom of speech in this country, we've got freedom of religion, which in a lot of countries you haven't, so I think Islam and Muslims in this country, yes, it's a good country to be in" (Dean). Similarly, Sumayyah said she feels she belongs in Britain because "we have mosques, we're allowed to pray, we have *halāl* meat, we're allowed to play Qur'an very loud and things… So I think it's a nice place to be Muslim because we're allowed to put mosques up anywhere" (Sumayyah). These comments from Dean and Sumayyah, which were echoed by several of the other converts, reveal a favourable assessment of the nation in contrast to other nations. They show the beginnings of a patriotism which celebrates the nation for virtues that other nations do not have. Moreover, these comments were often appended with harsh criticisms of Muslim-majority societies who were scathed for failing to allow freedom of religion. Generally, in the Muslim converts' direct comparisons between Muslim nations and the British nation, they often ranked Britain as superior and more deserving of their respect.

The Muslim converts also frequently extended this celebration of the nation to British citizens, whom several of the converts see as inherently virtuous. Aaron, a 21-year-old admin assistant, suggested that the non-Muslim Britons often personify Islamic characteristics more than Muslims, and that Muslims should learn these noble characteristics from non-Muslim Britons: "I see some non-Muslims who are better Muslims than some of the Muslims I know. I can't judge people but I know some Muslims who don't pray, who drink, who do drugs, this and that, and I know some Christians who are pretty much Muslims, if you know what I mean" (Aaron). Like several of the other interviewees, Aaron championed non-Muslim Britons in a manner that a patriot would champion the people of their nation. His preference of some non-Muslim Britons over some Muslims shows that his commitment to other people is not based on whether they are categorised as Muslim or non-Muslim, but rather, on whether they embody noble characteristics which he believes can be found amongst Muslims and non-Muslims. It is because many of the converts had the same perception that they remained friendly with non-Muslims whom they knew from before their conversion to Islam. Most of the converts maintained good relations with their non-Muslim friends, wanted to be a positive influence in their lives and even believed converting to Islam meant they are obliged to be even better friends in the same way many felt more dutiful to the nation after their conversion. Overall, conversion to Islam did not create individuals who were eager to detach from society, but often had the inverse consequence of encouraging the converts to become even more dedicated to their family, friends and society in general.

For most Muslim converts, conversion to Islam does not result in an abandonment of the nation or even feelings of animosity towards it. Rather, the converts showed signs of patriotism that included attachment to the nation, admiration of it, and a desire to belong. None of this sentiment was at the expense of a firm adherence to Islam. In fact, some of the most devout converts I interviewed were also the most defensive of being loyal citizens to the nation. The converts were therefore comfortable identifying with a hybrid identity as 'British Muslims'. They had what Nasar Meer (2010) refers to as "twoness". They fused two identities together, believed they were compatible, and in some instances mutually reinforcing, by which I mean they believed being a good Muslim meant being a good Briton and vice versa. The Muslim converts' hybridity contests the presumed incompatibility between holding a Muslim identity and European national identity concurrently. This notion of hybridity whereby the Muslim converts have multiple attachments simultaneously is evident in the way in which they frequently referred to themselves as some type of conduit between Muslims and non-Muslims. They desired to be 'bridge builders' whereby they mediate and seek reconciliation between Muslims and non-Muslims in this era when they are alleged to clash frequently. Several other researchers have also found this desire to be common amongst Muslim converts (Haddad 2006: 43; Jensen 2008: 401; van Nieuwkerk 2006: 5; Zebiri 2008: 84sqq.). Bakri, a 44-year-old holistic therapist, expressed a desire to 'build bridges' before I had even suggested it to him:

> I think again it's about building bridges between communities. Equally I've had a lot of people coming and asking me about... Like non-Muslims coming and asking me about Islam. I've had it from the other side too when people say: 'But why do [non-Muslim] people do that? Why do English people do that and this, that and the other?' (Bakri)

As with the numerous other converts who expressed a desire to fulfil this role of 'bridge building', Bakri demonstrates a dual belonging, as one would only care to build bridges between two entities if both sides of the bridge were deemed as important. The converts who took up this role of 'bridge building' show their concern for the nation in seeking to create harmony within that nation. Bakri acts as an ambassador to the nation, on behalf of Muslims, to whom he wants to explain Islam to, but also as an ambassador for the nation to Muslims, whom he educates about non-Muslim Britons. The converts here show a dual loyalty which Laura explained as follows: "I suppose you've got like a foot in both camps, haven't you?" (Laura). This tendency to defend Britain and non-Muslim Britons was common as several of the converts informed me that they regularly dispute with Muslims who make disparaging generalisations about non-Muslim Britons, showing again how the converts can be defensive of the nation. Alison, a 20-year-old undergraduate student, also explained how she took on that role:

"If I'm with my Muslim friends and they say something about the way non-Muslims act, I'll be quick to say: 'You can't judge them in that way, you can't make those assumptions, you can't think of them as that'" (Alison). Like Bakri, Alison is also defensive of non-Muslim Britons and in being so, reveals her affinity towards the nation and its citizens. In her research on Muslim converts, Laura Zahra McDonald also found this hybridity and merging of identities, in the tendency she observed for Muslim converts to begin using 'Islamic names' but also to continue using their non-Muslim British names (McDonald 2008). Like the converts I interviewed, these converts seemingly added to their existing identity rather than replaced it and were satisfied harmonising dual loyalties. Overall, the converts willingly testified as loyal to Britain, and as belonging within the nation. Aaron's comments show just how deep this patriotism could be:

> Just because it's not a Muslim State, it's still a beautiful, wonderful country... because the history of it is amazing, just the actual country itself, most of the people are lovely. You find it hard to find anywhere else like this in the world to live in because you're so free to practise your religion... At the end of the day, if something did happen in this country, then you're still gonna fight for this country... If someone attacked this country, and attacked my family, attacked my community, me as a Muslim, I'd be fighting alongside the non-Muslims against those who are trying to damage the community and trying to invade the country... At the end of the day, I am as much of a British citizen as the next guy.   (Aaron)

Aaron's passionate plea that he is 'as much of a British citizen as the next guy' reflects his awareness that some people doubt this is the case. Like several of the other converts, he seems to feel it is incumbent upon him to defend his attachment to the nation in order to wade off the misplaced assumptions that are held about him.

While I have thus far demonstrated that Muslim converts can be imagined as disloyal to the nation for converting to Islam even though many of them articulate a belonging to the nation, it is important to acknowledge that there have been numerous examples of Muslim converts around the world who have adopted radical hostility towards 'the West' in recent years and proudly attacked 'Western' nations and their citizens. These "small minority of converts are attracted to radical or militant Islam, although these have received a high profile in the media, creating the impression that they are more numerically significant than is in fact the case" (Zebiri 2008: 47). The most notorious of these extremist converts are Adam Gadahn (spokesman for al-Qaʻida), Zachary Chesser (sentenced to 25 years in prison for threatening South Park cartoonists in 2011), Richard Reid (attempted shoe-bombing on aeroplane in December 2001), Germaine Lindsay (suicide bomber on 7/7 2005), and Nicky Reilly (attempted suicide bombing in Britain in 2009). This handful of extremist converts are a minor fraction of the tens of thousands of Muslim converts in Britain, or the hundreds of thousands of Muslim converts worldwide, but the amount of news media coverage they receive can result in the perception that this type of treachery is more common than it is.

While the converts I interviewed were overwhelmingly comfortable as 'British Muslims' as I have already explained, there were some comments in the interviews that suggest that converting to Islam did diminish some of the converts' loyalty to Britain that are important to investigate. For example, Rizwan, an unemployed 55-year-old, was adamant that his Muslim identity comes before his British identity: "I'm British and I'm a Muslim; a Muslim first though. I don't... To me, my first person [sic] is Allah and I'm a Muslim. If I say that I'm British first and Muslim second, I can't, I don't see how that would work" (Rizwan). It is interesting that Rizwan ranks his allegiance in such a manner because indeed, asking Muslims in Britain whether they place their Muslim identity or British identity first is seen as the acid test of whether one is loyal enough or not. Rizwan's comments may be read as a direct confession of not being loyal enough to the nation, something that some are deeply troubled by. Indeed, minorities in contemporary Britain are not expected to voice such views because we live "[a]t a time when being a good Briton equals being a proud Briton... [when] all citizens, but especially minorities, are expected to reiterate their allegiance to Britishness and their pride in the nation" (Fortier 2008: 35). Elsewhere, Peter, a 35-year-old warehouse operator, expressed some discontent with British society after converting to Islam because he saw British culture as the antipathy of what it meant to be a Muslim. This led him to even consider leaving Britain to live in a Muslim-majority society:

> [Muslims cannot be truly at home in Britain] because of the society and culture of the country... We can't because it's too much sinful things around us; drinking on the streets... If you walk down any high street, at any time on weekends, thousands of people are pissed up, drunk on the street, women hardly dressed, sexually explicit and violent things on TV, you know, basically all the time. The fact is, to live a comfortable life, yes we can. To be truly free in our religion, no we can't, because there's too much sin around us... I think there are places which are better than other places. But you'll always get trouble and that, but on the whole there would be better countries [than Britain]. I've visited a few Muslim countries like Morocco and Tunisia and things, Egypt. I felt I could live there as a good Muslim. There are fewer temptations. (Peter)

Peter is antagonistic towards the nation because he perceives it to be engulfed in vice and sin. It is almost as if the nation has betrayed Peter and his Islamic morality which leads him to respond by rejecting the nation. He seems to undergo what Tina Gudrun Jensen found some Danish Muslim converts do, which is a "self-imposed exclusion" (2008: 396) based on a perception of Danish culture as being about "eating pork, drinking alcohol, participating in parties and sexual promiscuity" (2008: 395). In undertaking this 'self-imposed exclusion', Peter shows that he has considered whether he belongs in Britain and concluded that he belongs elsewhere, showing an emerging sense of having more affinity with other nations than the one in which he was born and raised. His conversion to Islam then has initiated a distancing from the nation as he believes the more of a 'good Muslim' one wants to be, the further away from the nation one has to move, both literally and metaphorically. Michael, a 28-year-old software programmer, echoed Peter's desire to quit Britain after converting to Islam when he told me: "For me personally, I'd like to immigrate to a different country" (Michael). His reasons were similar to Peter's in that he thought he could be a better Muslim elsewhere and face less restrictions and distractions.

The interviewee who most openly admitted that his allegiance to Britain had diminished after converting to Islam was Zach, a 25-year-old trainee teacher, who answered simply but confidently with "Dramatically" (Zach) when I asked him if his loyalty to Britain had decreased since becoming a Muslim. He made his loyalties clear when he said: "First and last I belong to the Muslim *umma* and that's it really" (Zach). Unlike Rizwan, Zach did not rank a British identity second; he did not rank it at all. He also said:

> My loyalty has changed hugely actually [since I became Muslim]. ...For a long time I wanted to be in the Armed Forces... And so I was supportive of my nation generally. It's only since becoming a Muslim that I've really become aware of the realities that exist in the world and that the way that the media portrays world events is not as it truly is... This has just opened my eyes in another way, completely. And because of this I cannot hold allegiance to Britain in the same way. It's a colonialist nation... or at least it was and still holds that legacy. And it supports a similar activity in its support of the United States. So... you know, it's a sort of matter of conscience isn't it? You can't support a nation which promotes so much injustice. (Zach)

Some might say that Zach deserves to be labelled as a 'traitor' because he admits that his conversion to Islam led him to relinquish his allegiance to Britain. However, while this conclusion may be appropriate based on this passage, other views expressed by Zach reveal a rather different understanding. For example,

Zach also believed that British people were generally admirable, that it was important to be law-abiding and that Muslims should seek to improve British society. While he was rather enthusiastic in expressing his disloyalty then, he had remained in Britain, had not made any plans to leave (three years since the interview he is still here), he did not boycott non-Muslims in any way, and he was generally a decent and peaceful citizen who contributed to the local economy and was striving to assist wider society by training to be a secondary-school teacher. This type of lifestyle was common amongst all of those converts who verbally positioned themselves as having shifted away from Britain and non-Muslim Britons. None of them were actively seeking to harm the nation or its citizens but were actually attached to the nation in some way and making a contribution to its prosperity. For instance then, returning to Rizwan, his comments make it clear that he does still identify as British even if it does come second. For Michael, even though he wanted to leave Britain for a Muslim-majority society, he still explained that he had an affinity towards Britain: "Wherever you're born, from whatever country you're born from, home is still home, isn't it? And this is my home… As much as you try… home is home" (Michael). Most striking though is the way in which Peter defended his Britishness at another part of the interview despite his earlier comments:

> Well sometimes when you hear people say this country is bad and all this and that and they complain about everything, what I say to Muslims and anyone: 'If you don't like it, don't stay here. Go somewhere else because we're free to go anywhere we want'. It's not just about living in this country, we all moan about work but in all truth if it was that bad we wouldn't be there. You'd just move on, wouldn't ya? And that's the thing … If people looked at things realistically, come on… It's not bad living in this country compared to other parts of the world… I am proud to be British… But that's the thing, it don't matter what anybody tells me. I'm who I am and I've always felt British and I always will be. Nothing can change that. I was born in this country. If I'm British, Pakistani, half-caste or whatever, at the end of the day, I'm British. (Peter)

Peter went from saying earlier: "[Muslims cannot be truly at home in Britain] because of the society and culture of the country…" and "there would be better countries [than Britain to live in as a Muslim]" to saying "I am proud to be British" and "I've always felt British and I always will be" (Peter). He offers a fascinating example that shows the way in which identity and belonging can be confused, contradictory and in flux. He is similar to some of the other converts who had various attachments that ebbed and flowed, some of which they were not always aware of when asked directly about them. Their identities and belongings were constantly renegotiated and while these reconciliations are not always straightforward or without tension, they almost always result in the converts feeling both Muslim and British. This multilayered sense of self is vital to emphasise because those who discuss the belonging of Muslims in Britain often assume Muslims must choose either loyalty to Islam or loyalty to the nation. This simplicity does not reflect the experiences of many for whom identity is much more dynamic, shifting in emphasis not only on a daily basis, but even minute by minute as happened within the interviews I conducted. Anyone who believes that converts 'defect to the other side' after converting to Islam needs to be reminded that they may 'defect back' at any moment, or more accurately, may always retain a degree of loyalty whether they are prepared to admit that or not. More importantly though, those who may at first be seen to be disloyal and betraying the nation, may actually only be doing so to the extent that they express disquiet about aspects of the nation and its governance, perhaps reflecting their concern for the nation that they hope to see celebrated after improvement. These converts have a cautionary belonging that requires clarification but a belonging nonetheless, as is evident in Justin's comments: "[Muslims can be at 'home' in Britain] without a doubt. Erm… yes. I mean, British culture, British life, yeah, no problem. Obviously as Muslims we don't feel happy about the foreign policy aspects that the British government has towards people living in Muslim lands…" (Justin). This type of indirectly patriotic critique of the nation is monumentally different from the holistic rejection which the fringe terrorists named earlier embark on with their indiscriminate violence against anyone and anything that seems to have a connection to the nation. Muslim converts may dissent against the nation, but this is typically only verbal posturing and in practical terms, many remain loyal, or they dissent against the nation in a manner which is about its betterment rather than its destruction. What is also clear here is that the definition of who makes a good citizen and the extent to which one has to prove this can vary between diffierent people. Whereas some may expect overt support of the military to be considered as a valued member of the nation, others may feel that it is possible to both criticise the nation's military escapades and still be considered a fully-fledged member of the nation. There is not only one definition of belonging then, but the Muslim converts construct their own ways of expressing attachment that makes them as integrated as any other typical citizen. These efforts may not satisfy the expectations of non-Muslims who have expressed a desire to hear the converts make more forthright and totalistic pledges of allegiance to the nation, rather than through demonstrating it via indirect means.

My findings echo much other research that has consistently made the same observations about Muslims in general and Muslim converts specifically, as loyal and well-integrated citizens. These contributions are supported by numerous polls. For example, the following has been revealed about Muslims in Britain: 86 per cent feel they belong in Britain (Gale/Hopkins 2009: 11sq.), 82 per cent identify themselves as loyal to Britain (Gardham 2009; Green 2009), 80 per cent are proud to be a British citizen (Dunt 2011), 78 per cent self-identify as British (Gourlay 2009), and 93 per cent are against political violence while large majorities support integration including working with the police to expose terrorists and voting in elections (ICM 2005). These figures consistently find that around 80 per cent of Muslims in Britain consider themselves loyal to Britain and feel as though they belong. These polls should not be read as implying that 20 per cent of Muslims in Britain are disloyal, but rather, this minority may just feel less patriotic than the majority of Muslims in Britain, or express their belonging in different terms.

CONCLUSION

In this chapter I have demonstrated that the way in which Muslim converts are imagined is starkly different from how they imagine themselves. They seem to see themselves as decent citizens of European nations such as Britain, willing to contribute and live peacefully alongside other non-Muslim citizens. This does not stop them from being labelled as 'traitors', however, and more questions need to be asked about the possibility of this negative labelling actually manifesting into creating alienated and disenfranchised individuals who eventually abandon the nation. There is no reason why similar patterns would not be found amongst Muslim converts in other European nations and also with lifelong Muslims. Laura captured the typical belonging of the converts when she said: "I don't feel any more or less British to be honest. I'm still British, just different" (Laura). Most converts identify as British Muslims and find no fundamental incompatibility between both aspects of their identity, even though others perceive them to be in conflict.

REFERENCES

Allen, Christopher (2010): *Islamophobia,* Farnham: Ashgate.

Archer, Louise (2009): "Race, 'face' and masculinity: The identities and local geographies of Muslim boys", in: Hopkins, Peter / Gale, Richard (eds), *Muslims in Britain: Race, place and identities*, Edinburgh: Edinburgh University Press, pp. 74-91.

Bagguley, Paul / Hussain, Yasmin (2005): "Flying the flag for England? Citizenship, religion and cultural identity among British Pakistani Muslims", in:

Abbas, Tahir (ed.), *Muslim Britain: Communities under pressure*, London: Zed Books, pp. 208-221.

Brice, M. A. Kevin (2010): *A minority within a minority: A report on converts to Islam in the United Kingdom*. [online] Faith matters. Available at: http://faith-matters.org/images/stories/fm-reports/a-minority-within-a-minority-a-report-on-converts-to-islam-in-the-uk.pdf (accessed 5 January 2011).

Dalrymple, William (2002): *White Mughals: Love and betrayal in eighteenth-century India*, London: HarperCollins.

Dunt, Ian (2011): "Surprise poll shows widespread Muslim support for gay rights", in: *Politics*, [online] 27 June. Available at: http://www.politics.co.uk/news/2011/06/27/surprise-poll-shows-widespread-muslim-support (accessed 19 July 2011).

Elias, Richard (2008): "Al-Qaeda's white army of terror", in: *The Scotsman*, [online] 13 January. Available at: http://news.scotsman.com/latestnews/AlQaeda39s-white-army-of-terror.3667425.jp (accessed 16 March 2011).

Fortier, Anne-Marie (2008): *Multicultural horizons: Diversity and the limits of the civil nation*, London: Routledge.

Gale, Richard / Hopkins, Peter (2009): "Introduction: Muslims in Britain – Race, place and the spatiality of identities", in: Hopkins, Peter / Gale, Richard (eds), *Muslims in Britain: race, place and identities*, Edinburgh: Edinburgh University Press, pp. 1-19.

Gallup (2009): *The Gallup Coexist Index 2009: A global study of interfaith relations*. [online] Available at: http://www.euro-islam.info/wp-content/uploads/pdfs/gallup_coexist_2009_interfaith_relations_uk_france_germany.pdf (accessed 19 July 2011).

Gardham, Duncan (2009): "More Muslims Identify Themselves as British Than Rest of Population", in: *The Telegraph*, [online] 7 May. Available at: http://www.telegraph.co.uk/news/religion/5287105/More-Muslims-identify-themselves-as-British-than-rest-of-population.html (accessed 28 April 2011).

Gardner, David / Faulkner, Katherine (2010): "White Britons 'Called Steve and Gerry Killed Fighting for Al Qaeda in Pakistan' by U.S. Drone Missile", in: *The Daily Mail*, [online] 17 December. Available at: http://www.dailymail.co.uk/news/article-1339036/2-white-Britons-killed-fighting-Al-Qaeda-US-drone-missile-attack-Pakistan.html#ixzz18IAduIrW (accessed 2 August 2013).

Gilliat-Ray, Sophie (2010): *Muslims in Britain: An introduction*, Cambridge: Cambridge University Press.

Gourlay, Chris (2009): "UK Muslims are Europe's most patriotic", in: *Times online*. [online] 13 December. Available at: http://www.timesonline.co.uk/tol/news/uk/article6954571.ece (accessed 28 April 2011).

Green, Chris (2009): "Patriotic, respectful and homophobic: A portrait of British Muslims' State of Mind", in: *The Independent*, [online] 8 May. Available at: http://www.independent.co.uk/news/uk/home-news/patriotic-respectful-and-homophobic-a-portrait-of-british-muslims-state-of-mind-1681062.html (accessed 28 April 2011).

Haddad, Yvonne Yazbeck (2006): "The quest for peace in submission: Reflections on the journey of American women converts to Islam", in: van Nieuwkerk, Karen (ed.), *Women embracing Islam: Gender and conversion in the West*, Austin: University of Texas, pp. 19-47.

Home Office (2011): *Prevent strategy*. [online] Available at: http://www.homeoffice.gov.uk/publications/counter-terrorism/prevent/prevent-strategy/prevent-strategy-review?view=Binary (accessed 21 July 2011).

ICM (2005): *Muslim Poll*. [online] July 2005. Available at: http://image.guardian.co.uk/sys-files/Politics/documents/2005/07/26/Muslim-Poll.pdf (accessed 28 April 2011).

Jensen, Tina Gudrun (2008): "To be 'Danish', becoming 'Muslim': Contestations of national identity?", in: *Journal of Ethnic and Migration Studies*, 34:3, pp. 389-409.

Kundnani, Arun (2007): "Integrationism: The politics of anti-Muslim racism", in: *Race & Class*, 48:4, pp. 24-44.

Mansson McGinty, Anna (2007): "Formation of alternative femininities through Islam: Feminist approaches among Muslim converts in Sweden", in: *Women's Studies International Forum*, 30:6, pp. 474-485.

Matar, Nabil (2009): "Britons and Muslims in the early modern period: From prejudice to (a theory of) toleration", in: *Patterns of Prejudice*, 43:3-4, pp. 213-231.

McDonald, Laura Zahra (2008): "Conversion, identity and social activism: Making space for British Islam". Paper presented at the conference "The future of Islam in Britain: New Muslims perspective", University of Birmingham.

McGhee, Derek (2008): *The end of multiculturalism? Terrorism, integration and human rights,* Maidenhead: Open University Press.

Meer, Nasar (2010): *Citizenship, identity and the politics of multiculturalism: The rise of Muslim consciousness,* New York: Palgrave Macmillan.

Modood, Tariq (2005): "Foreword", in: Abbas, Tahir (ed.), *Muslim Britain: Communities under pressure*, London: Zed Books, pp. viii-xii.

Morris, Chris (2010): Four lions (Motion picture). United Kingdom: Optimum Releasing.

Nelson, Dean / Hall, Allan (2009): "Pakistan discovers 'village' of white German al-Qaeda insurgents", in: *The Telegraph*, [online] 25 September. Available at: http://www.telegraph.co.uk/news/worldnews/asia/pakistan/6226935/ Pakistan-discovers-village-of-white-German-al-Qaeda-insurgents.html (accessed 27 April 2011).

van Nieuwkerk, Karen (2006): "Introduction: Gender and conversion to Islam in the West" in: id. (ed.), *Women embracing Islam: Gender and conversion in the West,* Austin: University of Texas, pp. 1-16.

Özyürek, Esra (2009): "Convert alert: German Muslims and Turkish Christians as threats to security in the new Europe", in: *Comparative Studies in Society and History,* 51:1, pp. 91-116.

PEW (2011): *Muslim-Western tensions persist.* [online] Available at: http://pewglobal.org/files/2011/07/Pew-Global-Attitudes-Muslim-Western-Rela tions-FINAL-FOR-PRINT-July-21-2011.pdf (accessed 25 July 2011).

Poynting, Scott / Mason, Victoria (2007): "The resistible rise of Islamophobia: Anti-Muslim racism in the UK and Australia before 11 September 2001", in: *Journal of Sociology,* 43:1, pp. 61-86.

Roy, Olivier (2009): "Al-Qaeda in the West as a youth movement: The power of a narrative", in: Emerson, Michael: *Ethno-Religious conflict in Europe: Typologies of radicalisation in Europe's Muslim communities,* Brussels: Centre for European Policy Studies, pp. 11-26, [online] Available at: http://www.ceps.eu/ceps/dld/1622/pdf (accessed 10 December 2012).

Seddon, Mohammad Siddique / Hussain, Dilwar / Malik, Nadeem (2003): *British Muslims: Loyalty and belonging,* Markfield: The Islamic Foundation.

Slater, Julia (2010): "Muslim converts raise fears in Switzerland". *Swissinfo.* [online] 17 April. Available at: http://www.swissinfo.ch/eng/swiss_news/ Muslim_converts_raise_fears_in_Switzerland.html?cid=8693278 (accessed 27 April 2011).

Thomas, Pierre (2011): "Osama Bin Laden's anti-U.S. strategy: Exploit minority converts". *ABC News,* [online] 7 May. Available at: http://abcnews.go.com/ Blotter/osama-bin-ladens-anti-us-strategy-exploit-minority/story?id=13547780 (accessed 20 May 2012).

UPI (2010): "West fears converts who become bombers". *UPI News,* [online] 15 February. Available at: http://www.upi.com/Top_News/Special/2010/02/15/ West-fears-converts-who-become-bombers/UPI-53431266251352 (accessed 16 March 2011).

Weller, Paul (2008): *Religious diversity in the UK: Contours and issues,* London: Continuum.

Zebiri, Kate (2008): *British Muslim converts: Choosing alternative lives,* Oxford: Oneworld.

"I have become a stranger in my homeland": An analysis of the public performance of converts to Islam in Switzerland

SUSANNE LEUENBERGER

This chapter analyses a Swiss convert's speech delivered at an early conference of the organisation Islamischer Zentralrat Schweiz (Islamic Central Council Switzerland, ICCS). The conference was held at an event venue in Zurich in front of an audience of several hundred Muslim individuals on 14 February 2010. The ICCS was established in due time to witness and react to the approval of the minaret initiative in late 2009. Given the ostentatious Islamic habitus of the association's convert leader and committee, the council's activities and its convert protagonists were given intense media attention. Hence, in the first half of 2010, the convert committee was to dominate media coverage on Muslims in Switzerland (compare Imhof/Ettinger 2011). Thus, in the aftermath of November 29, 2009, the trope of the convert as a religious zealot and cultural renegade was to structure Swiss public debates on Muslims and Islam in Switzerland prominently.

Convert Gibril's speech was entitled "Zum Fremden in der Heimat geworden: Ansichten und Einsichten eines Konvertiten" (I have become a stranger in my homeland: views and insights of a convert).

Adapting a performative, poststructurally informed approach on subjectivation, this chapter analyses convert Gibril's talk as an interpellative speech modelled on the Pauline theme of the death of the old sinner and birth of new man (2 Cor 5, 17, and Rom 6) as characteristic of conversion narratives. In his speech, Gibril delivers an account of his becoming perceived as a "stranger" in various social scenarios (private sphere, army, media) through his adoption of an Islamic habitus differing from his (former) social environment. Thus, as will be explored, the introspective therapeutic theme of overcoming a personal inner crisis which characterises standard conversion accounts is replaced by an external observer's perspective conveying the theme of social crisis following Gibril's conversion to Islam. While standard conversion accounts refer to the invisible 'inner self' as the locus of self-transformation, given his adoption of visible Islamic dress habits and aesthetic assets, Gibril's alteration is located on his bodily surface. Following the narrative structure of his talk, the analysis shows how Gibril gradually adopts and thus subjectivises present public addressations of migrant (ethnic) minorities as "Muslim strangers" as they have become increasingly popular in Switzerland ever since 9/11. Gibril presents his 'becoming a Muslim' as the retroactive assumption of the Swiss public's gaze, and thus places his alteration under a social frame of reference. By juxtaposing contemporary Muslim experiences of social exclusion to episodes from Qur'an and *sunna* in the concluding section of his talk, the convert relocates his narrative under an Islamic frame of reference, and thus qualifies "becoming a stranger" in everyday social scenarios and media addressations as a constitutive momentum of 'being Muslim'.

As this chapter argues, Gibril's account of the perception of his individual transformation allegorically narrates the discovery and construction of 'Islam' as an object of public problematisation of migrant populations in Switzerland, as well as a category of self-cultivation of ethnic Muslim ('migrant') youth.

METHODICAL CONSIDERATIONS

The data described and analysed in this study were collected by participant observation at the venue of the ICCS in 14 February 2010. General observations were captured in field notes. The major part of the performances delivered during the event, including the speech analysed, were recorded by digital camera. Even though analysis is based on his spoken performance, the visual recording of convert Gibril's speech allowed the inclusion of gestural performances into analysis.[1]

Analysis followed a sequential procedure (see Bohnsack 2008). Particular attention was paid to the dramaturgical structure of the speech. The paper presents the sequential structure of the convert's narrative to show how arguments are

---

1 Apart from the sequences containing consecutive translation into Arabic, the German speech was completely transcribed. The transcription was given line numbers to identify used quotations. Quotations have been translated into English. The line numbers quoted refer to the German transcription.

developed and to trace the shifting of speaker perspectives assumed by the narrator in the course of his speech.[2]

CONTEXTUALISATION

The ICCS (Islamic Central Council Switzerland)

Gibril's speech was delivered as part of the first annual conference of the ICCS. The council was established on 25 October 2009[3], in due time to witness the Swiss voters' approval of the minaret initiative on 29 November 2009. The executive board of the organisation is headed by several Swiss converts of both genders, along with an equal number of second generation Muslims. The Council is constituted as a membership association. According to its statutes, the organisation aims to encourage projects of Islamic education among Muslims in Switzerland. The ICCS seeks to promote the constitution of a Swiss-Muslim identity which unites Muslims from diverse ethnic backgrounds along normative criteria. As the first basis organisation of Muslims in Switzerland, the ICCS aims to represent practicing Muslims' moral and orthopractical interests vis-à-vis the public and authorities.[4] Since spring 2010, the association also functions as an umbrella organisation for Islamic communities in Switzerland. In this latter function, it competes with representatives of umbrella organisations of ethnic mosques, such as KIOS (Koordination Islamischer Organisationen Schweiz, established in 2000) and FIDS (Föderation Islamischer Dachverbände Schweiz, established in 2006). The long-term goal of those competing umbrella associations is to achieve the recognition of Islamic communities as bodies of public interest, in order to gain access to additional benefits. In their public statements the ICCS argues from the perspective of equal rights, religious freedom, minority protection and anti-discrimination guaranteed by the Swiss secular constitution. The council also plans to set up a Swiss *dār al-iftā'* (Fatwa Council) and establish Islamic schools.

The ICCS offers its members educational and recreational programs such as seminars, workshops and family camps, as well as legal support and counselling. The organisation's homepage (http://izrs.ch) is made up professionally. It pre-

---

2   Redundancies, expletives and passages of little analytical interest have been left out. Pauses, stammerings, and slips of the tongue have not been reproduced.

3   For the history of the council, see their own account on http://izrs.ch/der-izrs-stellt-sich-vor.html (accessed 30 March 2013).

4   See http://izrs.ch/statuten.html (accessed 30 March 2013).

184 | SUSANNE LEUENBERGER

sents standpoints and goals and announces current events related to the organisation. It also posts photographs, videos and documents of past events and conferences. It maintains a comprehensive press review and regularly posts comments on current topics related to the ICCS. Members get news alerts through SMS-messages. To reach out to the non-Muslim public, the ICCS organises information campaigns and public relations events.

Today, the association counts, according to its own figures, around 2600 individual members, and represents the interests of 13 Islamic communities.[5]

According to a newspaper with access to member statistics, 80 per cent of the council's members are under 35 years old, 60 per cent are male, 40 per cent female. 60 per cent of the members possess a Swiss passport. Only 10 per cent are converts, according to the self-declaration on the membership application forms. Of this group, 60 per cent are housewives. The bulk of the members work in the technical or in the service sector, others have jobs in the public sector.

Even though the association's individual members mostly have an ethnic Muslim background, it is the Swiss converts heading the organisation that incite the interest of the public.

Public observations: The convert committee in the focus of media attention

Right from the start, the public appearance of the convert members of the ICCS was accompanied by media coverage. Unlike ethnic Muslim associations in Switzerland, the ICCS preferably holds its venues in central public spaces, such as the Volkshaus in Zurich, the Congress Center in Biel/Bienne, or community centers in minor towns and cities.

Thus, it was also the ICCS that organised a 'Kundgebung gegen die Islamhetze' (demonstration against Islamophobia) on 10 December 2009 on Federal Square, in front of the Parliament Building, in the aftermath of the voters' backing of the minaret ban. All through the preparatory phase of the demonstration, this event was accompanied by high media attention due to the announced performance of the notorious Salafi preacher Pierre Vogel, a German convert observed by German authorities. Vogel was denied entry at the Swiss border for fear of religious agitation and thus did not appear at the event.[6]

---

5   Same URL as in note 3.

6   Raaflaub, Matthias (2009). "Überraschung bei Islam-Demo blieb aus", in: *Der Bund,* [online] 14 December. Available at: http://www.derbund.ch/bern/berraschung-bei-IslamDemonstration-blieb-aus/story/20059081?g=bern (accessed 20 July 2011).

After this event, the convert protagonists in the committee continued to incite public interest and triggered a media hype due to their perceived 'extremist' views and self-assertive claims on public space. The converts appeared in various media forms between April and late June 2010 and dominated media coverage on Islam and Muslims in Switzerland in the aftermath of the minaret vote (Imhof/Ettinger 2011: 18, 32). They were invited to television discussion programmes, were profiled in news magazines and talked in radio shows. Notably, it was the public appearance of fully-veiled convert Nora Illi in April 2010, the newly designated council member responsible for womens' issues, that fuelled a nation-wide debate about banning the *'burqa'*. Pictures of *niqāb*-wearing Nora Illi, posing in front of the Aletsch Glacier, or posing at a beach in Ticino with her two children, covered the front pages of Swiss print media. Nora's portrait hauntingly resembled the notorious imagery of the anti-minaret poster campaign (see illustration on p. 300). An overwhelming majority (93%), according to a non-representative survey conducted by Switzerland's popular tabloid *Blick* in Zurich in June 2010 (Grosse Burkadebatte 2010), deemed Nora's Islamic dress practice as utterly opposed to Swiss culture and/or the achievements of a liberal and secular society, and was in favor of a *'burqa'* ban.

Due to their high profile on the committee board, the ICCS was often perceived as a Swiss converts' association, even though they only make up a minor part of the total number of members. In the course of the media hype in the early summer of 2010, the figure of the 'radical convert to Islam' as religious zealot and 'cultural renegade' – as opposed to the more relaxed 'born, ethnic' Muslim – became topical.[7]

Convert Gibril, whose speech is analysed here, also received media attention in early summer 2010, and again in spring 2011.[8] Up until May 2010, the young man in his mid-twenties served as a lieutenant in the Swiss army and aspired to

7   See for example Gut, Philip (2010): "Bin Laden in Biel", in: *Die Weltwoche*. [online] 8 April. Available at: http://www.weltwoche.ch/ausgaben/2010-14/artikel-2010-14-bin-laden-in-biel.html (accessed 5 March 2013); Kalberer, Guido (2010). "Konvertiten sind am radikalsten", in: *Tages-Anzeiger*. [online] 5 May. Available at: http://www.tagesanzeiger.ch/leben/gesellschaft/Konvertiten-sind-am-radikalsten/story/14217480 (accessed 21 July 2011); Stamm, Hugo (2010). "Fanatismus ist lernbar", in: *Tages-Anzeiger*. [online] 22 April. Available at: http://newsnetz-blog.ch/hugostamm/?s=fanatismus+ist+lernbar (accessed 21 July 2011).
8   See for example Marinka, Claudia (2010): "Militär: Fundamentalist plant Karriere in Armee", in: *Der Sonntag*. [online] 1 May. Available at: http://www.sonntagonline.ch/index.php?show=news&id=994 (accessed 22 July 2011).

become captain (Hauptmann).[9] In 2008, he had converted to Islam. Since then, the mechanical engineer had critised the army's inadequate policies concerning Muslim members' religious interests and needs, notably the lack of possibility for ritual prayer during shifts as well as the absence of provisions allowing seg-regated showering.[10] The convert was repeatedly subjected to safety checks. In early 2010, the responsible authorities assessed him to be a security risk for the army. According to a newspaper quoting extracts of the officials' report, it ar-gued that the convert's "absolute compliance to his religion" ("Hörigkeit gegenüber seiner Religion") and the "unconditioned and unquestioned practice of it" ("absoluten und unhinterfragten Ausübung derselben") conflicted with his army loyalty and allegiance to state interests.[11] He was to be exempted from his current post in the army headquarters. Gibril appealed against this decree to the Federal Court. In May 2011, the Federal Court turned down Gibril's appeal, backing the army's assessment (see n. 11).

The Conference

The conference at which Gibril's speech was delivered was the first such event organised by the ICCS. It started at 11 am and lasted until 5.30 pm. It was held in the *Volkshaus*, a popular event hall in the heart of Zurich. The topic of the conference was "Switzerland after the ban on minarets. Where is the debate on Islam heading to?".

In front of the premises, green posters bearing the Arab greeting "ahlan wa-sahlan" and its German equivalent "Herzlich Willkommen" advertised the event. Young Muslim men and women gathered around the entrance. Some passers-by stopped for a moment before the rather unusual sight. The *Volkshaus* is known for pop and rock events. A number of sturdy dark bearded security men con-

---

9 Switzerland's army is organised as a militia system.

10 Wedl, Johanna (2011): "Ich bete auch in einem Bunker", in: *Tages-Anzeiger*. [online] 5 May. Available at: http://www.tagesanzeiger.ch/schweiz/standard/Ich-bete-auch-in-einem-Bunker/story/21235270 (accessed 22 July 2011).

11 Furthermore, the responsible authorities ruled that the convert was to hand in his army weapon, and that he was to be denied access to weaponry and ammunition. In addi-tion, he was to be excluded from further education and promotion in his army career, and must not partake in peacekeeping missions abroad. See Hasler, Thomas (2011). "Zum Islam konvertierter Offizier ist ein Sicherheitsrisiko", in: *Tages-Anzeiger*. [online] 7 May. Available at: http://www.tagesanzeiger.ch/schweiz/standard/Zum-Islam-konvertierter-Offizier-ist-ein-Sicherheitsrisiko-/story/25579223 (accessed 22 July 2011).

trolled the entrance and oversaw the foyer of the *Volkshaus*. In the entrance hall, men and women browsed through information stands and book tables, from where they were guided by signposts and security staff to the gender-segregated seating areas. The men were seated in the hall in the ground floor, while the women and children moved to the upper galleries of the theatre.

The bulk of the audience, about 700 individuals of both genders, appeared to identify as Muslims. One could hear Swiss-German, Turkish, Albanian and Arabic voices. The men and women were mostly young, in their twenties or early thirties. There were a lot of children. They ran around in the entrance area and played on the staircase. Many of the men were bearded and wore a prayer cap. Some were even dressed in traditional Muslim *qamīs*es or *galabiyya*s, worn over cotton trousers in discreet colours. Other young men were clean-shaven and casually dressed in a sportive or elegant manner.

The majority of the women present, although not all, wore a headscarf of some sort. Some of the younger women were dressed in form-fitting colourful clothes, others, often mothers, wore long *abayas* in discreet colours. Less than a handful of women wore *niqāb*.

A dozen journalists had positioned their cameras and microphones in front of the stage. During lunch break, they interviewed organisers and visitors.

The logo of the newly founded organisation was attached to the front of the lectern on the left side of the stage. In the background towards the middle of the stage, the organisers, translators and the moderator were seated at a conference table. The table front was covered by a big poster carrying the motto of the conference "Lernen, mit dem Islam zu leben" (Learn to live with Islam), which was also the title of president Nicolas Blancho's greeting address. Convert Blancho had a long beard, dyed with henna. His head was covered with a white prayer cap. He wore a long black coat over a tieless black suit. Convert Abdel Azziz Qaasim Illi, equally notorious spokesperson of the ICCS also had a red beard. He too was wearing a white prayer cap and was dressed in a long black coat. After the lunchbreak, Illi would hold an intellectually demanding speech about "Das Irrationale in der Islamophobie" (The irrational in Islamophobia).

The conference was opened with a recitation from the Qur'an performed by a dark skinned recitator. Then a number of speeches, starting with the president's address, tackled topics related to the current political and social situation of Muslims in Switzerland. The program consisted of talks, the reading of poems, and open discussion. Besides Blancho, Illi, Gibril and another young convert, also two convert women gave speeches. One of them, judging from her voice a young woman, was wearing a *niqāb* and reading an essay she had written on her thoughts after the minaret ban. The other convert woman, wearing *'abāya* and headscarf, delivered a speech entitled "Die Rolle der islamischen Frau vor dem Hintergrund ihrer Rechte (The role of the Muslim woman in respect of her rights)."

GIBRIL'S SPEECH

"Not long ago, I was an Other": becoming Muslim as alteration

Gibril's speech was announced unter the title "Zum Fremden in der Heimat geworden: Ansichten und Einsichten eines Konvertiten" (I have become a stranger in my homeland: views and insights of a convert). It was one of nine contributions and was held in the afternoon, after the break for lunch and *dhuhr* prayer. As the entire event was also concurrently translated into Arabic, his talk was interrupted several times by the translator. Including these interruptions, his speech lasted for 25 minutes. Gibril entered the stage. He was dressed in a charcoal coat, worn over a long white *qamīs* and cotton trousers. His head was covered by an off-white turban, and he had a reddish beard. He placed himself behind the lectern and started his talk.

Figure 1: Convert Gibril opens his speech

Source: author's photograph.

Gibril opened his performance with a supplication prayer in Arabic. Then he started his narration, taking a retrospective stance. Right from the beginning, the underlying theme of alteration, of becoming an Other, was introduced:

> Not long ago, I was an Other / had you made my aquaintance at that time / I think you would not recognise me anymore / I don't want to lose many words about

who I was or what I did / *a'ūdhu bi-llahi*[12] / but *Allah ta'ālā*[13] the All-Merciful /
he had mercy for me / he showed me the way / and gave me comprehension / *al-hamdu li-llāh*[14] / he lifted the veil from my eyes / he broke the seal over my ears
and over my heart / and he made me / *al-hamdu li-llāh* the biggest present one can
be given in this *dunya*[15] / he made me Islam to be my Religion [er machte mir den
Islam zur Religion] / *subhāna llāh*[16]. (6-13)

His opening prayer places Gibril's speech under an Islamic frame of reference.
As the bulk of the present audience most likely does not have extensive command of Arabic, his speaking in the Qur'anic language qualifies him as a particularly virtuous Muslim. Following the Arab supplication, Gibril introduces his
present self as somebody, who "not long ago, [...] was an Other" (6) in the first
phrase of his talk. To convey the theme of alteration, the first person narrator assumes a retrospective stance. Gibril, however, does not "want to lose many
words about who [he] was" (7sq.). For the time being, the audience is left at a
loss concerning his former self and the quality of his alteration. To convey his
self-transformation, Gibril summons the audience as potential external observers
that would not identify present Gibril as the same individual ("you would not
recognise me anymore") (7), had it made his acquaintance "not long ago" (6).
After drawing up this biographical caesura, Gibril proceeds to specify his recent
and sudden alteration as "the biggest present one can be given in this *dunya*", a
merciful act of godly working (11sq.). Gibril is using well-known Islamic metaphors (the lifting of the veil, the breaking of the seal over his ears and his heart)
(9sq.) to describe the transitive moment of sensual rapture effecting "Islam to be
[his] religion" (12sq.). By summoning Allah as the transcendent force to account
for his alteration, Gibril qualifies it as a religious turn.

"I had become an Other for them [...] I had decided to become a stranger": conversion as both passive moment and active process

In this first sequence, Gibril posits himself as a passive object of godly workings
upon his body. He presents his turning point as the opening of his visual and au-

---

12 Gibril uses a lot of standard Arabic eulogies in his speech. In the following, trans-
    lations will be given in the footnote. *a'ūdhu bi-llāhi* means "I take refuge with God".
13 "God, the exalted".
14 "Praise to God".
15 "Immanent world" (in opposition to a transcendent godly realm).
16 "God be glorified".

ditory faculties, the unclosing of his chest, an overwhelming bodily rapture that will retrospectively mark a break between a former self and convert Gibril. Presented as a transcendent process of alteration this change is only communicable by allegorical language, for the narrator lacks of any self in this moment of passage. While Gibril summons this instance of passive rapture, where he is momentarily bereft of any agency whatsover, in the following passage, he posits himself as the subject of this revelatory process:

> But ever since I have decided to follow the straight way that *Allah subhāna*[17] has provided for his servants my living conditions began to change drastically / a procedure many of you might have also experienced or may *inshā-llāh*[18] experience / suddenly I was to my friends not the cool guy one can chill out with anymore / I had become an Other for them / a stranger [...] the fact that I acknowledge the *qur'ān al-karīm*[19] and the words of our beloved Prophet *'alayhi s-salātu wa-s-salām*[20] as the only universal truth led to a change in my attitudes and values / *subhāna llāh* I had decided to become a stranger. (14-23)

In the sequence above, Gibril abruptly assumes an active role. In the first line, the narrator presents himself as an ego assuming a deliberate reorientation, a change of heart of his own choice ("I have decided to follow the straight way") (14). While in the preceding passage, his alteration is introduced as sensual rapture induced by external force, in the opening of the sequence above Gibril goes over to present it as a religious choice he has actively taken. The acknowledgement and confession to the "universal truth" of Qur'an and *sunna* (21sqq.) draws a continuous line to his present Muslim self standing on the stage and professing his faith in front of the audience.

"I have decided to become a stranger": becoming Muslim, becoming a stranger

Right from the beginning of this sequence, Gibril introduces a parallel alteration storyline (15-18). Speaking from the position of his present Gibril self, he opens up a synchronical observation perspective, where he posits himself, again, as "an Other", qualifying his alteration as "becoming a stranger" (17sq.). Therefore, he

---

17　"God, glorified is he".
18　"If God wills".
19　"The noble Qur'an".
20　"Upon him praise and peace".

assumes the viewpoint of his non-Muslim environment. He invokes the scenario of "chilling out with them" (16sqq.), a pastime he has ceased since his becoming Muslim. Gibril accompanies his narration by caricaturing the casual gestures of his former friends that stand in contrast to his present bodily habitus. In this short imitation Gibril presents the audience with a hint about his former self. His change is communicated by taking the perspective of his non-Muslim friends. In this episode, Gibril describes the loss of social belonging. Invoking it as an experience possibly shared by the present audience, he assumes the position of a Muslim collective.

Figure 2: Gibril imitates the 'chilling out' habitus of his former self

Source: author's photograph.

As in the storyline conveying his religious conversion, in the first instance, Gibril introduces himself as a passive onlooker in this process of social differentiation, describing how in their eyes, "for them", he has "become a stranger" (17sq.). However, in the next passage, again, Gibril actively assumes the role assigned to him by external observation, when he ends this episode stating that he "ha[d] decided to become a stranger" (23).

In the following sequences leading up to the middle of the speech, Gibril continues to present a number of scenarios in contexts ranging from face-to-face interaction to media observation, in which the themes of external observation of (visible) habitual difference and exclusion are reiterated.

Choosing 'true religion': Gibril as active confessor

Following the presentation of the 'chill out' episode, where he takes the position of his onlooking environment, Gibril presents himself as a proactive confessor of his religion against a hostile non-Muslim environment. Gibril recounts his futile attempts to familiarise his family and friends with Islam (24-30). Gibril mimes a discussion with imaginary non-Muslim counterparts who question the desirability of his religious choice: "why did you choose such a difficult, such a strict religion" (31sq.). His interlocutors' objections figure as rhetorical counterpoint to present his conversion as the absolute acknowledgement of the "universal truth" (31) of "Islam".

Following the 'chill out' episode, Gibril assumes the active role of a strong advocate of 'Islam' as 'true religion' against an objecting environment. Again, the narrative pattern of moving from a passive position of being confronted by external addressation to an active stance of affirming the onlookers' interpellation is discernable in this episode.

"When I arrived on duty with full beard [...] they withdrew their trust in me": shifting allegiances

Leaving these private scenarios, in the next passage, Gibril recounts his experience in the Swiss army. Echoing the passive stance he assumes in preceding episodes, he recalls becoming a stranger in his army colleagues' perceptions. Again, it is his differing habitus, notably visible bodily features and routines, that renders him worthy of, this time, official army observation:

> Before I accepted Islam [...] I was in certain circles highly thought of and respected / I was officer in the Swiss army and have to my knowing always served to the army's satisfaction [...] when I arrived on duty with my full beard and served my daily prayers / when I quit eating the meat I was served and abstained from aperitif receptions with my officer colleagues / in other words when I quit drinking alcohol / what happened / I was told that my new ideas were likely to involve investigative measures / in other words they withdrew their trust in me / *subhāna llāh.*   (39-49)

In the episode presented above, Gibril constructs a plot of shifting allegiances. The before-and-after structure of the sequence introduces his former army-officer self as discontinuous to his present Muslim self, proposing the incompatibility of being both Muslim and Swiss army officer. Gibril summons shifting social routines (44sqq.) – the withdrawal from former eating and drinking habits, the performance of Islamic duties and visible markers (full beard) – to present his 'birth' as Gibril and his simultaneous 'death' as Swiss army officer. As in the passages above, Gibril gains his Muslim contours by differing from his face-to-face environment. In the army scenario, it is the category of 'Swiss citizenship' that comes undone in his person when Gibril "arrives on duty with full beard".

"The one who commands the right [...] he is the enemy of the state number one": public observation of Muslims

Continuous to the army episode, the following sequence of Gibril's speech iterates the theme of suspicion and unjust critique levelled against him (50sqq.). The scope of observation is widened from face-to-face interaction to the general level of the public and media (50sq.). While up until now, Gibril has invoked the perception given to his own person as a convert, he now shifts his first person position from singular to plural, coming to eventually represent any Muslim present ("how many times have some of us heard…", 60sq.):

> We can clearly detect the media's role in opinion making / even though I had always served to their [the army's, S. L.] satisfaction, the media is more trusted / and prejudice is more trusted / than in [personal] acquaintance with me [.,.] my beloved brothers and sisters / fear is instilled [...] how many times have some of us heard purportedly silly remarks like have you fastened the bomb belt [...] *a'ūdhu bi-llāhi* / the one who commands the right and forbids the wrong / he is the unjust / he is the enemy of the state number one. (50-64)

Gibril refers to himself as someone who is "commanding the good and forbidding the wrong" (62sq.).

Drawing on the well-known Qur'anic principle, he constructs his moral self within an Islamic frame of reference. However, his Muslim moral sense of 'the good' is contrasted to the public perception of him and his like as "being the enemy of the state number one" (63sq.). Again, the theme of mutual exclusion of being (a good) Muslim and being (a loyal) Swiss citizen is iterated.

Gibril as "clear bogeyman": subjectivising public observations

The following sequence marks the end of his biographical account. Gibril proceeds to assume the subject position as a member of the council, before he will again resume speaking for Muslims in general. To begin with, he refers to a recent article published in *20 Minuten*, a popular free daily newspaper. Gibril quotes a conservative member of parliament demanding surveillance of and security measures against the ICCS:

> I quote it can't be denied that the group [...] poses a security risk for Switzerland / they are a new danger not known before / the radicalisation of young moderate Muslims could lead up to religious riots [...] and I quote the organisation needs to

be observed and in case of further provocations needs to be monitored by state security / penal measures against the group are not feasible before something happens… end of quote / yes / brothers and sisters / there are masses of internet sites
attacking in a racist and inhumane manner Islam and Muslims / *a'ūdhu bi-llāh* /
hate campaigns without sense and logic […] with a clear bogeyman [klar gepräg-
tes Feindbild] […]   (68-80)

When Gibril reaches the end of this section, he accompanies it by the gesture of
pointing to himself as the "clear bogeyman" of media observation (79sq.). Citing
Swiss media, Gibril places himself in an observing stance vis-à-vis the media,
reverting the attribution of perpetrator and victim. In Gibril's account, the Muslims themselves are presented as the victims of irrational "hate campaigns"
(78sq.) purported by security measures and media campaigns.

Figure 3: Gibril as the "clear bogeyman"

Source: author's photograph.

In the last two sequences, the autobiographical focus of Gibril's account is suc-
cessively replaced by a general perspective on Muslims' experience of social exclusion. With his assumption of being the "bogeyman", Gibril relates, by synec-
doche, his experience as a religious convert to "any (born, practicing) Muslim's"
experience.

"We are not the first to be tried in this way": Introducing an Islamic frame of interpretation

The middle of the speech is marked by a caesura in the dramaturgy of his narration. Gibril interpellates the present audience as Muslims ("we are Muslims *al-
hamdu li-llāh!*") (82sq.) who should not leave the "straight path" (81-85). Gibril
invokes Qur'anic exhortations ("be steadfast and beware of evil detractors", Ver-

leumder und Einflüsterer, 90sq.) to gather the audience as a collective of virtuous Muslim believers.

From this point on, Gibril proceeds to reintegrate the conveyed experience of social exclusion into an Islamic frame of reference by citing episodes from Qur'an and *sunna*. Gibril moves from delivering a first-person autobiographical account to a third-person narration:

> We are truly not the first to be tried in this way / it is not the first time that a group of Muslims is confronted with such rejection and injust prejudice / remember our beloved Prophet *salla llāhu 'alaihi wa-sallam*[21] what pain and torment he was exposed to / when he arrived with the message of Islam / he was attacked by his own kind by the people of Quraish [...] can you imagine the hate [...] 'Uqba bin Abī Mu'ait[22] he poured bowels of / blood and camels' dirt over our beloved Prophet *salla llāhu 'alaihi wa-sallam* / while he was in the *sujūd*[23] / only to amuse the chiefs of the Quraish / what did he have to tolerate and what hardships did he suffer.   (94-107)

In the subsequent sequences, Gibril describes physical torments to which the Prophet was exposed. The narrator summons passages in which the Prophet's body is objected to physical violence perpetrated by the Meccans. The strong image of the "pouring camels' dirt [...] while he [is] in the *sujūd*" (105sqq.) introduces a Prophet bereft of recognition and agency, denied of his subject status. Gibril invokes the episode of Umm Jamīl telling lies about the Prophet, and placing thorn plants in this way and on his door steps (99-103), and recalls the story of Bilal being tormented and faced with physical extinction by his enemies, still acknowledging the truth of Islam (108-115).

Recalling the Prophet being beaten unconscious, Gibril starts to cry:

> It was Abu Bakr[24] that came to support our Prophet *salla llāhu 'alaihi wa-sallam* when the *mushrikūn*[25] beat him and hit him on the head until he lost consciousness / and he Abu Bakr approached them and asked / you beat a man who says *rabbī Allah* my lord is Allah and what did the *mushrikūn* do / they said Abu Bakr *al majnūn* / Abu Bakr the madman / and they continued to hit him.   (118-123)

---

21 "May Allah honour him and grant him peace."

22 Early opponent of the Prophet in pre-hijra Mecca.

23 The state of being prostrated in Muslim prayer.

24 Early companion of the Prophet who was to become first caliph after Muhammad's death.

25 "Unbelievers".

"May Allah [...] make us and our brothers and sisters strangers": subjectivising the Prophet's sufferings

While until this point, Gibril was in the position of a third-person narrator, he once again assumes a first-person plural position, representing the Muslim audience present. The Prophet's exposure to physical abuse is equated to the contemporary Muslims' experience of social exclusion:

> See my beloved brothers and sisters / he who believes Allah's messenger and follows his word and stands by his side / he sometimes has to bear a heavy burden / but how more hardship did the companions suffer than we do today / *Allāhu a'lam*[26] [...] they too have become strangers in their homeland / Amr Ibn Auf[27] *radhiya llāhu 'anhu*[28] narrated / the messenger Allah / Allahs blessings and peace be upon him said / Islam has begun strange and it will become strange as it began [...] blessed be those who bring into being [ins Leben rufen] what the people after me have neglected of my *sunna* / *sadaqa rasūl Allāh salla llāhu 'alaihi wa-sallam*[29] / may *Allāh subhāna Allāh ta'ālā*[30] grant us this mercy and make us and our brothers and sisters strangers / strangers like our Prophet / *salla llāhu 'alaihi wa-sallam* and his companions *radhiya llāhu 'anhum* [...].   (124-138)

With the supplication to become strangers, Gibril's narration comes to an end. The speech is finished by a Muslim invocation in German language (138-142). While the major part of the second half of Gibril's speech was structured as a third-person account (97-123), in the last sequence of his talk, Gibril comes back to assuming a first-person position (124-138). Thus, he subjectivises the Prophet's and his companions' experience of physical abuse as "hav[ing] become strangers" (130), juxtaposing it to contemporary (born) Muslims' experiences in the Swiss public. The social exclusion conveyed is reintegrated into an Islamic frame of reference. Gibril invokes Allah as the agent that is to render them strangers (136sqq.). To be a stranger is thus given a salvational interpretation, qualifying the contemporary Muslims' experience as godly willed ("grant us this mercy and make us and our brothers and sisters strangers") and, thus worthy, as an *imitatio Muhammadi*.

---

26 "God knows better".
27 Amr Ibn Auf is one of the first companions of the Prophet.
28 "May God be pleased with him".
29 "Thus truthfully says God's messenger, may God honour him and grant him peace."
30 „God, glorified be he, God, exalted be he".

A theoretical discussion of Gibril's speech now follows below. To understand the particularities of Gibril's speech, it examines how the convert's account is modelled on the Pauline theme of *metanoia* (gr. turn around, change of attitude) characteristic of conversion narratives, yet how it diverges from standard conversion narratives in terms of observer perspective and thematic topic, and the presented locus of (self)transformation. In a further step, it discusses Gibril's speech with a performative, poststructurally informed concept of subjectivation.

FROM ALLAH'S WORKINGS TO THE SWISS ENVIRONMENTS' OBSERVATION: SHIFTING GAZES, SHIFTING STORYLINES OF GIBRIL'S "BECOMING AN OTHER"

Modelled on Paul's experience of sudden inner change and *metanoia*, conveyed as "the falling of the scales from his eyes" that follow his blinding vision and godly calling (Acts 9, 1-18), William James' classical definition of religious conversion describes a radical process of self-alteration, dividing the converts' biography into a life 'before' and a life 'after' conversion (James 1902: 186; Nock 1933: 7; Wiesberger 1990: 9).

As James and successive scholars have observed, the conversion experience appears as both a passive process as well as an active volitional act assumed by the convert (see James 1902: 186, 198, 207sq.; Rambo 1993: 176; Wiesberger 1990: 9; Asad 1996).

Secular conceptions of religious conversion first appear in psychological research in the latter part of the nineteenth Century. In those phenomenological approaches, originating in the pietist-Methodist context of US society, religious conversion figures as the religious experience par excellence (Hall 1882; Starbuck 1897; James 1902; Nock 1933). James presents religious conversion as a process of inner maturing and psychological integration effected by the workings of the "subliminal self" (1902: 186), conveying the therapeutic, introspective theme of overcoming a deep inner crisis.

Secular models of "becoming an Other": Alteration as subjectivation

William James and successive liberal scholars focused on a secularised reading of the topic of individualised subjective redemption underlying conversion narratives since Paul and Augustine. Meanwhile, other secular approaches, notably from structuralist and subsequent poststructural perspectives, have taken an interest in the both transitive and intransitive moment inherent in the process of self-transformation described in religious narratives as related by Paul, Augustine as well as the Old Testament prophets, initiated by transcendent godly power.

The Pauline paradigm of conversion as a blinding and calling, induced by an external force and its retroactive constitution of a 'seeing' and confessing 'new' self has figured as the prime allegory of secular theories of signification and subjectivation, of becoming an addressable and intelligible self. From this perspective, religious conversion figures as a paradigmatic form of 'becoming a subject'. Transposed to a secular frame of interpretation, the transcendent godly gaze and calling initiating the process of subjectivation as 'seeing' has been replaced by secular notions of 'ideology' (Althusser), 'symbolic order' (Lacan), or 'discourse/power' (Foucault, Butler) as social substance preceding individual and collective subjects. Judith Butler recapitulates the ambivalent nature of subjectivation as such:

> 'Subjectivation' signifies the process of becoming subordinated by power as well as the process of becoming a subject [...] the subject is initated through a primary submission to power." (1997: 2)

Following Rimbauds well-known dictum that "I is another", structuralist thinkers like Lacan and Althusser share an inherent suspicion against the liberal idea of a sovereign self-identical subject. They have drawn from biblical allegories and their sensory metaphors to avow for the fundamental moment of exteriority and alterity in any process of subject formation. Reinterpreting Freud's notion of the "Schautrieb" (scopic drive) as the preferred pathway of libidinal arousal (1999 [1905]: 58sq.) with *Gestalt therapy* and hegelianism, Lacan's widely influential account of the mirror stage describes the excentric (specular) and retroactive nature of narcisstic identification (2000 [1949], Pagel 2002: 26-29). Furthermore, Lacan emphasises the dominance of visual faculties and their specular projective moment in his idea of "the Other's gaze" as constitutive for subject formation and symbolic integration. As a structural function it triggers the individual's desire to respond and catch up to his imaginary self-image and thus retroactively assume the external beholder's gaze in which he is caught. The split between the individual's limited 'eye' and the projected all-seeing 'gaze' institutes the dual relationship constitutive of the I *(je)* and the imaginary self *(moi)* in the subject (Lacan 1978: 78-81), driven by the desire to 'see more' and gain (self)recognition. Following Lacan, Althusser draws on the idea of the self-begotten and self-identical Hebrew God (I am that I am) as the burning bush (the blinding eye that sees but is not itself seen) and voice, the Subject with a capital S, always-already there to 'name' all other individuals, and thus call them into social existence as addressable and responding 'subjects' (id.: 178sq.; Evans 2002: 197; Butler 2001: 103sqq.).

Notably, Althusser's well-known concept of 'interpellation' echoes the religious notion of prophetic 'calling' (Althusser 1971: 180sq.) as both passive and active act. Althusser famously invokes the episode of a policeman shouting "Hey, you there!" toward a person walking on the street. The person being appealed turns around to respond and thereby recognises himself as the subject of the calling (id.: 174). The metaphor of turning around illustrates the specular and retroactive nature of becoming a subject (Butler 2001: 106). The called turns to respond and to recognise the gaze he has been caught by without seeing it himself. The symbolic order enabling the individual to assume a subject position has always-already been there (id.: 176). Following Lacan, Althusser calls the subject's self-recognition a constitutive "misrecognition" (méconnaissance) because it presents a retroactive fiction, covering the fundamental heterogeneity of the process of subjectivation fuelled by the imaginary Other's gaze (id.: 172; Lacan 1978: 81). As Butler puts it: "Subjectivity consists precisely in this fundamental dependency on a discourse we never chose but that, paradoxically, initiates and sustains our agency." (Butler 1997: 2).

Taking a performative approach:
Gibril's speech as interpellative practice

Adapting Lacan's concept of imaginary identification and his linguistic model of the symbolic order as the locus of intersubjective intelligibility and social integration, Althusser's concept of 'interpellation' has been an important influence for poststructuralist approaches towards subjectivation. Notably, Butler's concept of performativity adapts Althusser's notion of hailing. Butler conceptualises subjectivation as a social practice accomplished by repeated acts of discursive inscription. Following Freud's notion of the ego as a "bodily ego [...] not merely a surface entity, but in itself a projection of a surface" (Freud 1999 [1923]: 20), Butler emphazises the phantasmatic moment of subjectivation (Butler 1993: 13). Applying a deconstructive reading of both speech act theory and psychoanalysis, she understands subjectivation as realised by repeated citational practices of bodily inscription performed by individuals and collectives. According to Butler, these iterative interpellations bring into being the very subjects which they name (Butler 1990: 24sq., 1993: 232). Taking this performative stance, Butler sees the presupposition of a (sovereign) subject preceding the act of citation as a mere retroactive yet necessary fiction. Echoing Althusser, she understands subjectivation as a both transitive and intransitive practice of signification, of 'naming' a self.

Based on Butler's performative approach, Gibril's autobiographical narrative can be understood as an iterative citational practice that brings into being the Muslim subject it summons. In his self-observational speech, we can follow the 'interpellation' of his own Muslim self, as well as the Muslim audience present. As analysis has shown, Gibril not only produces his individual convert self by summoning and subjectivising the observers' gazes in his speech. In the course of his speech, he also comes to assume the subject position of a Muslim collective, thus summoning the audience present as 'Muslims' along moral and orthopractical categories.

DISCUSSION: GIBRIL'S BECOMING MUSLIM UNDER PUBLIC OBSERVATION

Compared to the therapeutic theme of inner healing related by conversion accounts modelled on the Jamesian tradition (see above p. 197), Gibril's narrative is characterised by the complete absence of an introspective stance, and lacks the psychological theme of inner crisis and personal search. His alteration is conveyed from a synchronic perspective as the effect of external observation, triggering a social crisis. Gibril summons the external perspective of the present audience to account for the "observable" difference ("had you made my acquaintance at this time / I think you would not recognise me anymore", 6sq.). His religious alteration is thus related as an external, visible difference to his bodily surface, qualified as "strangeness".

The Christian theme of personal inner redemption relating the 'death' of the sinner and 'birth' of the Pauline "new man" (2 Cor 5, 17, and Rom 6) is replaced by the theme of the 'social death' of Gibril's former self and of his birth as 'strange man' effected by his adoption of a visible Islamic habitus.

Thus, Gibril's narrative uses the before-after caesura of the Pauline theme to account for the birth of a Muslim self that comes into existence by public observation.

Stranger Gibril's speech traces and reproduces the discovery of Islam as a both publically observable and subjective (subjectivisable) category in Swiss society. As a Swiss who discovers Islam he mirrors Switzerland's discovery of its Muslims.

As media analyses show, following 9/11 as well as subsequent international key events of Islamic terrorism and radicalism, 'Islamic difference' subsequently came to figure as a new category of public, academic, and political observation and addressation of Muslim 'migrant' populations in Switzerland (Schranz/Imhof 2002; Ettinger 2008; Ettinger/Imhof 2009; Behloul 2009; Imhof/Ettinger 2011; Udris/Imhof/Ettinger 2011).

REFERENCES

Research reports of all projects in the Swiss National Research Programme NRP 58 on "Religions, the State, and Society" are available online at http://www.nfp58.ch.

Althusser, Louis (1971): "Ideology and ideological state apparatuses", in: id. (ed.), *Lenin and philosophy and other essays,* New York: Monthly Review Press.

Anonymous (2010): "Grosse Burkadebatte in der Schweiz: Wir wollen ihnen ins Gesicht sehen", in: *Blick,* 3 May. [online] Available at: http://www.blick.ch/news/schweiz/politik/so-denken-die-schweizer-146006 (accessed 19 July 2011).

Asad, Talal (1996): "Comments on conversion", in: van der Veer, Peter (ed.), *Conversion to modernities: The globalization of Christianity,* London: Routledge, pp. 163-175.

Behloul, Samuel M. (2009): "Discours total! Le débat sur l'islam en Suisse et le positionnement de l'islam comme religion publique", in: Schneuwly Purdie, Mallory / Gianni, Matteo / Jenny, Magali (eds), *Musulmans d'aujourd'hui: Identités plurielles en Suisse,* Genève: Labor et Fides, pp. 53-72.

Bohnsack, Ralf (2008[7]): *Rekonstruktive Sozialforschung: Einführung in qualitative Methoden,* Opladen: Budrich.

Butler, Judith (1990): *Gender trouble: Feminism and the subversion of identity,* New York: Routledge.

— (1993): *Bodies that matter: On the discursive limits of 'sex',* New York: Routledge.

— (1997): *The psychic life of power: Theories in subjection,* Stanford: SUP.

— (2001): *Psyche der Macht: Das Subjekt der Unterwerfung,* Frankfurt a. M.: Suhrkamp.

Ettinger, Patrik (2008): *The problematization of Muslims in public communication in Switzerland.* [online] fög. Forschungsbereich Öffentlichkeit und Gesellschaft (ed.). Discussion Paper 2008. 2008-0004. Available at: http://www.foeg.uzh.ch/staging/userfiles/file/Deutsch/fög%20discussion%20papers/2008-0004_the%20,problematisation%20of%20Muslims%20in%20public%20communication%20in%20Switzerland.pdf (accessed 12 June 2011).

Ettinger, Patrik / Imhof Kurt (2009): *Zentrale Merkmale der Öffentlichen Debatte über die Minarettinitiative: Inhaltsanalyse des fög. Forschungsbereich Öffentlichkeit und Gesellschaft,* Zürich: Universität Zürich.

Evans, Dylan (2002): *Wörterbuch zur Lacanschen Psychoanalyse,* Wien: Turia und Kant.

Freud, Sigmund (1999 [1905]): *Drei Abhandlungen zur Sexualtheorie,* Frankfurt a. M.: Fischer.

— (1989 [1923]): *The Ego and the Id,* New York: W. N. Norton.

Hall, Stanley G. (1882): "The moral and religious training of children", in: Princeton Review, IX, p. 26-45.

Imhof, Kurt / Ettinger, Patrik (2011): *Ethnisierung des Politischen und Problematisierung religiöser Differenz.* [online] Research report NRP 58.

James, William (1902): *The varieties of religious experience,* London: Collins.

Lacan, Jacques (2000 [1949]): "The mirror stage", in: du Gay, Paul / Evans, Jessica / Redman, Peter (eds): *Identity: A reader,* London: Sage, pp. 44-50.

— (1978): *Das Seminar von Jacques Lacan: Die vier Grundbegriffe der Psychoanalyse,* Olten/Freiburg im Breisgau: Walter-Verlag.

Nock, Arthur D. (1933): *Conversion,* New York: Clarendon.

Pagel, Gerda (2002): *Jacques Lacan zur Einführung,* Hamburg: Junius.

Rambo, Lewis (1993): *Understanding religious conversion,* New Haven: Yale University Press.

Schranz, Mario / Imhof, Kurt (2002): "Muslime in der Schweiz: Muslime in der öffentlichen Kommunikation", in: *Medienheft Katholischer Mediendienst und Reformierte Medien,* 18 December 2002.

Starbuck, Edwin D. (1897): "A study of conversion", in: *The American Journal of Psychology,* 8:2, pp. 268-308.

Udris, Linards / Imhof, Kurt / Ettinger, Patrik (2011): "Problematisierung des Fremden in der direkten Demokratie", in: fög. Forschungsbereich Öffentlichkeit und Gesellschaft (ed.), *Jahrbuch 2011: Qualität der Medien. Schweiz – Suisse – Svizzera,* Basel: Schwabe, pp. 377-407.

Wiesberger, Franz (1990): *Bausteine zu einer soziologischen Theorie der Konversion: Soziokulturelle, interaktive und biographische Determinanten religiöser Konversionsprozesse,* Berlin: Duncker und Humblot.

Islamic fields and Muslim techniques of the self in a German context

JÖRN THIELMANN

In this paper I present new types of Muslim actors visible in the emerging Islamic fields in Europe.[1] Fields are not simply used as a heuristic metaphor, but understood in a refined Bourdieu'ian sense, where I adapt his model to the Islamic case. Introducing the notion of 'religious disposition' allows taking account of both individual and collective activities and mind sets. The complex interactions and struggles for recognition inside and outside of Islamic fields, involving ethnic and cultural heritage and traditions as well as new forms of a de-culturalised, de-historicised, and de-nationalised Islam will thereby come into focus. The latter form of Islam is quite often promoted by born-again Muslims, or reverts, and by converts to Islam. The role model for a true Muslim life is the Prophet himself. Complex "techniques of the self" (Michel Foucault) help overcoming the original habitus and form new Muslim selves, imitating the Prophet in everyday life.

THE ETHNISATION OF ISLAM

In the 1980s and 1990s, the public perception of Islam focused on 'political Islam' or 'Islamic fundamentalism'. After September 11, 2001 this perception sharpened: 'Islam' became the central paradigm not only for understanding the

---

1   Here, I present a generalisation. For a detailed ethnographic presentation of my local cases (Bad Kreuznach and Mainz) see Thielmann 2005. – I wish to cordially thank Gerdien Jonker, Susanne Leuenberger, and Andreas Tunger-Zanetti for their comments on this text.

Middle East, but also problems with migrants and their descendants in Germany and Europe, including non-Muslims. So, it is now normal to speak of 'the Muslims' when speaking about migrants with a supposedly 'oriental' background, without taking into account (lived) religiosity or the respective personal relationship with Islam or the socio-economic living conditions of the relevant persons. Thus, 'Islam' became ethnicised, mingling indissolubly with 'integration' and 'migrants'. Finding answers to the question who is a Muslim in Germany is therefore not easy (Spielhaus 2011). All migrants or their descendants – even fourth generation… – being identified by name or appearance as 'Muslims' are interpellated as such and their behaviour and their concrete situations explained by 'Islam'.

Here, the perceptions and prejudices of the German public meet with certain understandings of Islam by a number of Muslim actors (e. g. the advancing of an Islamic citizenship in Europe, stressing exclusively an Islamic identity), reinforcing each other, as becomes obvious with the so-called 'Salafites'/'Salafists'/'Salafis' and their 'Islamic dress', looking exotic and oriental, as in the case of the Swiss convert Gibril, presented by Susanne Leuenberger in this volume. The ethnisation of Islam is thus a twofold process, realised by the non-Muslim environment and Muslims alike.

ISLAMIC FIELDS: NORMS AND HABITUS

What are the structural features of Islamic fields? I use the term 'field' – following Pierre Bourdieu – for "a small and relatively autonomous social world, a micro-cosmos, inside a larger social world" (Bourdieu 2001a: 41, my translation). Fields are, according to Bourdieu, defined and regulated by their own *nomos*, their own structural regularities that distinguish them from other fields. They are structured by the accumulation of various forms of capital. The main forms are economic, social, symbolic, and cultural capital. Here, capital is understood as 'accumulated labour'. The different distributions of capital create power relations, with the poles dominant-dominated, and patterns characteristic for each field. The dominant powers want to preserve their position and tend towards routine and conservatism, whereas newcomers and dominated participants, by contrast, wish to restructure the field in their favour by subversion, quite often by a return to the sources and the purity of the origin (Bourdieu 2001b: 70). In all these processes rules for inclusion and exclusion exist as well as legitimate and illegitimate practices and discourses.

With regard to religious fields, Bourdieu bases his reflections (1971a; 1971b) on Max Weber's typology, stemming from Weber's understanding of Judaism, which identifies the magician, the priest, the prophet, and the layman as ideal typical competing actors in the religious field.[2] The magician and the prophet represent personal charisma, the priest the bureaucratic mandate. At stake are the administration of and the access to goods of salvation. Here, the prophet and the priest relate to a doctrine. Laymen are only objects and recipients of the good called 'salvation' distributed to them by professional actors. Thus, the professional actors are competing with each other over their followers. For Bourdieu, the constitution of a religious field goes hand in hand with an increase of religious capital of the religious specialists at the expense of the laymen. The Catholic Church serves as his model for the religious field.

Contrary to my previous understanding (Thielmann 2005: 164sq.), I am now convinced that Bourdieu's concept of the religious field needs a few, but clear modifications to be useful for an Islamic context. Otherwise his term 'religious field' functions simply as a heuristic one. In particular, the concentration on religious specialists and institutions and an understanding of the religious field as mainly related to them is problematic. Furthermore, to define the borders of a religious field or of religious fields in the plural, the inside and outside as well as to determine the overlapping between them and with other fields is a difficult enterprise.

First of all, the religious situation in Islam is totally different from the Catholic context, and to a large degree also from the Jewish one. Only a very weak religious-authoritative institutionalisation exists (if at all, one might find some institutionalisation in Shiite Islam with its hierarchised clerics). There are religious scholars, the *'ulamā'*, holding institutional charisma, like the Ottoman *şeyh ül-islām* and until today to a certain degree the *Shaykh al-Azhar*, or personal charisma, like the prominent sheikh Yusuf al-Qaradāwi (on the latter see Gräf/Skovgaard-Petersen 2009). Here, we find some analogies with the priest (institutional charisma) and the prophet (personal charisma) of Bourdieu's model, both also related to scripture-based religion. There might also be some Sufi shaykhs here and there to be understood as magicians, to make the Weber-Bourdieu personnel complete. In the course of the twentieth century, in large parts of the Islamic world existing religious institutions lost authority in the eyes of many Muslims, be it through state manipulation and instrumentalisation, or through the emergence of new authorities such as the 'Muslim intellectuals'. Here, the Egyptian doctor Mustafā Mahmūd (Conermann 1996), or the Syrian engineer Muhammad Shahrūr (Am-

---

2 For an overview of Bourdieu's sociology of religion see Dianteill 2002. For a short introduction to his sociological theory, in particular its relations to Durkheim, Weber, and Marx see Brubaker 1985.

berg 2009) serve as examples.[3] The increasing literacy of Muslims and access to education as well as the spread of old (radio, TV, audio-cassettes) and new (Internet, Web 2.0) media facilitate the religious learning of individuals and groups tremendously and shifts power, authority, and religious capital to lay people. Therefore, it seems more useful to me to describe actors in the religious field and their positions by their different religious dispositions (compare Verter 2003: 15). Here, I draw on earlier reflections, inspired by Werner Schiffauer[4], to speak of religiously more or less active groups (Thielmann 2005: 164). The term 'disposition', however, has the advantage to be applicable to both individuals and groups. Furthermore, it can be linked to the habitus concept of Bourdieu and fits also together with – as I will show below – Foucault's reflections on "techniques of the self".

Second, the conceptualisation of religious capital by Bourdieu is problematic. He envisages basically the Roman-Catholic sacramental theology: the priests administer the access to and distribution of goods of salvation. Such goods of salvation do not exist in Islam, if we leave some practices of 'popular Islam' aside. The possibility to pass the Day of Judgement and thereby to obtain salvation is based on individual observation of religious norms in practice, and not on the contribution by a third party. What can be distributed is only knowledge of religious norms and of the practice derived from them. Thus, "commanding the right, forbidding the wrong" (*al-amr bil-ma'rūf wan-nahy 'an al-munkar*, *sūra* 3, v. 104) is one of the most important individual and collective duties of Muslims (Cook 2000; Thielmann 2003: 25-60). The realisation of this duty is a litmus test for the 'Islamicity' of an individual Muslim or a group of Muslims. The relatively autonomous religious subject, who is constitutive for Islam, understands him or herself to be in direct relationship with God. It governs his religious orientation and in particular all his or her deeds by knowledge, either self-acquired or transmitted (stemming from binding authoritative religious sources). The layman, therefore, is the central figure in the Islamic religious field. The layman can also accumulate large quantities of religious capital through 'techniques of the self' without necessarily turning to transmitters, who administer and distribute this capital. Further, he can form a religious habitus that becomes active in society beyond the power struggles between religious professionals. It seems plausible that this is the reason why in Islamic religious fields there is no shortage of religious capital, contrary to Bourdieu's understanding (Verter 2003: 157). Every

---

3   For this phenomenon in the European context see the contributions of van Bruinessen/Allievi 2011.

4   Schiffauer in a personal communication on May 7, 2004.

Muslim can produce new (spiritual) capital at any time.[5] Thus, taking up Bradford Verter's proposal I suggest speaking of spiritual instead of religious capital (id., 157-169). If religious capital according to Bourdieu is something produced and accumulated by hierocratic institutions, spiritual capital can be understood as "a more widely diffused commodity, governed by more complex patterns of production, distribution, exchange, and consumption" (id., 158).

Spiritual capital is a form of cultural capital in three different manifestations (id., 159sq.): Firstly, it is embodied, defining not only the position in the field, but also comprising the religious disposition, the knowledge, abilities, taste and trustworthiness of a person in the religious field, as a result of an explicit educational or unconscious socialisation process. Secondly, it is materialised in symbolic goods, e.g. exegetic texts, ritual dress or votive offerings. Thirdly, it is institutionalised in organisations and families, but also explicitly extra-institutional.

According to Bourdieu, the specific *nomos* of a field regulates the distribution of capital, and thus the power inside a field, as well as the access to a field. This means, the definition of the borders of a field, what is inside or outside of it, and who is in and who is not. With regard to the Roman-Catholic Church and also to Judaism, this seems to be clear. With regard to Islam, it is not at all, as belonging to Islam is determined by the individual profession of faith in uttering the *shahāda*. At first instance, the observance of the four other pillars of Islam is secondary, as long as the relevant person does not openly deny the necessity of their observance, or of any other obligatory tradition. This, however, has changed through the spread of discourses and practices of *takfīr*, declaring someone an infidel, inspired by Wahhabism (or Salafism, as some would call it). So, it seems to me that inside an Islamic field there are sub-fields to which access is regulated by specific techniques of the self.

For Bourdieu the hierarchisation inside a field, which is produced by power struggles between the religious professionals, is central for the inner structure of a religious field. In my view, this does not hold true for Islamic fields and spiritual capital. The placing and valorising of specific forms of Islamic spiritual capital differ even inside Islamic religious fields. Therefore, I speak of them in the plural.

Fields – religious, political, economic, etc. – are not isolated from each other, but overlap: On the one hand, as fields as such, on the other hand by the moving of individuals across fields. Thereby, individuals can invest their various forms of capital in a variety of fields and valorise them.[6] Bourdieu ignores the interac-

---

5   See also Schrode 2010: 84-102 for shifts of authority and the strategies of legitimation in Sunni laymen's discourses.

6   Cf. the reflections of Paul Veyne on categorising and judging (Veyne 1988: 8, 15, 17).

tions between non-religious or other religious groups or fields with a particular religious field, which has to be taken into account in a multi-religious context.

BAD KREUZNACH, OR ISLAMIC FIELDS IN A SMALL TOWN IN SOUTH-WEST GERMANY

Over recent decades, differentiated Islamic fields have emerged in Germany, basically out of the particularities of Muslim presence in a diaspora. The Islamic community as a united *umma* is, of course, a common *topos*. However, this is usually not apparent to many Muslims, with the exception of the pilgrimage to Mecca. In Europe Muslims are – quite often for the first time – confronted with a multitude of Muslim traditions and cultures, thus experiencing the plurality of Islam in their daily life.

On the one hand therefore, we find ethnically, linguistically, and culturally homogeneous mosques, that comprise basically compatriots and their descendants. Nevertheless, these mosques are attended, of course, also by other Muslims from the neighbourhoods, for lack of alternatives or out of convenience. If the particular groups are large, further differentiations emerge following religious-political orientations, as happens with the Muslims of Turkish origin that reproduced the religious schisms of Turkey in Europe. Pro-Kemalists and anti-Kemalists were – and still are, to some extent – opposed. Groups that were already religiously active in their countries of origin (in most cases in opposition to the political system, e.g. the Kemalist state in Turkey) were the first to start mosque associations, such as the Millî Görüş, the Süleymancı (Verband der islamischen Kulturzentren, VIKZ), or Muslim Brothers from the Arab world. The pro-Kemalist associations started mainly as workers' associations, providing support and places in which to feel at home in the strangeness of Europe. Only after changes in migration policies in the early 1970s did religious activities emerge, leading finally to the establishment of Diyanet İşleri Türk İslam Birliği (DITIB) as the European branch of the Turkish Office for Religious Affairs. Events in the Islamic world, such as the Islamic Revolution in Iran in 1979, led to new dynamics in the Islamic fields in Europe and provoked further differentiations, like the Kaplan movement ("Caliphate State").

This even had repercussions in the small town of Bad Kreuznach. Located approximately 80 km north-west of Frankfurt and 40 km from Mainz, the capital of Rhineland-Palatinate, Bad Kreuznach is a district capital *(Kreisstadt)* on the river Nahe with 45 000 inhabitants. Due to the importance of the surrounding countryside, it has a better infrastructure than most other towns of this size. During the nineteenth century, Bad Kreuznach was a famous spa frequented by an international wealthy public. Today, the spa's activities are more modest in size and importance. Surrounded by vineyards and forests, Bad Kreuznach has also some industry and small and middle size enterprises. The French tire producer Michelin has a factory here. Until the year 2000 it also hosted an American garrison.[7]

Some Muslims left the main Turkish mosque, attracted first by Millî Görüş and its newly appointed mufti Cemaleddin Kaplan, afterwards following him into his own organisation, the later "Caliphate State", that was inspired by the Islamic state in Iran (Thielmann 2005: 158sqq.). These Muslims were not particularly revolutionary-minded. They only questioned the religious legitimacy of the board of their former association. They tried to rally followers with the call: "True Muslims pray with us!" Here, the process of how newcomers want to conquer their place in a field, described above, becomes visible: in our case by a subversive propaganda of a return to 'true Islam' and an effective engagement for the re-Islamisation of Turkey. In Bad Kreuznach – as well as in other places, as has been shown by Schiffauer (2000) – the question of power remained open for quite a while, before the Kaplan movement steadily radicalised and then became subsequently (self-)marginalised. Thus, the older Turkish Workers' Association (*Türkischer Arbeiterverein*) – perhaps also due to its alliance with the then founded DITIB and the resulting access to resources of the Turkish state – remained at the end the most powerful player in the Islamic field of Bad Kreuznach. This was confounded by the presentation of the mosque as primary in Bad Kreuznach.

Individual religiosity plays no role in most cases, with the exception of associations with a strong religious profile, like Millî Görüş, the VIKZ, or the Caliphate State. Compatriot-oriented mosque associations primarily support the social life of an ethnic community, offering social services, maintaining contact with the country of origin, and providing a meeting place to feel at home. Religious services are often restricted to the ritual prayer (sometimes not even held regularly), the celebration of the Islamic feasts, and religious education for children. Activists as well as visitors share a certain religious disposition, oriented towards preserving traditional religious forms. The religious personnel, e.g. the *hocas* coming from Turkey, are responsible for the preservation of these traditions. This means that in most cases the laymen do not compete with the religious professionals.

From the mid-1990s on, the established associations were again challenged by emerging new mosques, initiated by Muslims of non-Turkish origin who no

---

7   For a detailed description of Bad Kreuznach and its settings see Thielmann 2005. For the situation in Rhineland-Palatinate see Thielmann 2011.

longer wanted to pray in a Turkish dominated environment and listen to sermons in Turkish. They therefore searched for like-minded Muslims to set up their own supranational mosque. Furthermore, they also wanted to live more religiously. Here, processes of a religious resurgence became visible, not only among Muslims (Eickelman/Piscatori 1996: 142), but also in other religions worldwide. The new mosque in Bad Kreuznach – programmatically named Al-Hijra, reminiscent of the exodus of the first Muslims under Muhammad to Yathrib/Medina, the beginning of the Islamic calendar[8] – gathered around a shared understanding of Islam and how it should be practiced. Fraternity is valued and lived, as is personal religiosity. Both the individual and the collective in this mosque dispose of particular religious dispositions.

Interaction and contact between the mosques in Bad Kreuznach used to be a rare occurrence, but recent German public and political discourses on Islam have generally forced Muslim associations to establish joint structures and cooperation. In Bad Kreuznach, this particular situation may be caused by the monopolisation of public attention (and recognition) by the DITIB mosque. Nonetheless, a young activist of Pakistani origin tried to bring Al-Hijra mosque into the game by publishing articles about this mosque in the leading local newspaper.

Supra-national mosques are not *eo ipso* isolationistic. In any case, they have to internally negotiate new forms of Islamic practices. These forms are, in my view, necessarily de-culturalised, de-nationalised, and de-historicised to avoid conflict. This leads in many cases to an orientation toward the time of the Prophet Muhammad as the example of the perfect Islamic practice. Thus, the religious profile of and the lived religiosity in these mosques are higher than that of the average compatriot-oriented mosque. Adding to that is the fact that quite often these supranational mosques are initiated and run by charismatic figures, leading sometimes to frictions and break-offs. Some of these mosques also develop into 'family mosques' with totally new forms of collective religious action, no longer male dominated, and with German as the *lingua franca*.

Of course, the just mentioned imitation of the Prophet's life, as transmitted by the *sunna* and the *sīra* (biography) literature, in the true sense of an *imitatio Muhammadi* [sic] (Schimmel 1989: 27sq.), is known as a practice right from the

---

8   Some members explained the name to me as referring to their situation as migrants. However, the most common understanding is that of 'true believers leaving the city of the infidel'.

beginning of Islam.[9] Muhammad is the "beautiful example" (Schimmel 1989: 21-50, esp. 23-28). In the mystic tradition this plays a role, too. Fritz Meier mentions examples from Cairo from the sixteenth and seventeenth centuries (Meier 2005: 337) and points to the Tijaniyya (Meier 2005: 349-356) and the Sanusiyya, that turn the imitation to the political (id., 364). In the eighteenth and nineteenth century, Indian mystic movements called themselves explicitly "muhammadī-ye chālis [khālis, J. T.]", "aufrichtige Muhammadaner" (Schimmel 1989: 192).

In her research on the Süleymancı (VIKZ), Gerdien Jonker observed a re-actualisation of this Indian tradition, the Naqshbandi Mujaddidi, transmitted via Istanbul and then brought to Europe by Turkish migrants. Here, the imitation of the Prophet Muhammad is first of all an inner working, expressing itself in behaviour and speech, not in clothes or the shape of the beard (Jonker 2006: 80sqq.).

In sharp contrast, for today's so-called neo-Salafiyya or the 'Salafis'/ 'Salafists'[10] the meticulous – also bodily, and therefore visible and tangible – imitation of the Prophet is of central importance. Here, we see particular dresses, sometimes turbans and sticks, or specific forms of beards.

For me, however, the term 'Salafi' is highly problematic, because it is imprecise. The common classification established by an international consensus is a triple one: the purist or quietist (abstaining from politics), the political activist, and the jihadist (making also use of physical violence, even terror). But since spring 2012 developments in the Arab world prove this classification, which is particularly based on a political (or even security) perspective, to be too simplistic, if not outright wrong (see Lacroix 2012 or McCant 2012). In Egypt, 'Salafis' from all three sub-divisions have founded political parties competing with each other in parliamentary elections and winning seats. According to the 'pure' scientific model, this should never have happened.[11]

Furthermore, while the sheer outer appearance, e.g. the dress, cannot be a criterion, neither can the Qur'an and the *sunna*, the only sources of guidance and judgement. Here, a variety of groups join in who are in fierce opposition and strong, sometimes violent, animosity with each other. So, some German groups

---

9   The term 'the Muhammadan way' *(tarīqa muhammadīya)* appears as a book title first in the sixteenth century: Radtke 1999: 36. Thus, it seems plausible to assume that the term was not widely used as a proper concept before that date.

10 For current research on Salafism see Meijer 2009, also Amghar 2011.

11 There is also a general narrative of the genealogy of Salafism which has to be questioned (cf. Lauzière 2010).

calling themselves *ahl as-sunna*[12] (or similar) vigorously attack 'Salafi' groups which they call 'Wahhabi' or 'Takfiri' (from Arabic *takfīr*: to declare someone an infidel). They put forward traditional scholarship and the diverse and pluralistic Islamic intellectual history against the reductionistic Salafi black-and-white. Also in fierce opposition to Salafism and the Muslim Brotherhood is the so-called Habashiyya or al-Ahbash, the 'Ethiopians', a group originating from Lebanon. Their official name is Association of Islamic Charitable Projects (AICP) and they are inspired by the teachings of Sheikh 'Abdallah ibn Muhammad al-Harari al-Habashi (1910-2008).[13] All these groups opposing Salafism claim to follow the 'Muhammadan path' as well.

Criteria of differentiation can then only be their position concerning dogmatic faith, *'aqīda*, and a detailed analysis of their concrete everyday practices related to religion and piety as well as their dogmatic confessions – and not their supposed stance towards politics in general or democracy and elections in particular. Bernard Haykel (2009) seems to point in the same direction.

For a 'Muhammadan way of life' sound knowledge is needed: peer group learning and self-studying therefore play an important – and valued – role. The Internet is also gaining more and more influence.

MUSLIM TECHNIQUES OF THE SELF

The imitation of the life of the Prophet creates an Islamic practice which becomes manifest in a figure that I have so far (e.g. Thielmann 2005, 171sqq.) called 'perfect Muslim', following Klein-Hessling/Nökel/Werner (1999: 20). Now, I propose to give up coining a term in 'object language' and instead simply describe practices. The Muslim actor – as one who forms herself or himself actively as Muslim – can originate from a traditional or a non-practicing Muslim family, be a 'born-again' Muslim (revert), or a convert.

The former *amīra* of the Muslim Women Students Group in Mainz serves as an example for a Muslim with a traditional Muslim background. She grew up in a pious traditional family of Kurdish origin and was the first in her family to

---

12 See e.g. the website www.madrasah.de (accessed 13 December 2012) of the group "Minhaj Ahl as-Sunna".

13 See for the Ethiopian background Desplat (2010: esp. 171-182, 196-206, 215-222). For the doctrinal aspects of the conflict see Hamzeh/Dekmejian 1996 and Kabha/Erlich 2006. Websites of the group are www.aicp.org, or www.islami.de (accessed 13 December 2012).

study Islamic Studies *(Islamwissenschaft)* – thus Islam from the outside – and Turkology. In addition, she followed a two-year teaching programme of the Islamologisches Institut[14] of Amir Zaidan in Frankfurt, now based in Vienna (i.e. Islam from the inside). After puberty she decided to wear the hijab and to study Islam. She became an authority on religious issues both in her family and in her peer group. She took care of the religious education of her younger sisters and brothers and of the correct fulfilment of religious duties of the whole family. She tries to live 'true Islam' (cf. Amir-Moazami/Salvatore 2003: 59), overcoming traditional religious practices and habits and basing her practices only on Qur'an and *sunna*, instead of referring to cultural traditions.

The second type is represented by a young activist of Al-Hijra: Born in Germany, he grew up in a non-practising Muslim family. Some experiences during puberty and meeting a charismatic Muslim brought him to actively embrace the – until then neglected – religion of his parents and to study Islam. He can be called a 'born-again' Muslim, someone "reverting to Islam" (Jacobson 2011: 297sqq.).

The third type is the convert. The case of the Swiss convert Gibril (see Leuenberger, this volume), is exemplary. Through intense work on his inner self and bodily appearance, he totally altered not only his outer appearance, i.e. his dress (long white *qamīs*, turban, long coat) and form of beard, but also the way he speaks and behaves, making use of religious phrases in Arabic. This total shift of references, of social relations, and of dress and behaviour makes him a "stranger in his own homeland" (ibid.).

For many Muslims – traditional, reverts or converts alike – Islam functions as a source of meaning, pride, and guidance in life. The 'true Islam' becomes an identity marker of individuals and collectives. The pious lifestyle of these Muslims which resembles the Weberian rational lifestyle and inner-worldly asceticism, provides them with enormous symbolic capital – by valorisation of their spiritual capital accumulated through various techniques of the self.

With "techniques of the self" Michel Foucault (1993: 203) describes techniques allowing the individual to form his body, his soul, his thinking, and his behaviour by his own means and to change them, so that he reaches a state of perfection, of happiness, of supra-natural powers etc. Among these techniques are those who address the discovery and formulation of the truth about oneself, of utmost importance (id., 204). In Christianity, this eventually led to differenti-

---

14 Founded in late 2000, this private institute offers from the beginning courses and seminars in various towns in Germany, now extended to Austria. The students have to pay for the lessons and pass written examinations. See www.islamologie.info (accessed 13 December 2012).

ated confession practices (id., 210-221). In Islam, however, confession seems generally to be of lesser importance. Only in small strongly religious groups this may play a role.[15] The care for oneself[16] – for body and soul –, however, through the meticulous observation of the Sharia and the practices of the Prophet Muhammad to enable oneself to pass the Last Judgement and enter paradise is more central for Muslims. For Foucault (2000: 155), it is an attitude, "une certaine manière d'envisager les choses, de se tenir dans le monde". This requires a certain attentive self-perception and "actions que l'on exerce de soi sur soi, actions par lesquelles on se prend en charge, par lesquelles on se modifie, par lesquelles on se purifie et par lesquelles on se transforme et on se transfigure" (ibid.). Here, Islamic dressing habits, fasting, prayers with prosternations etc. come immediately to mind.

Power relations are crucial: Foucault proposes to make forms of resistance against various forms of power the starting point of an economy of power relations (Foucault 1982: 780). This economy of power relations defines the status of individuals as difference and is linked to the way knowledge circulates and functions, also in relation to power, what he calls "régime du savoir" (id., 781).

With regard to the young Muslims presented above, this means distancing themselves from the power of traditional Muslim or familial authorities as well as to the stigmatisations by the non-Muslim majority society. The young Muslims work in three fields on themselves: dress and body, knowledge, and religious practices (Jacobsen 2011: 295-359).

In the field of dress and body, pudency ('aura) and decency for men and women are important concepts. Body contact between men and women, such as shaking hands, is avoided. Women wear the headscarf (hijab) in such a way that not a single hair is visible. The language is formal, friendly, decent, the voice not loud. Good manners are important.

Knowledge is acquired by self-study and by peer group learning. Knowledge is sometimes more widely shared as in the case of the young revert, through lectures, seminars, and publications.

The observance of the 'ibādāt, the religious duties of man towards God, define the religious practices (see Jacobsen 2011: 329sqq.; Schrode 2010). Thus, these young Muslims prioritise the five daily prayers in everyday life (cf. Jouili 2012). Furthermore, additional fasting on a regular basis beyond the duty of fasting in Ramadan is quite often normal practice for them. The aim of these practices is to bring knowledge and everyday practices together and to form oneself

---

15 To my knowledge, the Gülen circles have some practices resembling confession and penance (personal information by Levent Tezcan).

16 Latin cura sui, in Greek epimeleia heautou (Foucault 2000: 145).

as Muslim. *Da'wa*, the propagation of the faith, thus becomes more and more a testimony, implicating the whole personality, given to oneself as a discovery and formulation of the truth about oneself (Foucault 1993: 204) and to both the Muslim and non-Muslim public. Hereby, the Muslim *dā'ī* (the propagandist) also takes care of him or herself by fulfilling a religious duty that requires a certain habitus to be trustworthy.

The dominant discourse, however, influences Muslims and Muslim groups. The Muslim techniques of the self just described transmit through and in individuals what Foucault describes as "gouvernementalité" (Foucault 2004; Tezcan 2008).[17] This means a complex set of regulations of society and individuals, consisting of politics and policies of a government and administration, but also of the power relations between individuals (e.g. between a teacher and his pupils, in a family) or in the individual itself (by interiorised norms governing the body and its expressions and the soul, leading to a subjectivisation).[18] Through techniques of the self specific religious dispositions among individual Muslims emerge which lead to the accumulation of spiritual capital and determine the place and status of actors in the Islamic fields.

UMMA – EURO-ISLAM – CULTURAL HERITAGE: UNITY AND DIVERSITY IN THE ISLAMIC FIELDS

These Muslims, possessing particular religious dispositions, are the individual, the supranational mosques the institutionalised promoters of changing beliefs and practices of faith. Traditions and habits from Muslim countries are refused if they are not rooted in Qur'an and *sunna*. The division between Sunna and Shia seems often to be irrelevant. The idea of the *umma*, experienced particularly in supranational mosques, becomes central. The exclusive focal point is a de-culturalised, de-historicised, and de-nationalised 'true Islam' – and this term 'true Islam' appears all over the Islamic world as a concept.[19] This does not mean a "Euro-Islam" as a normative construct (see Tibi 2000) postulating the emergence of new Islamic

---

17 But there can also be resistance by individuals to attempts to govern them in such a way (see Leuenberger, this volume, on Swiss convert Gibril).

18 For an unconventional introduction to Foucault's thinking in this field, see Veyne 2010: 113-135.

19 See Reichmuth 1998: 242-247 for Nigeria, Schulz 2008 for Mali, or Desplat 2010 for Ethiopia.

concepts and practices, informed by European enlightened ideas and practices and eventually leading to a specific European form of Islam.

The discourses over 'true Islam' in the Islamic fields in Germany, however, are most closely interwoven with global Islamic discourses and not restricted to Germany or Europe (see Al-Azmeh 2009; Conermann 1996; Salvatore 1997). Perhaps, we could speak of 'Islamic religion of German culture' with regard to these groups of Muslims, as German increasingly becomes the *lingua franca*. These Muslims – and not only the converts among them – are in most cases culturally, socially, and politically embedded in German customs and habits, even if in some cases merely in a constructed and performed opposition to them. Nevertheless the main stress in the supranational mosques lays on religion and the frame of reference is the global *umma* (see also Schrode 2010: 41-52), with a variety of concrete behaviour.

However, among the Turks of the DITIB mosque in Bad Kreuznach, the situation is different: They see themselves as Germans of Turkish origin who want to preserve their Turkish culture by religious instruction for their children. Here, culture and religion are inseparably mixed, with the national culture as reference.

THE STRUCTURING *NOMOI* OF THE ISLAMIC FIELDS

To sum up: the *tarīqa muhammadīya* is one structuring *nomos* of the Islamic fields and a clear marker of a specific type of 'being Islamic'. To follow the Muhammadan path through techniques of the self allows for the accumulation of individual and group-related spiritual capital that can be invested into both the Islamic fields and – when transformed into symbolic capital – the interactions with the non-Muslim German public. Thereby, recognition and respect inside and outside of Islamic fields can be acquired. To give an example: The young man mentioned above as a revert active in the supranational mosque Al-Hijra in Bad Kreuznach has a visibly pious lifestyle, even if he is not wearing oriental Islamic dress. This gives him credentials in his mosque community and invests him with spiritual capital, so that they trust him to write articles about the mosque and some of its leading figures for a local newspaper.

The mosque thus becomes visible for a larger (mostly non-Muslim) public and acquires some respectability for non-Muslims and Muslims alike by being presented in a recognised newspaper. The young man, on the other hand, could by this operation increase his personal symbolic capital in the public sphere and in the Muslim community and establish himself as an important local interlocutor on Islamic issues.

For supranational mosques this spiritual and symbolic capital compensates for the lack of economic capital and of professional personnel and theologians. It allows them to preserve their flock and to attract (perhaps) new followers, thus to expand their spiritual outreach. Hereby, they might also develop their economic basis.

The second *nomos* of the Islamic fields lays in the degree of proximity and distance to the concept of *umma* – understood as the community of the first believers and therefore as the prototype of a righteously lived Islam. The scale goes from equating Islam with one's own culture – this is at the far end from the idea of *umma* – to the identification of a de-culturalised, de-historicised, and de-nationalised 'true Islam' with Islam, and that means an orientation towards the *umma,* as an idea above time.

The *tarīqa muhammadiyya* is a *nomos* aiming first of all at the transformation of individuals by techniques of the self and thereby investing them with spiritual capital and placing them accordingly in the Islamic fields. The second *nomos,* the proximity or distance to the concept of *umma,* situates in my view specific groups of Muslims – aggregations of Muslims following the 'Muhammadan path' to various degrees or even not at all – on particular places in the Islamic fields, because *umma* as a concept of the ideal community of Muslims makes sense only in relation to collectives.

Hereby, new forms of lived Islam emerge in Germany and Europe, shaped by Muslim actors forming themselves by specific techniques of the self in reaction to post-modern and post-secular[20] living conditions in the context of non-Muslim majority societies. Contrary to common perceptions, even the appearance of 'oriental dresses' among these Muslims, such as in the case of the Swiss convert Gibril, does not mean a return to the Middle Ages, but is a quite modern valorisation of individual and collective concepts of life-worlds.

REFERENCES

Al-Azmeh, Aziz (2009): *Islams and modernities,* 3rd ed., London: Verso.

Amberg, Thomas (2009): *Auf dem Weg zu neuen Prinzipien islamischer Ethik: Muhammed Shahrour und die Suche nach religiöser Erneuerung in Syrien,* Würzburg: Ergon.

---

20 See Habermas 2008: "Today, public consciousness in Europe can be described in terms of a 'post-secular society' to the extent that at present it still has to 'adjust itself to the continued existence of religious communities in an increasingly secularized environment'", citing himself.

Amghar, Samir (2011): *Le salafisme d'aujourd'hui: Mouvements sectaires en Occident*, Paris: Michalon.

Amir-Moazami, Schirin / Salvatore, Armando (2003): "Gender, generation, and the reform of tradition: From Muslim majority societies to Western Europe", in: Allievi, Stefano / Nielsen, Jørgen S. (eds), *Muslim networks and transnational communities in and across Europe*, Leiden: Brill, pp. 52-77.

Bourdieu, Pierre (1971a): "Une interprétation de la théorie de la religion selon Max Weber", in: *Archives européennes de sociologie,* 12:1, pp. 3-21.

— (1971b): "Genèse et structure du champ religieux", in: *Revue française de sociologie,* 12:3, pp. 295-334.

— (2001a): *Das politische Feld: Zur Kritik der politischen Vernunft,* Konstanz: UVK.

— (2001b): *Langage et pouvoir symbolique,* Paris: Fayard.

Brubaker, Rogers (1985): "Rethinking classical theory: The sociological vision of Pierre Bourdieu", in: *Theory and Society,* 14, pp. 745-775.

Conermann, Stephan (1996): *Mustafa Mahmud (geb. 1921) und der modifizierte islamische Diskurs im modernen Ägypten,* Berlin: Klaus Schwarz.

Cook, Michael (2000): *Commanding right and forbidding wrong in Islamic thought,* Cambridge: Cambridge University Press.

Desplat, Patrick (2010): *Heilige Stadt – Stadt der Heiligen: Ambivalenzen und Kontroversen islamischer Heiligkeit in Harar, Äthiopien,* Köln: Köppe.

Dianteill, Erwan (2002): "Pierre Bourdieu et la religion: Synthèse critique d'une synthèse critique", in: *Archives des Sciences Sociales des Religions,* 118:2, pp. 5-19.

Eickelman, Dale F. / Piscatori, James (1996): *Muslim politics,* Princeton NJ: Princeton University Press.

Foucault, Michel (1982): "The subject and power", in: *Critical Inquiry,* 8:4, pp. 777-795.

— (1993): "About the beginning of the hermeneutics of the self: Two lectures at Dartmouth", in: *Political Theory,* 21:2, pp. 198-227.

— (2000): "Cours du 6 Janvier 1982", in: *Cités,* 2, pp. 143-178.

— (2004): *Geschichte der Gouvernementalität I: Sicherheit, Territorium, Bevölkerung,* Frankfurt a. M.: Suhrkamp.

Gräf, Bettina / Skovgaard-Petersen, Jakob (eds) (2009): *The global mufti: The phenomenon of Yusuf al-Qaradawi,* London/New York: Hurst / Columbia University Press.

Habermas, Jürgen (2008): Notes on a post-secular society, http://www. signandsight.com/features/1714.html (accessed 12 April 2013) [German original: "Die Dialektik der Säkularisierung", in: *Blätter für deutsche und internationale Politik,* 2008:4, pp. 33-46].

Hamzeh, A. Nizar / Dekmejian, R. Hrair (1996): "A Sufi response to political Islamism: Al-Ahbash of Lebanon", in: *International Journal of Middle East
Studies*, 28:2, pp. 217-229.

Haykel, Bernard (2009): "On the nature of Salafi thought and action", in: Meijer,
Roel (ed.), *Global Salafism: Islam's new religious mouvement*, London:
Hurst, pp. 33-57.

Jacobsen, Christine M. (2011): *Islamic traditions and Muslim youth in Norway*,
Leiden: Brill.

Jonker, Gerdien, 2006: "The evolution of the Naqshbandi-Mujaddidi: Sulay-
mançis in Germany", in: Malik, Jamal / Hinnell, John (eds), *Sufism in the
West*, London: Routledge.

Jouili, Jeanette S. (2012): "Von den Schwierigkeiten, beten zu lernen: Ṣalāt als
'moralische' Selbsttechnologie praktizierender muslimischer Frauen", in:
Schrode, Paula / Simon, Udo (eds), *Die Sunna leben: Zur Dynamik islamischer Religionspraxis in Deutschland*, Würzburg: Ergon, pp. 67-85.

Kabha, Mustafa / Erlich, Haggai (2006): "Al-Ahbash and Wahhabiyya: Interpretations of Islam", in: *International Journal of Middle East Studies*, 38:4, pp.
519-538.

Klein-Hessling, Ruth / Nökel, Sigrid / Werner, Karin (1999): "Weibliche Mikro-
politiken und die Globalisierung des Islam", in: Klein-Hessling, Ruth / Nökel, Sigrid / Werner, Karin (eds), *Der neue Islam der Frauen: Weibliche Le-
benspraxis in der globalisierten Moderne – Fallstudien aus Afrika, Asien
und Europa*, Bielefeld: Transcript, pp. 11-34.

Lacroix, Stéphane (2012): *Sheikhs and politicians: Inside the new Egyptian
Salafism*, Doha: Brookings Doha Center (Policy Briefing, June 2012).

Lauzière, Henri (2010): "The construction of Salafiyya: Reconsidering Salafism
from the perspective of conceptual history", in: *International Journal of
Middle East Studies*, 42:3, pp. 369-389.

McCant, William (2012): *The lesser of two evils: The Salafi turn to party politics
in Egypt*, Washington, DC: Saban Center for Middle East Policy at Brookings (Middle East memo Nr. 23, May 2012).

Meier, Fritz (2005): *Bemerkungen zur Mohammedverehrung: Teil II: Die
Tāṣliya in sufischen Zusammenhängen*, ed. by Bernd Radtke, Leiden: Brill.

Meijer, Roel (ed.) (2009): *Global Salafism: Islam's new religious mouvement*,
London: Hurst.

Radtke, Bernd (1999): "De betekenis van de Ṭarîqa Muḥammadiyya in de islami-
tische mystiek van de 18e en 19e eeuw", in: Buitelaar, Marjo / Ter Haar, Johan
(eds): *Mystiek: het andere gezicht van de islam*, Bussum: continho, pp. 35-44.

Reichmuth, Stefan (1998): *Islamische Bildung und soziale Integration in Ilorin
(Nigeria) seit ca. 1800*, Münster: Lit.

Salvatore, Armando (1997): *Islam and the political discourse of modernity*, Reading: Ithaca Press.

Schiffauer, Werner (2000): *Die Gottesmänner: Türkische Islamisten in Deutschland. Eine Studie zur Herstellung religiöser Evidenz*, Frankfurt a. M.: Suhrkamp.

Schimmel, Annemarie (1989): *Und Muhammad ist Sein Prophet: Die Verehrung des Propheten in der islamischen Frömmigkeit*, 2nd improved ed., München: Diederichs.

Schrode, Paula (2010): *Sunnitisch-islamische Diskurse zu Halal-Ernährung: Konstituierung religiöser Praxis und sozialer Positionierung unter Muslimen in Deutschland*, Würzburg: Ergon.

Schulz, Dorothea E. (2008): "(Re)turning to proper Muslim practice: Islamic moral renewal and women's conflicting assertions of Sunni identity in urban Mali", in: *Africa Today*, 54:4, pp. 21-43.

Spielhaus, Riem (2011): *Wer ist hier Muslim? Die Entwicklung eines islamischen Bewusstseins in Deutschland zwischen Selbstidentifikation und Fremdzuschreibung*, Würzburg: Ergon.

Tezcan, Levent (2008): "Governmentality, pastoral care and integration", in: Al-Hamarneh, Ala / Thielmann, Jörn (eds), *Islam and Muslims in Germany*, Leiden: Brill, pp. 119-132.

Thielmann, Jörn (2003): *Nasr Ḥāmid Abū Zaid und die wiedererfundene ḥisba: Šarī'a und qānūn im heutigen Ägypten*, Würzburg: Ergon.

— (2005): "The shaping of Islamic fields in Europe – A case study in Southwest Germany", in: Nökel, Sigrid / Tezcan, Levent (eds), *Islam and the new Europe: Challenge for continuity or chance for change?*, Bielefeld: Transcript, pp. 152-177.

— (2011): "Von der Vollbeschäftigung bis zur Islamischen Revolution und darüberhinaus: Muslime in der Pfalz", in: *Mitteilungen des Historischen Vereins der Pfalz*, 109, pp. 303-310.

Tibi, Bassam (2000): *Der Islam und Deutschland: Muslime in Deutschland*, Stuttgart/München: Deutsche Verlags-Anstalt.

van Bruinessen, Martin / Allievi, Stefano (eds) (2011): *Producing Islamic knowledge: Transmission and dissemination in Western Europe*, London/ New York: Routledge.

Verter, Bradford (2003): "Spiritual capital: Theorizing religion with Bourdieu against Bourdieu", in: *Sociological Theory*, 21:2, pp. 150-174.

Veyne, Paul (1988): "Conduites sans croyance et œuvres d'art sans spectateurs", in: *Diogène*, 143, pp. 3-22.

— (2010): *Foucault – Der Philosoph als Samurai*, Stuttgart: Philipp Reclam jun.

Part III

The many facing the 'other' (within)

The many facing the 'other' (within)

Andreas Tunger-Zanetti

If socially and politically relevant debates on Islam are taking place, this does not only imply some overlapping of various ideas about 'Islam', but also the existence of actors acting under certain epistemic conditions, as has been outlined by Samuel Behloul in the introduction to this volume. Since there is debate and not unison, there must be incongruity between positions articulated, be it due to a difference with part of the epistemic conditions, to the idea about the issue, or to differing interests. Part III of this volume sets out to analyse how specific actors or actor groups produce their positions and how the incongruities between them develop in the process of social practice.

'Islam' as topic for these debates has long been unmasked as an essentialised projection. "What I read about Islam in the media – that's not me", a young adult practising Muslim told me once. This feeling, widespread among Muslims in Switzerland, had a remarkable consequence in the run-up to the Swiss minaret vote: Muslims did not participate in the debate because they had the impression that this debate was not really about them. It was only after three years of public debate of Islam and five weeks before the minaret vote that two dozen young Muslims founded the Islamischer Zentralrat Schweiz (IZRS, Islamic Central Council Switzerland) to put something against the perceived lethargy and subservience of the existing umbrella organisations. Things went differently and started earlier in Austria and in Denmark as two of our chapters show. But even there the debates on Islam were not initiated by Muslims; certain Muslim actors just chose to participate in the specific constellation of the debate.

Therefore the question remains: Who, if not primarily Muslims, is debating 'Islam' in Western Europe? How are they doing it? And returning to 'the Muslims': Who among them gets involved in the debate, and in what way?

It is in the nature of the debate on Islam that every actor tries to construct his own homogeneous 'we' against an allegedly homogeneous 'other'. Under the conditions of liberal democracy competing actors offer competing versions of these constructions in order to mark specific positions. These positions are tested in elections and in the Swiss case also in frequent referenda. The preliminary character of any results yielded by a democratic system helps to put into perspective what appears as a majority on one occasion; inevitably, alliances will have shifted in the next poll. Therefore, in the context of debates on Islam, there is no such thing as a uniform 'majority society'. There is constant discussion and adjusting of positions among and within political parties, parliaments, governments, law courts, media, and civil society organisations including religious communities.

The struggle over the definition of the societal self confers the debate its importance and its totalising character. Therefore, everybody is under pressure to position himself in this totalising debate. Muslims, irrespective of their personal religious preferences, do not escape this logic, which is why they are included among the actors figuring in the following chapters.

The chapters in this part have selected varying combinations of the possible frames and actors just enumerated, and they analyse different forms of interactions among them, observable in publications, public speech, campaigning, practice, laws and regulations, and reflected by the media, direct observation or in surveys.

Austria is unique among the Western-European states for counting Islam among the officially recognised religions on its territory since 1912. This remnant of the multi-ethnic Habsburg Empire fell into oblivion for decades, but was rediscovered in the 1960s when Muslims were present again, and in growing numbers, in what was now the Republic of Austria. At this point Farid Hafez scrutinises how different Muslim groups, composed along ethnical or ideological lines, began struggling for predominance within this form offered by the hazards of history, and how this struggle has always taken into account broader societal positions towards the Muslim community, long before the typical debate on Islam developed in the 1990s. Contrary to what one could have expected, this unique legal frame, according to Hafez, has not led to a 'churchisation' of Austrian Islam. Rather, the Islamische Glaubensgemeinschaft in Österreich as the official representative of Austrian Islam fulfils just "the function of a religious interest group towards the state and the society, while religious life in the narrow sense of the word still is a domain of the Muslim organisations [at the local level, A. T.-Z.]".

Compared to Austria's Muslims who had their constitutionally secured shelter when hit by rough xenophobic winds, Muslims in Denmark in 2005-2006 faced a sudden, big storm in the plain. As Lene Kühle argues, the cartoon crisis triggered or accelerated several developments: For one thing it led to a securitisation of the political debate and state action in Denmark. For another thing it forced all sorts of people to take a position for or against the publication of the cartoons, for or against the religious sensibilities of Muslims and lifted the value of freedom of expression to a much more prominent place than before. Finally, it led to the formation of new Muslim organisations and to a more explicit search for 'representatives' of the Muslim community. Where the practice of the state towards corporative Muslim ambitions and demands had been inconsistent and somewhat random before the cartoon crisis, it became much more self-reflexive, coherent and focused.

The Swiss case is examined from different angles in the three following contributions. While the life of Muslims in Switzerland is similar in many respects to that in Denmark or Austria, the incorporation regime differs considerably. It is especially marked by a federal system which leaves it to the 26 cantons to organise domains like education or church-state relations in their own way. Some competences such as cemeteries or certain aspects of schooling are even regulated at the municipal level. At the same time, political debates are mostly conducted on a scale transgressing cantonal borders to encompass a whole linguistic region or the whole national territory. Amplified by the media, debates with a totalising tendency are quick to keep busy parliaments and authorities of more than one municipality or canton.

An indispensable perspective is therefore opened by Marius Rohrer's case study on how authorities and politics in Basel try to cope with Muslim parents who refuse to let their daughters participate in compulsory swimming lessons in public schools. Rohrer shows what concepts the actors use in order to grasp the 'problem' generated by diversity. Interestingly, they see the issue not exclusively in religious or 'cultural', but also in economic terms. Moreover, the systems theoretical and functionalist approach allows the author to show that because of the clash of different systems logics within the Swiss frame the 'problem' must almost inevitably remain unsolved.

Another perspective is highlighted by Andreas Tunger-Zanetti's contribution on the popular initiative to ban the construction of minarets. It focuses on the dynamics linking the single, local case to the nation-wide debate in the run-up to a federal referendum. The media and their very unequal use by different actor groups play an important role. However, this is not sufficient to explain the surprise result of the minaret vote. Tunger-Zanetti argues that the uninformed, ambivalent and uncertain attitude of a majority of Swiss citizens, including the elites, towards religion in general is necessary to understand the actual development in the minaret case.

The triad of Swiss perspectives is completed by Matteo Gianni's assessment of integration policy. In common understanding, the 'generalised Muslim' as the paradigmatic 'other' is of course the ideal-type 'foreigner' from whom 'integration' is demanded – although official statistics tell us that a quickly rising portion of Muslims in Switzerland (some 35 per cent in 2010) already hold the Swiss citizenship. Again, the debate largely misses the pretended target and reveals more about societal actors than about the issue debated.

Gianni works out the inconsistencies of the prevalent model of Swiss integration policy from the angle of political theory. He shows that 'integration' in this context usually is understood as adaptation of the newcomer to Swiss norms going far beyond mere conformity to the law. While the relevant Swiss law describes integration as a process of mutual obligations, the same law distributes the burden unevenly by spelling out the obligations of the receiving society in much less specific terms than those of the foreigner. Adding to this structural imbalance, the harsh reception which is widely practiced equals actual misrecognition, thus undermining the very concept of integration. One has only to go back to Marius Rohrer's chapter to see these inner contradictions of Swiss 'integration' policy become manifest in a concrete setting. Gianni ends by proposing a processual conception of integration to limit misrecognition. Such an understanding which implies political opportunities of participation for the newcomers, he pleads, would not only conform much better to basic values of Swiss democracy and the rule of law, but also significantly enhance an integration deserving that name.

Taken together, the contributions of the third part reveal an ambivalent picture: Once the superficial similarities of labour immigration from predominantly Muslim countries are left aside, the developments in Austria, Denmark and Switzerland start under quite different historical, legal and political conditions. Depending on the specific path, the debate on Islam in each country is not the same and does not lead to the same developments. Crises such as the cartoon crisis or the minaret vote may accelerate specific developments, especially the constitution of organisations serving the articulation of so far unrecognised and unrepresented interests. Specific actor groups may learn to deal more subtly with developments which bear the risk of destructive confrontation. At the same time, it is difficult to see a learning process encompassing broad strata of society and yielding a more relaxed attitude in questions related to religion, Europe and the self.

Institutionalised Austrian Islam: One institution representing the many

Farid Hafez

Islam and Muslims in Austria

The very first Muslims recorded in Austria lived in the Pannonian lowlands (on the southeastern borders of today's Austria) between 1080 and 1250. Two major historical events shaped the current situation of Islam and Muslims in Austria today. On a legal level, it was the occupation of Bosnia-Herzegovina in 1908 by the Austrian-Hungarian Empire and the Islam-law of 1912 (Potz 2010: 387sqq.), while on a social level it was the immigration of *Gastarbeiter*,[1] cheap, male, foreign workers from Turkey in the 1960s, and later waves of immigration due to the war in Ex-Yugoslavia in the 1990s, as well as the wars in Chechnya and Iraq. Thus the number of Muslims increased from 8000 in 1971 to 77 000 in 1981, 159 000 in 1991 and 339 000 in 2001 (Fliegenschnee/Goujon/Lutz 2004). The census of 2011 did not ask about the religious belief of citizens. Currently, estimates suggest that about 500 000 Muslims live in Austria, while the Islamische Glaubensgemeinschaft in Österreich (IGGiÖ, Islamic Council of Austria) registered 125 000 members in 2011 (compared to 5500 members in 2002). By the beginning of the 1960s, Muslim intellectuals (students mainly coming from Bosnia and Arab countries) started engaging in reviving the Islam-law from 1912, which already laid the basis to "manifest their religion in public, administrate their internal affairs autonomously and establish foundations for religious, educational and charitable purposes" (Schmied/Wieshaider 2004: 203). The few young students created the Muslimische Sozialdienst in 1964, an organisation

---

1   This term is generally used in German-speaking countries for seasonal workers.

whose main aim was to gain legal recognition as a 'church' of Austria's Muslims, which happened after a long struggle with Austrian authorities in 1979 (Hafez 2012: 40-45). Austria is thus in a rather unique institutional position concerning its Muslim population, as the historically built church-state relations determine the relation of the state and Islam to a high extent (Fetzer/Soper 2004). The IGGiÖ is now one of 14 recognised churches and religious communities in the Austrian Republic (Potz 2010).

DIVERSITY OF MUSLIM GROUPS IN AUSTRIA

While the first Muslim institutions that were built in Austria were mainly functional, Muslim movements from other countries settled down later. Functional here means that they were built to meet an immediate and very specific interest. The Muslimische Sozialdienst was created in 1964 due to the increasing number of Bosnian Muslim immigrants. This institution was founded in order to support its members in this new environment. The Moslemische Studentenunion (MSU) was established in 1968 because of the rising number of Muslim students who mainly stemmed from Arab countries. Only ten to twenty years later would the Muslim movements of (mainly) Turkish origin settle down as formal organisations in Austria. The migration of Turkish *Gastarbeiter* started in 1966. The small numbers of Muslims with Turkish background who arrived before 1966 organised themselves together with Muslims of other national and ethnic backgrounds – mainly Arabs – in the MSU. A more Turkish dominated organisation in those days was the Geselliger Verein türkischer Arbeitnehmer in Wien und Umgebung, which was an association for Turkish workers (Hafez 2006: 28). But it was only after 1966 that the number of Muslims arriving from Turkey substantially increased. In 1980, the Union Islamischer Kulturzentren, which is generally associated with the Süleymancılar-movement, was established as the first legal entity of Turkish Muslim movements (Jonker 2002). Only eight years later, was the Islamische Föderation, which is connected to the Millî Görüş movement, was established. In 1990, the Turkish embassy, via its attaché for religious affairs, also established the Türkisch Islamische Union für Kulturelle und Soziale Zusammenarbeit in Österreich (ATIB; Hafez 2006: 38-50, 69sq.).[2] This does not mean that they did not exist before. Rather, informal local networks of mosque-

---

2 A very similar pattern of organisations exists in Germany, where followers and sympathisers of different Islamic movements or institutions organised themselves in the IGMG, DITIB, ADÜTDF and the VIKZ.

organisations realised the necessity of organising in formal organisations and thus creating umbrella organisations for these already existing local associations. This wave of establishing legal entities reflects the fact that the former *Gastarbeiter* brought their families to Austria and had set themselves to live there permanently. Religious life thus had to have a clear organisational basis. In 1994, after masses of refugees from Ex-Yugoslavia came to Austria, the Dachverband Bosnisch-Islamischer Vereine was founded to coordinate Muslim prayer rooms caring for the religious needs of Bosnian Muslims (Hafez 2012: 27sq.). Muslims of Arab descent had already organised themselves in the 1960s and represent only smaller groups within the field of Austrian Muslim organisations. Nowadays, Muslim organisations of Turkish origin constitute the major part of Muslim organisations. Of 260 prayer rooms, about 200 belong to these umbrella organisations.

The fact that all of these organisations were established after the IGGiÖ reveals the Muslim movements to be late starters. While the early Muslim intelligentsia created the IGGiÖ, the quantitatively largest Muslim organisations were only an adjunct of this process. The followers of the Süleymancılar, the Milliyetçi Hareket Partisi (a nationalist political group, whose sympathisers established the Türkische Föderation in Austria) as well as of the Millî Görüş indeed participated in the elections (as individuals), but did not play a leading role in coalition building and the leadership of one of the competing electoral lists. The leadership was clearly in the hands of the intelligentsia that claimed presidency over the IGGiÖ and who had built this institution up from the late 1950s. Due to the lack of human resources that were able to manoeuvre the IGGiÖ through the political landscape of Austria, the then locally organised Turkish Islamic groups only acted as supporters in the election campaign for the two presidential candidates. Two blocs competed with each other in the very first election. Trenches between the two groups were so deep that the first election, which took place in 1980, even ended in acts of violence and had to be dissolved by the police. These frictions reflected the factions existing in Turkey at that time. The Milliyetçi Hareket Partisi and the Millî Selamet Partisi – which was the name of the political party of the Millî Görüş from 1973 to 1980, followed by the Refah Partisi from 1987 to 1997 – were competing in Turkish parliamentary elections. The situation became so tense, that members of different parties even fought in the street (Kubaseck/Seufert 2006: 95sqq.). These rivalries had their effects on the situation of Austrian Muslims of Turkish descent. While the two competing blocks could not reach an agreement, Ahmad Abdelrahimsai won the elections with the votes of the Islamische Föderation, while Smail Balić, who was supported by the Union Islamischer Kulturzentren and the Türkische Föderation lost the elections (Hafez 2012: 52sqq.). Since the election system works according to the principle "the winner takes it all", a major part of Muslim organisations was excluded from sharing power – executive as well as *de facto* legislative – and played no significant role in representing the IGGiÖ from the very beginning. This situation clearly contradicted the IGGiÖ's claim, as declared in its constitution, to represent *all* Muslims living in Austria. This was also due to the concentration of power of the president. Thus it happened that the Union Islamischer Kulturzentren and the Türkische Föderation were excluded from power in the IGGiÖ until Abdelrahimsai had an apoplectic stroke (and died two years later) and a new president was elected in 1997.

It is worth mentioning that at this time Muslim organisations had nearly no formal role to speak of. The formal structure of the IGGiÖ was based on different electoral lists consisting of individual members, who competed with each other. These lists were elected by individuals and later constituted different bodies of the IGGiÖ. Muslim groups were not even mentioned in the constitution of the IGGiÖ, since they were only founded after the IGGiÖ itself was established.

ATIB, THE TURKISH STATE IN AUSTRIA

While the Islamische Föderation, the Union Islamischer Kulturzentren and the Türkische Föderation were competing with each other and already realised the necessity of being part of the IGGiÖ, the Turkish state, which started seeing a danger in those non-governmental Turkish Islamic movements taking a monopoly in the Islamic religious field, only realised the importance of establishing a religious institution as an alternative to the existing movements in 1990. This is why the Turkish embassy in Austria set up the Türkisch Islamische Union für Kulturelle und Soziale Zusammenarbeit in Österreich, in short ATIB. In many respects, there was no necessity for ATIB to participate in the IGGiÖ for many years, one main reason being that all Muslim organisations except ATIB had to apply for a visa for their religious leaders, the imams, with the written approval of the IGGiÖ, whereas ATIB could rely on an inter-governmental agreement between Austria and Turkey. Imams of ATIB are sent by the Ministry of religious affairs of Turkey as diplomats and thus stay for a couple of years in order to switch to another workplace. In contrast, all the other Muslim organisations had to call imams from foreign countries because of the absence of Islamic theological and pastoral learning in Austria (Hafez 2006: 70). This seems to have been the major reason for Muslim organisations to participate in the IGGiÖ in the very first years, as the visa-issue was the main aspect of the IGGiÖ that directly had an impact on the everyday work of the different Islamic groups.

Already before establishing ATIB, the then ambassador of Turkey, Ecmel Barutcu had declared his fundamental opposition to the IGGiÖ. In a press release dated from April 1983 and quoted in an article by Abdelrahimsai, he wrote:

> We were informed that Islamic religious education should start this school year in some counties of Austria. [...] It is fundamentally questionable when people, who themselves have no Turkish citizenship and are not trained and qualified by our Turkish departments, give religious education to Turkish pupils. Religious teachers of other nationalities are extremely questionable. Considering this situation, it is demandable that our citizens stay observant and attentive. For that reason it is necessary that they turn to the respective school administration to declare that they will not approve an attendance of their children in such a religious class.   (Abdelrahimsai, quoted in Hafez 2012a: 67, my translation)

This press release demonstrates the fundamentally oppositional view of the Turkish state towards the IGGiÖ. In viewing their Turkish people, who are Muslims at the same time, first and foremost as Turkish nationals, the Turkish embassy refused to accept the religious leadership of the IGGiÖ and furthermore ignored the religious law of the republic of Austria, which puts religious affairs in the hands of the legally recognised churches and religious communities (Kalb/Potz/Schinkele 2003). Due to the fact that more than half of the Austrian Muslim population was of Turkish descent, Ahmed Abdelrahimsai feared this opposition and thus tried to find a compromise. After an interlocution between Abdelrahimsai and the Turkish embassy, the then president of the IGGiÖ went to Turkey where he negotiated an agreement which said that well-trained Turkish teachers of the Turkish republic should pass an aptitude test run by Abdelrahimsai to become teachers in Austria. About 30 teachers from Turkey came to Austria in the 1980s in this way (Hafez 2012: 68). Religious education at public schools was the most important aspect of the IGGiÖ's work between 1979 to 1997, when Abdelrahimsai headed the IGGiÖ. It was thus one of the main interests of the founders of the IGGiÖ from 1982. Another important issue within the IGGiÖ was the question of visas for the Imams which the Muslim organisations expected the IGGiÖ to resolve. As a president who had great power and influence, Abdelrahimsai was thus able to keep the Islamic movements on a short leash (Hafez 2012: 68sq.).

From dusk till dawn: the IGGiÖ after 1997

When Anas Schakfeh was elected executive president in 1997 for two years and was confirmed in his office in 1999, a new era of the IGGiÖ started. The IGGiÖ started building different institutions that belonged to the IGGiÖ itself or to the different Muslim organisations. Another achievement was the establishment of the Islamic Academy in Vienna in 1998, which trained future religious teachers for public schools. In 2001, a private school of the IGGiÖ was founded and another eight private Islamic schools were set up under the administration of Schakfeh (Hafez 2012: 82). For the first time since its existence, Islamic groups saw an added value in the IGGiÖ which transcended the issues of the visa-issue and religious classes. But still, the president, who enjoyed great power in the constitution until 2011, was not an active member in any of the Islamic movements, but an independent individual, who had gained the trust of the diverse Muslim groups. This trust was built on the fact that he had long experience in the IGGiÖ, which he had built up and to which he had belonged from the very beginning. Another reason was that the Islamic movements lacked human resources who would have been capable of doing this job. And so again, the Islamic movements were only standing in the second row.

It would be external factors which would eventually draw the IGGiÖ into the political arena. In 1999, the Austrian Freedom Party (FPÖ) organised a xenophobic election campaign. This alone was not new at all, but expected after the party's turn to the right that followed the coup of Jörg Haider in 1986. In the election campaign for the national parliamentary elections in 1999, after which the FPÖ came to power together with the conservatives, not only so called *Ausländer* (foreigners) were the target, but focus was given to the Muslim scapegoat. This lead to a higher sensitivity among a few more highly educated Muslims (mainly of Arab descent) in civil society, who later joined the IGGiÖ and participated in the elections in 2001. The rising Islamophobia, which became even stronger after the 9/11 attacks, brought Islam to the political scene. This had the effect that suddenly members of 'official' Islam – in other words the functionaries of the IGGiÖ – were asked to answer questions on Islam, encounter misconceptions and defend their religion. They were interviewed by daily newspapers, invited to talk shows on TV and started cooperating in the fields of anti-racism and human rights with other Austrian NGOs. Although representatives of Muslim organisations were also participating in public debates and some like the Islamische Föderation were also active in civil society, the functionaries of the IGGiÖ were regarded as the spokesperson for the officially recognised Islam (Hafez 2010b). Therefore, in order to have an impact on the public sphere as well as on state officials in their dealing with Muslim religious interests, one had to be working as part of the IGGiÖ. This became even more important after the right wing party FPÖ started to create an image of the Muslim as the bogeyman and stereotypical public enemy number one and thus subsequently tried to restrict the religious rights of the Muslim community (Hafez 2009; 2010; 2011; 2012b).

Islam had become a political topic, especially during the coalition government of the FPÖ with the conservative Österreichische Volkspartei (ÖVP) as the major and more experienced partner. Especially because the Austrian Republic, which has been a member of the European Union since 1995, was boycotted by the rest of the then 14 EU-member states because of the coalition of an extreme right-wing party (which was famous for its anti-Semitism and its xenophobia) in power, the ÖVP was eager to prove their good relationship with the Muslim community in Austria. This led to various initiatives of cooperation between the government and the IGGiÖ. When the capital city of Styria, Graz, was the European Capital of Culture for 2003, the Austrian Ministry of Foreign Affairs initiated the first so called European Imam Conference, which was organised jointly with the IGGiÖ and supported by different Austrian authorities. Cultural and/or scientific activities such as this conference helped the Austrian Republic in their cultural diplomacy towards the Muslim world. On the other side, the IGGiÖ profited from these considerations in Austria as well as internationally. This conference proved to be the first of its kind and was followed by another Austrian and two European conferences. With the support of institutions of the European Union, the supranational institution European Imam Conference became unique and played a leading role in the landscape of European Muslim organisations. In 2006 and 2010, further European conferences were held. Those conferences represented an invaluable opportunity to discuss questions which were of great importance in these days and which remain relevant today. This made Austria a vanguard for Muslim institutions not only in Austria but also on a European level. As a consequence, the political role of the IGGiÖ as the official representative body of Muslims was strengthened, and thus the interest as well as participation on the part of Muslims increased.

From 1999 to 2011, members of the Islamische Föderation and the Union Islamischer Kulturzentren were also part of the IGGiÖ. This means that their members were participating in the decision-making process of the different bodies on a regional as well as on a national level. In contrast, ATIB did not participate in the elections in 2001. The IGGiÖ had an indirect election system which divided Austria into four regions (Upper Austria and Salzburg; Lower Austria, Vienna, and Burgenland; Carinthia and Styria; Vorarlberg and Tyrol). While ATIB did not participate in three of the four regions at all, the argument in Vorarlberg and Tyrol was that the only possibility of participation would be to take all seats reserved for people of Turkish descent. The constitution from 2001

fixed a percentage of 30 per cent for people of one ethnicity in order that no ethnic community would dominate the other. When the Islamische Föderation and
the Union Islamischer Kulturzentren did not accept this proposal, ATIB boycotted the elections and even organised a protest march during the election process.
ATIB stayed out of the formal structure from 2001 until the next elections took
place in 2011 (Hafez 2006: 69sqq.). Like ATIB, the Türkische Föderation was
also structurally excluded from participating in the bodies of the IGGiÖ due to
its negligence of the elections. Another major portion among the Muslim organisations was the Alevis. One of the two Alevi groups, the Föderation der Aleviten
Gemeinden in Österreich (AABF), which was founded in 1998, never cooperated with the IGGiÖ. Because of the Alevi being regarded as Muslims by the state
and not having a separate legally recognised church, their special religious needs
were widely ignored. Due to their distance from mainstream Muslim theology,
the AABF was not considered as being a Muslim institution by the IGGiÖ. Only
a smaller group participated in Vorarlberg with the IGGiÖ with the aim of getting an Islamic cemetery established there (Hafez 2006: 71sqq.). But this cooperation seems to be more due the specific religious understanding of this local
Alevi group as Alevi Muslims, than due to local interests only. After all, the Alevi group also has different self-conceptions concerning its Muslim identity
(Gorzewski 2010).

BETWEEN OPPOSITIONAL CRITICISM AND COOPERATION

The IGGiÖ as the spokesbody of Islam and as the only negotiator with the
Austrian Republic in Muslim religious affairs also made the former oppositional Muslim groups aware of the increasing importance of this institution.
ATIB, the Türkische Föderation, some Shia groups and some individuals thus
started claiming that the IGGiÖ was not representative for them. Ahmed Rusznak, an Austrian convert, whose conversion to Islam was not recognised by the
IGGiÖ, began legal proceedings against the IGGiÖ decision, but the Constitutional Court agreed with the IGGiÖ on basis of the principle of home rule *(in-
nere Autonomie)*.[3] Rusznak, after having proceeded for years right up to the

---

3 As far as membership in the IGGiÖ is concerned, the institution faces a paradox in its
   claim to represent all Muslims in Austria as stated in its constitution on the one hand,
   but not having a compulsory membership and thus not registering individuals on the
   other. Contrary to the Christian churches who register infants (and non-Christian
   converts) with the liturgical act of baptism, Islamic tradition has no corresponding

Constitutional Court, became one of the leading oppositional figures against the IGGiÖ in the public sphere. Soon, other groups and Islamic movements shared his criticism and supported him in his demand that the IGGiÖ should not enjoy its representative status any more.

Also within the IGGiÖ itself, Anas Schakfeh was criticised for rallying functionaries with an Arab background and passing positions to people who were not elected, but nominated by himself, such as the commissioner for integration or his personal consultant and speaker. This argument was especially used by groups with a Turkish background. Harun Özdemirci, the head of ATIB, said in an interview in 2007:

> A representation based on majorities of the Muslim population does not exist in the Islamische Glaubensgemeinschaft in Österreich. We also disagree about issues concerning religious classes. That is why we are not members of the Islamische Glaubensgemeinschaft. That does not mean that we have no contact. Recently, our relations have become quite good. But we criticise the current election system. There are about 450 000 Muslims living in Austria but only 4000 are able to vote. It is slightly difficult to consider this as a democratic system. We are of the opinion that the president of the Islamische Glaubensgemeinschaft should be elected by all Muslims. (Ö1 2007; my translation)

Again, 25 years after the fundamental opposition, ATIB was still giving the IGGiÖ a wide berth. But this time, the opposition was not criticising the institution *per se*, but rather political processes within the system. This reveals the general acceptance of the institution IGGiÖ as *the* legal representative of all Muslims, no matter of what nationality Muslims were. Even on a practical level contacts did exist. Imams in the ATIB cooperated in some activities of the IGGiÖ such as the European imam conference, and ATIB formally had a seat in the advisory board of the IGGiÖ (Hafez 2006: 71). All of these activities revealed ATIB's awareness of the importance of the IGGiÖ in the life of Muslims in Austria. At the same time, ATIB raised criticism against the IGGiÖ in order to shape it according to the interests of some organisations/individuals, as we will see later.

The claim to revoke the representative status of the IGGiÖ became a central point of discussion in the media. Other groups were primarily founded in order

---

practice for children of Muslim parents nor has the IGGiÖ developed one. Therefore, formal registration of membership in the IGGiÖ depends on active enrolment preceded in the case of converts by pronouncing the *shahāda* (confession of faith declaring the oneness of God and the prophethood of Muhammad) in front of fellow Muslims.

to criticise the IGGiÖ. The most famous group was the Initiative Liberaler Muslime Österreich (ILMÖ; IIDZ 2009b), which declared that their goal would be to represent liberal Muslims and to "make the shortcomings of the IGGiÖ public". They even called for closing the IGGiÖ (IIDZ 2009a). Although the group never expanded to more than ten followers, the members of ILMÖ were active in shaping the image of the IGGiÖ by regularly publishing op-ed articles in daily newspapers and publishing press releases. The ILMÖ even went further in their criticism than ATIB when they claimed the IGGiÖ not to be liberal, but radical, supporting so called *Parallelgesellschaften* (parallel societies). Members of the ILMÖ even tried to put forward a motion at the Ministry of Education to set up a new legally recognised Muslim religious community called Islamisch Sunnitische Glaubensgemeinschaft in Österreich which was not successful. The aim was to weaken the sole representation of Muslims by the IGGiÖ (Hafez 2012: 177sqq.).

The contestation between the IGGiÖ and the group of the Alevi was taken to the court. One of the main issues between the IGGiÖ and the AABF was the quest by AABF for religious classes for Alevi Muslims. Since they disassociated themselves publicly from common/mainstream Islamic teachings, the IGGiÖ refused to accept them as a part of the Muslim community (Hafez 2006: 73). Finally, the AABF put forward a motion to legally recognise the Alevi group as a recognised religious community just as the IGGiÖ. Although different expert opinions had quite diametrical positions on this issue, the Islamisch Alevitische Glaubensgemeinschaft in Österreich (IAGÖ) was eventually recognised as a legal religious community[4] on 1 December 2010 due to an expert report for the Constitutional Court (Heine/Lohlker/Potz 2012: 92sq.). This initiative was important because it changed the idea of the *de facto* claim to sole representation by the IGGiÖ of all Muslims and the door was opened for other initiatives to follow. Shortly after this incident, a number of other groups tried to submit an application to receive legal recognition as a church or religious community. In contrast to the Alevi group, the ILMÖ and a small Shia group that was not supported by the major *Shia* umbrella organisation did not succeed.

The IGGiÖ responded to those critics and released a statement of support in which 45 national and umbrella organisations with 204 member associations expressed their solidarity with the IGGiÖ. The letter stated on 9 February 2009:

---

4   The Alevi group was registered as a *Bekenntnisgemeinschaft* and not a *Religionsgesellschaft*. After 10 years of existence and after meeting several other criteria, a *Bekenntnisgemeinschaft* would be able to become a *Religionsgesellschaft* or Church. Nevertheless, this paved the way for a completely equal religious community.

The undersigned Muslim organisations and mosque communities are increasingly concerned by the tendency to call into question the role of the Islamische Glaubensgemeinschaft in Österreich as the official representative of Muslims in Austria. We hereby declare that we will not allow a wedge to be driven between us. Authentic and lively inter-Muslim discussion is integral to finding solutions to different problems. We are composed to the full spectrum of the Islamische Glaubensgemeinschaft in Österreich. We see ourselves as made up of any in the Islamische Glaubensgemeinschaft who support and pursue the compatibility of a Muslim and Austrian identity and as such to make visible Muslims as part of Austrian society. (IGGiÖ 2009)

This statement reveals the enormous pressure which the IGGiÖ felt in the public sphere. The representatives of the IGGiÖ were accused on a regular basis of being non-representative of the Muslims in Austria. Statements such as "the Islamische Glaubensgemeinschaft is not a legitimate representation of Muslims" (FPÖ 2010) or "the Islamische Glaubensgemeinschaft only claims to be representative" (Schmidinger 2007) are only two examples of fundamental critics coming from the political right and the leftists after inner-Muslim rivalries became public.

A NEW BALANCE OF POWER

Contestations of the representativity of the IGGiÖ led to a new balance of power. From 2008 to 2010, the IGGiÖ worked on a new constitution to increase the participation of its members in the election process. The fact that only about 5500 people participated in the elections in 2001/2002 has always been an argument for many opponents to criticise the IGGiÖ. Another aspect was the evolutionary process of the IGGiÖ itself as well as of the different Muslim organisations. The IGGiÖ of 2008 was no longer that of 2001 (pre-9/11). The value of this institution as a religious interest group in the public sphere and towards state institutions was clear, and no longer reduced to the visa of imams and religious classes. That is why the different Muslim organisations exerted pressure to play a bigger role within the IGGiÖ. The former percental limitation of people of one ethnicity in a body of the IGGiÖ was expanded. In the past, no more than 30 per cent of the members of a body could belong to one ethnic group. The expansion of the limitation to 40 per cent would strengthen the Turkish Muslim movements which are the most organised among all Muslim groups.

Because of the low participation in the election in 2001/2002, the IGGiÖ and the informally associated Muslim groups started mobilising for enrollment in the

IGGiÖ. After the election had taken place, 125 000 people were now registered in the IGGiÖ. 27 000 people paid the yearly membership fee of 40 Euro and thus were entitled to vote, while 20 485 people in fact participated. 501 delegates were elected with 50 votes each (44 of them were female; Niederleitner 2011). Another reform was the formal incorporation of Muslim groups that had only been registered as associations according to the *Vereinsgesetz* (Law of associations) and by that had no connection to the IGGiÖ in a formal way. From now on, those Muslim groups could formally become members of the IGGiÖ as a *Fachvereinigung* and were thus formally integrated.

The position of organised Muslim groups was strengthened in the election system. From now on, it were not individuals, who voted lists, but electoral delegates. Each 50 people could vote one delegate, who then voted a list. With this system, organised Muslims were able to strengthen their position within the IG-GiÖ. The outcome was that for the first time in the history of the IGGiÖ, a candidate of a Muslim organisation, the Islamische Föderation, became president. ATIB also participated in the elections and became the second largest group within the IGGiÖ.

CONCLUSION

It can be concluded that the growing importance of the IGGiÖ for Muslim life in Austria enhanced the interest on the side of Muslim organisations. This led to more participation on one side and to more criticism on the other. The growing pressure resulted in the reform of the IGGiÖ's constitution and thus strengthened the role of organised Muslim groups, which have become the leading actors of the IGGiÖ. The role of the individual has been furthermore reduced due to the indirect election process of 50 individuals voting for one delegate who votes the candidate-list. Although internal rivalries within the Muslim community towards the IGGiÖ led to more participation, there is no reason to think that internal as well as external actors will soon stop contesting the IGGiÖ's representativity. But with ATIB being part of the IGGiÖ's main legislative and executive bodies, the strongest opposition in terms of quantity has now been integrated. There is reason to believe that rivalry will go on within the ranks of the IGGiÖ, as elections are to be held every four years.

Another aspect worth observing in the near future is the possible divide between the politics of Muslim organisations on one side and the IGGiÖ on the other side. Currently, some organisations such as the Islamische Föderation, of which the current president is a member, spoke out publicly against the Dialogforum Islam, a platform of the State Secretary of Integration of the Ministry of

Interior and the IGGiÖ, which aims at reforming many aspects of Muslim-state affairs such as the amendment of the Islam-law of 1912, the training of imams at university-level, etc. The Islamische Föderation argued that Muslim organisations had not been involved in this process (Kocina 2012). The example of the Dialogforum reveals that although Muslim organisations play a much bigger role than before, this does not mean that the president can be identified with a specific Muslim movement. Although the leadership of the IGGiÖ is accountable to the Muslim organisations via the delegates, who meet once a year, it seems that it develops a life of its own. The *Verkirchlichung* (churchisation) in the sense of a unification of a variety of Muslim groups is thus restricted to a certain level. As power is restricted to a period of legislation of four years, the unification of today can be dissolved tomorrow, depending on new political circumstances. But on the other side, the politics of the IGGiÖ have laid a basis for common action. Proclamations such as those issued during the Austrian and the European Imam Conferences are one example. The IGGiÖ seems to fulfil the function of a religious interest group towards the state and the society, while religious life in the narrow sense of the word still is a domain of the Muslim organisations.

Although the positioning of the IGGiÖ's current leadership is broader than in earlier years, this has not protected it from fundamental criticism, as press releases and public statements reveal (Albayati 2012). The fact that these internal rivalries were brought to the public can be considered as a sign of normalising the Muslims presence in Austrian society. Hence, Muslims are no more hidden behind the curtain but right in the middle of the public sphere. On the other side, this criticism has also been used by the political far right to regularly devalue the IGGiÖ because of its "lack of representation"[5] and to project an extremist agenda into the IGGiÖ (Hafez 2012: 137-151). Although internal rivalries have brought the diversity of Muslim communities to light, this has not led to a more factual and less stereotyped debate.

REFERENCES

Albayati, Amer (2012): ILMÖ Stellungnahme zur Islam-Rede des Herrn Bundespräsidenten. [online] 3 July. Available at: http://www.freidenker.at/index. php/blog/1153-ilmoe-stellungnahme-zur-islam-rede-des-herrn-bundespraesi denten.html (accessed 15 November 2012).

---

5 NEWS (2007). Streitgespräch 'Nachhause ins Morgenland!' NEWS 38/07.

Fetzer, Joel S. / Soper, Christopher J. (2004): *Muslims and the State in Britain, France and Germany,* New York: Cambridge University Press.

Fliegenschnee, Katrin / Goujon, Anne / Lutz, Wolfgang (2004): *Neue demographische Szenarien zur Zukunft der Evangelischen Kirche in Österreich,* Vienna Institute of Demography. Austrian Academy of Sciences. Working Papers 1/2004. [online] Available at: http://www.oeaw.ac.at/vid/download/WP2004_1.pdf (accessed 1 December 2012).

FPÖ (2010): Neubauer: Islamische Glaubensgemeinschaft ist keine legitime Vertretung der Muslime. [online] 25 August 2010. Available at: http://www.ots.at/presseaussendung/OTS_20100825_OTS0155/fpoe-neubauer-islamische-glaubensgemeinschaft-ist-keine-legitime-vertretung-der-muslime (accessed 1 September 2012).

Gorzewski, Andreas (2010): *Das Alevitentum in seinen divergierenden Verhältnisbestimmungen zum Islam,* Berlin: EB-Verlag (Bonner Islamstudien, vol. 17).

Hafez, Farid (2006): *Die Islamische Glaubensgemeinschaft in Österreich: Eine Analyse der Bodyisationsstruktur unter besonderer Berücksichtigung der Rolle muslimischer Spitzenverbände,* Diplomarbeit, Universität Wien.

— (2009): "Zwischen Islamophobilie und Islamophobie: Die FPÖ und der Islam", in: Bunzl, John / Hafez, Farid (eds), *Islamophobie in Österreich,* Bozen/Innsbruck/Wien: Studienverlag, pp. 105-125.

— (2010a): *Islamophober Populismus: Moschee- und Minarettbauverbote österreichischer Parlamentsparteien,* Wiesbaden: Verlag für Sozialwissenschaften.

— (2010b): "Österreich und der Islam – eine Wende durch FPÖVP? Anmerkungen zur Rolle von Islamophobie im politischen Diskurs seit der Wende", in: Baker, Frederick / Herczeg, Petra (eds), *Die beschämte Republik: Zehn Jahre nach Schwarz-Blau in Österreich,* Wien: Czernin.

— (2011): "Von der 'Verjudung' zur 'Islamistenpartei': Neue islamophobe Diskursstrategien der FPÖ im Rahmen des Wiener Wahlkampfs", in: Hafez, Farid (ed.), *Jahrbuch für Islamophobieforschung,* Bozen/Innsbruck/Wien: Studienverlag, pp. 83-98.

— (2012a): *Anas Schakfeh: Das österreichische Gesicht des Islams,* Wien: Braumüller.

— (2012b): "Jörg Haider and Islamophobia", in: Ansari, Humayun / Hafez, Farid (eds), *From the Far Right to the Mainstream: Islamophobia in Party Politics and the Media,* Frankfurt a. M. / New York: Campus, pp. 45-68.

Heine, Susanne / Lohlker, Rüdiger / Potz, Richard (2012): *Muslime in Österreich: Geschichte – Lebenswelt – Religion: Grundlagen für den Dialog,* Wien: Tyrolia Verlag.

IIDZ (2009a): Open letter. [online] 12 July 2009. Available at: http://web. archive.org/web/20100914023406/http://www.iidz.at/brief2.html (accessed 18 December 2012).

IIDZ (2009b): Open letter. [online] 13 July 2009. Available at: http://www. iidz.at/Brief_DR_Schmied.pdf (accessed 1 September 2010)

IGGiÖ (2009): Wir sind die Islamische Glaubensgemeinschaft! Erklärung der muslimischen Dachverbände, Organisationen und Moscheegemeinden. [statement, released 9 February 2009, online]. Available at: http://www. derislam.at/?c=content&p=beitragdet&v=beitraege&cssid=Stellungnahmen &navid=710&par=70&bid=52 (accessed 1 December 2012).

Imperial Council I (1912): Islam-law in English: [online]. Available at: http:// derislam.at/?c=content&cssid=Englisch&navid=886&par=10&navid2=906 &par2=886 (accessed 1 September 2012).

Jonker, Gerdien (2002): *Eine Wellenlänge zu Gott: Der Verband der Islamischen Kulturzentren in Europa,* Bielefeld: Transcript.

Kalb, Herbert / Potz, Richard / Schinkele, Brigitte (2003): *Religionsrecht,* Wien: WUV.

Kocina, Erich (2012): Österreichs Muslime: Interner Konflikt über Dialog. [online] 2 April. Available at: http://diepresse.com/home/panorama/religion/ 745787/Oesterreichs-Muslime_Interner-Konflikt-ueber-Dialog (accessed 15 November 2012).

Kubaseck, Christopher / Seufert, Günter (2006): *Die Türkei: Politik, Geschichte, Kultur,* München: Beck.

News (2007): Streitgespräch 'Nachhause ins Morgenland!' NEWS Weekly Newspaper 38/07.

Niederleitner, Heinz (2011): Islamische Glaubensgemeinschaft: Rücktritt und Prä-sidentenwahl. Oberösterreichische Nachrichten. [online] 25 June. Available at: http://www.nachrichten.at/nachrichten/politik/innenpolitik/art385,657995 (accessed 1 September 2012).

Ö1 (2007): Wer hat das Sagen? Am Kernpunkt der Debatte. [01.01.2007]. Available at: http://oe1.orf.at/artikel/210282 (accessed 1 September 2010).

Potz, Richard (2010): "Das Islamgesetz 1912 und der religionsrechtliche Diskurs in Österreich zu Beginn des 20. Jahrhunderts", in: Olechowski, Thomas / Neschwara, Christian / Lengauer, Alina-Maria (eds), *Grundlagen der öster-reichischen Rechtskultur,* Vienna: Böhlau, pp. 385–408.

Schmied, Martina / Wieshaider, Wolfgang (2004): "Islam and the European Union: The Austrian Way", in: Potz, Richard / Wieshaider, Wolfgang (eds), *Islam and the European Union,* Leuven/Paris/Dudley: Peeters, pp. 199-218.

Schmidinger, Thomas (2007): Der Kuschel-Imam und die öffentliche Sicherheit. Die Presse, 9 January, [online]. Available at: http://diepresse.com/home/ meinung/gastkommentar/55750/Der-KuschelImam-und-die-oeffentliche-Sicherheit (accessed 1 September 2012).

'We are in this together':
How the cartoon crisis changed relations
between the Danish state and Muslim Danes

LENE KÜHLE

When it comes to engagement in relations with its Muslim population most European countries have their determining incidence. In the UK this would be the 1989 Rushdie crisis (while the 2005 London bombing may be a second one), in the Netherlands the 2004 murder of Theo van Gogh, and in Spain the 2004 Madrid bombing. The incidences are not at all equal in substance, but they may be seen to correspond in effect: they triggered a debate on the place of Islam and Muslims in that society and may be 'focusing events' which open windows of opportunity for significant policy changes of the state vis-à-vis its Muslim populations (Bleich 2010: 10) as well as internal changes within the Muslim environment.

In Denmark the 2005/6 cartoon crisis provided such a focusing event. Like most of the above mentioned events it was not only a local event. The important part of the cartoon crisis may in fact be the interaction between local and global occurrences (Klausen 2009; Olesen 2007; Riis 2007, Warburg 2010). This paper will however discuss the consequences of the crisis from a local perspective: How did the debate following the cartoon crisis prompt a re-formation of the normative 'taken for grantedness' of Muslims in Denmark on the one hand and of the Danish majority society on the other? The argument put forward is that the cartoon crisis has had important consequences for the embeddedness of Islam and Muslims in Danish society.

The similarities between the experiences and developments in different European countries may tend to overshadow the fact that the encounters of Muslim minorities with the different European countries are happening in contexts which may vary widely. The legal framework of church-state relations and religion in general, former experience with religious minorities and the size and constitution of the Muslim minority group as well as the political culture and ideas on integration and citizenship indicate that the circumstances of Muslim minorities in the different European countries are more diverse than the concept of 'Muslims in Europe' suggests. Developments do however often follow similar patterns (Maréchal et al. 2003).

Denmark has a population of 5.5 million, and estimates hold that in 2010 about 230 000, about 4 per cent of the population in Denmark, have a Muslim background (Jacobsen 2011: 166). Because religious adherence is not registered in Denmark the exact number of Muslims is unknown, and estimations rest on statistics of ethnic background combined with surveys asking for religious self-identification. The history of Danish Muslims is similar to the story in many other Western European countries: Very few Muslims lived in Denmark before the end of the 1960s, but the abundance of possibilities for unqualified labor attracted (primarily) men from Morocco, Pakistan, Turkey and Yugoslavia to Denmark, most of them self-defining as Muslims. The crisis of the early 1970s led to a stop to labor immigration, but by the law on family unification of 1974 immigrants residing in Denmark were allowed to invite their families (Simonsen 2012: 17). The number of Muslims in Denmark has increased from about 30 000 in 1980 to about 230 000 in 2010. Islam has in this period become the largest minority religion in Denmark.

The main religious organisation in Denmark is the Folkekirke, the Evangelical Lutheran Church, which holds a position as a state church, sanctioned by the *Constitutional Act*. The executive leader of the church is a politician, the Minister of Ecclesiastical Affairs, and church legislation goes through parliament. The Folkekirke performs functions for the state, among other things civil registration of all Danes (and burials of most). The Folkekirke has an impressive, but declining membership (with a rate of 0.5% point every year) of 79.5 per cent of the population as by January 2012. There are about 28 000 Buddhists, about 12 000 Hindus and 7000 Jews in Denmark. The largest minority Christian religious organisation in Denmark is probably the Catholic Church with its membership of 38 000 (Ahlin et al. 2012).

A shift in Danish attitudes to and discourses on integration took place in the early 1980s from an apparently tolerant and liberal stance on immigration to what has been described as an extremely cultural racist discourse with strong anti-Muslim elements (Wren 2001). Whether 9/11 *per se* created a shift in this discourse is difficult to determine as 2001 also saw the rise of the neo-nationalist Dansk Folkeparti, the Danish People's Party, to power as a support party for the Liberal-conservative government. Dansk Folkeparti is often presented as responsible for processes of 'othering' and moving the boundaries of what it is acceptable to say about immigrants and Muslims (Larsson/Lindekilde 2009: 364; Riis 2011: 22; Sheikh/Crone 2012: 176). In the 2001 election, which took place in November, their path of rising electoral support continued and an additional nine seats in parliament were won, making Dansk Folkeparti the third largest party in parliament.

This chapter begins with a description of the state of affairs in Denmark before the crisis followed by a short description of the crisis itself. The bulk of the chapter will describe the changes which have taken place since 2005-6. Analysis of the cartoon crisis has tended to view its consequences as part of a greater landscape of *Kulturkampf* or 'value struggle' contributing to the 'securitisation of Islam' (Klausen 2009; Riis 2011; Sheikh/Crone 2012). The present article will however discuss whether the cartoon crisis may also be seen as having acted as a catalyst for a 'normalisation' and 'integration' of Islam in Denmark.

DANISH MUSLIMS BEFORE 2005

The establishment of the first purpose-built mosque predates all public debates on Islam. The mosque was inaugurated in 1967 in Hvidovre, a Copenhagen suburb. The organisation behind the mosque, the Ahmadiyya movement, also undertook the first full Danish translation of the Qur'an (by A.S. Madsen in 1967). Considered apostates by many Muslims, the Ahmadiyya mosque did not however fulfill the need for places to congregate for communal prayers and from the early 1970s local prayer halls were put up in Copenhagen and different places around the country. One mosque, Islamisk Kulturcenter, initially set-up with support from ambassadors from a number of Muslim countries, attained a special – and economically advantageous – position due to its position as the official institution for *halāl* certificates for Danish meat export to Muslim countries. This mosque was also one of the first Muslim groups to attain the position as a recognised religious community in Denmark, which among other things entails the right to perform civilly valid marriages.

By 1976 legislation enforced the enrollment of immigrant children into the Danish school system, but liberal Danish legislation in regard to achieving public funding for private schools meant that the first Muslim state-supported school could open in 1978. In the 1980s and 1990s new groups of Muslims arrived in Denmark as refugees from conflicts in – among others – former Yugoslavia, Iran, Iraq, Palestine, Somalia and Afghanistan. The new immigrants, many with a Muslim family background (though some were in fact fleeing from religious domination in Iran), were setting up their own mosques and associations. Much of this happened outside the public eye. More Muslim schools were subsequent-

ly inaugurated, and though some were closed again later (some for purely internal reasons; others due to state pressure to comply with regulations), during the
course of the 1990s the number of Islamic schools came to exceed 20. For some
religious groups the state supported schools came to constitute an important economic and organisational feature, by providing space for meetings and employment possibilities for key persons within the organisations (Kühle 2006).

Other organisations found other ways to sustain a living in Denmark: Many
local Turkish mosques found it advantageous to enroll under the Danish branch
of Diyanet, the Danisk-Tyrkisk Islamisk Stiftelse (Kühle 2006). Diyanet, the
Turkish state authority of Islamic affairs, would from 1985 send *hocas*, imams,
to mosques in Denmark (Pedersen 1999: 44). The conditions set by Diyanet were
that Diyanet would pay for the imam, but the local association would have to
buy a building to house the imam and the mosque room. Further, the Libyan Islamic Call Society and the Saudi Muslim World League were active in the
1980s, sending imams and supporting mosques financially and in other ways
(Simonsen 2012).

Until the 1990s there was little public debate on Islam, little public
knowledge about Islam and Muslims in Denmark and there were almost no Islamic voices present in the public sphere. Organisations representing Muslims in
the public sphere were immigrant organisations, representing immigrants rather
than Muslims, even if members were in fact Muslim. If a specific Muslim view
point was needed in the media or by state institutions, Ahmadiyya Muslims were
at hand. From the late 1980s a handful of Muslim youth organisations entered
the public sphere. These youth organisations, though representing a relatively
small group of altogether perhaps 6-800 members (Schmidt 2003) came to stand
in the middle of a thunderstorm as the presence of Islam and Muslims gradually
became more controversial. Many aspects of Muslim presence in Denmark
which had hitherto been uncontroversial now came under important discussion
in public space, including the wearing of the veil, state supported Muslim
schools and the political participation of Muslims.

After the intense public debates on Islam before and after 2001, the youth
organisations largely withdrew from the public sphere. The now open positions
of Muslim authority in the public space came to be occupied by imams (Nielsen
2010: 231). A few imams, in particular the imams of Islamisk Trossamfund (Islamic Religious Community), Abu Laban and Abdul Wahid Pedersen, a convert
to Islam, who has been initiator and leader of several Muslim organisations and
initiatives came to represent Islam in Denmark.

Two things are important to understand the situation of Muslims in Denmark
prior to the cartoon crisis. First, the public picture of Muslims in Denmark was a
restricted picture of what was going on among Muslims. For one thing the many

mosques and prayer halls, about 120 in 2005 (Kühle 2006) were rarely visible to the public eye: In a few instances Muslims groups had built mosques, but in an architecture which did not reveal their function as a mosque. Diyanet was by far the biggest Islamic organisation in Denmark, and with its more than 30 mosques buildings (among which only two purpose-built) and 20 imams also the best organised (Kühle 2006). Yet Diyanet was virtually unknown by the public. Newspapers reported about what they found to be relevant for their readers, but this focused on the controversies and seldom included 'ordinary' Muslim life. According to Jørgen Nielsen "The Danish political elites had previously taken little notice of the growing Muslim community in Denmark, and public awareness was based on hearsay and media stereotyping rather than direct experience" (Nielsen 2010: 228).

Second, most mosque associations and Islamic organisations had a local perspective. In terms of organisations, local mosque associations were set up from the start and though transnational Islamic organisation were also setting up mosques and sending in imams (for instance Muslim World League and Diyanet; Simonsen 2012: 21-24), the aim was to serve local needs. The organisation of Islam in Denmark was very ethnically defined. Diyanet catering for the group of Muslims with a Turkish background while its activities were virtually unknown outside the Turkish population is a good example, but in reality much Muslim organisational activity, including the youth organisations, had an ethnic profile, which meant that their connections to other Muslim organisations would be limited.

THE CRISIS IN SHORT

On 30 September 2005 the Danish daily newspaper *Jyllands-Posten* published twelve cartoons of the Prophet Muhammad. According to the text adjacent to them the reason they were published was to test whether Danish illustrators exercised self-censorship due to fear of reaction from Muslim radicals. The fact that a popular Danish comedian had publically announced that he wouldn't dare 'bullshitting' Islam, a Danish illustrator of a kid's book depicting the Prophet insisted on anonymity, and several museums had removed pieces of art in order not to insult Muslims, were all mentioned as reasons for taking a stance for freedom of expression against demands for special treatment out of consideration for their religious feelings by some Muslims (Rose 2005, 2008). The wider context of the *Jyllands-Posten* cartoons was evidently a post-9/11 context which indirectly also included the murder of Theo van Gogh and the bombs in Madrid and London.

The publication led to few immediate *media* reactions, but something was building up behind the scenes. Some corner stores owned by Muslims stopped selling the paper and a demonstration in central Copenhagen two weeks after the publishing gathered about 3000 participants. The cartoons had already then been mentioned at bi-lateral talks between Denmark and Egypt and a group of eleven ambassadors from Muslim countries had written a letter to the prime minister urging him to take affair. In November the issue evolved from the diplomatic level to public reactions in a number of Muslim countries and the issue was discussed in a meeting of the Organization for Security and Co-operation in Europe. In December the UN intervened through the High Commissioner for Human Rights, Louise Arbour. In January 2006 the question exploded with massive boycotts from a number of Muslim countries, demonstrations and riots, including the burning down of the Danish embassies in Syria and Iran and the General Consulate in Lebanon, and the calling back of the ambassadors in Denmark by Saudi Arabia. Likewise Danish diplomats were withdrawn from Indonesia, Afghanistan, Yemen, Syria and Palestine due to the risk of riots (Klausen 2009; Larsen 2007).

The cartoon crisis, often named the largest foreign policy crisis in Denmark since the Second World War (Larsen 2007: 1), had a number of immediate consequences for Denmark: boycotts on Danish products in a number of Muslim countries and by Muslim consumers in the West, recommendations that Danish travellers in Muslims countries should not identify as Danes and restrain from discussing religion. That Denmark and in particular *Jyllands-Posten* and the cartoonists had become priority targets was evidenced by direct threats on websites and on a broadcast on Al Jazeera by leading al-Qaʻida ideologues (Jensen 2007). It is also difficult not to see a direct connection between the cartoon crisis and the leading position of the Danish intelligence service and the Danish Ministry of Integration in attempts to fashion, along with British and Dutch colleagues, a new policy of countering 'radicalisation'.

Another direct consequence of the cartoon crisis was the immediate polarisation of the debate. All Danes, Muslim or not, had to relate to the dichotomies of the debate: freedom of speech versus respect for religious symbols/minorities. As a majority of Muslim Danes, 81 per cent according to a survey, felt that the cartoons were offensive (see table 1), in the heat of debate Muslims were generally regarded as supporting respect for religious symbols and being against freedom of expression. This of course ignores the fact that some Muslims vigorously attempted to distance themselves from the group of imams who were active in drawing international attention to the cartoons (Ammitzbøll/Vidino 2007). In fact half of the interviewees found the reactions the cartoons caused in the Middle East to be unacceptable, while only 11 per cent understood them fully (table 2).

Table 1: Reaction of Muslim Danes

How do you feel about the publication of the cartoons?	Per cent
Very offended	49
Offended	32
Not offended	16
Don't know/decline	3

Source: Survey data collected by Catinet Feb 2006. 841 respondents (A4 2006).

Table 2: Reactions of non-Muslim Danes

How do you feel about the Muslim reactions in the Middle East? (burning of flags, boycott, attack on embassies)	Per cent
I understand fully	11
I understand partly	36
I cannot accept	49
Don't know/decline	4

Source: Survey data collected by Catinet Feb 2006. 841 respondents (A4 2006).

The fact that non-Muslim Danes were divided was however so obvious that it could not be ignored (Riis 2011: 26): Headlines in for instance the major tabloid paper described the Danish population as divided as about half did not think the cartoons should not have been published in the first place (BT 2006).

These are important immediate consequences of the cartoon crisis, but some of them remained isolated from the main crust of life in Denmark and some were not of lasting importance. The export of Danish dairy products is back on and even exceeding pre-cartoon crisis standards and surprisingly the cartoon crisis has not had a noticeable impact on the foreign policy of Denmark (Larsen 2007). And though policies against radicalisation have been implemented, most Danes, Muslim or not, have never heard about them. In terms of terrorist plots, the three largest cases of home-grown Islamist terrorism were exposed in 2005, 2006 and 2007, but, save an attempt (by an individual) to murder one of the cartoonists in Denmark in 2010, terrorist attempts to punish the publication of cartoons have been international – from the two Chicago-based men who planned to bomb *Jyllands-Posten* (2009) to the one-legged Chechen boxer (2010) and a carful of Swedish Muslims, who has been convicted of planning a reel bloodbath in the quarters of *Jyllands-Posten* in Copenhagen (2010). This indicates that the Danish intelligence service now has to deal primarily with international terrorists targeting Denmark. In terms of risk for Danish travellers abroad the Danish security service maintains that militant Islamist groups may have a priority for Danish targets, but also that "the primary terrorist threat to Danish nationals abroad is connected with the fact that Danish nationals typically congregate in places frequented by other Westerners, such as tourist areas, nearby tourist attractions, embassies, etc. These places may generally be singled out by terrorists as potential targets" (Politiets Efterretningstjeneste, n. d.).

Based on material from the European Value Study, sociologist Peter Gundelach ascribes one major value shift to the cartoon crisis. Where the concept of freedom of expression before the crisis was a value not often evoked in debates, this changed during the crisis and the mentioning of freedom of expression has remained much more common than before. Where freedom of expression before the cartoon crisis was associated with the political left, it is now a value evenly shared across the political spectrum (Gundelach 2011: 26). In terms of general tolerance of immigrants he finds a steady increase in tolerance in the period from 1981 to 2008. Whereas 18 per cent wouldn't have wanted an immigrant as a neighbor in 1981, this number was down to seven per cent in 2008. Similarly the 53 per cent which in 1990 preferred Danes to immigrants was reduced to 25 per cent of respondents in 2008.

Other changes however, though sometimes indirectly rather than directly related to the cartoon crisis, may have larger consequences for the evolving relationship between Denmark and her Muslims.

FORMATION OF NEW MUSLIM ORGANISATIONS

The cartoon controversy led to a unique mobilisation of Danish Muslims (Larsson/Lindekilde 2009: 366). The formation of two organisations, The Committee for the Defense of the Honour of the Prophet and Democratic Muslims, was a direct consequence of the crisis. The Committee for the Defense of the Honour of the Prophet was formed a few days after the publishing of the cartoons and consisted of a number[1] of mainly Arab-dominated Muslim organisations and mosque committees. The Committee for the Defense of the Honour of the Prophet was instrumental in bringing the existence of the cartoons to the attention of leaders and audiences in the Muslim world and came to represent the

---

1   The exact number was contested, because some of the organisations mentioned as part of the committee claimed that they were in fact not.

Muslim antagonism towards the cartoons. Another organisation, the Democratic Muslims, was established in February 2006, at the height of the cartoon controversy, by among other politicians Naser Khader. The aim of the organisation was unite 'moderate' Danish Muslims through adherence to what the organisation called "The Ten Commandments of Democracy" (Khader 2006). Democratic Muslims have had much organisational trouble and many of its leading figures have left the board, partly because of problems of setting new agendas for the association, and the organisation seems to more or less have died out (Nielsen 2010: 233). The Committee for the Defense of the Honour of the Prophet likewise seems to have been dismantled. Important as they both were for the developments of the cartoon crisis neither of these organisations made a lasting impact on the Islamic milieu in Denmark. Of a more lasting importance is the later establishment of a number of less ad-hoc organisations and the changed behavior of already existing organisations.

UMBRELLA ORGANISATIONS

The formation of two umbrella organisations, United Council of Muslims (Muslimernes Fællesråd, MFR) and Danish Muslim Union (Dansk Muslimsk Union, DMU) in the after-math of the cartoon crisis represents the first lasting establishment of representative organisations for Danish Muslims. Former initiatives to build representative organisations for Danish Muslims had failed. The establishment of MFR and DMU, without pressure and little support from the state, represents probably the most important legacy of the cartoon crisis. The United Council of Muslims (MFR), formed in 2006, being an association of fourteen different Muslim organisations, owes its success in representing Danish Muslims to this (though it is also possible to become an individual member). Former attempts to establish an organisation for Danish Muslims were built on individual membership. MFR boasts a membership of 30 000 – 35 000, about one out of seven Danish Muslims. The membership includes a broad variety of Sunni organisations with different ethnic profiles: organisations with mainly Pakistani, Turkish, Somali, Afghan, Arab background, but several of the organisations claim a specific Danish-Muslim approach (e.g. Muslimer i Dialog). MFR is very active in the public sphere, and campaigns for environment protection and initiatives for sick and elderly Muslims have been on the agenda of the organisation. They often send out press releases and engage in cooperation with other civil society actors, including Christian organisations (Nielsen 2010: 233). The policy of radicalisation prevention has demonstrated a need for ministries and municipalities to engage with those with knowledge of Islam in Denmark and MFR has put itself at their disposal. MFR was for instance invited to comment on the policy of countering radicalisation and has also contributed with comments to recent law proposals. The fact that MFR has on several occasions been regarded as a partner by the Copenhagen municipality and the Ministry of Integration, and has also has received money from the Ministry of Integration to do a project on Women and integration is something which however became highly contested in the media as well as in the court room (Helqvist 2010). The court partly dismissed former Minister of Welfare Karen Jespersen's claim that MFR was a fundamentalist organisation supporting stoning: She was allowed to call them fundamentalist, but not to claim that they support stoning.

The second umbrella Danish Muslim Union (DMU) was officially founded in March 2008. The initiative came from a working group, which during 'several years' had worked to establish union objectives, structure, workflow, etc. The initiative for the formation of the union was taken by Millî Görüş and consists of associations representing Muslims from different ethnic backgrounds, including Pakistani, Turkish, Bosnian, Arabic, Somali and Danish. Six Muslim organisations and 31 local associations and youth divisions, including Minhaj ul-Qur'an and the Association of Bosnian Muslims, are members of DMU. DMU claims to have about 25 000 members. The activities in which DMU is involved in include a conference on prevention of radicalisation (and they were also invited to comment on the government's plan of preventing radicalisation), but their activities are otherwise less outward oriented and more internal and religious. An example of an activity arranged by DMU is a staging on world famous Qur'an recitations. DMU makes a point of distinguishing itself from MFR by stating that "DMU is not a council, as we know it from other associations, whose primary function is to be advisory. Because DMU is something different and more than a council: "We are a Union, an organ for uniting Muslim organizations, associations and institutions in Denmark [...]" (Dansk Muslimsk Union, n. d.; my translation).

Despite their differences, DMU and MFR have several similarities. First, they are both aware of their responsibility in terms of representing Muslims in the Danish public sphere. Though the subject of radicalisation is so broadly defined by Danish authorities that it is not easily appropriated by religious Muslims, who may face the risk of becoming categorised as 'radical', both DMU and MFR have engaged in activities to prevent radicalisation (Kühle/Lindekilde 2010). Second, the leaders of the organisations do not have specific religious authority. The initiative for MFR came from a private practice physician and the chairman of DMU is affiliated to a Muslim private school. Generally, the two organisations encompass 'secular leaders', that is personalities who may be religiously qualified but who among their assets include secular education and positions. The possession of some amount of secular education is the norm for religious leaders in Denmark, where for instance ministers in the Folkekirke have received six years of training in state universities. The new Muslim leaders are therefore more similar to other religious leaders than the 'imams' of the cartoon crisis.

CHANGE IN EXISTING ORGANISATIONS

Another interesting phenomenon is the changes taking place within already existing organisations. The most important change is probably the public emergence of Diyanet. Before the cartoon crisis Diyanet wasn't known publicly at all. Not recognised as a religious community, and not visible on the national level, few knew that Diyanet was in fact the largest Muslim organisation in Denmark. It says a lot about Diyanet's public strategy that they built two mosque buildings which did not have the appearance of mosques from the outside. The years after the cartoon crisis have meant major changes within Diyanet. For one thing Diyanet has applied for and has received recognition as a religious community and has joined the MFR and participates in its activities including interreligious dialogue. But most importantly perhaps Diyanet is working to get accepted its position as the major Danish Islamic organisation (though retaining ties to its Turkish support base). Many of the local Diyanet mosques have interacted with local communities for many years, but now Diyanet is taking this on as a larger organisation. This includes study groups for the imams stationed in Denmark in order for them to embrace the daily realities of life in Denmark, and the new publicly known mosque project which will be discussed below. Diyanet is also in the process of launching a new more expanded and welcoming home page. Eventually this homepage will also be available in Danish. In comparison to the activities of other Muslim groups and even Diyanet branches in other European countries this may not sound substantial, but in relation to the prior-2005 situation this amounts almost to a revolution. Other organisations which were given a 'boost' by the crisis included 'Muslimer i Dialog' (Muslims in Dialogue), Dialogforum, (Dialogue Forum), a group inspired by the Gülen movement, and 'Forum for Kritiske Muslimer' (Forum for Critical Muslims), an organisation inspired by Tariq Ramadan's call for a European Islam (Nielsen 2010: 233).

In sum the establishment of a number of new organisations as well as changes within existing organisations which followed the cartoon crisis represent a shift of Islamic authority in the public sphere (Kühle 2012: 83). The cartoon crisis was a traumatic experience for many Danish Muslims and though blame was put on *Jyllands-Posten* for publishing the cartoons, many Danish Muslims also felt that the group of Muslims actively involved in The Committee for the Defense of the Honour of the Prophet and Democratic Muslims, generally known in the public as 'the imams' were to be blamed for the dichotomies of the debate following the publications. Some also blamed themselves for not getting more involved in the debates, because they had been so unprepared. The establishment of the two umbrella organisations and the changes taking place within other organisations largely responds to this demand. DMU and MFR regularly publish press releases in which they condemn terrorism as well as comment about Muslims. The leaders of these organisations tend to be well-educated, new secular leaders, and possess a feeling of responsibility in furthering good relations between the Muslim community and Danish society. The way that the umbrella organisations can now represent Islam in Denmark and the way that the question 'how to be a Danish Muslim' has (re)appeared suggests that Islam in Denmark is coming of age. This does not mean that Danish Muslims are now more in agreement than before the cartoon crisis. In fact the converse is true. Before the cartoon crisis most Danish Muslims did not know about the activities and positions of other Muslims outside their own national-ethnic background. Now representatives of the different Muslim organisations are cooperating with those with whom they feel they have something in common.

FROM *AD HOC* TO A RELIGIOUS MINORITY POLICY?

In sum the cartoon crisis led to a transformation of the Muslim environment in Denmark. The question to be asked is the extent to which the policies of the general Danish society also changed. In the book *Mosques in Denmark: Islam and Muslim prayer halls* I described the Danish state's policies towards the Muslims population as ad hoc and inconsistent. The state is, for instance, acting favorably towards Muslim practice in a number of ways: The Danish system of free schools allows for state support for confessional schools, a system characterised by Jørgen Nielsen as one of the most liberal in Europe (2004: 80-82) and Danish legislation allows for *halāl* slaughtering (Bergeaud-Blackler 2007) to give examples of practical aspects of Muslim life which are well provided for in Denmark.

A major inconsistency came however from the different attitudes of local and national authorities, and the different practices of local authorities. In relation to burial practices, hospitals and funding some municipalities have stretched legislation. In relation to provision of funding for mosque associations even to the degree that provisions borders on unlawfulness and is not granted to other religious communities. Though this funding was given to help Muslim communities, it was as concessions rather than rights and their un-systematic nature often led to frustration for the Muslims. The cartoon crisis appears to have resulted in changes in these policies. Few municipalities would now provide 'dubious' funding for Muslims communities, but would treat them on an equal footing with other religious communities. Further, the inauguration of a Muslim burial ground in 2007 allows Muslims to become buried in Denmark in a proper Islamic way without having to rely on the brokerage and facilitation of local burial authorities, often *in casu* ministers in the Folkekirke (Simonsen 2012: 26).

The cartoon crisis created a need for Danish authorities to have direct access to Muslims in Denmark. This requirement is often instrumental, representing the need of authorities to engage Muslim representatives in problem-solving, something which appears to be a major aspect of the strategy of employing more imams in Danish prisons to counter radicalisation and/or further resocialisation (Furseth/Kühle 2011). Yet the consequence for prison life is that religious services are provided to Muslim prisoners. It is hard to tell how much interaction between the Danish state and Muslim organisations has increased since the cartoon crisis, but examples abound from 'Ramadan dinner' (*iftār*) in Parliament and municipalities, procedures of requesting hearing statements on law bills and policies from Muslim organisations, to the major celebration of '*īd al-fitr* in August 2012 arranged by Danish public television (DR; Andersen 2012). The changes in the way the state relates to religion is dependent on the changes within the Muslim environment, where the presence of umbrella organisations with a public agenda allows state and local authorities to relate to the Muslim population in a more systematic, public and sustained way. Islam is on its way to finding a continual and institutionalised position in Denmark.

The changes in the Muslim environment and in the relationship between the state and the Muslim population are not just of academic interest. They condition the goals that Muslim Danes are able to achieve. One area concerns the extent to which mosque associations receive recognition as religious communities in Denmark. Another area regards plans to erect a large and beautiful purpose-built mosque, symbolising the lasting presence of Muslims in Denmark. Being used, mostly in American media, as a measure of the poor conditions of Danish Muslims, the cartoon crisis placed these two topics high on the agenda.

IT TAKES TWO TO TANGO: RECOGNITION OF RELIGIOUS COMMUNITIES

The practice of recognising religious communities goes back to pre-constitutional days. The status of recognised religious communities has historically involved different things, but the right to perform civilly valid marriages has always been considered central. In the recent decade the right to obtain temporary resident visa for foreign 'preachers' has also been bestowed on the recognised religious communities. Previously, this privilege was granted more ad hoc and inconsistently.

When it was alleged during the cartoon crisis that Islam is not recognised in Denmark, this was in fact not true. The first Muslim mosque association to achieve recognition was the Nusrat Djahan mosque under the Ahmadiyya Community, which achieved recognition in 1974. In the 1970s the Muslim World League (1975) and the Islamic Cultural Center (1977) also became recognised religious communities. In the course of the 1980s an additional three Muslim communities achieved recognition. In the 1990s seven more followed, bringing the count to thirteen. In the 2000s nine more communities were recognised, five of which received their position after the cartoon crisis. Some of the Muslim communities are congregations, while others are denominations with several congregations, a fact which should be remembered when counting recognised communities. In 2011 there were 22 Islamic communities encompassing in total 66 congregations (Religion i Danmark 2011). More than half of these congregations have received their recognition since the cartoon crisis. The main factor behind the change is not so much the establishment of new Muslim organisations, but a changing strategy of existing organisations, most noticeably Diyanet. Diyanet received recognition as a denomination in 2006, and now includes 30 congregations.[2] Over the years the procedure has become more transparent so it is simpler for religious communities to apply for recognition, and a website now not only features the forms needed for the application but also the name and addresses of the recognised religious communities.

BUILDING OF PURPOSE-BUILT MOSQUES

The fact that Denmark only holds one building which can be identified as a mosque building from the outside (namely that of the Ahmadiyyas), came to symbolise the alleged oppression of Islam in Denmark during the cartoon crisis. In the aftermath of the cartoon crisis non-Muslim political entrepreneurs and public intellectuals suggested that Danish society as a whole should unite to help Muslims build a mosque as a kind of reimbursement for the sufferings caused by the cartoons. This project was fruitless as commercial interest in investing in

---

2 Ankestyrelsens Familieretsafdeling (n. d.). The board is responsible for handling the recognition of religious communities.

mosques building projects dropped after the cartoon crisis lost its grips on the markets. Until the 1980s and early 1990s Danish authorities were relatively accommodating in terms of Muslim mosque building plans. In 1992 a plot of land was in even set aside in the district plan for Copenhagen for a cultural institution, for instance a mosque (Lægaard 2010: 65), but disagreement among groups of Muslims meant that the plan was not realised. The new landscape of Muslim organisations is directly linked with new mosque building projects. A private investor bought the lot in Copenhagen in 2006 and soon engaged in negotiations with the United Council of Muslims on plans to include a mosque in the bigger project. The project is however only one of a handful of mosque projects all likely to be implemented in the course of the next few years. Several mosque projects have building permission at hand so mosques will be built whenever money has been collected to fund the buildings.

This integration of Islam into 'official' Danish life is – at least partly – an outcome of the cartoon crisis. It is part of a general phenomenon of "progressive normalisation of Islam in European public space" (Saint-Blancat/Perocco 2006: 108). Danish authorities are now developing ways in which Islam may fit into the general fabric of religion-state relations. Islamic organisations and mosque associations are engaging more actively with each other and with other civil society organisations as well as with state agencies. Many of the changes taking place in post-cartoon-crisis Denmark were on its way before the crisis and may eventually have happened anyway. But the pace with which they have appeared justifies talking about the cartoon crisis as a catalyst for the changes.

CONCLUSION

From a Danish-Muslim perspective the cartoon crisis was not a good thing. According to a survey made in 2006 almost all Muslim Danes found the cartoons to be blasphemous and offensive. The global reactions led Denmark into the largest foreign policy crisis for more than 60 years, including attacks on Danish embassies around the world as well as a massive boycott of Danish products in some Muslim countries. The cartoon crisis led to a heated debate in Danish media on the balance between freedom of expression and protection owed to religious minorities. But while two out of three found that the initial publication was justifiable, almost 60 per cent found that the republishing of the cartoons by *Jyllands-Posten* in 2008 was not (Westh 2008). According to a survey done by Zapera for *Ugebladet Mandag Morgen* in February 2006, at the culmination of the crisis", 31 per cent of the respondents found that the crisis has made them realise that they needed more knowledge on Islam (Pedersen/Redington 2006). A market for knowledge on Islam was created by the cartoon crisis. Media attention to Muslims and Islam remains high, but presentation appears to be more even-handed, catering for conflict-related issues as well as general curiosity about Islam. It says a lot about media attention as well as the growing level of cooperation between Muslim organisations and 'official Denmark' that a new phrase, 'Ramadan dinner' has entered the Danish language forcefully since the crisis.

The effects of the cartoon crisis include the formation of new umbrella organisations and these along with the larger publicity of mainstream Muslim organisations as for instance Diyanet means that the presence of Muslims in the public sphere has been normalised. And though the cartoon crisis is not forgotten many Danish Muslims have come to the conclusion that it was not the Prophet the cartoons depictured, following the argument that the Prophet in Islamic thinking is known to have been very beautiful, which inarguably none of the cartoons captured. Or as MFR wrote in a press release following the publication of a book by Flemming Rose, editor at *Jyllands-Posten*, which republished the cartoons: "The cartoons have nothing to do with Islam's last prophet, Muhammad, but portray only the ignorance that prevails about his work" (Muslimernes Fællesråd 2010; my translation). The new Muslim organisations are in this way helping to prevent a new cartoon crisis. The changes caused by the cartoon crisis were big, though it must be said that the cartoon crisis enhanced and speeded processes which were already taking place before the cartoon crisis rather than creating a whole new situation. Autumn 2011 meant the fall of the right wing liberal-conservative government and the installment of a new Social democratic led government. Whether the new government represents a change in discourses and policies remains to be seen. On the grounds of a small word count, documenting a peak in the use of words 'integration', 'Muslim' and 'imam' in national newspapers in 2005-6 and a subsequent decline to a level similar to or below the 2001-level ever since, *Jyllands-Posten* announced in May 2011 that the societal debate on Islam has died down. To illustrate these quantitative changes *Jyllands-Posten* points to the qualitative changes mentioned by politicians and commentators in the article: the debate is less polarised and the general view on Muslims much more nuanced. Discussion on Islam has been replaced by discussions of the financial crisis. Most astonishing is perhaps the change in the position of Dansk Folkeparti, where the 'new' enemy is said to be eastern European workers (Broberg/Kristensen 2012).

REFERENCES

A4 (2006): "Hver tiende muslim accepterer flag afbrænding", in: *Ugebladet A4.* [online] no. 10, 13 March 2006. Available at: http://www.ugebreveta4.dk/ 2006/10/Baggrundoganalyse/Hvertiendemuslimacceptererflagafbraending.as px (accessed January 21, 2013).

Ahlin, Lars et al. (2012): "Religious diversity and pluralism: Empirical data and theoretical reflections from the Danish Pluralism Project", in: *Journal of Contemporary Religion*, 27:3, pp. 403-418.

Ammitzbøll, Pernille / Vidino, Lorenzo (2007): "After the Danish cartoon controversy", in: *Middle East Quarterly*, XIV:1, pp. 3-11.

Andersen, Katrine Jo (2012) "Satsning: Danmarks Radio fejrer eid med stor folkefest", in: *Politiken*, 10 August 2012, p. 3.

Ankestyrelsens Familieretsafdeling [The Division of Family Affairs at the National Social Appeals Board] (n. d.): Anerkendte og godkendte trossamfund og menigheder. [online] Available at: http://www.familiestyrelsen.dk/samliv/ trossamfund/anerkendteoggodkendtetrossamfundogmenigheder (accessed 10 March 2013).

Bergeaud-Blackler, Florence (2007): "New challenges for Islamic ritual slaughter: A European perspective", in: *Journal of Ethnic and Migration Studies*, 33:6, pp. 965-980.

Bleich, Erik (2010): "State responses to 'Muslim' violence: A comparison of six West European countries", in: Bleich, Erik (ed.), *Muslims and the State in the post-9/11 West*, London/New York: Routledge.

Broberg, Mads Bonde / Signe Lund Kristensen (2012): "Islam er taget af plakaten", in: *Jyllands-Posten*, 11 May 2012, p.12.

B. T. (2006): "Danskerne har delte holdninger til Muhammedtegninger", in: *B. T.,* 5 February 2006, p. 11.

Dansk Muslimsk Union [Danish Muslim Union] (n. d.): Om DMU [About DMU]. [online] http://www.dmu.nu/index.php?id=18 (accessed 25 February 2013).

Furseth, Inger / Lene Kühle (2011): "Prison chaplaincy from a Scandinavian perspective", in: *Archives de Sciences Sociales des Religions*, 56:153, pp. 123-141.

Gundelach, Peter (2011): "Stabilitet og forandringer" [stability and changes], in: id. (ed.), *Små og store forandringer: Danskernes værdier siden 1981*, Copenhagen: Hans Reitzels forlag, pp. 11-29.

Helqvist, Iben (2010): "Muslimske interesseorganisationers samarbejde med Integrationsministeriet", in: *Tidsskrift for Islamforskning*, 2, pp. 104-116.

Jacobsen, Brian (2011): "Denmark", in: Nielsen, Jørgen S. et al. (eds), *Yearbook of Muslims in Europe*, vol. 3, Leiden: Brill, pp. 165-180.

Jensen, Michael Taarnby (2006): *Jihad in Denmark: An overview and analysis of jihadi activity in Denmark 1990-2006*, København: DIIS Working Paper 35.

Khader, Naser (2006): The 10 Commandments of Democracy. [online] Available at: http://www.radikale.dk/cms/vis.aspx?aid=53297 (accessed 25 February 2013).

Klausen, Jytte (2009): *The cartoons that shook the world*, New Haven/London: Yale University Press.

Kühle, Lene (2012): "Mosques and Organizations", in: Nielsen, Jørgen (ed.), *Islam in Denmark: The challenge of diversity*, Lanham: Rowman & Littlefield, pp. 81-94.

— (2006): *Moskeer i Danmark: Islam og muslimske bedesteder*, Højbjerg: Univers.

Kühle, Lene / Lindekilde, Lasse (2010): *Radicalization of young Muslims in Aarhus*, Aarhus University. [online] Available at: http://cir.au.dk/fileadmin/site_files/filer_statskundskab/subsites/cir/radicalization_aarhus_FINAL.pdf (accessed 21 February 2013).

Larsen, Henrik (2007): "The cartoon crisis in Danish foreign policy. A new balance between the EU and the US?", in: *Danish Foreign Policy Year Book 2007*, pp. 51-85. [online] Available at: http://dcism.dk/graphics/Publications/Books2007/Yearbook2007/yearbook07_hole.pdf#page=51 (accessed January 21, 2013).

Larsson, Göran / Lindekilde, Lasse (2009): "Muslim claims-making in context: Comparing the Danish and Swedish Muhammad cartoons controversy in comparative perspective", in: *Ethnicities*, 9: 3, pp. 361-383.

Lægaard, Sune (2010): "Grand-Mosque' projects in Copenhagen: Intersections of respect, tolerance and intolerance in the distribution of Public Space", in: *Politics in Central Europe*, 6:3, pp. 60-80.

Maréchal, Brigitte et al. (eds) (2003): *Muslims in the enlarged Europe: Religion and society*, Leiden: Brill.

Muslimernes Fællesråd [United Council of Muslims] (2010): Pressemeddelelse vedrørende: Udgivelse af bogen 'Tavshedens tyranni' af Flemming Rose. 29 September. [online] Available at: http://www.mfr.nu/index.php?option=com_content&view=article&id=1&Itemid=59 (accessed 10 March 2013).

Nielsen, Jørgen (2010): "Danish cartoons and Christian-Muslim relations in Denmark", in: *Exchange*, 39:3, pp. 217-235.

— (2004): *Muslims in Western Europe*, Edinburgh: Edinburgh University Press.

Olesen, Thomas (2007): "The porous public and the transnational dialectic: The Muhammed cartoons conflict", in: *Acta Sociologica*, 50, pp. 295-308.

Pedersen, Lars (1999): *Newer Islamic movements in Europe*, London: Ashgate.

Pedersen, Poul Anders / Redington, Noa (2006): "Den danske befolkning: islam er foreneligt med demokrati", in: *Ugebladet Mandag Morgen,* February 13, 2006. Available at: http://www.mandagmorgen.com/www_coexistenceofcivilizations_org/filer/Ugebrevsartikel%20-%20Islam%20foreneligt%20med%20demokrati.pdf. (accessed January 21, 2013).

Politiets Efterretningstjeneste [Danish Security and Intelligence Service] (n. d.): Threats to Danish interests abroad. [online] Available at: https://www.pet.dk/English/Threats%20to%20Danish%20interests.aspx (accessed 25 February 2013).

Religion i Danmark (2011): [online] Yearbook on Religion in Denmark. Available at: http://teo.au.dk/csr/rel-aarbog11/god-tro (accessed 21 June 2011).

Riis, Ole (2011): "Rejection of religious pluralism", in: *Nordic Journal of Religion and Society,* 24:1, pp. 19–36.

— (2007): "Religious pluralism in a local and global perspective", in: Beyer, Peter / Beaman, Lori (eds), *Religion and globalisation,* Leiden: Brill, pp. 433-453.

Rose, Flemming (2008): "Why I published those cartoons", in: *Washington Post,* 19 February 2006, p. 3. [online] Available at: http://multimedia.jp.dk/archive/00080/Avisside_Muhammed-te_80003a.pdf (accessed 21 February 2013).

— (2005): "Muhammeds ansigt", in: *Jyllands-Posten,* 30 September 2005, [online] Available at: http://www.washingtonpost.com/wp-dyn/content/article/2006/02/17/AR2006021702499.html (accessed 21 February 2013).

Saint-Blancat, Chantal / Perocco, Fabio (2006): "New modes of social interaction in Italy: Muslim leaders and local society in Tuscany and Venetia", in: Césari, Jocelyne / McLoughlin, Seán (eds), *European Muslims and the secular state,* Aldershot: Ashgate, pp. 99-112.

Schmidt, Garbi (2003): "Muslimske Ungdomsforeninger I Danmark", in: Paulsen Galal, Lise / Liengaard, Inge (eds), *At være muslim i Danmark,* Frederiksberg: Anis, pp. 51-73.

Sheikh, Mona Kanwal / Crone, Manni (2012): "Muslims as a Danish security issue", in: Nielsen, Jørgen (ed.), *Islam in Denmark: The challenge of diversity,* Lanham: Rowman & Littlefield, pp. 173-195.

Simonsen, Jørgen Bæk (2012): "Denmark, Islam and Muslims: Socioeconomic dynamics and the art of becoming", in: Nielsen, Jørgen (ed.), *Islam in Denmark: The challenge of diversity,* Lanham: Rowman & Littlefield, pp.173-195.

Warburg, Margit (2010): "Globalisation and religious diasporas: a reassessment in the light of the cartoon crises", in: Christoffersen, Lisbet et al. (eds), *Religion in the 21st century: Challenges and transformations,* Farnham: Ashgate, pp. 215-228.

Westh, Asger (2008): "Danskerne om Muhammedtegningerne: Rigtigt første gang – ikke anden", in: *Jyllands-Posten,* 17 March 2008, p. 1.

Wren, Karen (2001): "Cultural racism: something rotten in the state of Denmark", in: *Social and Cultural Geography,* 2:2, pp. 141-162.

Basel's 'swimming refuseniks'[1]
A systemic study on how politics observe
Muslim claims to diversity in state schools

MARIUS ROHRER

INTRODUCTION

According to Nentwich, Steyaert and Liebig (2010: 263), Switzerland is an
"amazingly diverse country" with regards to its four official languages, many religions and 26 sovereign administrative entities (cantons) given its comparatively
small population. It seems only natural, then, that diversity is increasingly becoming a political issue. The political negotiation of diversity is a global issue
(Benhabib 1996: 4), and the question of how it is or should be treated has often
been framed in terms such as "multiculturalism", "equality" (Cooper 2004), and
"immigration" (Kymlicka/Keith 2006) or "integration" in a German-speaking
and Swiss context (D'Amato/Suter 2012; Gianni 2009; Niederberger 2004;
Wichmann/D'Amato 2010). For the past decade, in Switzerland and many other
European countries, Muslims have been perceived as "paradigmatic 'others'"
(Allenbach/Sökefeld 2010: 9). Thus, an analysis of the governance of religious
diversity seems apt and will be demonstrated by looking at the case of several
Muslim parents refusing to send their children to coeducational swimming les-
sons in state primary schools in Basel.

---

1 The media quickly coined the German term 'Schwimmverweigerer' for the Muslim
parents refusing to let their children attend swimming lessons. Cf. *Basler Zeitung*, 9
December 2010, http://bazonline.ch/basel/stadt/Schwimmverweigerer-muessen-zahlen/
story/17776087 (accessed 24 March 2012).

The findings presented in this article are based on empirical data from various sources which are thematically concerned with the issue of the 'swimming refuseniks' in Basel. They include (a) a data corpus of 26 newspaper articles from January 2008 to April 2012, (b) ten semi-structured interviews (lasting 50 to 90 minutes each, transcribed verbatim) with eleven informants (one double-interview), six of whom were employees of Basel's Department of Education (DoE) at the time of the interview, and (c) a corpus of 22 case-relevant administrative, legal and political documents. All data were analysed according to a modified version of the Distinction Theory Text Analysis (Titscher et al. 2007: 185-197) as described in the methodology section below.

'SWIMMING REFUSENIKS': RELIGIOUS DIVERSITY AND PUBLIC EDUCATION IN BASEL

In Basel's state schools, religious diversity has been observed as a potential source of tension between the educational mandate of state schools and parental authority (Kanton Basel-Stadt 2007: 3). Issues include exemptions from school on religious holidays; Christian ceremonies (Easter, Christmas); sports and swimming lessons; field trips and overnight stays; and the issue of wearing religious symbols (ibid.).

The question as to whether Muslim students should be obliged to attend compulsory swimming lessons in public primary schools has been widely discussed in both the legal and political sphere due to two conflicting Federal Supreme Court rulings in 1993 and 2008.[2] In 1993, the Federal Court ruled in favour of the claim that compulsory mixed-sex swimming lessons contravened Islamic beliefs, which were to be protected under the principle of the freedom of religion (Bundesgericht 1993). In a second Federal Court verdict in 2008, however, the 1993 ruling was overturned. This time, the verdict considered the public interest of compulsory education to be more important than private religious freedom (Bundesgericht 2008), basing this decision on four main interrelated arguments: It was argued that, compared to 1993, the "religious composition" of Swiss society had changed considerably, particularly with regard to Islam. Secondly, more of a "multicultural school reality" (ibid.) could be observed than fifteen years prior which demanded a particular effort with regard to the "acclimatisation" and "inclusion" of pupils into state schools and Swiss society (ibid.). Thirdly, because of this change, integration measures had been given a central

---

2   For a legal analysis see Reich (2009).

position overall, such as in a new law concerning foreigners issued in 2005 (ibid.). The verdict finally acknowledged the importance of state schools in the process of social integration.

Roost Vischer states that the 2008 verdict "led to a stricter management of exemption requests on the cantonal level" (2010: 126) and that in Basel, the issue of exemption from swimming lessons due to religious reasons constituted the main conflict regarding religious diversity in 2008 (ibid.; Roost Vischer 2011: 376). Whereas prior to that change in law and the directive issued by the DoE, Muslim children in Basel's schools had been exempt, this was now no longer possible. To the contrary, the policy change also enabled the DoE to issue fines in cases of non-compliance by parents or pupils (id.).

However, from August 2008 onwards, five families refused to send their seven children to the mandatory swimming lessons despite the new regulations. In September 2008, the parents were informed about the possibility of a fine and a meeting between the parents and the head of the Education section at Basel's ministry of education was held, but no agreement could be reached. The conflict escalated and in July 2010, the DoE eventually issued fines due to "repeated violation of parental duties" (to send their children to class) to the amount of CHF 350 (ca. EUR 300) per parent and child (Administrative Court of Basel 2010: 2).[3] One family, with the financial help of a third party, decided to appeal the verdict, first on the cantonal, then on the federal level. In a fashion similar to the Federal Court case, they argued that the religious education of their children (to which the parents are, by law, solely entitled until the child reaches the age of 16) could not be successfully achieved if their children were to attend coeducational swimming lessons from the start of primary school, i.e. at the age of seven. These parents also regarded the compromise of their girls wearing a *burqini*[4] as unsatisfactory, as the issue of seeing lightly dressed people in the lessons remained (Interview with Department of Education, DoE[5], Basel, 1 December 2010). In March 2012, however, the Federal Court ruled against the claimants, reasserting its 2008 ruling that compulsory schooling and integration are more important than religious commandments (Bundesgericht 2012).

---

3   One family with two parents and two children was therefore fined to the amount of
    CHF 1400.

4   A burqini is a swimsuit fully covering the whole body except the face, the hands and
    the feet. Cf. http://www.ahiida.com (accessed 5 March 2012).

5   Names withheld.

METHODOLOGY: SYSTEMS THEORY, DIVERSITY AND FUNCTIONAL ANALYSIS

The research presented in this article builds on sociological systems theory as put forward by Niklas Luhmann.[6] Fundamentally, this strand of systems theory contends that meaning-based psychic and social systems operate through *observation* (Fuchs 1999: 47), "an operation using a distinction for indicating one side of the distinction and not the other" (Luhmann 1993: 485). Being the basic principle of the construction of reality,[7] observation draws a distinction (Spencer-Brown 1969: 3), marking one side while leaving the other side unmarked. Words in textual data, then, are forms distinguishing what they indicate from other (excluded) possibilities (Hafen/Gretler Heusser 2008: 229). This means that every distinction is a *two-sided distinction*: even if only one side is indicated and named (e.g. the form for inclusion into the political system, 'citizen'), every observation carries with it the other, unmarked side of the distinction (the corresponding form for political exclusion, 'foreigner') (Luhmann 2002a: 212; Stichweh 2005: 76sq.). The unity of the difference between the two sides is called *form* ('citizenship' = citizen | foreigner) (Spencer-Brown 1969: 4). Whenever an observation is carried out using a particular form (such as 'citizenship'), the system cannot at the same time see the outside, its *blind spot* (Titscher/Wodak/Vetter 2007: 187). In our example, this could be any other attribute of a person: marital status, job position, favourite pastime or another quality.

While diversity and diversity management are well-established concepts in business administration and organisational research, it is still rarely used in political analysis (Riedmüller/Vinz 2007: 143). In the few contributions that employ the term 'diversity', it is understood as "a normative politics" (Cooper 2004: 8) or as an effect of an "act of differentiation" (Differenzhandeln; Fuchs 2007: 17). Riedmüller and Vinz emphasise the *constructedness* of differences in diversity politics, arguing that differences form only through their "indication" (2007: 144). In this respect, Luhmann's notion of the fundamental cognitive operation of observation as "distinction and indication" (1995: 44) proves analytically helpful. I will argue that diversity can be framed as an *observation of difference (not identity, and particularly in the form of a quality attributed to a person) made by systems*, and applied to the study of governance or political management of diversity.

---

6 In English: Luhmann (1995 [German original: 1984]) or, introductory, Borch (2011).

7 According to Spencer-Brown, "a universe comes into being when a space is severed or taken apart" (1969: v), or in other words, reality is created by drawing distinctions, distinguishing something from other possible things and thereby creating its identity.

Titscher, Wodak and Vetter (2007: 185-197) offer a method to "reconstruct the distinctions in utterances" (id., 187) appearing in textual data, which is called "Distinction Theory Approach" (DTA; id.). However, whereas the authors psychologically define the distinctions appearing in texts to represent "the only visible aspect of perceptual frameworks" (id., 187), I argue that, in line with a systems theoretical framework, distinctions and forms appearing in a text should be interpreted as *observations made by social systems*. Following Luhmann's hypothesis of the functional differentiation of modern society, dividing it into manifold contextures[8] of function systems (like law, economics, or politics) each operating by its own binary code (1995: 53), one can then interpret a text as a "poly contextual, multidimensional performance of society" (Vogd 2005: 77). In other words, a text is not seen as a manifestation of the psychological constructs of its authors, but rather as a *polycontextual interplay of systemic observations* which reproduce social systems (and with them, society) through that text. From here, one can employ a research strategy called "functional method" (or "functional analysis") (Luhmann 1995: 52sqq., Knudsen 2010) in order to ask which problem the use of a specific distinction at a particular point (in a text, for example) solves, or what *function* it serves. In brief, functional analysis treats social phenomena as one possible solution to a problem of meaning, and it is its task to (re)construct that problem (Knudsen 2010). Thereby, the method shifts "manifest" structures and functions into the context of other possibilities, exposing them to comparison and treating them as contingent (Luhmann 1995: 56sq.). In sum, systems theory and functional analysis provide a basis with which to conceptualise how systems cope with diversity and to understand "how contingent[9] forms of communication stabilize themselves as systemic structures, as well as the functions of these specific communication structures" (von Groddeck 2010).

---

8   A contexture is a "binary structural domain, i.e. a binary logic (true/false or yes/no)" (Sütterlin 2009: 61).

9   Not to be confused with arbitrary, but more in the sense of a lack of exclusive determination. According to Luhmann (1995: 106), the concept of contingency results from excluding necessity and impossibility: "Something is contingent insofar as it is neither necessary nor impossible, it is just what it is (or was or will be), though it could also be otherwise. A societal reservoir of communicative forms, so to speak, is (re)produced through communication" (the selective processing of information, utterance and understanding; Luhmann 1995: 147). But at no point is the use of one particular form (and not another) exclusively necessary or impossible. Rather, the forms could have evolved differently.

HOW POLITICS COPE WITH DIVERSITY:
DISCIPLINED INCLUSION, POTENTIAL, EXPULSION

The politics of education[10]: Discipline and include[11] religious claims

One document in particular marks the shift in the approach Basel's public education takes towards diversity in general, and in dealing with the 'swimming refuseniks': An administrative directive concerning religious diversity issues at school (Kanton Basel-Stadt 2007). According to one of the contributors to the directive, the main goals of the document included "finding a balance to the area of tension between the rights to freedom and equality which is particularly salient in schools, and to consider the parents' right to education as well as the school's mandate to education and integration" (Roost Vischer 2010: 126).

Crucial to the 'swimming refuseniks' case is the form of 'puberty'. This form is used in the directive to determine when to switch from coeducational to monoeducational swimming instruction:

> Swimming and sports classes are mandatory. Exemptions can only be issued to students, who have reached puberty (thus, from about twelve years of age)[12], if swimming lessons have to be taught coeducationally. For gender-separated swimming lessons, no exemptions can be allowed. Exemptions are to be restricted in time.   (Kanton Basel-Stadt 2007: 8)

The distinction *prepubescent | pubescent* (and not, for example, a form concerned with *psychological* development) is then used to observe religion regarding its

---

10 In reference to Luhmann's book series on "the politics, economy, law, art (etc.) of society" (e.g. 2002a/b), the three strategies of coping with religious diversity presented here are called "the politics of (education, integration, migration)" since they represent communicative networks belonging to (are subsystems of) the political system: The politics of education does not concern itself with marking pupils' essays, but tries to reach a collectively binding decision on the implementation of swimming lessons at schools in the canton of Basel-City, which by Luhmann's definition (1990: 73), makes it political communication on education, not educational communication.

11 In reference to Foucault's (1995) account of coercive measures and institutions of the modern nation-state.

12 As of 2011, swimming lessons in Basel are being taught monoeducationally from fifth grade onwards, compared to sixth grade before (Roost Vischer 2011: 378).

stance on gender-relations and coeducation. The directive deduces that "no religion prescribes the compulsory separation of girls and boys before puberty. In consequence, the question of exemption from swimming lessons only becomes salient *after* puberty" (ibid., my emphasis). The Qur'an is explicitly mentioned as "demanding for both men and women clothing which mostly covers the body from the onset of puberty" (ibid.). The directive then progresses to construct knowledge about "the Islamic cultural sphere", which is seen to "value the protection of intimacy very highly" (Kanton Basel-Stadt 2007: 9), and in consequence infers strategies of governance: "In these cases, particular conditions for swimming classes should be offered", including separate changing rooms and shower stalls, the possibility to wear particular swimwear (like a *burqini*) and teachers of the same sex as students (ibid.). The directive argues that "hereby, religiously motivated morals can largely be met and requests for exemption can be avoided, without compromising tuition or the right to education" (ibid.). However, other possible observations of governability and self-governance remain a blind spot.

As far as reflective observations of politics are concerned, one significant form is 'social order' *(coexistence | chaos)*. In an interview with a high ranking civil servant of the DoE, the state is seen as the warrantor of social order, and its authority must not be undermined, or else chaos will break out (Interview DoE Basel I, 15 December 2010). To this interviewee, issuing fines is also a (political) means to uphold the state's authority. In the same vein, he observes a third party's offer to pay for the fines in place of the Muslim parents as legally permitted, yet politically unwanted (ibid.). Blind spots include the position and potency of the state to guarantee social order in general, as well as other possible forms of social order (e.g., self-organised local communities).

However, another DoE official used the form of 'trade-off': "yes, they have to swim, but in return the school pays attention that religious feelings are not being hurt" (Interview DoE Basel II, 10 November 2010). The usage of this form (just like the measure suggested in the directive to avoid exemptions) signals a degree of co-dependency between public administration and its audience and suggests that it is not the state as such that is at stake here. Reflective observations of the educational system rather point to a problem of that very system: *ensuring the inclusion of all children into public education*. This can be seen as one of the central expectation structures of that system since its emergence in the late eighteenth century (Luhmann 2002b: 137), and its semantics are still reproduced today: Public education is seen by two interviewees as a "societal bracket" – perhaps even "the last one", providing *social coherence*, and as being threatened by claims to diversity (religious and otherwise). Reflections on the actual possibility of total inclusion into public education and social coherence more generally remain blind spots. This expectation of total inclusion is then used by one inter-viewee as one side of the "norm"[13] form, comparing the norm to compromise made in class. When asked about a case where a headmaster had allowed Mus-lim children to attend private swimming lessons (prior to the publication of the directive), the interviewee, a high ranking official of the DoE, replied:

> There you've got the solution in practice, haven't you? One starts to make com-promises. In the end it becomes wishy-washy and then the whole system breaks apart and this is dangerous, isn't it? The next one will come and say: 'this French teacher is useless, my mother tongue is French and I'm going to teach it myself.' And so you start to give in and in the end the idea of public education is just gone.
>
> (Interview DoE Basel I)

On the other hand, the problem of controlling educational objectives is used to argue against allowing private schooling. It is interesting to note that all these concerns are not limited to religious diversity but "individual claims" and "opin-ions on education in general" including questions such as which school snack is considered healthy (Interview DoE Basel III, 1 December 2010).

The interviewees evaluated the governmental effectiveness of the fines as predominantly positive[14], drawing a positive causal link between the penal measure and a cessation in exemption requests: "Because of this regulation [the directive, MR], perhaps also in combination exactly with the fine, requests for exemption are gone, [...] and there are no exemptions anymore" (Interview DoE Basel II). Just like with the form of governance, reflection on the possibility of governance in general remains a blind spot, as does the question of unintended consequences or 'side-effects' of regulative measures.

The following table summarises the forms as well as their blind spots dis-cussed so far:

---

13 In the sense of the unity of difference (the two sides of the form) between compliant and non-compliant expectations. The "norm"-form can be used to observe deviation from an expectation (Krause 2005: 199).

14 The mass media would disagree here, according to my analysis. Also, a recent report criticised the negative effect of fines issued to 'swimming refuseniks' in the neigh-bouring canton of Basel-Land. See http://www.telebasel.ch/de/tv-archiv/&id=366791623 (accessed 19 April 2012). However, all of the interviewees at one point critically ob-served the mass media as drawing a disproportionate amount of attention to the re-fuseniks' case.

Table 1: Selected relevant forms in directive and interviews with members of Basel's DoE

Indication	As distinct from	Form	Blind spots
pubescent	prepubescent	puberty	psychological development
offering particular conditions	no particular conditions	governance	governability, self-governance
coexistence	chaos	authority of state	possibility of social order, different forms of order (self-organisation)
participation	respect for religious feelings	trade-off	possibility of total inclusion into public education
practice (non-compliant)	norm (compliant)	norm	reflection of expectation itself
prevention of exemption requests	no prevention	governance effect	governability, 'side effects'

Source: Author's compilation.

Table 1 shows a predominance of forms related to governance, norm and state authority, while the actual *possibility* of governance – governability or the expectation of successfully causing a direct effect through governance – as well as the possibility of constructing and upholding social order and the reflection of norms itself remain blind spots.

If we once again turn to the question of function, we can see that the communication of a fine offers latency protection for a crucial expectation structure of the educational system: total inclusion of society through its children. In other words, it relieves the education system of having to reflect the contingency of public education – after all, people can send their children to private schools if they see their religious, pedagogical or other needs better suited there. This also makes plausible the form of trade-off which represents a compromise in state power: while expulsion from school would be an imaginable alternative, it would compromise the goal of extensive inclusion – as would granting private swimming lessons or exempting students from swimming would. While the relevance of swimming lessons can be disputed from an integration policy perspective focussing on the potential of migrants, pupils' attendance to swimming classes remains vital to the educational system in order to uphold its expectation of total inclusion. Therefore, we might best characterise the educational politics approach to diversity as "discipline and include"[15]: Accepting diversity as long as it does not compromise the systemic structure of total inclusion.

Hypothetically speaking, there would be another solution which would allow for the inclusion of 'swimming refuseniks' into public education: monoeducational swimming lessons for all school levels. However, this would mean significant change on the *organisational level* of schools: More teachers, more budget and more infrastructure would be needed – making it not the easiest task to justify politically in the light of the quantitative marginality of the conflict.[16] The following two sections will look at other approaches to the 'swimming refuseniks' conflict put forward by integration and parliamentary politics.

The politics of integration: Diversity as a potential

In 1999, Basel's governing council commissioned a mission statement and action plan for the canton's integration policy (Ehret 1999). It was slightly revised in 2004 but is still in effect as of today. The mission statement builds on three principles and subsequently defines appropriate implementation proposals:

– To make use of the potential, the "achievements, abilities and skills of the involved parties" as the foundation for integration policy.
– To consider integration as a concern for society as a whole, where "the totality of all members of society is brought into focus of observations and efforts".
– The conscious and diligent approach to difference: "Neither must socially or structurally caused problems be superficially culturalised or ethnicised, nor must gender-specific aspects be ignored or neutralised" (Ehret 1999: 4).

The mission statement derives implementation proposals following from these principles, including the fields of education, employment, neighbourhood development, public awareness campaigns and political participation for migrants. Through an analysis of the distinctions and forms used in the text, an interplay between political and economic modes of observation becomes evident.

---

15 In reference to Foucault's (1995) analysis of governmental control mechanisms, and Dhamoon's notion of "disciplining" diversity (2010: 256).
16 This argument is taken up by Roost Vischer (2010: 127) who argues to consider the "aspects of feasibility and commensurability" in the "swimming refuseniks" case and calls on "all groups" for raised "resource awareness" (ibid.).

Political inclusion/exclusion

Unsurprisingly, one of the most central forms in the mission statement observes the inclusion/exclusion of persons into or out of the *political system*. On the one hand, persons (to be included) are being observed according to their quality of *citizenship: (Swiss) citizen | foreigner*. Following Luhmann we can observe the form of citizenship as a genuinely political one which appeared in the aftermath of the French revolution and European nation-building processes of the late eighteenth century (2002a: 212). By being a political contexture, it blocks out other observations of persons, be they economic, legal, scientific, religious, medical or otherwise, and the question of their inclusion into those function systems at the same time.

However, political instruments are also being observed: do they allow for the inclusion of non-nationals or not? This observation again fades out the question of inclusion into (or exclusion of) other systems. The mission statement diagnoses an asymmetry regarding opportunities of political participation: "They [nonnationals, MR] possess neither the right to vote nor the right to participate in initiatives or referendums. [...] They don't have [...] a real political voice" (Ehret 1999: 11, my translation). In the action plan of the statement, goals to reverse this asymmetry are being formulated, ranging from the cantonal right to vote for all residents, naturalisation according to EU norms after five to ten years of regular stay in Switzerland, to the introduction of the *ius soli*[17] (Ehret 1999: 22). Ten years after the ambitious goals were supposed to be achieved in 2002, none of them is fully implemented as of today. This is not intended as criticism, I merely want to point out the problematic nature of governance and of the expectations vis-à-vis politics regarding the governance of society. This is the subject of the next group of forms.

Economic observation of difference and consequences for political action

This group contains a series of forms which structure the *observation of difference*, and the (observed) consequences of these observations for political action. Three particularly important forms emerge: First of all, we can observe a distinction regarding approaches to difference. If we turn again to the third principle of

---

17 Recognition of citizenship according to a child's place of birth, as opposed to the 'inheritance' of citizenship through parents *[ius sanguinis]* which is in effect in Switzerland; see Gilbertson (2006).

the mission statement (see above), dealing with difference is observed (in second order) through a two-sided distinction: *reflective | nonreflective*. Already the statement hints at the consequences of the (negatively evaluated) 'nonreflective' side of the distinction: doing so could lead to culturalisation or ethnicisation, or ignorance of gender-related issues.

Secondly, a form that structures the observation of difference and their consequences for political action appears, namely *causal attributions explaining the social status of migrants* (*intrinsic deficiencies | external opportunity structures*):

> Future integration policy measures are guided by the to-date little used cultural capital and potential of migrants (mutlilingualism, intercultural competence, the idea of the cultural broker, etc.). This realignment signifies a gradual, systematic dismissal of the dominant idea (since the 1970s) of a general need of migrants to catch up (deficiency approach), which had dominated both research and mass media. The fact that foreign employees and their families have difficulty gaining social status in mainstream society shall no longer be explained a priori by their deficiencies. (Ehret 1999: 22, my translation).

These causal attributions are a distinction of reasons that serve to answer the question as to why migrants are less dispositioned (socioeconomically in particular) than Swiss nationals – which is in itself an observation based on the form of citizenship. The 'outdated' deficiency approach explained this asymmetry through the migrants' deficiencies, as discussed above. Subsequently, integration policy measures aimed at compensating these deficiencies – without guaranteeing access to status positions (Ehret 1999: 5). The mission statement observes the implemented compensatory measures as *failed* since they did not "lead to the desired success" (ibid.).

From this observation of failure, the legitimacy of the 'new' potential approach is drawn[18]: "As a consequence, in the future new integration policy measures have to be pursued which increasingly take into account the *competences* of migrants and their children" (ibid., my emphasis). On the level of political action, this leads for example to the formulation of the goal to systematically promote the employment of foreign personnel in state administration and state-

---

18 We might call this form ,cognition' (as opposed to ,form', see above): "Expectations that are willing to learn are stylized as *cognitions*. One is ready to change them if reality reveals other, unanticipated aspects" (Luhmann 1995: 320, original emphasis). In our case, we are presented with a second-order observation of a policy measure in the temporal dimension: (earlier) failure / (future) alignment.

subsidised organisations (id., 18). Specifically, "in the selection and recruitment process [...] their [i.e. the foreigners', MR] specific language skills and their intercultural competence (should be) assessed as qualifications" (ibid.).[19]

And thirdly, the way in which attributions of qualities to migrants (which are observed as *different*) are interpreted and evaluated. Non-natives are seen to have at their disposal a *cultural capital*[20] or *potential* in the form of *multilingualism and intercultural competence* (Ehret 1999: 4). If we look at the temporal dimension, this future-oriented attribution is distinguished (by the mission statement itself) from an earlier attribution focusing on the *deficiencies* of migrants. Here we witness a second-order observation of migration and integration policy over time: how have migrants been perceived in earlier days, compared to nowadays – and possibly the future? The mission statement's answer seems to be: *from deficiency to potential*.

Equally interesting is the distinction of migrants as 'employees': this observation refers to a system-specific role, to their inclusion into the *economic* system – while they could have been observed in their role as parent, patient, plaintiff or consumer. This goes hand in hand with the desired effects the document sees in the implementation of the 'potential approach'. It constructs a business case for using the potential of migrants:

> In the long term, such measures will affect the canton's overall situation in a productivity-increasing and innovation-enhancing way. A comparison with Europe shows that the *positive economic positioning* of immigrants – and particularly their children – has a highly integrative effect on a society.
>
> (Ehret 1999: 5, my translation, original emphasis).

Several keywords – productivity, innovation – and their use in a comparative degree ('enhancing') point towards an *economic* observation: it *is beneficial* to use the migrants' potential (or vice versa: not tapping it would result in a *loss*). This argument is reinforced in the second sentence by a causal attribution between *prosperity* and *integration*.

---

19 Without wanting to dismiss the good intentions underlying this policy, it remains unclear why exactly foreigners are seen to possess these skills – intrinsically, because they are foreigners? Or because they actively acquired them? My point is to hint at the fact that this equation "foreigner = interculturally competent" might prove to be a problematic (or perhaps disappointing?) one.

20 For the sociological notion, see Bourdieu/Passeron (1990).

Basel is not the only city where this realignment towards using the potential of migrants can be observed. Similar policy shifts have occurred in Toronto, Vienna, or Frankfurt am Main (Heinrich-Böll-Stiftung 2008). Observed from a governmentality[21] perspective, this shift "from governance in the sense of a welfare-state-like regulation of the social [...] towards the governance of individuals" can be ascribed to a "currently dominant neoliberal rationality" (Piñeiro/ Haller 2009: 156) and give cause for moral concern. Through the looking glass of systems theory and functional analysis, however, another question comes into focus: *which problem* does this reference to an economic vocabulary of diversity management solve in the context of integration policy?

We start our search for the problem with the citizenship form and the attribution of responsibility for success of integration to both 'sides'. As discussed above, in the mission statement, the form of citizenship – and with it the positive value of Swiss nationality – becomes contingent, and Swiss nationals are starting to be held equally responsible for integrative success of society. As a result, the *scope* of integration policy is being widened beyond 'foreigners'. This allows integration policies to acknowledge and to cope not only with foreign, but also 'domestic' diversity – diversity which cannot be distinguished by the category of nationality. In the case of religious diversity in public education, the functionality of the semantical shift from deficiency to potential becomes evident: Educators increasingly face claims from Muslims, who might no longer be 'aliens'[22], as well as from Jehova's witnesses, fundamental Christians or non-religious parents of Swiss nationality (Interview DoE Basel III, 1 December 2010).

With regard to the 'swimming refuseniks' case, the coordinator for religious issues at Basel's Office for Integration stated that as almost all cantons lack swimming pools to systematically enforce obligatory swimming lessons (Roost Vischer 2010: 127), a promotion of swimming classes outside of state schools would make sense and reduce "a lot of tensions [...] without having to abandon important elements of integration" (ibid.). This emphasis on reducing tension through extracurricular education stands in stark contrast to the actual measures the Department of Education took against the 'swimming refuseniks', as we have seen in the last section. The proposed solution of extracurricular tuition

---

21 In general, proponents of governmentality studies observe (and sometimes criticise) a neo-liberal, economic take-over of politics and social phenomena in general. For an overview, see Dean (2010) or, with a more critical attitude towards the notion of governmentality, Lemke (2000).

22 At least one of the 'swimming refusenik' parents had been naturalised years ago, by his own account (Interview with father, Basel, 3 February 2011).

may solve an integration policy-specific problem (allowing for diversity instead of problematising it), but not those of the educational system (total inclusion) and of educational politics (producing a collectively binding decision on swimming instruction without overburdening educational organisations).

In the following table, the forms discussed in this section shall be displayed again in brief:

Table 2: Relevant forms in Basel's mission statement on integration policy

Indication	As distinct from	Form	Blind spots
citizen	alien	citizenship	other qualities or systemic status (legal, economic, religious, medical etc.)
inclusion	exclusion	inclusiveness of political system	inclusiveness of other systems
potential	deficiency	interpretation of migrants' qualities	reflection of attribution of qualities to migrants and of 'migrant' as category
benefit	loss	economic effect of tapping potential	political, legal, econonomic and other consequences

Source: Author's compilation.

The above table shows how the analysed source uses economic semantics alongside to political semantics when making a point for the benefit of integration policy: tapping the potential of immigrants economically benefits the Basel area.

THE POLITICS OF MIGRATION: EXCLUSION OF DIVERSITY

In April 2010, Sebastian Frehner, a member of the right-wing Schweizerische Volkspartei (SVP, Swiss People's Party[23]) and of Basel's cantonal parliament, along with 32 other members of the cantonal parliament (out of 100 members in total) signed a motion "concerning withdrawal of residence permits of parents keeping their children from attending obligatory swimming lessons" (Kanton Basel-Stadt 2010). Even though this motion was not actually submitted to the

---

23 The party's national website (http://www.svp.ch) is only available in German and French. For their international website aimed at Swiss expatriates, see http://www.svp-international.ch/index.php?lang=en (accessed 25 June 2012).

government council, its content is insightful in terms of the governance of diversity:

> Migrants should only have the right of residence in our canton if they are willing to integrate. Integration requires the willingness of those concerned to observe our laws and adapt to our customs. [...] The undersigned hold that foreign parents who do not, even after repeated requests, exercise their duty to send their children to obligatory swimming lessons, should have their residence permits withdrawn, as they apparently lack the will to integration. (ibid.).

In this motion, the role of migrants is further specified withing the education system, as foreign *parents*. The motion observes the act of refusal by parents to send their children to swimming lessons at school from a *legal* perspective, as a breach of (school) law: *within the law | outside the law*. It then couples this legal distinction to a *moral*[24] one: *willing | not willing to integrate*. And in consequence it demands to *politically exclude* these persons by withdrawing their residence permits.

It becomes obvious that the entire argument of the motion rests on the political form of citizenship. After all, expulsion would not be an applicable measure to 'swimming refuseniks' of Swiss nationality, but only to *foreign parents* as quoted above. This drastic measure therefore only makes sense within the political system, and we can again ask what problem it solves: It evidently does not solve an educational problem, since the public educational system (at least in Basel) will be unable to educate the children once they have been expelled from the system. Since problems are always system-problems (Fuchs 1997: 102sq.), it seems that the answer is rather to be found in the function of the political system, that is to provide the capacity for enforcing collectively binding decisions. Withdrawing the parents' residence permits solves the problem of ensuring the collectivity of a decision, such as holding mandatory coeducational swimming lessons until puberty in state schools. *Excluding diversity* by using a political measure

---

24 Morality "relates to the question whether and under what conditions human beings esteem or disdain one another" (Luhmann 1995: 235), esteem meaning a "generalized recognition and evaluation which honors the fact that others accord with the expectations one believes must be assumed for social relations to continue" (ibid.). In this light, the swiming refuseniks' actions is observed as an unwillingness to integrate, as a moral wrong, which is then subjected to expulsion.

– expulsion – means removing those who are considered different.[25] And on a semantical level, the expulsion strategy also serves to reproduce the expectation of a unified identity: It enables the construction of a homogeneous national collective by excluding diversity. Societal ideas that allow for or are even based on diversity thus remain a blind spot.

CONCLUSIONS

This article conceptualises diversity as an *observation of difference by systems*. Therefore, strategies of managing religious (and other forms of) diversity are always seen as system-specific and closely related to the respective system's *function* and *expectational structures*. I have argued that by drawing on sociological systems theory, it is possible to analyse the first- and second-order observations in textual empirical sources and make visible the polycontextual interplay of systemic structures in the communicative processing of social phenomena. Issues connected to social diversity, such as the claim of Basel's 'swimming refuseniks' in public education can then be seen as a multi-problem, as *multiple observations of religious (and other) diversity* to which multiple, system-relative solutions are produced: (1) Employing an economic notion of diversity as a potential in order to adapt integration policy to conditions of increasing 'domestic' diversity, (2) 'disciplining and including' diversity to uphold the crucial expectation of the education system that all children must be included in public education, or (3) excluding diversity through political expulsion in order to facilitate collective acceptance of decisions and to reproduce the expectation of a unified national identity.

Using a systems theoretical and functionalist approach to study the governance and management of diversity implies consequences both for research and its use outside academia that can only be touched upon briefly here. The differentiation of society into social systems serving particular functions and observing their environment in a particular way means coexisting polycontextual and heterarchical modes of observation and communication (Fuchs 1992). This in turn implies a growing probability of *dissent*, undermining the primacy of the

---

25 The effectivity of this measure can be disputed: The possibility of becoming a Swiss citizen through naturalisation, as one of the 'swimming refuseniks' did (cf. note 22), makes it very difficult to expel a person or withdraw their citizenship (cf. Federal Office for Migration, http://www.bfm.admin.ch/bfm/de/home/themen/buergerrecht/schweizer_buergerrecht.html (accessed 23.04.2012).

political system and its capacity to produce collectively binding decisions. Instead of focusing on the "dream of consensus" (Wefer 2004: 86), it may therefore be more apt (but certainly more complex) to consider these limitations in a conception of "postheroic" (id., 218sqq.) politics operating in an environment of self-organising systems, self-reflectively coping with contingencies, dissent and diversity. The approach used in this article contributes (a) to the reconstruction of the different systemic logics that determine a particular outcome as well as (b) to enabling self-reflection about these logics to provide an understanding of their contingency and a starting point for change in diversity management practices. Beyond the system of academia, educational organisations and their political administration could then be consulted as to whether it is a promising strategy trying to counteract social-structural change by sanctioning individuals, or if there is a way to allow for social evolution while coping constructively with contingency, dissent and diversity of all kinds.

REFERENCES

Administrative Court of Basel (2010): Ruling VD.2010.226. Available at http://www.rwi.uzh.ch/lehreforschung/alphabetisch/kiener/Vorlesungen/hs11/menschenrechte/unterlagen/VerwG-BSSchwimmunterricht.pdf (accessed 22 April 2012).

Allenbach, Brigit / Sökefeld, Martin (2010): "Einleitung", in: Allenbach, Brigit / Sökefeld, Martin (eds), *Muslime in der Schweiz*, Zürich: Seismo, pp. 9-40.

Baecker, Dirk (2007): Form und Formen der Kommunikation, Frankfurt a. M.: Suhrkamp.

Benhabib, Seyla (ed.) (1996): *Democracy and difference: Contesting the boundaries of the political,* Princeton: Princeton University Press.

Borch, Christian (2011): *Niklas Luhmann,* London/New York: Routledge.

Bourdieu, Pierre / Passeron, Jean-Claude (1990): *Reproduction in education, society and culture,* London: Sage.

Bundesgericht [Swiss Federal Supreme Court] (1993): Ruling 119 Ia 178 – swimming lessons. Available at http://www.servat.unibe.ch/dfr/a1119178.html (accessed 21 April 2012).

— (2008): Ruling 2C 149/2008 – exemption from swimming lessons due to religious reasons. Available at http://jumpcgi.bger.ch/cgi-bin/JumpCGI?id=24.10.2008_2C_149/2008 (accessed 21 April 2012).

— (2012): Ruling 2C_666/2011 – obligation to attend coeducational swimming lessons. Available at http://jumpcgi.bger.ch/cgi-bin/JumpCGI?id=07.03.2012_2C_666/2011 (accessed 21 April 2012).

Cooper, Davina (2004): *Challenging diversity: Rethinking equality and the value of difference,* Cambridge: Cambridge University Press.

D'Amato, Gianni / Suter, Christian (2012): "Monitoring immigrant integration in Switzerland", in: Bijl, Rob / Verweij, Arjen (eds), *Measuring and monitoring immigrant integration in Europe,* The Hague: Netherlands Institute for Social Research, pp. 326-243.

Dean, Mitchell (2010): *Governmentality: Power and rule in modern society,* London: Sage.

Ehret, Rebekka (1999): *Leitbild und Handlungskonzept des Regierungsrates zur Integrationspolitik des Kantons Basel-Stadt.* [online] May 1999. Available at: http://www.welcome-to-basel.bs.ch/leitbild_vollversion.pdf (accessed 25 June 2012).

Foucault, Michel (1995): *Discipline and punish: The birth of the prison,* New York: Vintage.

Fuchs, Martin (2007): "Diversity und Differenz – Konzeptionelle Überlegungen", in: Krell, Getraude / Riedmüller, Barbara / Sieben, Barbara / Vinz, Dagmar (eds), *Diversity Studies: Grundlagen und disziplinäre Ansätze,* Frankfurt a. M.: Campus, pp. 17-34.

Fuchs, Peter (1992): *Die Erreichbarkeit der Gesellschaft,* Frankfurt a. M.: Suhrkamp.

— (1997): *Das seltsame Problem der Weltgesellschaft: Eine Neubrandenburger Vorlesung,* Opladen: Westdeutscher Verlag.

— (1999): *Intervention und Erfahrung,* Frankfurt a. M.: Suhrkamp.

Gianni, Matteo (2009): "Citoyenneté et intégration des musulmans en Suisse: adaptation aux normes ou participation à leur définition?", in : Schneuwly Purdie, Mallory / Gianni, Matteo / Jenny, Magali (eds), *Musulmans d'aujourd'hui: Identités plurielles en Suisse,* Genève: Labor et Fides, pp. 73-92.

Gilbertson, Greta (2006): *Citizenship in a globalized world.* [online] Migration Information Source. Available at: http://www.migrationinformation.org/Feature/display.cfm?ID=369 (accessed 15 April 2012).

Hafen, Martin / Gretler Heusser, Simone (2008): "Diversity management – Mittel zur Anti-Diskriminierung, neoliberales Phänomen oder alter Wein in neuen Schläuchen?", in: *Gruppendynamik und Organisationsberatung,* 39:2, pp. 225-237.

Heinrich-Böll-Stiftung (2008): Dossier 'Diversity politics'. [online] July 2008. Available at: http://www.migration-boell.de/downloads/diversity/Dossier_Politics_of_Diversity.pdf (accessed 15 April 2012).

Kanton Basel-Stadt (2007): *Handreichung: Umgang mit religiösen Fragen in der Schule [Directive: coping with religious issues at school].* [online].

Available at: http://edudoc.ch/record/38671/files/BS_2007_d.pdf (accessed 5 April 2012).

— (2010): *Motion betreffend Entzug der Aufenthaltsbewilligung für Eltern, die ihre Kinder vom obligatorischen Schwimmunterricht fernhalten* (Geschäft Nr. 10.5080.01). [online] Grosser Rat, 14. April 2010. Available at: http://www.grosserrat.bs.ch/dokumente/100347/000000347635.pdf (accessed 12 March 2012).

Kaur Dhamoon, Rita (2010): "Security warning: Multiculturalism alert!", in: Ivison, Duncan (ed.), *The Ashgate companion to multiculturalism*, Farnham: Ashgate, pp. 255-276.

Knudsen, Morten (2010): *Suprised by method – Functional analysis and systems theory*. [online] FQS, 11(3), Art. 12. Available at: http://www.qualitative-research.net/index.php/fqs/article/view/1556/3067#g2 (accessed 25 June 2012).

Krause, Detlef (2005): *Luhmann-Lexikon,* Stuttgart: Lucius & Lucius.

Kymlicka, Will / Banting, Keith (2006): "Immigration, multiculturalism, and the welfare state", in: *Ethics & International Affairs,* 20:3, pp. 281-304.

Lemke, Thomas (2000): "Neoliberalismus, Staat und Selbsttechnologien: Ein kritischer Überblick über die 'governmentality studies'", in: *Politische Vierteljahresschrift*, 1, pp. 31-47.

Luhmann, Niklas (1990): *Political theory in the welfare state,* Berlin/New York: De Gruyter.

— (1993): "Observing re-entries", in: *Graduate Faculty Philosophy Journal,* 16:2, pp. 485-498.

— (1995): *Social systems,* translated from German by John Bednarz Jr. with Dirk Baecker, Stanford CA: Stanford University Press.

— (2002a): *Die Politik der Gesellschaft,* Frankfurt a. M.: Suhrkamp.

— (2002b): *Das Erziehungssystem der Gesellschaft,* Frankfurt a. M.: Suhrkamp.

Nentwich, Julia / Steyaert, Chris / Liebig, Brigitte (2010): "Diversity made in Switzerland: traditional and new plurality meets the business case", in: Klarsfeld, Alain (ed.), *International Handbook on Diversity Management at Work*, Cheltenham: Edward Elger, pp. 263-282.

Niederberger, Josef Martin (2004): Ausgrenzen, Assimilieren, Integrieren: die Entwicklung einer schweizerischen Integrationspolitik, Zürich: Seismo.

Piñeiro, Esteban / Haller, Jane (2009): "Neue Migranten für die Integrationsgesellschaft: Versuch einer gouvernementalen Gegenlektüre des Prinzips 'Fordern und Fordern'", in: Piñeiro, Esteban / Bopp, Isabelle / Kreis, Georg (eds), *Fördern und Fordern im Fokus: Leerstellen des schweizerischen Integrationsdiskurses*, Zürich: Seismo, pp. 141–170.

Reich, Johannes (2009): "Switzerland: Freedom of creed and conscience, immigration, and public schools in the postsecular state – compulsory coeducational swimming instruction revisited", in: *International Journal of Constitutional Law*, 7:4, pp. 754-767.

Riedmüller, Barbara / Vinz, Dagmar (2007): "Diversity politics", in: Krell, Getraude et al. (eds), *Diversity Studies: Grundlagen und disziplinäre Ansätze*, Frankfurt a. M.: Campus.

Roost Vischer, Lilo (2010): "Alle Kinder sollen schwimmen lernen", in: Christoph Merian-Stiftung (ed.), *Basler Stadtbuch*, 130, pp.125sqq.

— (2011): "Weder Assimilations- noch Differenzzwang: Islam und gesellschaftliche Integration – Reflexionen aus der Basler Praxis", in: Allenbach, Brigit / Sökefeld, Martin (eds), *Muslime in der Schweiz*, Zürich: Seismo, pp. 359-390.

Spencer-Brown, George (1969): *Laws of form*, London: Allen & Unwin.

Stichweh, Rudolf (2005): *Inklusion und Exklusion: Studien zur Gesellschaftstheorie*, Bielefeld: Transcript.

Sütterlin, Petra (ed.) (2009): *Dimensionen des Denkens*, Norderstedt: Books on Demand.

Titscher, Stefan et al. (2007): *Methods of text and discourse analysis*, London: Sage.

Vogd, Werner (2005): "Komplexe Erziehungswissenschaft jenseits von empirieloser Theorie und theorieloser Empirie: Versuch einer Brücke zwischen Systemtheorie und rekonstruktiver Sozialforschung", in: *Zeitschrift für Erziehungswissenschaft*, 8:1, pp. 113sq.

von Groddeck, Victoria (2010). *The case of value-based communication – Epistemological and methodological reflections from a system theoretical perspective.* [online] Forum Qualitative Social Research, 11:3. Available at: http://www.qualitative-research.net/index.php/fqs/article/view/1551/3061 (accessed 25 March 2012).

Wefer, Matthias (2004): *Kontingenz und Dissens: Postheroische Perspektiven des politischen Systems*, Wiesbaden: VS Verlag.

Wichmann, Nicole / D'Amato, Gianni (2010): *Migration und Integration in Basel-Stadt: Ein Pionierkanton unter der Lupe.* [online] Forschungsbericht no. 55, Neuchâtel: SFM. Available at: http://www.welcome-to-basel.bs.ch/sfm _55_complet.pdf (accessed 24 March 2010).

'Against Islam, but not against Muslims'
Actors and attitudes in the Swiss minaret vote

ANDREAS TUNGER-ZANETTI[1]

On 29 November 2009, Swiss voters in a national referendum decided to add a single phrase to Article 72 of the constitution: "The construction of minarets is forbidden." 57.5 per cent of those going to the polls voted in favour of this amendment. The vote is remarkable in several respects: Firstly, an unusually high percentage of 53.8 of those entitled to vote actually went to the polls, the average for 2000-2010 being 44.7 per cent. Secondly, the proposition was accepted against the recommendation of nearly all major parties and civil society organisations. Thirdly, surveys prior to the vote predicting the rejection of the proposal proved wrong. Fourthly, the outcome caused widespread bewilderment nationally and internationally and triggered discussions among the political elite on some aspects of direct democracy. The Swiss public, voters and non-voters alike, considered the vote important even before the result was known, as shown in a survey taken after the vote (Demoscope 2010a, question S06).

Certainly, the popular initiative proposing the ban and the result itself are a landmark in Switzerland's political history. But what does it stand for? What was being negotiated, and by whom? How can we explain the unexpected approval of the ban? To answer these questions, I will describe the dynamics of public communication in the run-up to the vote with a new focus.

---

1   I am grateful to my co-editors and to Ursina Marty for their comments on a draft version of this chapter. I am also grateful to Werner Reimann of Demoscope, Adligenswil, for making the original tables of the Demoscope survey available to me. The title of this chapter is inspired by the headline of an online news article (Anon. 2010).

Scientific analysis so far has treated several aspects of the Swiss debate on 'Islam'. Samuel Behloul (2009a; 2009b) has highlighted the totalising character of the dominating discourse. Several researchers (Ettinger/Udris 2009; Ettinger 2010; Ettinger/Imhof 2011) have analysed the nature and quality of Swiss media reporting on the minaret initiative and its interdependence with the political process. Adrian Vatter (2011) and his team have analysed the minaret vote in detail and situated it in historical perspective, showing that the minaret ban is part of a series of measures taken against religious and other minorities by means of direct democracy. Jean-François Mayer (2011), however, has argued that the minaret ban was more than just 'another case' in that record, but is part of a general European trend. Other researchers have described the composition of the Swiss Muslim population and how they construct their identity (Schneuwly Purdie 2009), Swiss Muslims' own perception of being integrated in society (Gianni 2010) or the way Swiss society and politics conceive of integration and, consequently, design their 'integration policy' (Gianni, this volume).

Integrating these previous contributions I attempt to show that the dynamics leading to the minaret ban cannot be explained without two interrelated phenomena. The first is widespread 'religious illiteracy', one of the salient features of the more general religious landscape of Switzerland alongside growing plurality and a rapidly increasing portion of non-affiliated. Religious illiteracy, I will argue, shapes political debates on religion by leaving many actors unsure about how to handle the topic, thus blocking a substantial public debate and instead favouring one-sided communication in a segmented public. The second phenomenon is what I term the 'second public sphere' in which an important part of public communication beyond mass media took place.

IMMIGRANTS TAKING ROOTS

There are good reasons for thinking that the proposal to ban minarets indicates a general identity crisis of the Swiss collectivity rather than a factual problem with Islam (Ettinger/Imhof 2011: 37). I therefore content myself with highlighting only a few relevant features here.

Islam in Switzerland has no homogenous structure. By 2010 some 440 000 individuals or 5.5 per cent of the Swiss population were of Muslim background (Lathion/Tunger-Zanetti, forthcoming). Ethnically, more than half have their origin in one of Yugoslavia's successor states, one fifth in Turkey and less than 10 per cent in Arab countries. Biographically, the Yugoslav and Turkish guest workers of the 1960s and 1970s were joined by their families in the 1980s and by fellow countrymen in the wake of the Balkan wars in the 1990s. Refugees from other conflict zones in Africa and Asia added more diversity. Only a minority of 10 to 20 per cent is involved in one of the mosque associations with a prayer hall. These associations and a diverse spectrum of umbrella organisations are still mostly headed by first generation immigrants. Islam in Switzerland is far from having any organisational unity, unlike for example in Austria (see Hafez, this volume), because of the linguistic division of the country and because church-state relations are in the competence of each of the 26 cantons.

The low economic and social profile of Swiss Islam becomes obvious through its buildings. Nearly all places of worship are 'invisible' backyard mosques, lodged in industrial premises, office buildings or even apartments. Only two among the half a dozen purpose-built mosques follow classical models and include a minaret: the Mahmud mosque in Zurich, built in 1962-63 by the Ahmadiyya movement, and the Saudi-financed mosque in Geneva, built in 1975-78. They belong to an era which saw only one sacred building constructed every three years, all immigrant religions taken together, and knew no problems with minarets.[2]

A new era in the visibility of immigrant religions began in the mid-1990s when the majority of immigrants finally knew that they would stay and their religious communities began to strive for more adequate places of worship. A buddhist temple, five Orthdox churches, a Sikh gurdwara and a zendo preceded the third overall minaret in the country which, at little more than 3 m high, was set up without any opposition on a converted industrial hall in Winterthur in 2005.

Minaret projects numbers four to six, however, launched independently from each other in 2005 and 2006, turned out to be the catalyst for the anti-minaret campaign. They indicated nothing more than the fact that the immigrant first generation had given up the return perspective and just wanted 'a real mosque' for their permanent stay.[3] Only the first of these three minaret projects was realised, bringing the total in the country to four.

---

2   The project "Cupola – Temple – Minaret" of the University of Lucerne has documented recognizable places of worship of immigrant religions in Switzerland since 1945 and is constantly updated online: www.religionenschweiz.ch/bauten. Some results are presented in Baumann/Tunger-Zanetti 2011: 160sq.

3   The ideas of Muslims in Western Europe, especially first generation immigrants, and non-Muslims about the typical appearance of 'a real mosque' marked by a cupola and a minaret converge (cf. Jasarevic, Alen: "Anders! Das Islamische Forum in Penzberg", in: Beinhauer-Köhler/Leggewie 2009, pp. 102sq.). The difference is in the context: immigrant Muslims try to reconstruct an element of the culture of their country

The case of the fourth minaret holds the key to subsequent developments. A Turkish community in the village of Wangen near Olten (canton of Solothurn), who asked for permission in 2005 to build this "symbolic minaret" as it was termed in the construction request. The structure, erected after four years of litigation in January 2009, is six meters high and sits on top of the lift shaft of a former factory building, bringing the top of the minaret to 16 m above the ground. In June 2006, the Albanian community in the small nearby town of Langenthal (canton of Berne) submitted a similar project providing also a flat cupola next to the minaret on top of the one-storey building bought from a club of Italian guest-workers.[4] In August 2006, protest was also heard in the small town of Wil (canton of St. Gallen) after the imam of the Albanian congregation had shown plans for a mosque with a minaret in an interfaith group, although his congregation had not even bought a building lot at the time.

The projects in Wangen and Langenthal were opposed by neighbours and their local political allies and soon received nationwide media coverage because formal administrative processes had started and entailed litigation. The project in Wil, still lacking a building lot, was pursued by its promoters more discreetly until well after the minaret vote.

The opponents, however, began their campaign anyway. They were preconditioned by developments in the broader European context among which earlier mosque conflicts, comparatively researched by Stefano Allievi (2010b) and his team of national correspondents, but also the well-known chain of events since the Rushdie affair. The last link in this chain was the Danish cartoon crisis (cf. Kühle, this volume). As Ettinger and Imhof (2011: 13) have shown, the cartoon crisis was most important among several key 'communication events' because it provided the reference point for claiming that the religious values of Islam were *per se* incompatible with liberal Swiss values. Earlier, campaigns with anti-immigrant and anti-Muslim colouring, orchestrated by the populist and nationalist-conservative Swiss People's Party (SVP) in other contexts in 2003 and 2004, had helped to prepare the ground (Mayer 2011: 12sq.).

It is against this backdrop that local opponents of the specific projects, allied political entrepreneurs, local authorities, the judiciary and the media were acting. They are the next actors to be portrayed here.

---

of origin as they remember it, for non-Muslims it is something belonging to distant countries known through travel or mass media. These preconceptions recur in most construction plans as well as in pictographs or non-Muslim mosque representations (cf. also the campaign poster on p. 195).

4   For a detailed presentation of the Langenthal case see Kestler 2013: 276-282.

WANGEN, LANGENTHAL, WIL

Swiss construction law gives owners of neighbouring estates the right to oppose building projects within a certain deadline from the date of publication of the plans. The building commission of the municipality, usually composed of citizens elected for a specific term, discusses controversial projects and facilitates negotiations between the owner of the project and the opponents. If no agreement is achieved, the commission has to decide on the basis of law. The defeated party can bring the decision to court. In the case of Langenthal, opposition was not only voiced through neighbouring owners criticising a variety of aspects of the projects, but also through petitions signed by considerable numbers of other residents asking for an unspecified possibility for "the people" to have a say in decisions on the construction of minarets or cupolas.[5] In Wangen the collective appeal ("Sammeleinsprache") of some 381 among the 5000 residents argued that a mosque was not admissible in the industrial zone. In Langenthal, a town of 15 000 inhabitants, 3476 individuals signed the petition which was dismissed by the authorities; here it was the opponents who took the building permission to court. In both cases the public debate created considerable pressure on the local authorities, who in the case of Wangen gave in.

Clearly only a minority of those signing the Wangen appeal and the Langenthal petition were neighbours or in other ways directly affected by the projected structures. They signed to support the 'soft' arguments of urban planning, aesthetics and preservation of cultural heritage, as the Langenthal petition put it. They wanted to prevent the intrusion of an icon linked to distant countries into 'their own' realm. Of course actual neighbours may have had more concrete reasons for opposition, for example for fear of increased traffic, unauthorised parking or noise at inappropriate times. These aspects are much easier to deal with, as the regulations give quite detailed instruction, for example on the calculation of the number of parking lots required for a public building. Claus Leggewie (2009: 122sq.) calls them "teilbare Konflikte" (divisible conflicts) which can be solved by negotiating a 'more or less solution'. "Unteilbare Konflikte" (indivisi-

---

5   The central demand of the Langenthal petition reads as follows: "The undersigned oppose the building of minarets and domed structures for reasons of urban development, aesthetics and cultural heritage, and demand that religious and structurally prominent symbols are not granted within normal planning-permission proceedings. It is important that no political-religious realities are created through the building authorities without allowing the people to have a say and be involved in decision making" (my translation). The whole petition can be found in Tanner 2007, 79.

ble conflicts) by contrast are characterised by an 'either – or' logic which in practice excludes a compromise.[6] In all three cases mentioned the opponents went for an indivisible conflict and used the 'either – or' strategy.

The evidence of many conflicts around mosque building (or conversion) projects throughout Western Europe shows that usually arguments of both types of logic are being advanced. It is very much in the hands of the authorities to deal with the problem in such a way as to create as little discontent or damage as possible without ending up beyond the law.

In the case of Wangen this goal was clearly missed. The local authorities sided with the opponents and refused building permission. Subsequently, the judiciary had to cancel this decision against the minaret. This in turn left the opponents with a sense of having been 'betrayed' by 'their own' judiciary against 'foreigners' and made them think of ways to set new rules for the judges to follow.

The reasons for this failure to manage the process are several and not restricted to Wangen. For one thing small municipalities are less likely to have at their command the competence and experience of how to deal with such rare projects as a new place of worship; building commissions are composed of ordinary citizens among whom usually only a few are familiar with planning and construction. Secondly, these citizens are 'near to the people' and may be more susceptible to public opinion in a controversial project like a mosque than they would be in a bigger municipality. Third, in Wangen in particular, communication was difficult from the beginning. This was certainly not only the fault of the municipality but also of the Turkish congregation. The Olten Türk Kültür Ocağı, founded in 1978 in the nearby city of Olten (18 000 inhabitants), had bought the premise in Wangen in 2002 after giving up the search for an affordable place for its grown congregation in Olten itself. They asked for building permission without first preparing the ground and looking for local allies. Given their firm Turkish nationalist outlook, making friends among the long-established residents was not their priority. Additionally, the pastor of the Protestant church happened to be a German, resident in the parish for many years after having left the heavily Turkish-populated neighbourhood of Berlin-Kreuzberg in Germany. He was personally opposed to the minaret project. Thus, contrary to other cases, a possible mediator was not available to help promote mutual understanding.

---

6   Allievi (2010a: 89) categorises the motives advanced for opposition into those expressing "real" or "cultural" apprehensions. These categories roughly cover Leggewie's categories of "divisible" and "indivisible" conflicts but do not allow the same clear distinction in a specific case.

Another opponent was Roland Kissling, a former member of the Liberals, in 2006 vice-president of the more right-wing and nationalist Swiss People's Party (SVP). He was the person who not only collected the 381 signatures from residents opposed to the minaret, but he was also a member of the group which formally launched the popular initative on the national level (see next section).

What reasons did Kissling and like-minded people advance for opposing the minaret?

- No place for another 'culture': "We know two officially recognised churches here – and now a completely alien culture is about to enter the village? We people of Wangen do not want this" (Kissling, quoted in Studer 2006).
- Risk to religious peace: Kissling "warned against creeping subversion by Islam" (Studer 2006). "We are Christians. Religious peace is endangered by the minaret" (Kissling, quoted ibid.).
- Lack of reciprocity: The building of churches in Islamic countries should be tolerated first, before a minaret is accepted in Switzerland: "Why must we Swiss always be the first to allow something?" (ibid.).
- Unfair procedure by the newcomers: "What annoys me most is the procedure of the Turkish cultural association, its divide and conquer tactics" (Kissling, quoted ibid.).[7]
- Unwanted traffic: one resident expressed "fear of foreign pilgrims from the Islamic camp", his main argument being that Wangen already suffered from too much traffic. Another was afraid of "Islamists from half of Europe seeing the minaret on their way through Wangen and stopping to pray to Allah" (Müller 2006).
- Trouble emanating from particular Muslim customs: Kissling referred to the Danish cartoon crisis as an example for the trouble a larger number of Muslims with their peculiar customs would entail; to prevent this the best attitude would be to "nip it in the bud!" (ibid.).

The arguments advanced show a mixture of general xenophobic motives, some of them taking on an Islamophobic colour, with general anxiety about the future development of the local setting.[8] For one thing they express the fear of having

---

7   According to Kissling the association had at first only looked for a place for its meetings, it had then established prayer rooms, it wants a minaret now and will certainly want to broadcast the call to prayer using loudspeakers at some point in the future.

8   This is in line with Jörg Stolz' study (2005: 564) which shows, based on an extensive survey conducted in Zurich in 1994-1995, that "Islamophobia is [...] strongly linked to general xenophobia".

to face more 'foreigners'.[9] These 'foreigners' are furthermore perceived as strangers about whom fantasies are constructed rather than facts known or personal encounters sought. The newcomers, many of whom were not residents in Wangen and came just because the mosque happened to be there, were not known personally and were pereceived as not integrated, the underlying concept of integration being one of assimilation rather than an exchange process (see Gianni, this volume). The core of the arguments advanced in Wangen remained the same for Langenthal, Wil and later on throughout the four year campaign against minarets on all levels. At the same time they became more stereotyped, as the minaret opponents advanced and propagated them more systematically.

FROM THE LOCAL TO THE SUPRA-REGIONAL SCALE

Early on the opponents tried additional ways to prevent the minaret in Wangen. As well as addressing the media directly, every parliamentary move and every step in the formal process concerning the building permission and the subsequent litigation provided another occasion for reporting and for publicising their own opinion.

Roland Kissling opened the media campaign with a letter to the editor of the local newspaper on 7 September 2005 (Bretscher 2009: 83). He and his allies were ready to present their views to each and every media. For one and a half years the Wangen case was a constant media topic (in detail Wäckerlig 2011: 17-30; id. 2013: 316-332). This made it known nation-wide and prepared the ground for political moves on a broader scale. From September 2006 onwards an additional element allowed the opponents to add scandal to the minaret project: the flag of the Turkish congregation outside its premise showing the Turkish nationalist symbol of the 'grey wolve'. A further occasion for public discussion was however created as early as November 2005 by Roman Jäggi who, supported by 15 other members of the parliament of the canton of Solothurn, formally asked the cantonal government to change construction law in a way that would prevent the new construction and conversion of any "buildings with religious architecture". The parliament clearly rejected this demand in June 2006.

---

9   Strictly speaking some 20% of the resident population in Switzerland hold a foreign passport. Nationalist circles distinguish however between naturalised Swiss citizens, still seen as 'foreigners', on the one hand and a vague concept of 'Eidgenossen' (confederates by oath), seen as the only true Swiss.

Similar moves were launched in the cantonal parliaments of Zurich (April 2006), St. Gallen (September and November 2009), Ticino (October 2006) and Berne (March 2007). All failed to win a majority in the respective cantonal parliaments. However, they helped create the sense amongst the public that minarets were somehow a problem.

By summer 2006 minaret opponents in Wangen and Langenthal had realised that within the existing laws there was little hope of opposing minaret projects successfully on the municipal level, and that their attempts in the cantonal parliaments were likely to fail as well. Therefore they began to think of still more powerful strategies.

The final step from the local to the supra-regional level can be dated precisely and linked with a name. It was on 6 September 2006 that a group of people like Roland Kissling and Roman Jäggi met in Egerkingen, a small village near Olten to found the Egerkingen Committee (Egerkinger Komitee) in order to coordinate opposition against minarets nation-wide. The person who reported on the meeting in the weekly SVP news bulletin was Ulrich Schlüer. He was a member of the National Council and, born in 1944, had gained his first and lasting political experience as the secretary of James Schwarzenbach, right-wing nationalist and father of a xenophobic popular initiative which had almost been successful in 1970. Drawing on that experience and a long career in the SVP, Schlüer proved a very effective coordinator of the anti-minaret campaign. He was certainly the most experienced but by no means the only political entrepreneur in the Egerkingen Committee. Other participants of the first meeting were Roland Kissling together with another resident from Wangen, three residents from the Langenthal region; Roman Jäggi, then SVP speaker and member of the parliament of the canton of Solothurn, Lukas Reimann, member of the cantonal parliament of St. Gallen, and Walter Wobmann, besides Schlüer the second member of the national parliament. Soon the group was reinforced by Daniel Zingg from Langenthal and Christian Waber from the village of Wasen in Emmental, both members of the evangelical splinter party Eidgenössisch-Demokratische Union (EDU; Federal Democratic Union), and SVP members from other regions. The core group thus clearly represented the three hotspots of minaret discussions: Wangen, Langenthal and Wil.

The group presented themselves to the public as willing to take a firm stand against what they called "the creeping Islamisation of Switzerland"[10]. They proposed to amend the federal constitution by the sentence "The construction of minarets is forbidden." Using the means provided by direct democracy they

---

10 See www.minarette.ch (accessed June 9, 2012).

started on 1 May 2007 to collect at least 100 000 signatures within 18 months from Swiss citizens entitled to vote, in order to bring about a national referendum. During this period four of the six attempts to achieve a minaret ban on a cantonal level were turned down, each time giving fresh publicity to the topic. On 8 July 2008 they submitted 114 895 signatures to the federal chancellery.

ONWARDS TO THE NATIONAL AND INTERNATIONAL SCALE

The debate now reached a new stage by involving the federal government and the Federal Assembly as well as the international public.

The federal government was embarrassed. It was forced to formulate its own position vis-à-vis the initiative and to bring it before the two chambers of the national parliament. Bearing in mind Switzerland's image in the international arena, its strategy was to downplay the proposition and to minimise publicity. This explains why the government rejected the proposal with unusual haste in a public statement on the very day of its submission and weeks before delivering its official recommendation to parliament (Schweizerischer Bundesrat 2009a).[11]

Switzerland's image in the world subsequently was a motive in the Swiss debate, but not the dominating one. Foreign pressure on the Swiss institution of bank secrecy and the Libya crisis[12] were present throughout the debate on the popular initiative. Both themes may have increased in many Swiss citizens the feeling of being unjustly treated by foreign powers, leading to a defiant attitude, whereas the federal government and export-oriented segments of the economy opted for a more diplomatic approach.

The two chambers of parliament as well as civil society organisations like churches, Muslim organisations and NGOs dealt with the popular initiative in

---

11 A Swissinfo article linked the first statement explicitly to the fact that the Organisation of the Islamic Conference on its summit in Dakar in March 2008, in its final communiqué, had alluded to Switzerland along with Denmark (cartoon crisis) and the Netherlands (Geert Wilders) as examples of rising Islamophobia in Europe without naming these countries explicitly (Swissinfo: "Initiative gegen Minarette eingereicht". 8 July 2008 [online] Available at: http://www.swissinfo.ch/ger/Home/Archiv/ Initiative_gegen_Minarette_eingereicht.html?cid=6784116, accessed 4 January 2013).

12 Following the arrest of Hannibal al-Qadhafi in a hotel in Geneva on 2 July 2008, the Libyan dictator Muammar al-Qadhafi reacted by arresting two Swiss businessmen in Libya who were not released until 2010 after nearly two years of diplomatic quarrel.

the usual way.[13] They practically all denied the existence of any problem and they dismissed the demand as violating several principles of the Swiss constitution and international treaties, supported in this by nearly all jurists. Some of the institutions published carefully elaborated tracts arguing against the initiative (for example SEK 2008). All this was reported by the media, creating the impression of an overwhelming majority leaving the initiative with no chance.

National-conservative parties and their allies were the only ones to argue for the initiative, claiming that the 'political elite', by rejecting the idea of a ban, was far from the feelings of the people. Their main line of argument went like this: Since Islam does not separate religion and the state the minaret is a religio-political symbol of power expressing totalitarian claims of a 'religious ideology' towards society; forbidding minarets thus would send a strong signal that Swiss society does not accept such claims and that foreigners have to assimilate.[14]

This line of argument was repeated unchanged again and again throughout the campaign. It takes account of the fears and motives as expressed in the first phase of the controversy in Wangen (cf. above p. 7). Since the promoters of the ban offered no positive perspective for establishing anything visibly Islamic, the insistence on 'integration' can only be understood as assimilation.[15]

MEDIA

The developments so far had yielded plenty of occasions for the media to add more chapters to a story which was very much to their taste: controversial, appealing to the popular imagination, connecting local as well as international dimensions. With the popular initiative set on the institutional track, the date of the

---

13 Lacking a constitutional court, the Swiss parliament decides whether or not a popular initiative is to be submitted to the voters. As in similar cases during the last decade or so, the majority decided *in dubio pro reo*, thus creating the possibility, considered improbable, of a popular vote in favour of a demand considered as improper.

14 A whole set of arguments, examined in detail by Lienemann (2009), is still available online at http://minarette.ch/argumente/index.html (accessed 26 April 2013).

15 "Ausländer, die sich anpassen und hier nach unseren Regeln leben, sind willkommen" ("Foreigners who assimilate and live here under our rules are welcome"). Yvette Estermann, a born Slovakian and federal MP for the SVP, quoted in the local newspaper *Zentralschweiz am Sonntag,* 22 November 2009 and in the SVP party program 2011-2015 "SVP – die Partei für die Schweiz", p. 54. The argument recurs countless times in online forums related or not to minarets.

national referendum was becoming the focus and the provisional end of the story to which everything converged.

The media are vital especially for this last phase, for two reasons: firstly, because reporting facts and opinions on topics of national referenda are a *sine qua non* for mainstream media, and secondly, because the dynamics of this phase are to a large degree detached from the factual situation on the ground. Analysing the whole discourse related to the minaret debate by presenting all relevant actors, roles, motives and stages of the dynamics is beyond the scope of this chapter. Indeed, much of this has already been done by Patrik Ettinger (2010) and by Oliver Wäckerlig (2011; 2013). I therefore restrict myself to some remarks concerning the actors and the key elements which influenced the dynamics of the overall Islam debate.

The media and journalists, although considering themselves as neutral, influence debates by their choice of topics, of interview partners and of framing their contributions. The very idea of having a product to sell and a 'story' to tell indicates a broad global tendency of the last decades putting the accent more and more on promptness and an appealing form to the detriment of accuracy, quality of sources and thorough reflection (cf. Ettinger/Imhof 2011: 7; Dahinden 2009: 4). This 'new structural transformation of the public sphere' manifests itself in the organisation of editorial boards where the specialist knowing his dossier *à fond* is an endangered species. Editorial boards do not investigate topics related to religion on their own initiative, but only react if the topic seems to have some 'news value' (id., 6).

If journalists are ignorant concerning religion, any religion, and are unable to understand its 'language', a resulting poor quality of reporting is no surprise. In the case of the minaret debate it consisted mainly of collecting statements from the 'usual suspects' whenever a new development had been noticed. Critical inquiry into the motives of these actors and into their arguments was rare.

The Islamic congregations in Wangen and elsewhere, mostly represented by first generation immigrants, after having had initially mixed experiences with the media, largely refrained from an active management of this domain. For one thing they lacked specialists in communication capable of handling the media smartly, a lack they share with other small religious groups (id., 3). For another thing, representatives of some major umbrella organisations in a meeting in March 2009 explicitly opted for a low profile strategy. They calculated that Swiss public opinion would not appreciate "loud interference of representatives of co-citizens who are in the majority foreign and thus not entitled to vote" (Hanel 2009); a correct assessment of Swiss mentality and Swiss political usage, but with an unforeseen effect.

All this played into the hands of the minaret opponents who were well-versed in handling the media. They were the most prominent single actor group present in public reporting related to the initiative (Ettinger 2010, second graph). Differing views by Muslims, political opponents, civil society organisations and experts were also regularly reported, however, and, taken together, outweighed the quotations in favour of the ban. The superficial impression showed a broad alliance leaving the minaret opponents with no chance. This was reflected in three surveys conducted before the vote. The ballot count, however, as shown in table 2, revealed that the determination of what had appeared as a minority position had in fact been decisive.

Table 2: Surveys and ballot count (all figures in per cent)

	Yes	No	Undecided
Survey March/April 2009	37	49	14
Survey October 2009	34	53	13
Survey November 2009	37	53	10
Ballot count on 29 Nov 2009 Turnout: 53,8	57.5	42.5	

Sources: Isopublic 2009; Milic/Freitag/Vatter 2010, 21.

The enormous difference between the surveys and the actual result of the vote calls for an explanation. It can be found in the specific constellation of the voters, their attitude towards religion, the topic submitted for decision and the functioning of political discourse in Switzerland.

RELIGION – A PROJECTION SCREEN

Taken at face value, the referendum was about minarets, an architectural element that had until then not caused any general problems. As the popular voices and the arguments of minaret opponents show (cf. p. 291), the arguments put forward were much more general. The thing to keep out of Switzerland was 'foreign culture', driven by a religion with claims to shaping society or, at the least, to show prominently in public. 'Islam' did not only serve as the most prominent codeword for everything unknown. Seemingly Islam – as depicted by the opponents – also put into question the arrangement found for religion in Switzerland. This arrangement has two aspects, one institutional and one social.

298 | Andreas Tunger-Zanetti

The institutional aspect is characterised by minimal regulation. The federal constitution grants freedom of belief and conscience (comprising freedom of religion) in article 15. Article 72 confers the authority for each canton to regulate the position of 'the church'. All but two cantons have some form of official recognition linked to certain privileges (tax collection) usually granted to the Roman Catholic and the Protestant churches, in some cantons also to the Old Catholic Church and to a Jewish community. Obstacles for obtaining this status are high for denominations which do not enjoy it and they differ among the cantons.

The aspect of social reality, on the other hand, has evolved enormously in recent decades. Religious practice among the affiliates of established churches has eroded dramatically, the figures of religious affiliation show a somewhat less sharp, but constant decline. Religious plurality has increased considerably, although not very visibly. The most important single trend is the sharp increase of the number of people without affiliation to a religious denomination. According to the 2010 census, they make up 20.1 per cent of those aged over 14 years (Bundesamt für Statistik 2012). On the individual level religion has been very much relegated to the private sphere, understood by most people as the private home and the interior of churches, temples or mosques.

These are only the most salient symptoms of the fundamental change of the individual's religious profile (Stolz et al. 2011). In order to manage this change in a society making much use of direct democratic decisions, the citizen needs certain competences: a certain basic understanding of what religion means to religious people, of the internal variety of religions and of how religions work. One could call this 'religious literacy' (Prothero 2007, cf. Wood 2011). Clearly, one can be 'literate' in this sense without being religious. At the same time religious people may lack this understanding. Formal education certainly helps to gain some degree of religious literacy, but is no guarantee. Minority experience may enhance it, but is no guarantee either.

The fundamental trends mentioned above have however not stimulated religious literacy, but undermined it. Perhaps it was never flourishing in Switzerland, as earlier discriminatory direct democratic decisions dating back as far as 1893 (Vatter 2011) suggest. In any case, statistics show that religion has been losing importance on a personal level for the majority of people for decades (Stolz 2011: 17-21). At the same time the need for religious literacy has grown due to increasing religious plurality, but is less likely to increase, because of decreasing overall religious practice and reflection.

Although 'religious illiteracy' as such needs more research, its effects for the minaret debate are manifest (in more detail: Tunger-Zanetti forthcoming). Religious convictions are rarely spoken about in private or in public. 'Religious illiteracy' has deprived the individual and society of a language in which to adequately conceptualise and discuss matters related to religion, be it in the context of personal belief or in the context of institutional arrangements. This does not prevent religion of being the topic of newspapers and magazines. However, this happens under changed conditions. One is the above-mentioned 'new structural transformation of the public sphere'. Another is that most journalists, being religious illiterates themselves, cannot act as 'interpreters' between the shrinking habitat of religion and an illiterate public. Nor can the rare media contributions of excellent quality be understood by a religiously illiterate reader, as comments in online forums show.

Nonetheless, one might object that media do not always thematise religion in a negative way with favourable reporting about the Dalai Lama and other manifestations of 'Asian' religions as evidence. The degree of accuracy, differentiation and background knowledge, however, is not higher in these cases. Rather these cases show the tendency of allocating the roles of 'good' versus 'bad' religions (Dahinden 2009: 5). Journalism about religion thus often tells more about the journalist's level of religious literacy than about the actual topic. Moreover, by its deficiencies, it produces and reproduces projection screen for the supposed demands of the readers who are religiously illiterate as well in their majority.

This constellation becomes virulent when religion enters the public sphere with a statement or a claim. This applies not only to 'new' religions, but increasingly also to new manifestations of established churches or independent churches.[16] The claim demanding a reaction lays bare the lack of concepts for dealing with it in a differentiated, adequate way. The strangeness of religion *per se* combines with the strangeness of Islam, a religion especially disconcerting by the emphasis it lays on visible othopraxy rather than on confessed orthodoxy. Apparently, in the minaret case two insights which had enabled earlier arrangements were largely absent: firstly, that religion inevitably also has a social and a public side, and secondly that there are more subtle and less contradictory means than prohibition to manage this side. The personal experience or the abstract knowledge that could have activated either of these insights seems to to have been lacking or blocked.

---

16 This can for example be seen when an independent church wants to build a bigger complex in a small municipality, as in the case of Harvest Network International's project in Seon in 2010. Bell ringing by long-established churches, crosses on hilltops or crosses and crucifixes in classrooms have also been a matter of dispute and sometimes litigation.

In this setting, the promoters of the minaret ban were able to convince many people that religious freedom, understood in the narrow sense of freedom to believe and to associate *in private*, was in no way affected by the initiative, but that the erection of minarets posed a threat to the established order. The amendment, they argued, was in no way directed against Muslim people, but solely against 'Islam' which is, according to them, a religious-political ideology trying to expand and to gain supremacy (cf. references given in n. 13). This blurring of the distinction between religion and politics, but also between religion and culture, was a tactical necessity against the argument that a minaret ban would violate the freedom of religion. It proved especially successful among people with little formal education (Longchamp et al. 2010; Hirter/Vatter 2010).

For the SVP this was just a variant in its long tradition of sharp polemics against foreign influence, aimed at restricting the number of foreign residents in Switzerland as well as their access to rights and benefits. This time the SVP's campaign was more explicitly directed against a symbol rather than people than on other occasions. It depicted the danger that Swiss people would be ever more marginalised in their own country by 'arrogant' Islam and one day acustically terrorised by the call to prayer if further minarets were admitted. This frightening perspective was visualised in the main poster for the Yes campaign:

Figure 1: Anti-minaret poster, 2009

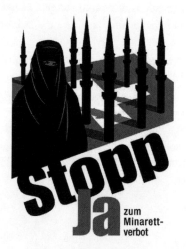

Source: www.minarette.ch

The poster shows the Swiss flag being perforated by seven Ottoman style minarets; the prominent black figure in full veil to the left represents the social consequences if 'Islam' is allowed to realise its alleged programme. The poster instantly became iconic and was soon adapted for other anti-Muslim campaigns in Europe.[17]

The strategy of the Egerkingen Committee clearly was to make the debate a debate on Islam instead of the more general – and quite abstract – principle of religious freedom. This was easy because everybody in the country had some idea, however partial or distorted, about 'Islam'. Islam – once more in Western history – was the ideal projection screen and bogeyman for everything. It has to bear all disadvantages of any religious topic and additionally the extremely negative image accumulated through centuries and vigorously updated by 9/11, the Madrid and London bombings in 2004 and 2005 and continuous news reporting on violence in Iraq, Afghanistan etc.

THE 'SECOND PUBLIC SPHERE'

The projection screen offered the opportunity to talk about anything Islamic and link it to the minaret initiative. This was extensively done by the supporters of the proposal. They organised public lectures with Islamophobic speakers such as Mark A. Gabriel or Israeli propagandist Avi Lipkin, alias Victor Mordecai. They distributed tracts, filled online discussion forums and 'letters to the editor' columns with snippets from their arguments. It was by no means only the Egerkingen Committee that was active in the supporter's camp. For organisations such as the Schweizerischer Bund aktiver Protestanten (Swiss Union of Active Protestants, www.chbap.ch), politically sympathetic to the EDU initiators of the minaret ban, the campaign fitted neatly with their general programme in which warnings of Islam are a constant element. Also individuals spent much time mobilising their personal networks, as was seen in the case of Julia Onken, a Swiss psychologist and women's book author who urged some 4000 former clients of her seminars to vote for the ban (Sandl 2009).

All these activities were very much at the grassroot level. They constitute what I call in this context a 'second public sphere' as opposed to the one and only public sphere in the original Habermasian model. This alternative sphere was 'public' since it was in principle accessible to everybody, it was 'second' because it constitutes clearly a sphere aside the primary public sphere, with au-

---

17 A quick internet search delivers examples from the British National Party, the Front National in France, a local case in Warsaw, and the 'Libertarian' blog rebellog.com using the EU flag.

thorities, political parties, civil society organisations and mainstream public media as its main actors. The wider public could have concluded the existence of the second public sphere only from occasional reporting in mainstream media as in the case of Julia Onken or when a group of Muslims reported Avi Lipkin for discriminatory speech.[18]

The senders of messages in this sphere chose their starting point among several topics depending on the sender and combined at their discretion: Islam as the forces of Antichrist, Islam as a backward religion, persecution of Christians in Islamic countries, the second class status of women in Islam, the presence of Muslim foreigners in Switzerland, 'Islamic' Turkey under 'Islamist' president Erdoğan asking for EU membership.

This spectrum of sceneries, mostly situated abroad, was vaguely linked to Switzerland. The reasoning went like this: 1) Terrible things are happening in Islamic countries and Western countries are having troubles with their Muslim minorities, 2) the Muslim presence in Switzerland is becoming more firmly rooted, 3) so let us prevent trouble by breaking the spearhead of this 'creeping Islamisation' and ban minarets. This reasoning was garnered *ad libitum* with facts taken out of their context (Turkish premier Erdoğan's public quoting of a verse by nationalist author Ziya Gökalp equating minarets to bayonets; Egerkinger Komitee 2007: 13), invented stories (a Swiss teacher pasting over little pigs in her class textbooks in an act of preemptive obedience to avoid protest from Muslim parents; Moser 2009), distortion, misinterpretation and illogical conclusions. However, the supporters repeated their limited arsenal of stereotypes and erroneous arguments unwaveringly throughout the campaign, appearing thereby convicted themselves and convincing many of the uninformed people, especially in the centrist camp. These favourite topics of the second public sphere were only rarely taken up by other actors in the traditional public sphere because their poor connection to the proposed ban was all too obvious.

In the opposite camp there was consensus to reject the initiative, but not about which argumentative strategy to follow, neither was there effective coordination among organisations and resources. Other researchers have elaborated on the roots and general features of this discourse (Behloul 2009a; 2009b), on the arguments advanced by the supporters of the ban (Lienemann 2009; Mayer 2011) and on the dilemma through which the established as well as the independent churches sought their way with little determination (Mathwig 2009). In

18 For the Lipkin case see http://chronologie.gra.ch/index.php?p=4&y=2009&a=1 (accessed 19 April 2013). For the second public sphere see Tunger-Zanetti (forthcoming).

panel discussions, opponents of the ban faced the dilemma of trying to correct distortions about Islam, thus remaining fixed to shadow-boxing, or to engage in a demanding discussion about the content of religious freedom and the place of religion in society and the state. Only a minority of them seem to have been conscious enough of this dilemma. Moreover, local parish committees and the media set an 'Islamic' frame for public discussions. Getting away from that frame would have required a major effort.

Why did the camp opposed to the ban not mobilise the same degree of missionary zeal shown by the opposite camp? Was it because the *classe politique* had ignored the people? Many citizens shared this view.[19] This seems however to be rather the symptom than the cause of the defenders of the *status quo*. I see four main reasons why engaging against the idea of the ban was unattractive: Firstly, opponents of the ban felt the sympathy of many people for the proposed ban and avoided to confront it. Secondly, they shunned the effort to make the abstract and unfamiliar issue of church-state relations a topic of debate. Thirdly, it is difficult to prove that increased visibility of a newly established actor does *not* exceed the ordinary measure and that the existing legal framework is sufficient. Fourthly, the efforts seemed to be a waste of time since the surveys showed that a comfortable majority would reject the ban anyway. All this created an impression of little determination to fight the initiative. Again, the situation on the public billboards illustrates this drastically. Posters in favour of the initiative confronted the citizens throughout the country, whereas posters from the opposite camp were practically invisible.

This reticence must have had two effects, as can be inferred from German demoscope Elisabeth Noelle-Neumann's research: One effect was that the elites gave away the chance to influence the formation of public opinion on a sensitive issue, even among their own followers. This effort can be crucial in a climate of shifting opinion or watching out for orientation (Noelle-Neumann 2001: 322; id., 1993: 218sq.). The second effect is equally important: "In attempting to avoid those who think differently from themselves, people lose their quasistatistical ability to assess correctly the views of their environment." (Noelle-Neumann 179; id., 1993: 124). This loss of sensibility made the elites, including demoscopes, blind to the impact of tendencies opposed to their own opinion and caused the surprise of the actual result on 29 November 2009.

---

19 56% agreed to the proposition that the vote was only accepted "because *all* parties had
    neglected many people's apprehensions over current developments" (Demoscope
    2010a, question Q04, my emphasis).

This constellation of actors with their preconditions, interests and strategies led to an ambiguous situation in the run-up to the vote: On the one hand, arguments against the proposed ban had been widely elaborated and disseminated in the primary public sphere through the channels of *courant normal*, i.e. mainstream media and the associational press, but lacked ardent propagators, Muslim or non-Muslim; no major effort to convince the undecided was visible. On the other hand, the proposition of the ban was ubiquitous on the billboards and equally prominent through a simplistic imagery and discourse. However disconnected to Swiss reality that this may have been, it was constantly actualised within the 'second public sphere', not perceived by the social and political elites who were fixed on the primary public sphere. As a result the opposing parties contented themselves with trying to win sympathy for their position, but avoided a real debate about the core arguments (Ettinger/Imhof 2011: 29sq.).

The voters thus had the choice to trust the considerations of their elites cutting a rather pale figure in the campaign or to follow their sentiment, concordant with popular mood, and express their uncertainty about how to deal with 'Islam' by casting a 'yes' vote. Many chose the second option thus punishing the elites for their hesitant attitude. They found this all the easier as most of them had no personal interests at stake.

WHO? WHY?

The surprise result of the vote on 29 November 2009 prompted many questions: What were the characteristics of those voting 'no' and 'yes'? What had been their motives? Why had nobody foreseen the outcome? What now?

The high turnout (53%) of the minaret vote was similar to other votes shortly before this one on issues concerning foreigners. According to the VOX surveys carried out after each federal vote it was not people with a generally negative attitude towards foreigners who were more mobilised than usual, but those people who try to balance modern and more open attitudes with more traditional ideas (Vatter/Milic/ Hirter 2011: 146); apparently, they saw the identity of Switzerland as being at stake. These voters, in their majority sympathising with the centre parties, Liberals and Christian democrats, were the decisive factor: they voted against the recommendation of their parties' conventions by a margin of 2 : 1, whereas voters to the left and nationalist right had made their decision early on in opposite directions (Longchamp et al. 2010; Demoscope 2010a, question S07). Regularly surveyed fundamental attitudes would have given enough reason to suspect a 'yes' tendency within this group, but this had been neglected over the expressed intention for the vote. It seems plausible that many respondents, especially in the centrist camp, apparently felt that their inclination was not the socially desirable one and dissimulated it (Milic/Freitag/Vatter 2010: 16-22).

The VOX survey, conducted by Claude Longchamp (2010), asked voters to give the two most important reasons for casting a 'yes' or 'no'. Among the 'yes' voters the most frequent first-named reasons were: minarets are symbols of is-lamisation (25%), minarets are not a necessary element for mosques (15%), Christian faith has to be defended, especially because of building obstacles for Christians in Islamic countries (14%), minarets do not fit the Swiss landscape (13%), Muslims do not follow 'our' laws (9%). The reasons given first by 'no' voters were: the ban violates fundamental rights or freedom of religion (31%), general negative comments on the initiative (15%), minarets have not bothered me so far (13%), the ban is intolerant (11%) (Vatter/Milic/Hirter 2011: 160).

The VOX survey also tested arguments and opinions related to the ban pro-posal. Most remarkably, 64 per cent of the voters agreed fully (22%) or quite (42%) that "Swiss and Muslim ways of life are compatible with each other". At the same time 87 per cent shared the opinion that women are oppressed in Islam. Other arguments expressing a general suspicion against Islam scored between 54 and 61 per cent, except for the claim that mosques with minarets are generally strongholds of extremists (34%) (id., 161sq.).

These seemingly contradictory figures reflect the artificial nature of the Is-lam debate in Switzerland. Living and working together with Muslims is experi-enced as being without major problems. Most people probably do not even know for sure whether their neighbour or colleague from Kosovo is a Muslim or for example a member of the Catholic minority. Religion is just no major issue for most Swiss, Muslim or not. The Islam debate however has created or fostered images and stereotypes which were able to overrule the unproblematic personal experience. The figures of the post-vote surveys are echoed in the general am-bivalent attitude as shown by Stolz et al. (2011: 32): Freedom of religion is val-ued high, yet regularly followed by a 'but' concerning public appearance of reli-gion. In other words, the figures reveal a deficit in religious literacy, a lack of re-sistance against the powerful anti-minaret campaign. This is in turn to some de-gree a consequence of the little engagement of the camp opposed to the ban dur-ing the campaign.

AFTER THE VOTE

What effect did the result have on the 'Islam' debate in Switzerland? On the even-ing of 29 November 2009 and for several days following it, there were spontane-ous demonstrations by non-Muslim Swiss citizens expressing shame for their country. The government issued a statement expressing its will to respect the verdict and at the same time trying to minimise the damage of Switzerland's international reputation by explaining that the existing four minarets would remain and mosques (without minarets) could still be built. The statement was given in German, French, Italian, English and Arabic (Schweizerischer Bundesrat 2009b).

The supporters of the ban, taken as much by surprise as everyone else, did not boast too loudly about their success. The Egerkingen Committee however did not dissolve but continued its internet presence and kept nurturing anti-Islamic attitudes. Meanwhile it has announced plans to launch another popular initiative in 2013, this time directed against the full veil. They must have felt all the more encouraged to do so as Christophe Darbellay, president of the Christlichdemokratische Volkspartei (CVP; Christian Democratic People's Party), immediately after the minaret vote proposed to ban the Islamic full veil as well as separate cemeteries for Muslims and Jews. A national newspaper interpreted this move as an attempt to regain control over sympathisers who had not followed the party's recommendation to refuse the proposed minaret ban (Mooser 2009).

Many Muslims, functionaries or not, were shocked by the vote. So were people engaged in interfaith groups for years. However, after a shock period of several months most of them resumed their activity because they saw no alternative.

The single most important development is probably the foundation of the Islamischer Zentralrat Schweiz (Islamic Central Council Switzerland, ICCS) five weeks *before* the vote. The anti-minaret campaign as such had motivated some twenty young Muslims, headed by converts Nicolas Blancho and Abdel Azziz Qaasim Illi, to set up an organisation which would take a more active stand in the future than the traditional organisations had done so far. Though highly controversial in the general Swiss public and among Muslims, the ICCS has become the most powerful single Muslim player in the country with more than 2600 individual members by beginning of 2013 (see also Leuenberger, this volume).

On the political level, the vote made several actors think about ways to prevent similar disasters in the future, all the more as Swiss direct democracy had faced several other popular initiatives violating international law. National Councillor Andreas Gross of the Social Democrat Party advocates a constitutional amendment which would allow to block this type of issues from being submitted to the voters at all.[20] The cross-party discussion forum Club Helvé-

---

20 For Gross' ideas see Wolf Südbeck-Baur: "Verfassungsrevision steht an", in: *Aufbruch*, no. 179, 3 February 2011, [online] http://www.andigross.ch/html/site984.htm (accessed 15 February 2013).

tique confirmed its demand of 2007 for a Constitutional Court.[21] Engaged individuals such as Daniel Thürer and Jörg Paul Müller, both professors of international law, proposed a constitutional amendment stating the obligation of religious communities to act according to the principle of tolerance and promote it among their followers (Müller/Thürer 2010). None of these moves have led to tangible results so far. Some of them are being treated by the Federal administration (in detail Mader 2012).

Three and a half years since the minaret vote it is safe to say that the vote has left a more important trace in public debate than in the factual conditions for Muslim life in Switzerland. It has been a wake-up call for many actors in the camp opposed to the ban. However, it has not led to a more thorough self-investigation of Swiss society and its relation to religion in general. This relation is heavily dependent on megatrends of social change is marked by high religious illiteracy. This in turn is one of the reasons why no real debate about the core arguments took place in the minaret case.

REFERENCES

Research reports of all projects in the Swiss National Research Programme NRP 58 on "Religions, the State, and Society" are available online at http://www.nfp58.ch.

Allievi, Stefano (2010a): *La guerra delle moschee: L'Europa e la sfida del pluralismo religioso,* Venezia: Marsilio.
— (ed.) (2010b): Mosques in Europe: Why a solution has become a problem. In collaboration with Ethnobarometer. Network of European Foundations (NEF); Initiative on Religion and Democracy in Europe. London. [online] Available at http://www.alliancepublishing.org/mosques-in-europe-why-a-solution-has-become-a-problem (accessed 2 April 2013).
Anon. (2010): "Nicht gegen Muslime, aber gegen den Islam: Vox-Analyse zur Abstimmung über das Minarettverbot", in: Neue Zürcher Zeitung, 25 January. [online] Available at: http://www.nzz.ch/aktuell/startseite/vox-analyse-zur-minarett-initiative-1.4616364 (accessed 5 March 2013).

---

21 See n. 12. Cf. no. 6 among its theses on the constitutional state. Club Helvétique: *Rechtsstaat. Sechs Thesen des Club Helvétique zum Rechtsstaat,* December 2007 [online] http://www.clubhelvetique.ch/clubhelv/index.php?CH_Thesen:Rechtsstaat (accessed 15 February 2013).

Baumann, Martin / Tunger-Zanetti, Andreas (2011): "Wenn Religionen Häuser bauen: Sakralbauten, Kontroversen und öffentlicher Raum in der Schweizer Demokratie", in: Baumann, Martin / Neubert, Frank (eds), *Religionspolitik – Öffentlichkeit – Wissenschaft: Studien zur Neuformierung von Religion in der Gegenwart,* Zürich: Pano, pp. 151-188.

Behloul, Samuel M. (2009a): "Discours total! Le débat sur l'islam en Suisse et le positionnement de l'islam comme religion publique", in: Schneuwly Purdie, Mallory / Gianni, Matteo / Jenny, Magali (eds), *Musulmans d'aujourd'hui: Identités plurielles en Suisse,* Genève: Labor et Fides, pp. 53-72.

— (2009b): "Minarett-Initiative: Im Spannungsfeld zwischen Abwehr-Reflex und impliziter Anerkennung neuer gesellschaftlicher Fakten", in: Tanner, Mathias et al. (2009): *Streit um das Minarett: Zusammenleben in der religiös pluralistischen Gesellschaft,* Zürich: Theologischer Verlag, pp. 103-122.

Beinhauer-Köhler, Bärbel / Leggewie, Claus (eds) (2009): *Moscheen in Deutschland: Religiöse Heimat und gesellschaftliche Herausforderung,* München: Beck.

Bretscher, Simone (2009): (K)eins aufs Dach? Über realisierte und geplante Minarette in der Schweiz, Licence thesis, University of Basel. [online] Available at http://www.religionenschweiz.ch/pdf/bretscher-minarette.pdf (accessed June 9, 2012).

Bundesamt für Statistik [Swiss Federal Statistical Office] (2012): Medienmitteilung, corrected version, 10 October. [online] Available at: http://www.bfs. admin.ch/bfs/portal/de/index/news/medienmitteilungen.Document.159960. pdf (accessed 5 March 2013).

Dahinden, Urs (2009): *Die Darstellung von Religionen in Schweizer Massenmedien: Zusammenprall der Kulturen oder Förderung des Dialogs?,* Chur: Hochschule für Technik und Wirtschaft. Research report NRP 58.

Demoscope (2010a): Tables of the CATI-BUS survey, conducted 22-27 January 2010 among 1006 individuals over 15 years.

— (2010b): Signal der Bevölkerung an die politischen Parteien, press release, 29 January.

Egerkinger Komitee (2007): Islam-Argumentarium: Grundbegriffe, 4 May. [online] Available at: http://minarette.ch/downloads/argumentarium-komplett-d.pdf (accessed 19 April 2013).

Ettinger, Patrik (2010): "Qualität der Medienberichterstattung zur Minarettinitiative", in: Forschungsbereich Öffentlichkeit und Gesellschaft (ed.): *Jahrbuch 2010: Qualität der Medien Schweiz,* Basel: Schwabe, p. 267-274.

Ettinger, Patrik / Udris, Linards (2009): "Islam as a threat? Problematisation of Muslims in the mass media and effects on the political system", in: Marsden,

Lee / Savigny, Heather (eds): *Media, religion and conflict*, Farnham: Ashgate, pp. 59-79.

Ettinger, Patrik / Imhof, Kurt (2011): Ethnisierung des Politischen und Problematisierung religiöser Differenz. Research report NRP 58 (Accessed 2 April 2013).

Gianni, Matteo et al. (2010): *Vie musulmane en Suisse: Profils identitaires, demandes et perceptions des musulmans en Suisse*, Rapport réalisé par le Groupe de Recherche sur l'Islam en Suisse (GRIS). 2e édition du rapport 2005, Berne: Commission fédérale pour les questions de migration CFM. Bern. [online] Available at: http://www.ekm.admin.ch/content/dam/data/ekm/dokumentation/materialien/mat_muslime_f.pdf (accessed 11 May 2013).

Hanel, Muhammad M. (2009): Am Sonntag, dem 15.3.09 [etc.]. Report of one of the participants. [online] Available at: http://www.iphpbb.com/board/ftopic-43715060nx17898-33-15.html#704 (accessed 19 April, 2013).

Hirter, Hans / Vatter, Adrian (2010): Analyse der eidgenössischen Abstimmungen vom 29. November 2009. VOX-Analyse des Forschungsinstituts gfs.bern und Institut für Politikwissenschaft, Universität Bern. [online] Available at: http://www.gfsbern.ch/portals/0/vox-analysen/2009-11-29_VoxD.pdf (accessed 4 March 2013).

Institut für Politikwissenschaft (2010): "Kirchen", in: Année Politique Suisse / Schweizerische Politik, ed. by Institut für Politikwissenschaft at University of Berne [online] Available at: http://www.anneepolitique.ch/de/aps-online.php (accessed 8 January 2013).

Isopublic 2009: Minarettinitiative: Die Situation Ende März / anfangs April 2009. Gallup Tele Omnibus, Schwerzenbach: Isopublic. [online] Available at: http://www.isopublic.ch/publikationen/pdf/Tabellen20090424.pdf (accessed 11 May 2013).

Kestler, Annegret (2013): „Steine des Anstosses: Diskurse um religiöse Gebäude und Bauvorhaben in der Schweiz", in: Uehlinger, Christoph / Lüddeckens, Dorothea / Walthert / Rafael (eds): *Die Sichtbarkeit religiöser Identität: Repräsentation – Differenz – Konflikt*, Zürich: Pano, pp. 271-311.

Lathion, Stéphane / Tunger-Zanetti, Andreas (forthcoming): "Switzerland", in: *Yearbook of Muslims in Europe*, 5, 2013.

Leggewie, Claus (2009): "Warum es Moscheebaukonflikte gibt und wie man sie bearbeiten kann", in: Beinhauer-Köhler, Bärbel / Leggewie, Claus (eds), *Moscheen in Deutschland: Religiöse Heimat und gesellschaftliche Herausforderung*, München: Beck, pp. 117-218.

Lienemann, Wolfgang (2009): "Argumente für ein Minarett-Verbot? Eine kritische Analyse", in: Tanner, Mathias et al. (eds): *Streit um das Minarett: Zusammenleben in der religiös pluralistischen Gesellschaft*, Zürich: Theologischer Verlag, pp. 123-139.

Longchamp, Claude et al. (2010): VOX 101. GFS.Bern / Universität Zürich / Universität Bern / Université de Genève. Neuenburg: SIDOS.

Mader, Luzius (2012): Volksinitiativen und Völkerrecht: Vorschläge zur besseren Vereinbarkeit, presentation at the 5th Solothurner Landhausversammlung, 31 March 2012, [online] http://www.landhausversammlung.ch/v01/images/stories/5landhausversammlung/PPP_L_Mader_Vortrag_vom_31__M%C3%A4rz_2012_2.pptx (accessed 15 February 2013).

Mathwig, Frank (2009): "Das Kreuz mit den Minaretten: Theologische Bemerkungen zur Rolle der Kirchen in der Minarett-Diskussion, in: Tanner, Mathias et al. (eds), *Streit um das Minarett: Zusammenleben in der religiös pluralistischen Gesellschaft*, Zürich: Theologischer Verlag, pp. 141-187.

Mayer, Jean-François (2011): "A country without minarets: Analysis oft he background and meaning of the Swiss vote of 29 November 2009", in: *Religion*, 41:1, pp. 11-28.

Milic, Thomas / Freitag, Markus / Vatter, Adrian (2010): Der Einfluss von Umfragen auf den direktdemokratischen Meinungsbildungsprozess. Bern/ Konstanz: Universität Bern / Universität Konstanz, http://www. srgssrideesuisse.ch/fileadmin/pdfs/2010-08-17_Studie_Freitag_Vatter_de.pdf (accessed 6 March 2013).

Mooser, Hubert (2009): "Nach dem Minarett-Verbot: Darbellay auf Kreuzzug", in: *Tages-Anzeiger*, 4 December. [online] Available at: http://www.tagesanzeiger. ch/schweiz/standard/Nach-dem-MinarettVerbot-Darbellay-auf-Kreuzzug/story/ 28122419 (accessed 20 April).

Moser, Urs (2009): "Die Islam-Debatte kommt auf den Hund", in: *Aargauer Zeitung*, 16 November.

Müller, Jörg Paul / Thürer, Daniel (2010): "Toleranzartikel", in: Gross, Andreas et al. (eds): *Von der Provokation zum Irrtum – Menschenrechte und Demokratie nach dem Minarett-Bauverbot*, St-Ursanne: Editions le Doubs, p. 277-285.

Müller, Martin (2006): "Grosses Bangen in Wangen", in: *Beobachter*, 16 February. [online] Available at: http://www.beobachter.ch/justiz-behoerde/ auslaender/artikel/religion_grosses-bangen-in-wangen/ (accessed 20 April 2013).

Noelle-Neumann, Elisabeth (1993): The spiral of silence: Public opinion – our social skin. Chicago: The University of Chicago Press, 2nd ed.

— (2001): *Die Schweigespirale: Öffentliche Meinung – unsere soziale Haut*, 6th, enlarged ed., München: Langen Müller.

Prothero, Stephen (2007): *Religious literacy: What every American needs to know – and doesn't*, San Francisco: Harper.

Sandl, Ida (2009): "Julia Onken kämpft gegen Minarette", in: *Tages-Anzeiger*, 17 November. [online] Available at: http://www.tagesanzeiger.ch/schweiz/

standard/Julia-Onken-kaempft-gegen-Minarette/story/11032319 (accessed 9 June 2012).

Schneuwly Purdie, Mallory (2009): "Sociographie de l'islam en Suisse", in: Schneuwly Purdie, Mallory / Gianni, Matteo / Jenny, Magali (eds), *Musulmans d'aujourd'hui: Identités plurielles en Suisse,* Genève: Labor et Fides, pp. 23-36.

Schweizerischer Bundesrat [Federal Council] (2009a): *Volksabstimmung vom 29. November 2009: Erläuterungen des Bundesrates,* Bern: Bundeskanzlei.

— (2009b): 'Yes' to popular initiative against the construction of minarets, press release of 29 November, [online] http://www.admin.ch/aktuell/00089/index.html?lang=en&msg-id=30430, with Arabic version attached (accessed 12 February 2013).

SEK (2008): Zwischen Glockenturm und Minarett: Argumentarium des Rates des Schweizerischen Evangelischen Kirchenbundes (SEK) zur Volksinitiative "Gegen den Bau von Minaretten". Vom Rat SEK verabschiedet am 2. Juli 2008, Bern: Schweizerischer Evangelischer Kirchenbund [Swiss Union of Evangelical Churches]. [online] Available at http://www.kirchenbund.ch/sites/default/files/stellungnahmen/Argumentarium_Zwischen_Glockenturm_und_Minarett.pdf (accessed 4 January 2013).

Stolz, Jörg (2005): "Explaining Islamophobia: A test of four theories based on the case of a Swiss city", in: *Swiss Journal of Sociology,* 31:3, pp. 547-566.

Stolz, Jörg et al. (2011): Religiosität in der modernen Welt: Bedingungen, Konstruktionen und sozialer Wandel, Research report NRP 58 (accessed 15 April 2013).

Studer, Ruedi (2006): "'Wir sind Christen!' Minarett-Gegner Roland Kissling ist vom Entscheid des Kantons Solothurn enttäuscht", in: *Basler Zeitung,* 14 July, p. 5.

Tanner, Mathias (2007): *Mediation in Minarettkonflikten: Beschreibung, Kontextualisierung und Analyse des Minarettkonflikts in Langenthal im Hinblick auf die Frage, was Mediation zu seiner Lösung beitragen könnte,* licence thesis, Universität Bern. [online] Available at www.religionenschweiz.ch/pdf/tanner-mediation.pdf (accessed 11 May 2013).

Tanner, Mathias et al. (2009): *Streit um das Minarett: Zusammenleben in der religiös pluralistischen Gesellschaft,* Zürich: Theologischer Verlag.

Tunger-Zanetti, Andreas (forthcoming): "Religious illiteracy and segmented public spheres: Why the Swiss minaret ban came as a surprise", in: Loch, Dietmar (ed.): *Migrants in the political sphere of European societies: Between normative values, political participation and social rights,* Basingstoke: Palgrave Macmillan.

Vatter, Adrian (ed.) (2011): *Vom Schächt- zum Minarettverbot: Religiöse Minderheiten in der direkten Demokratie,* Zürich: Neue Zürcher Zeitung.

Vatter, Adrian / Milic, Thomas / Hirter, Hans (2011): "Das Stimmverhalten bei der Minarettverbots-Initiative unter der Lupe", in: Vatter, Adrian (ed.): *Vom Schächt- zum Minarettverbot: Religiöse Minderheiten in der direkten Demokratie,* Zürich: Neue Zürcher Zeitung, 144-170.

Wäckerlig, Oliver (2011): Das Fanal von Wangen: Diskursanalyse des Konflikts um ein Minarett. Unpublished master thesis, University of Zürich.

Wäckerlig, Oliver (2013): „Das Fanal von Wangen: Diskursanalyse des Konflikts um ein Minarett", in: Uehlinger, Christoph / Lüddeckens, Dorothea / Walthert / Rafael (eds): *Die Sichtbarkeit religiöser Identität: Repräsentation – Differenz – Konflikt,* Zürich: Pano, pp. 313–348.

Wood, Susan K. (2011): "Religious illiteracy", in: *Marquette Magazine,* Winter. [online] Available at: http://www.marquette.edu/magazine/recent.php? subaction=showfull&id=1295026841&archive=&start_from=&ucat=6& (accessed 15 April 2013).

Protecting democracy, misrecognising Muslims?
An assessment of Swiss integration policy

Matteo Gianni

It is quite well known that the Swiss model of incorporation is assimilationist and based on an ethnic conception of citizenship (Koopmans et al. 2005); that it entails a naturalisation procedure which is (according to international standards) very restrictive (Huddleston et al. 2011) and, in some cases, unfairly discretionary (Helbling 2008); and that it goes along with the constant politicisation of the issue of foreigners, which has characterised the Swiss political landscape since the xenophobic popular votes of the 1960s (traditional immigration) to the more recent debates on the effects of the bilateral agreements (new immigration; see Mahnig 2005). Although these aspects of Swiss immigrant policy have been extensively analyzed, it is arguable that there is something peculiar in the revival of assimilationist discourses which have focused on Muslims for the last decade (Gianni 2009). What is particularly striking is that the pressure put on Muslims (as a group) to assimilate is generally justified in the media and public debate, by the necessity to protect and to preserve basic democratic norms, values and practices, such as gender equality (Ettinger/Imhof 2011; Gianni/Clavien 2012), i.e. what are considered Swiss core political and cultural values. Islam and Muslims have been therefore increasingly constructed as potential threats that should be securitised (Gianni 2013) in order to preserve Swiss democracy.

Such a trend raises important theoretical and political issues regarding the contemporary Swiss modalities of management of cultural differences, especially with regards to integration and, more generally, citizenship. The aim of this chapter is to scrutinise whether the (new) public philosophy of integration which prevails in Switzerland with regard to Muslims is suited to fostering an actual and fair democratic integration. In the first part of the paper, after a presentation of some general features about Muslim presence in Switzerland, I will show that the Swiss revival of assimilationist discourses and practices follows a conception of integration which is seen as entailing the mere *adjustment* (or normalisation) of the 'Other' to (supposedly) 'common' democratic and liberal norms. This results from the fact that Muslims are often portrayed in Swiss public discourse as being opposed to democratic norms and gender equality and that public institutions should therefore pressure them to adapt to such democratic standards. On this basis, I argue that integration as adaptation raises a case of democratic misrecognition (in the sense of lack of public respect and of status subordination that denies Muslims the opportunity to live up to the standards of the principles of liberty, equality or autonomy). The case of democratic misrecognition is based on three main aspects; first, integration as adjustment creates a dichotomy between 'good' and 'bad' citizens that calls into question the democratic equality inherent to citizenship; second, adjustment entails a progressive *de-politicisation of citizenship* as a category of practice. In order to be accepted in Swiss polity, Muslims are implicitly compelled to uncritically endorse the content and scope of Swiss democratic norms and practices; I maintain that such symbolic requirements call into question the transformative power inherent to democratic citizenship. Such transformative power is also called into question by a third factor: integration as adjustment is based on a categorical mistake that raises important political consequences: the requirement to adapt to fundamental democratic principles is based on the idea that such values are by definition universal and therefore intangible. This is perhaps true with regards to the values expressed in very abstract terms, but certainly not with regards to the specific modalities of implementation (norms, laws, procedures, etc.) to provide actual content. Therefore, to require individuals to unequivocally adjust to specific values can strongly limit their democratic empowerment and, I contend, their democratic integration. In the last part of the article I will sketch the general features of an alternative conception of integration, namely integration as a process, that may avoid the undemocratic aspects inherent to integration as adjustment. In particular, I will support a conception of integration conceived as an inter-subjective process of negotiation of principles and values structuring the Swiss shared identity. I will therefore suggest that in order to minimise misrecognition, integration has to be understood as a *process* finalised to establish the conditions for the inter-subjective (re)definition of common norms and principles. This normative requirement is not only grounded on an ideal theory of integration; it also emerges from the contextual possibilities/options offered by Swiss institutions. In fact, although it has never been labelled in this way, the intuition inherent to the processual conception of integration is historically part of the Swiss political and institutional culture (i.e. what is usually termed consensus democracy).

MUSLIM PRESENCE IN SWITZERLAND: CONTEXTUAL ASPECTS

The issue of Muslim integration in Switzerland has been given very high international resonance since the vote of the popular initiative "against the minarets".
The initiative, which sought to forbid the building of minarets in Switzerland,
was presented by the initiators as respecting the right of Muslims to practice
their religion, yet providing a clear symbolic message and legal limitation to
what the Swiss People's Party (Schweizerische Volkspartei, SVP) termed the *Islamisation* of Swiss public space. In November 2009, 57.5 per cent of Swiss voters accepted the ban, providing an unreported procedural democratic legitimation to a decision which clearly misrecognises Muslims (or discriminates against
them – according to Vatter 2011).

Unsurprisingly, the campaign on this vote has led to a very emotional and
harsh public debate on the Muslim presence in Switzerland[1]. In particular – as in
other European countries (Bousetta/Jacobs 2006; Modood/Triandafyllidou/
Zapata-Barrero 2006; Parekh 2008) – issues relating to multiculturalism or integration have been increasingly structured by narratives based on a construction
and representation of Islam in terms of fear, distrust and hostility. In a sense, the
debate about minarets has functioned according to a metonymic logic: starting
from the particular details on the meanings and functions of minarets, it has led
to very broad considerations on Islam, such as its (assumed) lack of potential to
fit with democracy or the risks of Islamisation and radicalism and, hence, to the
broader issue of the protection of Swiss values and democracy against religious
and political threats. Among the topics raised during the campaign, one was particularly salient, namely gender issues. In fact, the debate on minarets progressively shifted to a debate on Muslim women's condition[2].

---

1   The initiative was launched in May 2007 and succeeded in collecting the required
    100 000 citizen's signatures. It was deposited at the Federal administration in August
    2008, and the vote took place on 29 November 2009.
2   This is exemplified by the main poster from the group behind the popular initiative: it
    represents a Swiss map full of minarets (pointing to the sky as missiles); in the fore-
    ground there is a Muslim woman wearing a *niqāb* (see illustration on p. 300). This
    poster is very interesting for two reasons: first, it clearly demonstrates the metonymic
    logic of the debate; second, it suggests a compelling reason for which Swiss citizens
    should ban the construction of new minarets, namely the protection of women's rights
    and autonomy (see Parini/Gianni/Clavien 2012).

With regard to the diachronic peculiarities of the debate on Islam that have emerged in the last decade, it is reasonable to think that the decision by Swiss voters is not the simple result of contingent factors, but mainly of a wider structural frame of representations that construct Muslims as (the new) figures of otherness in the country (Gianni/Clavien 2012; Behloul 2009). This has happened since the rapid increase in the demographic, social and political visibility of the Muslim population has taken place. In fact, the settlement of Muslims in Switzerland is a very recent phenomenon: the Muslim population has increased by almost 20 times between 1970 and 2000 (from about 16 000 to 311 000), amounting at 4.3 per cent of the residents. According to the most recent estimations concerning 2010, the Muslim population has increased to 440 000, or 5.5 per cent of the overall population. While the presence of the first generation of immigrants was considered as temporary (because of the *guest worker* status), many Muslims are now permanently settled in Switzerland. They come from three main geographic areas: Turkey, the Balkans and North Africa[3]. It is then its social and ethnic heterogeneity which characterises this population, and not homogeneity as it is suggested by the essentialising representations voiced in the public debate. It is also important to note that, contrary to other European countries, Muslims living in Switzerland are mainly foreigners, although the proportion of Muslims holding a Swiss passport is increasing: while in 2000 only 11.7 per cent of them were Swiss citizens, estimates based on recent data suggest that 31 per cent or more of the Muslim population are Swiss citizens (Federal Statistical Office 2012).

In recent years, Muslims have become the second religious group (if Catholics and Protestants are considered part of a single Christian religious group). Moreover, socially and politically, Muslim presence has gained higher public visibility during the last decade. On the one hand, because of the advent of some Muslim religious leaders or intellectuals in the media and in the political debate through some claims for recognition (what I might roughly summarise, referring to Hirschman's typology [Hirschman 1970], as a shift from *loyalty* to *voice*). Contrary to the (mostly) silent attitude of previous immigrant groups, the leaders of Muslim associations have progressively voiced their willingness to be integrated into Swiss polity and society not *despite*, but *with* their cultural particularities. Individual cases in which local authorities have opposed Muslim practice (as, for instance, wearing of the headscarf, Muslim cemeteries, slaughtering procedures, mixed sport activities, etc.) have therefore contributed, following 9/11,

---

3   For more systematic accounts of Swiss immigration dynamics and policy, see Mahnig (2005) and Piguet (2004).

to the creation of a 'Muslim problem' which has become an important feature of the Swiss political debate (European Monitoring Center on Racism and Xenophobia 2006; Commission fédérale contre le racisme 2006). On the other hand, issues related to the Muslim presence in Switzerland have increasingly been thematised by political actors. Through direct democracy, the increasing politicisation of Islam by right-wing parties (in particular the SVP) has fostered during the last decade several votes and political campaigns asking for more restrictive measures on the integration of foreigners and asylum policies (see Betz/Meret 2009). Although the right-wing SVP is certainly the actor who mobilises the most around the implications of the Muslim presence in Switzerland (individual members of this party, together with counterparts of an evangelical splinter party launched the initiative for the ban of minarets), all the main political forces have expressed, formally or informally, the idea that it is important to put strict limits to demands for recognition claimed by Muslims leaders or inherent to Muslim practices[4]. Therefore, while it is true that the SVP started to politicise the issues, the other political parties, although they reacted by denouncing such practices, ultimately aligned themselves with some key elements of the SVP claims[5].

One of the most relevant features of the politicisation of the Muslim presence is the discursive (re)affirmation of (supposedly) authentic and universal democratic values. Unsurprisingly, such a discursive process has progressively transformed Muslim public invisibility and private diversity into (deviant) Muslim otherness. It is characterised by the central place occupied in the public space by the figure of the 'generalised Muslim' (van den Brink 2007), the one portrayed as possessing given and fixed cultural-religious attributes, as being deeply opposed to the ethos of democracy and gender equality (Modood 2007: 130sq.), as being a threat of violence, and, more generally, a problem for democracy because of his (and not her) religious radicalism. In other words, through a logic of essentialisation, Muslims have been depicted as being driven by a (religious)

---

4 As for instance the decision of the Federal Court to rule out the request of some Muslim parents to the school authorities to implement non-mixed swimming lessons (cf. Roher, this volume), or the idea to introduce forms of 'integration agreement' (*contrat d'intégration*). These decisions are mostly supported by all the main political forces of the right and the left.

5 For instance, on 28 September 2012 the National council decided (93 against 87) to avoid banning the *'burqa'* from Swiss public places. It is interesting to notice that, on such a non-problem (there is not a *'burqa'* issue in Switzerland, at least for the moment; the number of women wearing the *niqāb* is also extremely small) the SVP was able to gain at least 20 votes from representatives of other parties.

overwhelming conception of the good which strictly determines their behaviors, political culture and capacities of integration[6].

Recent data and analysis[7] shows that this hegemonic representation of Muslims is empirically unsound. The reality of Muslims living in Switzerland is more complex and much less homogeneous than stereotypes in the public debate suggest. For instance, it is a matter of fact that some Muslims support assimilationist policies, while others oppose to them; some ask for better forms of accommodation of Islam, while others share the secularist perspective of Swiss non-Muslim citizens; some define themselves as Muslims because of their cultural origin, while other define themselves as Muslims strictly because of their religious faith; the majority of Muslims support the right to build minarets in Switzerland, but more than 20 per cent of them consider that it is better to ban them. Moreover, contrary to the widely spread perception of Muslims as a threat to democracy, data shows that, first, a very high proportion of Muslim respondents consider that in order to be integrated in Switzerland Muslims should obey the law (on a 0-10 scale, the mean Muslim response is 9.5); second, Muslims consider themselves as well integrated in Switzerland (on a 0-10 scale, the average is 8); third, Muslims living in Switzerland express a higher degree of attachment to Switzerland, than to other Muslims; fourth, Muslims have a score of trust in institutions (as the government, the parliament and the judicial system) which is higher than the score of Swiss respondents. Finally, the Swiss model of integration is very much valued by Muslim respondents, but such an opinion

---

6 Volpp (2000) shows that 'problematic' behaviours are presented and explained very differently in the (US) media and political discourses depending on the ethnic background of the individuals involved. For instance, "[...] we consider early marriage by a Mexican immigrant to reflect ‚Mexican culture'. In contrast, when a white person commits a similar act, we view it as an isolated instance of aberrant behavior, and not as reflective of a racialized culture" (p. 90). The consequences is that "this tendency to submerge only certain groups into the forces of culture is linked to the assumption that the behaviour of devalued and less powerful groups is somehow more culturally determined – that they behave in certain ways and make particular choices because they follow cultural dictates. [...] The notion that non-Western people are governed by culture suggests they have a limited capacity for agency, will or rational thought" (p. 96).

7 For a more in-depth empirical analysis of Muslims in Switzerland see Gianni, Giugni and Michel (forthcoming). This research, financed by the Swiss National Science Foundation, is based on a survey administered to a sample of 900 Muslims and 300 Swiss non-Muslims (functioning as a control group). It aims at analysing the political, social and cultural attitudes and behaviours of the Muslim population in Switzerland.

does not entail that Switzerland is perceived as heaven by Muslims. For instance, about 1/3 of the respondents has felt discriminated against at least once; about 60 per cent of them consider that Islam/Muslims should be more recognised by Swiss authorities, for instance by exemptions from some existing laws. Moreover, from the analysis of the answers provided by 300 non-Muslim Swiss, it emerges that a substantial part of the latter group has a quite negative perception of Muslims. For instance, they present a low degree of trust towards mosques and Muslim associations (an average of 4 on a 0-10 scale) and a relatively high share of them (between 13 and 29 per cent depending on the question) is not happy to enter into relations with Muslims. Unsurprisingly, the Swiss non-Muslim citizens mostly support an assimilationist and strongly secularist conception of the State and of the public space when it comes to the accommodation of Islam in Switzerland (Gianni/Giugni/Michel, forthcoming).

This raw/empirical data provides a more heterogeneous and fluid picture of Muslim subjectivity and heterogeneity which is largely obscured by the essentialised figure of the Muslim which dominated the public debate before the vote on minarets (and other previous votes). The frame of representations essentialising Muslim identity entails the misrecognition of the plurality of voices and subject positions constituting the Muslim population. Certainly, the fact that a total homogenisation of individual subjectivities does not empirically exist is not, analytically speaking, a big surprise; what is more interesting to analyse are the normative and political implications of these results with regard to the conception of integration prevailing in Switzerland.

THE UNDEMOCRATIC LOGIC OF INTEGRATION AS ADJUSTMENT

What is the link between the figure of the 'generalised Muslim' and the conception of integration prevailing in Switzerland? In this section I first argue that the essentialisation of Muslims as figures of otherness and the dominant conception of integration prevailing in Switzerland (namely integration as adjustment) reinforce each other. Second, that this entails important consequences on citizenship and, ultimately, the normative quality of Swiss democracy. In fact, the conception of integration as adjustment leads to the misrecognition of important symbolic resources that Muslims would need in order to be considered as democratic equals. I am not referring here specifically to the right to vote, which is certainly a central aspect of democratic integration (Carens 2005) and which is still unavailable to the majority of Muslims; but mainly to the symbolic factors allowing an individual to be considered by others as a full citizen and perceive himself as having actual political agency.

Let's start by briefly defining integration. It is generally acknowledged that the "term integration implies the idea of a process of give and take on both sides [and] the term assimilation suggests that the immigrants must do the adjusting" (Klausen 2005: 10). It is therefore the inter-subjective dimension inherent to integration that makes the difference (both at the political and normative levels) with assimilation, namely the adjustment of foreigners to the immigration societies' norms. In particular, integration can be seen as

> a long lasting process of inclusion and acceptance of migrants in the core institutions, relations and statutes of the receiving society. For the migrants integration refers to a process of earning a new culture, an acquisition of rights, access to positions and statuses, a building of personal relations to members of the receiving society and a formation of feelings and belonging and identification towards the immigration society. (Heckmann 2005: 15, quoted in Grillo 2007: 983)

If one scrutinises this definition thoroughly it quickly emerges that the actual scope and breadth of the elements composing it are still very poorly defined. For instance: which rights should be necessarily granted to immigrants to foster integration? I suggest here that the vagueness of Heckman or Klausen's definition is very much dependent on the ontological characteristics of the concept of integration. In fact, integration is an essentially contested concept (Gallie 1955), in the sense that it is constituted by both an empirical and a normative dimension which are too symbolically loaded to obtain a unique and commonly accepted sense. The fact that the meaning of integration is contested entails the existence of different public philosophies of integration (Favell 1998), namely different ways to transpose it into actual public policies or into political decisions determining which values and behaviours of cultural/religious minorities are acceptable or not acceptable in the public sphere.

As already mentioned above, in Switzerland the contemporary political debate is very much structured around the idea of compelling immigrants to adjust to local democratic norms (Gianni 2009). The central aspect of such philosophy of integration is the emphasis put on the *willingness* of immigrants to integrate themselves in the host society.[8] In other words, with regard to immigrants, the Swiss state follows a strict liberal-individualistic perspective on integration. The

---

8   Foreigners must have "la volonté [...] de s'intégrer". Federal Office for Migration: Exigences en matière d'intégration selon le droit des étrangers. [online] Available at: http://www.auslaender.ch/content/bfm/fr/home/themen/integration/foerderung/vereinb arungen.html (accessed 24 March 2013).

consideration of immigrants as *groups* or of *vertical* (or political) forms of integration, as for instance the public recognition of cultural differences of foreigners, are (almost) absent as means to foster integration. This carries at least two implications: first, the willingness to adjust concerning mainly the 'different', the burden of integration by adjustment is not fairly shared by the newcomers and the receiving society. For instance, while the duties of immigrants are clearly established in Swiss law, which stipulates that "Integration requires willingness on the part of the foreign nationals and openness on the part of the Swiss population" (Swiss Federal Assembly, 2005, art. 4, al. 3, official translation), the duties of the host society towards the immigrant are much more vaguely expressed. In this light, integration as adjustment calls into question the give and take dynamic that is generally supposed to characterise integration. Second, because of the emphasis put on the individual willingness to integrate, it is not surprising that group or individual claims for the collective recognition of some cultural/religious differences is perceived as a lack of willingness to adjust to the existing norms and rules, and therefore as a lack of integration.

In my view, these two aspects corroborate the claim that a philosophy of integration based on the unilateral requirement of adjustment to existing norms and laws entails important forms of *misrecognition* that ultimately call into question the moral and the democratic characters of such integration policy. Theories of recognition (see Thompson 2006) provide several reasons to support this view, reasons that I will only sketch here. For instance, the ban of minarets can be seen as concealing the idea that the cultural particularities of Muslims are not worthy enough to be socially visible (the issue about minarets is mainly an issue about visibility). As Galeotti (1993: 597) asserts "if a social difference is denied public visibility and legitimacy in the polity, the group associated with it inevitably bears social stigmata", and this can impact on its societal esteem, respect and autonomy. For Honneth (1995) such a denial of social esteem is a case of misrecognition. With regard to the principle of "parity of participation" suggested by Fraser (2005), the pressure put on Muslims to adjust shows that participation as equals is not granted and therefore that they suffer a condition of status subordination. Finally, according to Taylor (1994), both the negative representations of Muslims and the restriction of their civil rights through the ban of minarets are incompatible with the normative standards inherent to democratic recognition[9].

---

9 According to Taylor, "equal recognition is not just the appropriate mode for a healthy democratic society. Its refusal can inflict damage on those who are denied it [...]. The projection of an inferior or demeaning image on another can actually distort and oppress, to the extent that the image is internalized" (1994: 36).

According to such theoretical standards, therefore, there is little doubt that the pressure put on Muslims to unilaterally adjust their behaviours and beliefs in order to integrate into Swiss polity and society is at odds with what the theory of democratic recognition requires. Obviously, to call into question the idea of adjustment to common norms/principles is not to say that there shouldn't be limits to the demands for recognition articulated by Muslim groups in democratic polities or to (supposed) Islamic practice; neither it is to suggest that there aren't some non-negotiable common democratic principles that must be preserved in all democratic multicultural societies. After all, to state that a community of citizens must be organised around a minimal core of common values to promote social stability and justice is intuitively legitimate (Rawls 1993). My argument against integration as one-sided adjustment is that it denatures the meaning of integration itself. If integration means a total adaptation to the majority's norms and values, then we are no longer talking about integration but about assimilation. The latter is precisely what, generally, theories of recognition struggle against. So, what might integration be?

LIMITING *MISRECOGNITION*? THE *PROCESSUAL* VIEW OF INTEGRATION

So far I have argued that the conception of integration as adjustment produces forms of misrecognition. What forms does this misrecognition take? In this section I first present three arguments about the negative impact that integration as adjustment has on citizenship and democracy. In the second and final part, I provide the main theoretical elements of an alternative view of integration, that I call integration-as-process. I suggest that such a conception of integration is suited to limit misrecognition and therefore increase the democratic quality of integration in Switzerland by empowering Muslims as political and social actors.

The first argument against integration as adjustment is the restriction of one's activity as a political subject or citizen and the subsequent normalisation of citizenship as a category of practice. With regard to citizenship, or more generally agency, the moral perfectionism inherent in the requirement to adapt to given norms *de facto* strongly normalises one's activity as a citizen. Besides the fact that it creates the opposition between 'good' and 'bad' citizens, the perfectionist and *thick* (Walzer 1994) moral content of the model of integration as adaptation also entails a lack of *political* opportunities to foster the societal integration of the members of minority groups into the polity, in particular when it concerns the forms of participation to the definition of new or revised common values. In other words, the requirement to adapt to norms represented as non-negotiable imply a drastic reduction (if not the annihilation) of the 'give and take' dynamic which is supposed to be present in most conceptions of social and political integration. This goes against the idea that integration should be conceived as the opportunity, both politically and symbolically, provided to subjects to be part of the process of inter-subjective determination/revision of the best modalities to implement fundamental principles. This idea, which resonates with Nancy Fraser's principle of parity of participation, does not only concern the level of the societal recognition of minority groups, but also the idea that the plurality of individual views and voices inherent to cultural-religious minority groups must be given channels of expression and be taken into account in the process. To avoid misrecognition, citizenship rights and resources should be enriched by democratic procedural opportunities allowing Muslims to be integrated into the arenas where collective determination of common values takes place. Loyal and integrated Muslims should not be expected – as everybody else functioning as members of a polity – to *uncritically* adjust to Swiss democratic values and practices. This would mean that they are not considered worthy or autonomous enough to participate in decisions or discussions concerning their identities/interests.

The first argument is linked to a second important limit of integration as adjustment, namely its tendency to *de-politicise* citizenship as category of practice (see Brown 2006). Such form of integration indirectly provides a *quasi-extra-political* status to the values, laws and practices to which immigrant should adjust. In other words, these become almost *non-negotiable*, and this significantly reduces Muslims' political agency as citizens. In other words, instead of being a place in which common values can be inter-subjectively reassessed, citizenship turns into a place where certain values, considered as characterising and constituting the polity itself, are only reaffirmed. Therefore, citizenship as the *locus* of political definition of common values is so constrained by the symbolic imposition of *pre-political* assumptions that the political deliberation basically becomes an actualisation of the latter. This is inconsistent with the idea that the democratic legitimacy of citizenship relies on the fact that citizens are allowed to freely determine (that also means, in liberal terms, to *revise*) the terms of their social and political contract, and, therefore, the values underlying it.

Finally, integration as adjustment entails a categorical mistake which is inherent to the requirement to adapt to the fundamental democratic principles. Much empirical evidence shows that almost all the claims to recognition articulated by Swiss Muslims in the public space do not call into question fundamental democratic values in themselves, but the modalities of their implementation/interpretation by legal and political acts or decisions. There is a categorical difference between the contestation of fundamental democratic rights/principles and the criticism of *one* of its possible interpretations or embodiment in public policies or legal-political decisions. It is precisely this categorical mistake that spoils integration as adaptation at its core. In the public debate, it is often asserted that Muslims should adapt to fundamental liberal democratic norms and principles. Taken as such, this requirement is intuitively fair and legitimate: the idea that the democratic character of a polity is enhanced when principles such as liberty, equality and autonomy are protected and are a constitutive part of its symbolic and moral grounds is quite uncontroversial. Having said this, it is also evident that the collective acceptance of such general principles does not logically entail that there is *just one way* of implementing them in actual laws and public decisions. It is even fair to say that politics is precisely the competitive activity which allows actors to allocate specific procedures and material or symbolic resources in order to embody abstract principles in actual collective decisions. Now, when Muslim individuals or groups take a position against specific laws or public decisions, they mainly criticise the implementation/interpretation of a given general principle. Such an attitude does not necessarily entail an opposition to the general principle. This is the case, for instance, with regard to laws occasioning forms of discrimination (and therefore conflicting with the principle of equality of treatment), or when the constitutional principle of religious freedom is not interpreted broadly enough to protect the right to build minarets. The willingness to protect the principle of equality between men and women, which I consider as one of the fundamental pillars of any democratic system, does not automatically entail either the requirement to ban the Islamic headscarf, or the moral obligation to allow it without any restrictions in all social settings. Therefore, the fact of contesting a particular way to implement the principle does not necessarily entail being at odds with it. Almost all the controversial issues opposing Muslims and Swiss public authorities do not call into question the intrinsic validity of Swiss democratic values, *but* mostly their contextual *interpretation* and the modalities of their actualisation in legal and political acts or decisions (see Kymlicka 2000: 148). This distinction is crucial (and much understated in the public and political debates on Muslims), for there is a huge difference between contesting a democratic fundamental principle and demanding a possible reinterpretation of its legal or political scope and modality of application.

Laws, procedures and norms are the product of historically and contextually situated interpretations and decisions. The fact of considering (wrongly, on the basis of a categorical mistake) laws and norms as non-negotiable as if they were universal principles (assuming that these exist), contradict the main aspects of what integration as *process* is supposed to be. More specifically, the social and political framing of norms or laws as if they were non-negotiable implicitly entails that only a *formal-legal* approach to integration, based on unidirectional adjustment, is suited to accommodate Muslims' presence/claims. I argue that this view precludes other important options, as for instance the focus on *procedural-democratic* modalities to promote accommodation through a process of collective reinterpretation or revision of the contents of common norms.[10] The formal-legal accommodation is grounded on the idea that the existing norms and principles are intrinsically good. This leads to a situation where the political debate does not involve exchange between the cultural majority and the cultural minorities about the content of new shared values and common principles, but merely as a discussion among the members of the cultural majority about what they are supposed to do about the minority groups or individuals.[11] In this case, the majority asks from the minority loyalty to contingent norms, laws or decisions which are not necessarily endorsed morally and by sound arguments, but politically enforced.

To avoid such forms of misrecognition, struggles for the reinterpretation of particular modalities of implementation of general principles should be part of the political dynamic; but this requires the existence of adequate democratic procedures. Their justification can be grounded on different normative theories of recognition, such as reciprocity (Gutmann/Thompson 1996), parity of participation (Fraser 2005), precondition to deliberation (Pourtois 2002), or as struggle against disrespect (Honneth 1995). I do not intend to suggest here that one of these principles is superior to others; what I want to emphasise is that, whatever the best principle might be, it will ineluctably conflict with the normativity inherent to and the political implementation of integration as adjustment. Therefore an alternative conception of integration is needed to limit democratic misrecognition.

The *processual* conception of integration may be such an alternative. I say to 'limit' and not to 'avoid' misrecognition because I assume, following Tully, that there are good sociological reasons to believe that "struggles over recognition, like struggles over distribution, are not amenable to definitive solutions beyond further democratic disagreement, dispute, negotiation, amendment, implementation, review" (Tully 2000: 477). It is precisely on this ontological assumption that integration as process is grounded. Broadly inspired by a Habermasian logic, its main normative intuition relies in the idea that all subjects concerned by political acts or decisions should be included in an inter-

---

10 For an empirical presentation of these two logics of societal regulation, see Gianni (2005).

11 I completely agree with Phillips that "when policies are worked out for rather than with a politically excluded constituency, they are unlikely to engage with all relevant concerns" (1995: 13).

subjective process of redefinition/reinterpretation of common norms. Processual integration is not suited to erasing misrecognition as a socio-political dynamic for good, but it consists in a political and procedural framework in which the effects of misrecognition or the acts producing it can be articulated, discussed, assessed, and, ultimately, revised. In this light, processual integration aims at contributing to the reduction of misrecognition by transforming the latter into a political issue. In other words, integration would be less about culture than about political resources giving individuals the opportunities to protect or amend their cultural values. To conceive integration in political terms means that the integration of Muslims is not an issue of cultural charity or politeness, but a democratic imperative needed to provide moral and political legitimacy to the overall democratic polity.

It is worth emphasising that the processual view of integration suggested in this paper is not only an ideal theoretical construction; it is also – and more importantly – a crucial (although, perhaps, implicit) pillar of the Swiss political and institutional culture. Considered as a consensus democracy (Lijphart 1999), the Swiss polity is very much built around a very large set of formal or informal political procedures to foster agreement between actors belonging to territorialised cultural and linguistic groups. The situation is almost the opposite concerning non-territorialised minority groups. The case of Muslims illustrates this trend well. Broadly speaking, almost nothing has been done with regard to democratic procedures or political opportunities allowing the leaders of the Muslim community to participate to the determination of decisions about their claims; no Muslim association has obtained the public recognition from the state as an association of general interest; very few specific procedures of conflict management have been implemented when pragmatic forms of accommodation fail and the debate becomes public and highly emotional. Some exceptions to this trend do exist, as for instance a successful case of a procedural accommodation of conflict around an Islamic cemetery (see Gianni/Varone 2007); but they mainly concern issues not involving very relevant rights and/or values or that can be dealt at a local level. Besides such exceptions, when a conflict occurs the institutional response is mostly based on law or formal decisions, not through political devices intended to build post-conventional identities based on an inter-subjective recognition of all actors concerned (Williams 1995). Therefore, integration as adaptation blocks the opportunities for minority groups to be part of a process of renegotiation and of reinterpretation of the common norms, and this leads to forms of democratic misrecognition.

It seems to me that such a trend is not only problematic with regard to a general theory of democratic recognition, but also with regard to the basic shared principles on which Swiss democracy is built, as for instance the commitment to compromise, to a strong conception of democracy, and to the idea that values are not *external* to politics, but the product of political participation and deliberation (Barber 1984). The strong republican stance embedded in Swiss political culture and in its understanding of active citizenship offers the institutional and cognitive knowledge to think of *processual means* to foster forms of integration. Or in the case of integration as adjustment, the normativity embedded in the Swiss public philosophy of integration of cultural-religious minorities conflicts with some aspect of the normativity embedded in the overall polity. In my view, therefore, the decision of not employing them is not only a case of democratic *mis*recognition in ideal terms, but also according to contextual standards (on this approach, see Carens 2000; 2004).

CONCLUSION

In this article I attempted to show that a conception of integration as adjustment entails the weakening of democracy as the medium to promote forms of common understanding. Instead of being a locus where *voice* is a resource to create loyalty, adjustment entails a pre-political loyalty to norms, principles and practices that define the scope of freedom for the members of cultural minority groups. Muslim presence in Europe compels public authorities and intellectuals to find better ways to actualise and implement democracy, not against them, but with them. Such a processual and inclusive perspective on integration and citizenship does not mean that all demands to recognition claimed by Muslims should be necessarily granted. There are issues opposing some Muslims to public authorities, as for instance practices pertaining to gender, to the equality between men and women, or to the protection of children's rights, that cannot be recognised, and therefore indirectly legitimised, by liberal-democratic states. This does not mean, however, that democratic procedures aiming at establishing modalities of deliberation, effective participation and mutual listening to arguments and ethical stances should not be fostered and envisioned. There is something important to gain by implementing such democratic processes: it is the fact that, although the public recognition of a specific issue can fail, the symbolic recognition of Muslims as morally autonomous individuals and as equal participants to the common definition of values and norms is a very crucial step towards social and political integration. The overall quality of citizenship, and hence democracy, will be enriched, although conflicts or controversies about the specific contents, meanings and moral assessments of the debated claims will inevitably persist. Nothing is very surprising in such a dynamic: ultimately, this is what democracy is about.

References

Barber, Benjamin (1984): *Strong democracy,* Berkeley: University of California Press.

Behloul, Samuel M. (2009): "Discours total! Le débat sur l'islam en Suisse et le positionnement de l'islam comme religion publique", in: Schneuwly Purdie, Mallory / Gianni, Matteo / Jenny, Magali (eds), *Musulmans d'aujourd'hui: Identités plurielles en Suisse,* Genève: Labor et Fides, pp. 53-72.

Betz, Hans-Georg / Meret, Susi (2009): "Revisiting Lepanto: the political mobilization against Islam in contemporary Western Europe", in: *Patterns of Prejudice,* 43, 3-4: 313-334.

Bousetta, Hassan / Jacobs, Dirk (2006): "Multiculturalism, citizenship and Islam in problematic encounters in Belgium", in: Modood, Tariq / Triandafyllidou, Anna / Zapata-Barrero, Ricard (eds), *Multiculturalism, Muslims and Citizenship: A European Approach,* New York: Routledge, pp. 23-36.

Brown, Wendy (2006): *Regulating aversion,* Princeton: Princeton University Press.

Carens, Joseph (2000): *Culture, citizenship, and community: A contextual exploration of justice as evenhandedness,* Oxford: Oxford University Press.

— (2004): "A contextual approach to political theory", in: *Ethical Theory and Moral Practice,* 7, pp. 117–132.

— (2005): "The integration of immigrants", in: *Journal of Moral Philosophy,* 2:1, pp. 29-46.

Commission fédérale contre le racisme (2006): *Les relations avec la minorité musulmane en Suisse.* Bern.

European Monitoring Centre on Racism and Xenophobia (2006): *Les musulmans au sein de l'Union Européenne: Discriminations et islamophobie,* Vienna.

Favell, Adrian (1998): *Philosophies of integration,* Basingstokes: Macmillan.

Federal Assembly (2005): Bundesgesetz vom 16. Dezember 2005 über die Ausländerinnen und Ausländer [Federal Act on Foreign Nationals], [online] English version available at http://www.admin.ch/ch/e/rs/142_20/index.html (accessed 28 December 2012).

Federal Statistical Office (2012): Ständige Wohnbevölkerung ab 15 Jahren nach Religions- und Konfessionszugehörigkeit in den Sprachregionen (revidierte Daten vom 11.10.2012). [online] Available at: http://www.bfs.admin.ch/bfs/portal/de/index/news/04/01.Document.159819.zip, file su-d-01.06.02.03.01 .xls (Accessed 28 December 2012).

Fraser, Nancy (2005): *Qu'est-ce que la justice sociale?,* Paris: La Découverte.

Galeotti, Anna-Elisabetta (1993): "Citizenship and equality: The place for toleration", in: *Political Theory,* 21:4, pp. 585-605.

Gallie, Walter Bryce (1955): "Essentially contested concepts", in: *Proceedings of the Aristotelian Society*, New series, 56, pp. 167-198.

Gianni, Matteo (2005): "L'intégration comme enjeu culturel à Genève: le cas de la minorité musulmane", in: Mahnig, Hans / Cattacin, Sandro (eds), *Histoire de la politique de migration, d'asile et d'intégration en Suisse depuis 1948,* Zürich: Seismo, pp. 344-374.

— (2009): "Citoyenneté et intégration des musulmans en Suisse: adaptation aux normes ou participation à leur définition?", in: Schneuwly Purdie, Mallory / Gianni, Matteo / Jenny, Magali (eds), *Musulmans d'aujourd'hui: Identités plurielles en Suisse,* Genève: Labor et Fides, pp. 73-93.

— (forthcoming): "Securitizing democracy, de-securitizing citizenship? The case of Muslims in Switzerland", in: Guillaume, Xavier / Huysmans, Jeff (eds), *Security and citizenship: The constitution of political being*, London: Routledge.

Gianni, Matteo / Clavien, Gaëtan (2012): "Representing gender, defining Muslims? Gender and figures of otherness in public discourse in Switzerland", in: Flood, Christopher et al. (eds), *Political and cultural representations of Muslims: Islam in the plural*, Leiden: Brill, pp. 113-129.

Gianni, Matteo / Giugni, Marco / Michel, Noemi (forthcoming): *Musulmans en Suisse: Profils et intégration,* Lausanne: Presses polytechniques et universitaires romandes, collection Le savoir suisse.

Gianni, Matteo / Varone, Frédéric (2007): "Les délégués cantonaux à l'intégration en Suisse: gardiens d'un Etat laïque et du pluralisme confessionnel?", in: *Ethique publique,* 9:2, pp. 36-50.

Grillo, Ralph (2007): "An excess of alterity? Debating difference in a multicultural society", in: *Ethnic and Racial Studies,* 30:6, pp. 979-998.

Gutmann, Amy / Thompson, Dennis (1996): *Democracy and disagreement,* Cambridge MA: Belknap.

Heckmann, Friedrich (ed) (2005): *Integration and integration policies: IMISCOE Network Feasibility Study,* Bamberg: EFMS Intpol Team.

Helbling, Marc (2008): *Practising citizenship and heterogeneous nationhood: Naturalisations in Swiss municipalities,* Amsterdam: Amsterdam University Press.

Hirschman, Albert O. (1970): *Exit, voice, and loyalty: Responses to decline in firms, organizations, and states,* Cambridge MA: Harvard University Press.

Honneth, Axel (1995): *Struggles for recognition,* Cambridge MA: MIT.

Huddleston, Thomas et al. (2011): *Migrant integration policy index III,* Brussels: British Council and Migration Policy Group.

Klausen, Jytte (2005): *The Islamic challenge,* Oxford: Oxford University Press.

Koopmans, Ruud et al. (2005): *Contested citizenship: Immigration and cultural diversity in Europe,* Minneapolis: University of Minnesota Press.

Kymlicka, Will (2000): "Les droits des minorités et le multiculturalisme: l'évolution du débat anglo-américain", in: *Revue de philosophie et de sciences sociales*, pp. 141-171.

Lijphart, Arend (1999): *Patterns of democracy: Government forms and performance in thirty-six countries*, New Haven: Yale University Press.

Mahnig, Hans (ed) (2005): *Histoire de la politique de migration, d'asile et d'intégration en Suisse depuis 1948*, Zürich: Seismo.

Modood, Tariq (2007): *Multiculturalism*, Cambridge: Polity, pp. 130-131.

Modood, Tariq / Triandafyllidou, Anna / Zapata-Barrero, Ricard (eds) (2006): *Multiculturalism, Muslims and citizenship*, London: Routledge.

Parini, Lorena / Gianni, Matteo / Clavien, Gaëtan (2012): "La transversalité des questions de genre dans le débat médiatique sur l'Islam et les musulmans dans la presse Suisse francophone", in: *Cahiers du genre*, 52:2, pp. 197-218.

Parekh, Bikuh (2008): *The new politics of identity*, London: Palgrave Macmillan.

Phillips, Anne (1995): *The politics of presence*, Oxford: Oxford University Press.

Piguet, Etienne (2004): *L'immigration en Suisse*, Lausanne: Presses polytechniques et universitaires romandes.

Pourtois, Hervé (2002): "Luttes pour la reconnaissance et politique délibérative", in: *Philosophique*, 29:2, pp. 287-309.

Rawls, John (1993): *Political liberalism*, New York: Columbia University Press.

Taylor, Charles (1994): "The politics of recognition", in: id., *Multiculturalism: Examining the politics of recognition*, edited and introduced by Amy Gutmann, Princeton: Princeton University Press, pp. 25-74.

Thompson, Simon (2006): *The political theory of recognition*, Cambridge: Polity Press.

Tully, James (2000): "Struggles over recognition and distribution", in: *Constellations*, 7:4, pp. 469-482.

Vatter, Adrian (2011): *Vom Schächt- zum Minarettverbot: Religiöse Minderheiten in der direkten Demokratie*, Zürich: NZZ.

van den Brink, Bert (2007): "Imagining civic relations in the moment of their breakdown: a crisis of civic integrity in the Netherlands", in: Laden, Anthony S. / Owen, David (eds), *Multiculturalism and political theory*, Cambridge: Cambridge University Press, pp. 350-372.

Volpp, Leti (2000): "Blaming culture for bad behavior", in: *Yale Journal of Law & the Humanities*, 12, pp. 89-116.

Walzer, Michael (1994): *Thick and thin: Moral argument at home and abroad*, Notre Dame: University of Notre Dame Press.

Williams, Melissa (1995): "Justice toward groups: Political not juridical", in: *Political Theory*, 23:1, pp. 67-91.

Epilogue

On relating religion to society and society to religion

REINHARD SCHULZE

I

In what follows, I will once again raise the question of the relationship between Islam and secularity. This question preconditions a macro-sociological
perspective. It calls for shaping the texture of Islamic traditions in such a way
that it can be linked to a process of secularisation, no matter how this relationship is established. At first glance, this question seems simple, but in fact, it is
difficult to find an appropriate method through which to give a satisfactory answer. If, following Charles Taylor, one understands 'secularisation' as a process signifying a radical humanism which is linked to a disenchantment of the
world and thus to a separation of religion from its force of enchantment, it is
necessary to identify a process which has deeply influenced and transformed
Islam from the outside.

Admittedly, many observers often draw attention to endogenous factors in
the history of religions, which have been adjusting this process to the
respective religion in a very different way. In Christianity for example,
secularisation refers to the Reformation. But generally, the idea prevails that
exogenous factors paved the way for the secularisation of the social worlds.
Thus, in respect of Islam, two questions come up: a) Was there an endogenous
process leading to the secularisation of life worlds which can be related to one
of the traditions of Islam? b) Which exogenous factors transformed Islam so
that it has lost its power of enchantment, hence its power over the temporal
orders?

In most cases, the description of the relationship between Islam and secularity is spontaneously linked to normative perspectives. These conditions are

mostly established by readings of the Qur'an or the entire prophetic traditions which are used to determine the relationship between Islam and secularity. As a result of this 'consultation of Islamic sources', the following opinions are developed: Islam is characterised by a) the lack of the separation of religion and state, b) the lack of determination of an autonomous subject, and related to this, c) the lack of historicisation of the Islamic religious canon.

We could add the assertion of sociology of religion that the 'secularist disbelief' has not extended to all social strata. But this discourse cannot explain some cultural facts. Firstly, the fact that many people linked in one way or another to Islam certainly behave in a secular way. By splitting the modern conjunction of norms and values, they refer to Islam as a system of values and submit their life worlds to the standards of a secular *Dasein*. Consequently, they restrict the legitimacy of the state to enact these values morally and keep away the claim of ultra-religious Islamists to impose their norms as social rules by means of the state. Secondly, the fact that there is an Islamic self-explanation which assesses the delimitation of ultra-religious validity claims positively and accepts Islamic values as standard of an autonomy of civil and political realms, without denying the role of Islam in the moral; hence, autonomy is regarded as a value that is an integral part of civilisation.

Usually, these facts are explained by the interpretation that there are exogenous forces that have an important influence on Islam without having led to a fundamental transformation of the social order. This interpretation is further supported by the consensus that secularisation is considered to be specific to and marked by the history of the Christian religion. As Talal Asad maintains, secularisation is defined by specific experiences in the history of Christian religion, despite the universalism which connotes the term itself. Following José Casanova, secularisation is indeed an experience particular to Protestantism, and similar processes in Catholicism should be termed independently in order to avoid the interpretation that Catholic secularisation is considered a protestantisation of Catholicism. The more secularisation is discussed as a particularity within the history of the Christian religion, the more the question becomes important as to how we can understand the entry of other religions into Charles Taylor's "immanent frame". As for the Catholic Church, secularism has indeed become a frame for positive self-interpretation. In a publication of the Congregation for the Doctrine of the Faith in 2002, we read:

> For Catholic moral doctrine, the rightful autonomy of the political or civil sphere from that of religion and the Church – *but not from that of morality* – is a value

that has been attained and recognized by the Catholic Church and belongs to inheritance of contemporary civilization.[1]

Secularism is autonomous vis-à-vis religion, but not vis-à-vis morality:

> While a plurality of methodologies reflective of different sensibilities and cultures can be legitimate in approaching such questions, no Catholic can appeal to the principle of pluralism or to the autonomy of lay involvement in political life to support policies affecting the common good which compromise or undermine fundamental ethical requirements. This is not a question of 'confessional values' *per se*, because such ethical precepts are rooted in human nature itself and belong to the natural moral law. (ibid.)

If the entry into the "immanent frame" is particular in time and tradition, we must ask how Muslims have achieved to live in a secular world. Investigations by sociologists of religion have shown that a large majority of Muslims has actually entered this framework; in Turkey, about 75 per cent of respondents supported positions that are usually attributed to a secular attitude, yet about the same number of respondents described themselves as "religious". On average, two-thirds of the population in the old-Islamic world believe that religious professionals should not play a political role. At the same time, two-thirds say that Sharia should be a moral source of the legal order.[2]

Therefore, we should ask what is the actual genealogy of secularity in Muslim countries that was unveiled during the contemporary revolts in the Arab countries? To understand secularity in Muslim countries, and to understand how Islam can contribute to the creation/reconstruction of a genealogy of secularity, I would like to propose a modest model, which could serve as a starting point.

II

A look at the writings of the nineteenth century, written in European languages as well as in oriental languages, reveals that the term 'secular' is basically an interpretation of society seen from the perspective of religion. Here, the interpretation Niklas Luhmann suggested proves true: "If society is described from the

---

1   Congregation for the Doctrine of the Faith 2002, p. 13 (original emphasis), referring to Second Vatican Council, Pastoral Constitution *Gaudium et spes,* p. 76.

2   See Schulze 2010a.

point of view of religion as secular, religion is described from the point of view of society as culture."[3] Luhmann explained this relation as follows:

> Secularization is a term by which the system of religion describes the condition of aggregation of its social environment. The need for such an aggregation is in itself a product of social development. It occurs only when the system of religion being/as society does not orientate itself towards the personal environment of the system of society in the first place, but being/as a subsystem of society towards the inner-societal environment; in this respect, secularization displaces sin as the central concept for experienced incongruity.[4]

As a supplement to Luhmann's definition of secularisation, I use the word secularity – the concept actually meant the temporal jurisdiction of the Church – to denote the factuality of a secular state of social reality. This word is a category by which religious actors explain society, and as, at the same time, the concept of 'culture' is a category of explanation by which societal actors want to interpret religion, the result is a discursive separation between religion and society, which exactly reproduces the distinction between the religious and the secular.

Both the concept of 'society' and the concept of 'religion' as normative categories stem from a pre-modern transcendental order in which there was only one order of truth. As such the two concepts – religion and society – have a common genealogy: they represent normative orders that refer to each other and that complement each other. From the point of view of religion, society seems in principle 'secular', and from the point of view of society, every religion seems

---

3 Luhmann 1996: 313: "Wenn von der Religion aus gesehen die Gesellschaft als säkularisiert beschrieben wird, so von der Gesellschaft aus gesehen die Religion als Kultur." It is noteworthy that Max Scheler aiming at Max Weber and his school of thought vehemently rejected to interprete religion as culture, see Max Scheler. Vom Ewigen im Menschen. Bd. 1. Religiöse Erneuerung. Leipzig: Der neue Geist, 1921, p. 648.

4 My translation from Luhmann 1982: 227sq.: "'Säkularisierung' ist ein Terminus, mit dem das Religionssystem den Aggregatzustand seiner gesellschaftlichen Umwelt bezeichnet. Der Bedarf für eine solche Aggregation ist selbst ein Produkt der gesellschaftlichen Entwicklung. Er tritt erst auf, wenn das Religionssystem sich nicht mehr in erster Linie als Gesellschaft an der personalen Umwelt des Gesellschaftssystems, sondern als Teilsystem der Gesellschaft an der innergesellschaftlichen Umwelt orientiert; insofern löst Säkularisierung Sünde ab als Leitbegriff für erfahrene Nichtübereinstimmung." – See also Luhmann 2013.

basically 'cultural'. These two interpretations are mutual, and they are only possible within this reciprocity:

Table 1: Mutual interpretations of society and religion

OBJECT

		Society	Religion
	Society	autonomy	Culture
SUBJECT	*Religion*	Secular	autonomy

Source: Author's compilation.

The discursive interdependence of these two orders becomes apparent when both orders accept the respective categorical ascription as a self-interpretation. Thus when the societal actors interpret society as 'secular', they can construe culture as "secular religion"[5] or religion as "secular culture"[6]. And when religious actors interpret religion as 'cultural', they can construe the secular as 'cultural society' or society as 'secular culture'. Both strategies still reflect the claim that it is legitimate to gain control over the contrapositive order by subjecting it to the logic of self-interpretation. The concept of order 'society' then performs its self-description by accepting the reading religious actors have construed and, in parallel, religion increasingly stressed its self-interpretation by using the attribute which societal actors have assigned to religion. In addition, it is then possible to provide the societal attribute called 'secular' to a specific religion and the religious attribute called 'cultural' to a specific society. Relating Islam to society dates back to the middle of the eighteenth century. The Jesuit scholar Joseph de

---

5   I found the first evidence for the use of this syntagma in the work of the English Baptist dissenter Robert Robinson (1735-1790; *The History and Mystery of Good-Friday*, London: Lephart, 1782, p. 35: "The whole farrago of a secular religion is a burden, an expence, a distress to government, and every corrupt part and parcel of it is some way or other injurious to civil polity. Consider a kingdom as one large family, sum up the priesthood into one domestic chaplain, compare what he costs with the good he does, and judge whether the family gains as it ought, or loses as it ought not by his chaplainship." It is true, however, that as in French, the qualification of religion as secular has gained general acceptance not before the 1940s.

6   This English syntagma came into use in the 1870s.

Menoux (1696-1766) used this expression (de Menoux 1758: 93), and the French royalist politician Louis-Gabriel-Ambroise de Bonald (1754-1840) stated: "[…] so that it is true to say that the Muslim society is, as that of the Jewry, a religious society rather than a political society."[7] Later in 1828, François Guizot (1787-1874) introduced this term in his discussion of 'civilisations':

> They also found themselves in juxtaposition with two civilizations, not only different from their own, but more advanced; the Greek on the one hand, and the Mahommedan on the other. There can be no doubt that the Greek society, although enervated, perverted, and falling into decay, had upon the crusaders the effect of a more advanced, polished, and enlightened society than their own. The Mahommedan society afforded them a spectacle of the same nature.[8]

I would like to add two other examples. First, the pharmacist Victor Fontanier (1796-1857) who, having been sent by the French Government to visit the Persian Arab Gulf, noted in 1834: "The Crusades were nothing else but a struggle of the Christian civilization against the Mahometan civilisation."[9] And the politician and French literary critic, Saint-Marc Girardin (1801-1873) pointed out:

> Although it is easy to say that the Qur'an is favorable to republican equality, and it is even easy to point out that Mahomet did not outlaw either Jews or Christians, and that there should not be hate but against the idolators, it is nonetheless true that the Muslim society is founded on the idea of Muslim superiority over all other people. Between Muslims, equality exists, as it existed in Athens between all citizens, so the people could make a general a passer-by, a leather currier or a

---

7   My translation from de Bonald 1796, p. 350: "[…] ensorte qu'il est vrai de dire que la société Musulmane est, comme celle des Juifs, une société religieuse plutôt qu'une société politique."

8   Guizot 1856 : 154, corresponding to the French original in id., 1828: 21sq., and id., 1835 : 239: "Ils se sont trouvés d'ailleurs en relation avec deux civilisations, non seulement différentes, mais plus avancées; la société grecque d'une part, la société musulmane de l'autre. Nul doute que la société grecque, quoique sa civilisation fût énervée, pervertie, mourante, ne fît sur les croisés l'effet d'une société plus avancée, plus polie, plus éclairée que la leur. La société musulmane leur fut un spectacle de même nature." Cf. Eugène Daumas, *La vie arabe et la société musulmane*, Paris: Michel Lévy, 1869.

9   My translation from Fontanier 1834, pp. XVI sq.:"Les croisades n'étaient autre chose que la lutte de la civilisation chrétienne contre la civilisation mahométane."

butcher, if we believe Aristophanes, the sultans often took viziers for porters or hewers of wood.[10]

As in French usage, the term 'culture' was introduced quite late, the first statement on 'Muslim culture' that I found is of Ernest Renan, who wrote in 1852:

> In fact, Arab philosophy was taken seriously only by the Jews. In Islam, the philosophers were insulated men, obnoxious, persecuted, and the two or three princes who protected them incurred the anathema of sincere Muslims. Their writings are found almost only in Hebrew translations or in transcriptions in Hebrew characters, made for the usage of the Jews. All literary culture of the Jews in the Middle Ages is nothing but a mirror of Muslim culture, far more similar to their genius than the Christian civilisation.[11]

In 1853, Arthur Gobineau related Islam to culture as follows:

> The Muslim civilisation as such never penetrated [in Abyssinia, R.S.]. In the true sense of the word, its rationale was to be an ethnic composition very different from that of the Abyssinian population. These simply limited themselves to spelling the Semitic scoop of Muslim culture, and until our days, they, Christians or Mohammedans, did not have anything else, and they did not have more, and

---

10 My translation from Girardin 1858, p. 966: "On a beau dire que le Coran est favorable à l'égalité républicaine, on a beau même faire remarquer que Mahomet n'a proscrit ni les juifs, ni les chrétiens, et qu'il n'a de haine que contre les idolâtres: il n'en est pas moins vrai que la société musulmane est fondée sur l'idée de la supériorité du musulman sur tous les autres peuples. Entre musulmans, l'égalité existe, comme elle existait à Athènes entre tous les citoyens, si bien que le peuple pouvait faire général le premier venu, un corroyeur ou un charcutier, si nous en croyons Aristophane, de même que les sultans ont souvent pris pour viziers des portefaix ou des fendeurs de bois."

11 My translation from Renan 1852, p. 137: "La philosophie arabe n'a réellement été prise au sérieux que par les juifs. Les philosophes n'ont jamais été dans l'islamisme que des hommes isolés, mal vus, persécutés, et les deux ou trois princes qui les ont protégés ont encouru l'anathème des musulmans sincères. Leurs œuvres ne se retrouvent guère que dans les traductions hébraïques ou dans les transcriptions en caractère hébreu, faites pour l'usage des juifs. Toute la culture littéraire des juifs au moyen âge n'est qu'un reflet de la culture musulmane, bien plus analogue à leur génie que la civilisation chrétienne."

they did not cease, as in the most distant ancient times, being the end, the radical termination and the application of the frontier of this Greco-Semitic civilisation.[12]

In the French and English context, it was by far more common to qualify Islam by the term 'civilisation'. Again, it was François Guizot who popularised this interpretation:

> The Arabs, on the contrary, were both conquerors and missionaries; the power of the sword and that of the word, with them, were in the same hands. At a later period, this character determined the unfortunate turn taken by Mussulman civilization; it is in the combination of the spiritual and temporal powers, in the confusion of moral and material authority, that the tyranny which seems inherent in this civilization originated. This I conceive to be the cause of the stationary condition into which that civilization is everywhere fallen.[13]

This practice was already used in a small treatise named *Mélanges de pensées et de quelques observations détachées, sur les préjugés du siècle des lumières*, published in 1820. Speaking of the Crusades, the anonymous author maintained:

> In the explanatory statements to the expeditions, no contemporary author speaks about trade, about benefits of illegal speculation and about profitable speculations. Therefore, these expeditions miss the only ennoblement known for legitimate, avarice; in addition, they were favoured by the clergy. Does one need more to de-

---

12 My translation from Gobineau 1853, p. 49: "La civilisation musulmane proprement dite ne pénétra jamais bien. Dans sa plus belle expression, elle avait pour raison d'être une combinaison ethnique trop différente de celle des populations abyssines. Ces dernières se bornèrent simplement à épeler la portion sémitique de la culture musulmane, et jusqu'à nos jours, chrétiennes ou mahométanes, elles n'ont pas eu autre chose, elles n'ont pas eu davantage et n'ont pas cessé d'être la fin, le terme extrême, l'application frontière de cette civilisation gréco-sémitique, comme dans l'antiquité la plus lointaine."

13 Guizot 1851: 53, corresponding to id., 1835: 17sq.: "Les Arabes, au contraire, étaient conquérans et missionnaires; la force de la parole et celle de l'épée étaient chez eux dans les mêmes mains. Plus tard ce caractère a déterminé le tour fâcheux de la civilisation musulmane; c'est dans l'unité des pouvoirs temporel et spirituel, dans la confusion de l'autorité morale et de la force matérielle, que la tyrannie, qui paraît inhérente à cette civilisation, a pris naissance; telle est, je crois, la principale cause de l'état stationnaire où elle est partout tombée."

serve the anathema of philosophy? The philosophy should rather lease the benefits of Mohammedan civilisation, and this is perhaps one of its regrets.[14]

Since then, the taxonomic categorisation has become commonplace, as shown in a passage of Abel-François Villemain (1791-1870):

> For five centuries, two large movements have been spread in the world and have been acting in contrary directions, the Christian civilisation and the Muslim civilisation, the Muslim caliphate, and, one can almost say, the Christian caliphate.[15]

In a certain sense, 'society' and 'civilisation' still meant the same conceptually. Michel Chevalier (1806-1879), who published a small book on the Universal Exhibition in London of 1851, addressed the "Muslim/Mohammedan civilization" in social and economic terms. The same trend can be found in many books on the French colonisation of Algeria published before the 1850s. At the time, it was already common practice to use the phrase "culture and civilisation". In his *Cours de philosophie positive*, Auguste Comte (1798-1857) preferred the French term 'civilisation' to the word 'culture', and at the same time, he tended to use the word 'culture' when refering to epistemology, methodology, empiricism, mentality, morality, aesthetics and science; by contrast he used the word 'civilisation' to denote a specific 'quality' of history, of regions, of traditions, of temporality, of sociality and even of denominational orders.[16] While it is true that this distinction was not used in the public of the nineteenth century as a routine, the French word 'culture' rather referred to symbolic hermeneutics, whereas the term 'civilisation' was applied to describe a social status.

These certifications show that from the early nineteenth century on, Islam, as other religious traditions, was reinterpreted by being elevated to the level of cul-

---

14 My translation from D.A.C.B.L.A.F. 1820, p. xxx: "Aucun auteur contemporain ne parle du commerce, des bénéfices de l'agiotage et de spéculations lucratives, dans l'exposé des motifs de ces expéditions. Elles manquent donc du seul ennoblissement connu pour légitime, la cupidité; elles ont de plus été favorisées par le clergé. En faut-il tant pour mériter les anathèmes de la philosophie? Elle loueroit plutôt les bienfaits de la civilisation Mahométane, et c'est peut-être un de ses regrets."

15 My translation from Villemain 1830, p. 171: "Depuis cinq siècles, deux grands mouvemens s'étaient déployés dans le monde et agissaient en sens contraire, la civilisation chrétienne et la civilisation musulmane, le califat musulman, et on peut presque dire le califat chrétien."

16 Febvre 1930.

ture. Needless to say, this 'culturalisation' of religion was made possible by a secular perspective, when society appropriated secularisation as self-identity. This interpretation was the subtext of statements like that, which the philosopher and sociologist Gustav Ratzenhofer (1842-1904) made in 1893:

> In spite of the civilisational value of the pure monotheism, Islam absorbed with the research-hostile characteristic of the fully declining West-Asian cultures the germ of its own decline. Now the civilisation is sharply struggling against this Mohammedan culture.[17]

Certainly, in the writings of the eighteenth century, an opposition between 'civil society' and 'religious society' was often discussed. In Moses Mendelssohn's (1729-1786) *Jerusalem*, one can read for example:

> In one word; civil society, as a moral entity, may have compulsory power; nay, was actually invested with it by the social compact; religious society lays no claim to it; nor can all the compacts in the world confer it on it. The state possesses perfect rights; the church, only imperfect rights.[18]

Here, Mendelsohn still had implicitly spoken of the Church as an institution, and not of the society which could be civil or religious, or both, as many authors later upheld. Certainly, the idea of 'modern society' was formed mainly in demarcation with respect to the state, but, in the beginning, it was the opposition to religion which became normative. The differentiation between society and the state assumed a distinction between society and religion insofar as, at the time of the Enlightenment, there was a sharp distinction between religion and the state.

---

17 My translation from Ratzenhofer 1893, p. 428: "Trotz des civilisatorischen Wertes des reinen Monotheismus nahm der Islam mit dem forschungsfeindlichen Grundzug der im vollen Niedergang begriffenen westasiatischen Culturen den Keim des eigenen Niedergangs in sich auf. Gegen diese mohammedanische Cultur steht nun die Civilisation im vollen Kampfe."

18 Mendelssohn 1838, p. 22 = id., 1783, p. 29, and id. 1787, p. 25: "Mit einem Worte: die bürgerliche Gesellschaft kann, als moralische Person, Zwangsrechte haben, und hat diese auch durch den gesellschaftlichen Vertrag würklich erhalten. Die religiöse Gesellschaft macht keinen Anspruch auf Zwangsrecht und kann durch alle Verträge in der Welt kein Zwangsrecht erhalten. Der Staat besitzet vollkommene, die Kirche blos unvollkommene Rechte."

The formation of the social as 'society' corresponded to the normative constitution of a particular tradition as 'religion' and of a lordship/rule/governance as 'state'. This transformation had in common to essentialise society, religion and state, and to derive from the then established 'essence' the respective 'normative orders'. Rabbi Ludwig Philippson (1811-1889) approached this idea already in 1848 as follows: "Just as religion being a religion of the individual must become a religion of society, society as a society of individuality should become a society of an organic whole, should become religious."[19] Contrary to William Warburton (1698-1779) who had argued in 1738:

> But now Civil and Religious Society, having Ends and Means entirely different, and the Means of Civil Society being coercive Power, which Power therefore the Religious consequently hath not; it follows, that the Administration of each Society is exercised in so remote Spheres, that they can never possibly meet to Clash. And those Societies which never Clash, necessity of State can never bring into Dependency on one another. (Warburton 1738, p. 237)

Philippson proceeded from a de-sacralised state of religion, which necessarily appeared in the form of society (or 'societalised'). He specified this idea in a text of 1874:

> What is [...] now the necessary consequence of this? That religion simply interchanges its self-conception and its position. Instead of being in its nature a religion of the individual, it must become a religion of society, and in its manifestation: instead of being a formal and cloistered association, it must become the free action of the individual.[20]

---

19 My translation from Philippson 1848, p. 64: "Sowie die Religion aus einer Religion des Individuums eine Religion der Gesellschaft werden muß [...], muß die Gesellschaft aus einer Gesellschaft der Individualität eine Gesellschaft der organischen Gesammtheit, muß eine religiöse werden."

20 My translation from Philippson 1874, p. 213: "Was [...] ist nun hiervon die nothwendige Folge? Dass die Religion diese ihre Auffassung und diese ihre Stellung geradezu mit einander vertauschen, geradezu umwenden muss. Statt in ihrem Wesen eine Religion des Individuums zu sein, muss sie eine Religion der Gesellschaft werden, und in der Erscheinung: statt eine äusserliche, abgeschlossene Vereinigung zu sein, muss sie die freie Bethätigung des Individuums werden."

The triangulation of the normative order by means of the terms society, religion and state, offered manifold opportunities for a mutual 'hostile takeover': the religion by the state ('nationalisation of religion', an idea of the *Kulturkampf*), religion by society ('socialisation of religion'), and the state by society and society by the state. Thus, the normative content of a concept could easily travel to other concepts resulting in a new semantic formation (cf. Hegel's "Society of the State", the "state of society" to describe a polis), the 'state of religion' for medieval orders, the 'religion of state' to paraphrase ancient orders, 'society of religion', 'religious society', 'religion of society' etc.).

This societalisation of religion – or the realisation of religion as society[21] – was already early identified with Protestantism. Catholic critical journalists like Carl Muth (1867-1944) argued that the "Reformation should be considered the highest form of national societalisation of religion".[22] The thesis of secularisation, derived from this evidence inevitably limited secularisation of the Christian tradition. This shows to what extent religion and society – and their mirror images culture and secularity – are strongly intertwined due to their common genealogy.

III

Contrary to the terms that are part of the immanent frame, the concepts in question are clearly normative, and as normative concepts they define the rules for the social world and interact within a process of functional differentiation. If both levels concord that "the privatization of religious decisions" as well as "the enactment of social decisions" bear, as Luhmann said, a "socio-structural rele-

---

21 The English term 'social religion' (originally referring to the congregational character of religion) is rather old. See for example "Godliness takes into it our Love to godly People. There must be a social Religion; *not forsaking the assembling of our selves together, but considering one another to provoke unto Love and good Works, and so much the more as you see the Day approaching.*" Thomas Bradbury. (1677–1759): *Mystery of godliness consider'd in LXI sermons [...].* vol. 1, London: Cox, 1726, p. 113 (original emphasis).

22 My translation of the phrase "Reformation als grösste Form einer nationalen Vergesellschaftung der Religion", *Neues Hochland,* 13 (1916), p. 228, cited in Schulze 2010a, p. 197.

vance",[23] a secular structure occurs because the starting point is the societal order, and not religion. Religion involved in the social decisions in the public sphere is thus part of secularity, in that it recognises the society as field of reference. In this case, religion is 'societalised' or, so to speak secular. Religion can of course raise validity claims without reference to society and attempt to circumvent the power position of the society by positing itself as a field of primary reference. This is exactly what happened in the process we know as fundamentalism, which includes normative doctrines in the social field. While classical Islamists such as Muhammad Abduh (1849-1905) remained faithful to the primary reference to society or to the state as its legal substitute and construed a 'societalised Islam', early Islamic fundamentalists of the 1920s defined Islam as the antithesis to society in two types: either as a functional replacement (Islam takes the place of the society or the state, however, by adopting its structure), or in the form of a difference of principle. The latter meant to construe Islam as a pure order of norms freed from values, which conventionally and in a Durkheimian sense legitimates norms.[24]

Recombining Islam and society could even lead to an explicit confirmation of the common genealogy of religion and society. The Iranian sociologist Ali Shari'ati (1933-1977) defined society as an order established by/in the transcendence, which finds its radical expression in Islam. This allowed him to argue that "God manifests himself in society, and society is a manifestation of God" (Shari'ati 1955).

Anybody who now studies modern Islamic traditions will see that the categorical (non-institutional) separation of religion and society is constitutive for their interpretation of the world. The Muslim scholars, at least those of the nine-

---

23 "We may comprehend secularisation as the relevance of the *privatisation* of religious arbitration for the *structure of society*." My translation (original emphasis) from Luhmann 1982, p. 232: "Säkularisierung können wir begreifen als die *gesellschaftsstrukturelle* Relevanz der *Privatisierung* religiösen Entscheidens." See also Luhmann 1984.

24 It was the French sociologist Emile Durkheim who saw the social order to be based on the conformity of norms and values. Durkheim brought into accord two concepts of order: German neo-Kantian philosophy of values and French positivism. Broadly speaking, neo-Kantianism defined values as original and primordial (linked to culture respectively to religion), whereas positivism conceived norms as being progressive, representing in a teleological sense the rules of a future social condition (linked to society). According to Durkheim it is religion which expresses values; the neo-Kantian Rickert considered culture to be the real place of values. Since then, it has become possible and commonplace to speak of "cultural values" and "social norms".

teenth and early twentieth century could refer to texts from their own tradition in which, as in the works of Ibn Khaldun, a relationship between 'the social cosmos' (*hay'a ijtimā'īya*) and religion was discussed. The differentiation between the social world (*dunyā*) and a world of cult referring to transcendence (*dīn*) was so constitutive that it has been possible to accommodate to the modern scheme 'religion and society' without major debates since the nineteenth century. This, however, presupposes a reinterpretation of the concept of *dīn*: Only when this category no longer described the practice within a world of worship, but denoted religion in the modern sense, could society be recognised as a worldly order. We know that this reinterpretation of the concept of *dīn* can be verified in many texts from the sixteenth century on, but we do not know much about the genealogy of the concept of society as a partner of differentiation.

It is striking that the old terms of 'social cosmos' (*hay'a ijtimā'īya*) or 'assembly' (*ijtimā'*) have been replaced by the neologism *mujtama'* since the mid-nineteenth century, when the term 'society' became important. This indicates that there was a need to make, at least in Arabic, a clear differentiation between religion and society. Scarcely had this terminological distinction crystallised when the Luhmannian formula took effect: religionists believed that society is determined by its own laws and recognised a secular society. First, however, the naming of this recognition was flickering. The Arab term *dahrī* was privileged. The societal actors, however, could not identify themselves with this word, because it was still strongly tied to Islamic scholastic traditions of the Middle Ages and even to the concept of a time of destiny, well known in pre-classical Arabic poetry. The tradition of Arabic Christian literature proved to be more useful for the new self-interpretation. It offered the term *'almānī*, derived from Syriac, which designated the *saeculares*, namely laymen who were not subject to the authority of the rules (*regulae*) of monastic communities. In the mid-nineteenth century, the term was widespread in Syria and Lebanon in the context of the activities of missionaries in the Levant, who had used the word *'almānī* to stigmatise their opponents, which is the secular society. The Lebanese Jesuit Louis Shaykho, vehemently attacking secularists wrote in 1910:

> The word 'secular' is in their speech equivalent to someone who has no religion, and even the Freemasons do not conceal this anymore, they freely say [...] that God has no place in their intelligence and they should teach their children to despise religion and its representatives. (Shaykhō 1910: 16, my translation)

In the late nineteenth century this concept was popularised in Islamic discourses, too, and replaced the concept *dahrī*, of course integrating the interpretation Shaykho and others had proposed. Other thinkers, like the Egyptian writer

Salāma Mūsā (1887-1958), appropriated this concept in a positive way, reflecting the English usage proposed by anti-clerical author George Jacob Holyoake (1817-1906).

From the point of view of society, Islam now appeared as necessarily 'cultural'. When societal actors identified themselves with the attribute 'secular', they could integrate Islam as 'culture' in their own scheme of order. Under certain circumstances, they could even use Islam as an expression of their validity claims in the public sphere, regardless of their own denominational attachment.

Viewed from the outside, this double reference to Islam blurred the process of differentiation (whether from the point of view of religion or from the point of view of society). As the external master narrative was based on the proposition that secularisation was a privilege of Western traditions, it seemed to verify the statement having been made since the early nineteenth century, that Islam did not separate religion and the world. In fact, however, Islam now addressed two realities simultaneously: religion and secularity.

From an internal perspective, secularisation, that is the formation of the social order as a society, is a historical fact which cannot be denied for 'Muslim' countries. The competition between the two concepts of order, religion and society, has determined the public discourse in the so-called 'Islamic world' since the 1840s. This competition has been mostly unremarkable, as if there were a mutual and silent tolerance. This tolerance faded away when religionists raised a validity claim to exercise sovereignty over society, or when society actors strove to incorporate religion in their field of order. In both cases, the dualism was on the agenda for the debate between religionists and societal actors. And in both cases, there was a call for monistic (fundamentalist) solutions: the extremism of the 1920s was a radicalisation of the claims of Islamic religionists, and Atatürk's state fundamentalism mirrored the fundamentalism of societal actors. On a structural level, both discourses were akin, which is why Islamists such as Muhammad Rashid Ridha showed a fairly deep understanding for the religious policy of Atatürk in the 1920s. At the same time, when Ridha articulated his positive opinion on Atatürk, the interpretation of the secularisation paradigm proposed by Durkheim (individualisation) and Weber (rationalisation) became commonplace in the intellectual debate, later turning into the famous 'secularisation thesis', which was developed by referring to industrialisation, urbanisation, social mobilisation (David Martin), to the loss of the social significance of religion (Bryan Wilson) or to the "de-traditionalization of social ties" (Peter L. Berger). Nevertheless, critics like Ralph Dahrendorf found fault with this view as it underestimated the necessity and meaning of "ligatures", that is of social ties and traditions, for the social integration of a society. Dahrendorf maintained that religion also was a form of a social ligature. With certain constraints he noted referring to

religious fundamentalism: "Religions, however, furnish ligatures for a free society only, if they do not contain a claim based upon their absoluteness which cuts
down options and destroys in the long run."[25]

By defining religion as a social function (Durkheim), and by rooting the
modern structure of the origin of capitalism in religion (Weber), religion became
an objective of society and with it of sociology. In other words: if modern theology is the self-reflexive explanation of religion by 'religious' actors, sociology is
the self-explanation of the society by the societal actors. The two positions had
an interest in showing that secularisation did not lead to the loss of significance
of religion, but argued from very different perspectives for its functionality within society. And two positions had in common the basic idea that Christianity
should be considered as a starting point for a generic explanation of the secularisation thesis.

With reference to Islamic society, the idea of an 'Islamic society' appeared in
the 1960s. It is significant that the inverted version (a 'social Islam') had already
been proposed by Muslim intellectuals in the early twentieth century. This orientation towards the world meant a secularisation of the Islamic frame of reference,
which reflected the validity claims as highlighted by the Islamic elites in the
public sphere. But that does not necessarily stimulate the emergence of a "theology of society" in the sense of Heinz Dietrich Wendland, Paul Tillich, Helmut
Gollwitzer or Trutz Rendtorff. There was, however, a remarkable convergence,
as from the 1940s several Islamic religionists proposed theories of an 'Islamic
society' in which Islam should construe the social ethics. The derivation of this
Islamic normative order, however, followed paths which completely differered
from those of post-war Protestantism. Access to Islamic society was not theological, but ideological. The system of Islamic references itself used for the interpretation of the society was already substantially secularised to such a degree
that it did not produce a specific Islamic standard of secularisation.

IV

What does all this mean for the discussion on debating Islam and negotiating religion, Europe and the self? According to Luhmann's model, societies as well as
their subsystems are construed through communication in difference to their re-

---

25 My translation from Dahrendorf 2003, p. 46: "Allerdings liefern Religionen nur dann
    Ligaturen für eine freie Gesellschaft, wenn sie nicht einen Absolutheitsanspruch ent-
    halten, der Optionen einschränkt und am Ende zerstört."

spective environment. Communication is defined as self-referential social operation. This means that social systems are closed with regard to the operations which produce the structure of the system. This of course does not exclude dependence from environmental contributions, on the contrary, such contributions are of great importance for the self-definition of a society, as they create a structural linkage which defines this dependence. The borders of the domain of communication decide to what extent information flows from the environment to the system.

Debating Islam then, can be understood as a social operation which is part of a procedure by which the society as a system strengthens its self-referential conceptual autonomy. In other words, debating Islam is just a paradigm of social operations; it takes place within a set of conventional discourses without creating new forms of communication. Its primary function is to stabilise the autonomy of the society as a social system. That is why the 'code' of the society and the 'codes' of the societal subsystems (Europe, self, law, religion etc.) are put into the foreground of debating Islam. As I have argued, the code of society is epitomised by the term 'secular', which in the nineteenth century was still an epithet used by religionists to characterise society. Thus, debating Islam also means to determine whether Islam may enter into the secular frame which edges social operations that produce the structure of society. As a consequence, debating Islam does not mean to debate Islam, but to use Islam as a self-referential tool with which to debate society. No wonder, hence, that the borders of the domain of communication decide what information related to Islam is included in this debate.

In this respect, the gulf between society and religion is of great importance. As Islam is debated within the *autopoiesis* of society, Islam is not communicated as a 'religion', but as a 'societal other'. Therefore, Islam is conceived as a new environment of society and as a disturbance which influences or even threatens the self-referentiality of society and not of religion. Islam is not debated with respect to its „religious" frame of reference, but related to worldly affairs. That is why Islam has often been termed a 'political religion' (Schulze 2010b).

In correspondence, many Muslims, stressing that they are an 'element' of a societal system, claim the validity of Islam as a social operation of society. Again this presupposes the redefinition of Islam as 'societal', and it is exactly at this point where non-Muslim and Muslim societal actors meet. Islam has then to be read by using the 'codes' of society and its subsystems, a procedure to which Muslim intellectuals have been accustomed since the end of the nineteenth century. By relating Islam to the societal order or system, Islam has been radically secularised.

As we have seen, the autonomy of society depends on the autonomy of religion, and the autonomy of religion requires the autonomy of society. Thus the respective order construes the other as an environment and epitomises the other with its own codes (secular or cultural). As Islam, however, is not debated as a religion whose autonomy the society would accept, societal actors tend to create a rift within their own concept of religion and endeavour to identify common 'values' which gum up society and religion.[26] In our context, the codes 'Europe' and 'the West' represent these values. Societal actors then categorise certain religions as 'good' as long as these religions seem to conform to these values and others who do not conform as 'bad'.[27] Debating Islam thus also implies discourses on its moral quality.

Therefore, many Muslim participants in the debate acknowledge also moral principles as a starting point. Yet for them it is rather difficult to explain what Islam then means. As on the one hand they have to define Islam as social operation in order to mirror the societal definition of Islam and as on the other hand they accept the modern cleavage of society and religion, they have to enact Islam in two respects: as societal order and as religion. This of course meets and at the same time contradicts the expectations of the non-Muslim public that debates Islam, as the public demands that Muslim actors strictly confine Islam to the field of 'religion' and simultaneously ascertains that Islam is categorically not a 'religion' in the narrow sense of the word, but a 'system of life'. This double bind creates an *aporia* which Muslim actors can hardly avoid if they participate in debating Islam.

Though still popular in public discussions, this rather classical scheme of debating Islam, however, has come under attack. The main question is whether the bi-polar modern order of religion and society actually mirrors the social reality and the complex structure of social operations. The manifold contradictory and often contested statements on a "post-religious" [28] and "post-cultural"[29], respec-

---

26 "Moral value" has become a central issue in debating secularism (Charles Taylor, José Casanova, Hans Joas et al.) especially with regard to the neopragmatic school of thought. For a re-interpretation of moral values as economic values see Graber, David: *Toward an Anthropology of Value: The False Coin of our own Dreams.* New York: Palgrave, 2001.

27 The moral qualification of a religion was very common in the beginning of the nineteenth century. A recent example can be found in Wenzel, Uwe Justus (ed.): Was ist eine gute Religion? Zwanzig Antworten [What is a good religion? Twenty answers], München: Beck, 2007.

28 LaLonde 2007, p. 7: "By 'post-religious' I do not mean the total obfuscation of religious language, thought, experience, etc., from the reservoir or reach of human meaning. This is neither possible nor desirable. The term 'post-religious' rather denotes the

tively on "post-societal"[30] and "post-secular" [31] situation or "condition" at least suggest that 'society' and 'religion' are losing their discursive power as normative orders. In fact, debating Islam along the paradigm of modernity ignores the processes of functional differentiation which effects both orders, religion and society. If we try to comprehend the current social operations that construe Islam be it in the West or in the old-Islamic world, then we may tentatively identify at least four mainstreams: a predominant trend is what I would like to call *consumption-oriented event piety* as addressed for example by preachers like the Egyptian accountant ʿAmr Khālid (Wise 2003) or as expressed by certain Sufi networks;[32] next we come across a *post-Ikhwanism à la mode*[33]. I use this term to describe Islamic discourses and social practices which are genealogically linked to the realm of the Muslim Brotherhood (and of analogous Islamic organisations), yet have freed themselves from the normative order of Islamic "brotherism". Within the *post-Ikhwanist* discourses there is a multitude of conceptualisations which range from neo-pietistic spirituality to radical orthodoxy. The third

---

secular deflation and separation of religious worldviews that entail the acknowledgment of multitude religious traditions and streams within each religious tradition."

29 Rapport/Overing 2000: 268sq.; Muggleton/Weinzierl 2003.

30 A stimulating discussion of "post-societal" theories is offered by Mellor 2004.

31 Habermas (2006: 258): "This term refers not only to the fact that religion continues to assert itself in an increasingly secular environment and that society, for the time being, reckons with the continued existence of religious communities. The expression postsecular does not merely acknowledge publicly the functional contribution that religious communities make to the reproduction of desired motives and attitudes. Rather, the public consciousness of postsecular society reflects a normative insight that has consequences for how believing and unbelieving citizens interact with one another politically. In post-secular society, the realisation that 'the modernization of public consciousness' takes hold of and reflexively alters religious as well as secular mentalities in staggered phases is gaining acceptance. If together they understand the secularization of society to be a complementary learning process, both sides can, for cognitive reasons, then take seriously each other's contributions to controversial themes in the public sphere."

32 Others speak of "Market Islam". See for example Patrick Haenni (2005), who connects Islamic consumerism to neo-liberal, globally integrated economic development. Also: Izberk-Bilgin 2013.

33 Anne Sofie Roald (2001: 56) uses this term to designate those Muslim Brothers who accept the religious identity of Islam and reject "the political and organizational control". See Brook 2012: 33.

mainstream is represented by *neo-conservative Muslim Brothers* and their informal networks. Though their mindscape still reflects the traditional puritan world view according to which Islam should provide the basis for the morals of behaving as a Muslim and for societalising Muslims, Olivier Roy remarked that the Muslim Brotherhood or more generally speaking "Muslim Brotherism" may become a "Muslim church in Europe, which will pose little or no security threat, but will push for conservative moral and social values".[34] Finally we are confronted with a rather powerful heterogeneous *ultra-religious normative Salafism*, which enacts Islam as a radical normative order of clearly confined life worlds. In contrast to the neo-conservative 'brotherist' trend, which in a Durkheimian sense still focuses on the dependence of 'norms' on 'values', this *Salafism* is not value oriented, but bases its validity claim exclusively on a multitude of casuistic 'norms' which should govern life. For them, Islam has become a lived performance, and life in its totality has become the only expression of Islamic worship. As a consequence, debating *Salafism* becomes nearly impossible, because the public debate still relates religion to society by the code called 'value', which for *Salafism* has lost its meaning. For matter of convenience, I muster all these trends under the umbrella term lifestyle-Islam.[35] The social form of *lifestyle-Islam* (lifestyle Islamicity[36]) is not fixed: it may hover between bourgeois middle class culture[37] and radical social separatism.[38]

Thus independently from being enacted within the frame of specific symbolic traditions and references, the performance of Islamicity varies substantially:

---

34 Roy 2004: 276, also discussed in Lorenzo Vidino. The New Muslim Brotherhood in the West. New York: Columbia University Press 2010, p. 222sq.

35 This of course corresponds to non-Muslim definitions of Islam, see for example Furseth/Repstad 2006, p. 95: "However, Islam is also a lifestyle religion, where religiously based customs and rituals tend to dominate the everyday life of the believers. Such a connection between religion and everyday life might give Islam more of a protection against secularization than in the case for Christianity."

36 In order to avoid an essentialist definition of religion as lifestyle, I prefer to speak of "lifestyle religiosity". Accordingly, it would be adequate to render Muslim lifestyle religiosity with the term 'lifestyle Islamicity'. But as this term is difficult to understand, I use the expression 'lifestyle Islam' in the full knowledge that this expression may be confusing.

37 Nasr 2009. For a more substantial conceptualisation of Muslim bourgeois middle class culture ("Islamische Bürgerlichkeit") see Motadel 2009.

38 For the consequences with regard to the relation of Islam and the public see Schulze 2009.

today, it can be staged as a social event, reified as body culture or dramatised as life; it can serve to express a posture and even to structure as a new habitus. The 'code' of modern religion, internalised faith, is receding in behalf of visible performance. At this point, ultra-religionists have an advantage, as they 'show' their Islamicity. As the societal public is then 'debating Islam', when it assumes a violation of the borders which confine the domain of communication, 'debating Islam' in most cases rationalises the public perception of visible performance of Islamicity (Göle 2011). This perception, especially when turned into scandals, strengthens the validity claims of ultra-religionists.

The breaking up of the two normative orders of religion and society shows to what extent both orders have lost their discursive hegemony and their force to govern social integration. Thus analysts of discourses called 'debating Islam' should take into consideration that Islam as a religious category and Islam as a societal category are – at least in part – likely to lose their integrative capacity. In addition, 'debating Islam' has actually become a paradigm of 'negotiating religion' and even of 'negotiating Europe' as a code of society. In other words, negotiating religion and Europe has been enacted in a debate on Islam. The act of debating and negotiating then does not only mean to discuss the place and validity of Islam respectively religion in society. It also scrutinises the normativity of Islam respectively of religion, be it within the biography of individuals or in social life worlds or in the field of theoretical meaning.

REFERENCES

Brook, Steven (2012): "The Muslim brotherhood in Europe and the Middle East: The evolution of a relationship", in: Meijer, Roel / Bakker, Edwin (eds), *The Muslim Brotherhood in Europe,* New York: Columbia University Press.

Congregation for the Doctrine of the Faith (2002): Doctrinal note on some questions regarding the participation of Catholics in political life, Rome: The Holy See [online] 24 November http://www.vatican.va/roman_curia/congregations/cfaith/documents/rc_con_cfaith_doc_20021124_politica_en.html (accessed 16 February 2013).

D. A. C. B. L. A. F. (1820): *Mélanges de pensées et de quelques observations détachées, sur les préjugés du siècle des lumières: Recueil posthume,* Lyon: Théodore Pitrat.

Dahrendorf, Ralph (2003): *Auf der Suche nach einer neuen Ordnung: Eine Politik der Freiheit für das 21. Jahrhundert,* München: Beck.

de Bonald, Louis-Gabriel-Ambroise (1796): *Théorie du pouvoir politique et religieux dans la société civile*, vol. I.1., Paris: n. p.

de Menoux, Joseph (1758): *Notions philosophiques des vérités fondamentales de la religion*, Nancy: Baltazard.

Febvre, Lucien (1930): "Civilisation: Evolution d'un mot et d'un groupe d'idées", in: id. et al. (eds): *Civilisation – le mot et l'idée, Paris: la Renaissance du livre*, pp. 10-59.

Fontanier, Victor (1834): *Voyages en Orient entrepris par ordre du gouvernement français, de 1830 à 1833: Deuxième voyage en Anatolie*, Paris: Dumont.

Furseth, Inger / Repstad, Pål (2006): *An introduction to the sociology of religion: Classical and contemporary perspectives*, Aldershot: Ashgate.

Girardin, Saint-Marc (1858): "Les voyageurs en Orient", in: *Revue des deux mondes*, 14/2, 1858, pp. 950-975.

Gobineau, Arthur (1853): *Essai sur l'inégalité des races humaines*, vol. 2, Paris: Firmin Didot.

Göle, Nilüfer (2011): "The public visibility of Islam and European politics of resentment: The minarets-mosques debate", in: *Philosophy and Social Criticism*, 37:4, pp. 383–392.

Guizot, François-Pierre-Guillaume (1828): *Cours d'histoire moderne: histoire générale de la civilisation en Europe depuis la chute de l'Empire romain jusqu'à la révolution française*, Paris: Pichon et Didier.

— (1835): *Cours d'histoire moderne*, Bruxelles: Louis Hauman.

— (1856): *The History of Civilization: From the Fall of the Roman Empire to the French Revolution*, vol. I, London: H. G. Cohn. English translation of Guizot 1828 and 1835.

Habermas, Jürgen (2006): "On the relations between the secular liberal state and religion", in: de Vries, Hent / Sullivan, Lawrence E. (eds), *Political theologies: public religions in a post-secular world*, New York: Fordham University Press.

Haenni, Patrick (2005) : *L'Islam de marché, l'autre révolution conservatrice*, Paris: Seuil.

Izberk-Bilgin, Elif (2013): "Theology meets the market place: The discursive formation of the halal market in Turkey", in: Rinallo, Diego / Scott, Linda / Maclaran, Pauline (eds): *Consumption and spirituality*, London: Routledge.

LaLonde, Marc P. (2007): *From critical theology to a critical theory of religious insight: Essays in contemporary religious thought*, New York: Peter Lang.

Luhmann, Niklas (1982): *Die Funktion der Religion*, Frankfurt a. M.: Suhrkamp.

— (1984): *Religious dogmatics and the evolution of societies* [= chapter 2 of Luhmann 1982]. Translated with an introduction Peter Beyer, New York: Edwin Mellen, 1984.

— (1996): «Religion als Kultur», in: Kallscheuer, Otto (ed.), *Das Europa der Religionen: Ein Kontinent zwischen Säkularisierung und Fundamentalismus*, Frankfurt a. M.: Suhrkamp, pp. 291–315.

— (2002): *Die Religion der Gesellschaft*, ed. by André Kieserling, Frankfurt a. M.: Suhrkamp [English translation: Luhmann 2013].

— (2013): *A systems theory of religion*, ed. by André Kieserling, Stanford: Stanford University Press [German original: Luhmann 2002].

Mellor, Philip A. (2004): *Religion, realism and social theory: Making sense of society*, London: Sage.

Mendelssohn, Moses (1838): *Jerusalem: a treatise on ecclesiastical authority and Judaism*, vol. II, London: Longman [English translation of id., *Jerusalem oder über religiöse Macht und Judenthum*, Berlin: Friedrich Maurer, 1783, and Frankfurt a. M. / Leipzig: n. p., 1787.

Motadel, David (2009): "Islamische Bürgerlichkeit: Das soziokulturelle Milieu der muslimischen Minderheit in Berlin 1918-1939", in: Brunner, José / Lavi, Shai (eds): *Juden und Muslime in Deutschland: Recht, Religion, Identität*, Tel Aviver Jahrbuch für deutsche Geschichte 3.

Muggleton, David / Weinzierl, Rupert (eds) (2003): *The post-subcultures reader*, Oxford, New York: Berg.

Nasr, Vali (2009): *Forces of fortune: The rise of the new Muslim middle class and what it will mean for our world*, New York: Free Press.

Philippson, Ludwig (1848): *Die Religion der Gesellschaft und die Entwickelung der Menschheit zu ihr, dargestellt in zehn Vorlesungen*, Leipzig: Baumgärtner.

— (1874): *Entwickelung der religiösen Idee im Judenthume, Christenthume und Islam und die Religion der Gesellschaft*, Leipzig: Oskar Leiner.

Rapport, Nigel / Overing, Joanna (2000): *Social and cultural anthropology: The key concepts*, London: Routledge, 2000.

Ratzenhofer, Gustav (1893): *Wesen und Zweck der Politik: Als Theil der Sociologie und Grundlage der Staatswissenschaften*, vol. 3, Leipzig: Brockhaus.

Renan, Ernest (1852): *Averroès et l'Averroïsme: Essai historique*, Paris: Auguste Durand.

Roald, Anne Sofie (2001): *Women in Islam: The Western experience*, London: Routledge.

Roy, Olivier (2004): *Globalized Islam: The search for a new ummah*, New York: Columbia University Press.

Schulze, Reinhard (2009): "Islam im öffentlichen Raum oder der Islam als öffentliche Religion", in: Mariano Delgado / Ansgar Jödicke / Guido Vergauwen (eds), *Religion und Öffentlichkeit: Probleme und Perspektiven*, Stuttgart: Kohlhammer, pp. 141-166.

— (2010a): "Die Dritte Unterscheidung: Islam, Religion und Säkularität", in: Lienemann, Wolfgang / Dietrich, Walter (eds), *Religionen – Wahrheitsansprüche – Konflikte: Theologische Perspektiven*, Zürich: Theologischer Verlag, pp. 147-205.

— (2010b): "Der Islam als politische Religion: eine Kritik normativer Voraussetzungen", in: Assmann, Jan / Strohm, Harald (eds), *Herrscherkult und Heilserwartung*, Paderborn: Fink, pp. 107-149.

Sharī'ati, 'Alī (1955): *maktab-e wāsiṭa* [The Median School]. Mashhad 1335 [A. H.].

Shaykhō, Lūwīs (1910): *al-aḥkām al-'aqlīya fī madāris al-'almānīya al-lādīnīya*, Beirut: al-ābā' al-yasū'īyīn.

Villemain, Abel-François (1830): *Cours de littérature française: Littérature du moyen âge*, vol. 1, Paris: Pichon et Didier.

Warburton, William (1738): *The divine legation of Moses demonstrated, on the principles of a religious deist*, London: Fletcher Gyles.

Wise, Lindsay (2003): 'Words from the heart': New forms of Islamic preaching in Egypt. M. phil. thesis, St Anthony's College, University of Oxford.

Index

Contributors

Barras, Amélie completed her PhD at the London School of Economics in the Department of Government in Spring 2011, and she is currently a Swiss National Science Foundation post-doctoral fellow at the University of Montreal working with the Chair on Religion, Culture and Society and the Canadian Religion and Diversity Project (www.religionanddiversity.ca). Her research interests focus on studying the interactions between the politics of secularism, religion and gender. Her most recent publication on this topic is: "Devout Turkish Women Struggle for Full Citizenship", in: MERIP2, pp. 32-35.

Behloul, Samuel M. is Senior Lecturer at the Department for the History of Religions at the University of Lucerne. Since January 2013 he has the position of National Director at migratio, the Office of the Swiss Bishop Conference for the Pastoral Care of Migrants and Itinerant People. He received his PhD in 2000 in Arabic and Islamic sciences (Free University Berlin). The main focus of his research work is on Muslim migrant communities in West Europe and in particular in Switzerland. His recent publications include: "Religion or Culture? The public relations and self-presentations strategies of Bosnian Muslims in Switzerland compared with other Muslims", in: Valenta, Marko / Ramet, Sabrina (eds), The Bosnian Diaspora: Integration in Transnational Communities, Ashgate2, pp. 301-318.

Bleisch Bouzar, Petra is Lecturer in religion and ethics at the College of Education and in Islamic law at the University of Fribourg. Currently, she is working on a PhD project which adopts narratological approaches to explore learning processes of female converts to Islam in Switzerland. Her research interests include Islam and Muslims in Switzerland, Islamic Law as well as narratological and cognitive approaches in the study of religions. Among her publications figures: "'She is simply present' – female leadership and informal authority in a Swiss Muslim Women's Association", in: Kalmbach, Hilary / Bano, Masooda (eds), *Women, Leadership, and Mosques. Changes in Contemporary Islamic Authority*, Brill, pp. 279-300.

Gianni, Matteo is Associate Professor of political theory at the department of Political Science and International Relations of the University of Geneva. He is a founding member of the Group of Researchers on Islam in Switzerland (GRIS) and has (co)directed several research projects about the Muslim's immigration and integration in Switzerland, inter alia a project on gendered representations of Muslims / Islam in the Swiss public discourse. His main research area is the political theory of multiculturalism and citizenship.

Hafez, Farid holds a PhD and a M.A. in political science (University of Vienna) and a M.Sc. in civic education (University of Krems). He has lectured and conducted researches at the University of Vienna, and currently teaches political science at the Muslim Teachers Training College (Vienna). Research interests are: Islam in Europe, Islamophobia and Islamic political theory. Hafez is the editor of the German Yearbook of research on Islamophobia (www.jahrbuch-islamophobie.de). His latest publications include (co-edited by Humayun Ansari): *From the Far Right to the Mainstream. Islamophobia in Party Politics and the Media*, Leiden: Brill2.

Kühle, Lene is Associate Professor in sociology of religion at the Department of Culture and Society, Aarhus University. She received her PhD in 2004 with a dissertation on the development of religious pluralism in Denmark. Her research interests comprise religion-state relations, religion and politics and Muslims in Europe. Her most relevant recent publications include (with Marie Vejrup Nielsen): "Religion and state in Denmark: Exception among exceptions", in: *Nordic Journal of Religion and Society*, 24:21, pp. 173–188.

Leuenberger, Susanne has submitted her PhD in Science of Religion at Berne University in 2013. In her doctoral thesis, she reconstructs how the public entry of a number Swiss Converts to Islam in the aftermath of the approval of the minaret initiative has structured the Swiss Muslim debate. Her research interests include conversion to Islam, secularism, theories of subjectivation, performativity. Her most recent publication is: "Der Heimelige Islam. Konversion als Zwischenraum zur Neuaushandlung familiärer Bezüge. Eine Einzelfallstudie", in: Lienemann, Christine / Lienemann, Wolfgang (ed.): *Religionswechsel, Konfessionswechsel und Bekehrung in religiös pluralen Gesellschaften*, Harrassowitz2, pp. 115-140.

Moosavi, Leon is Lecturer in Sociology at the University of Liverpool. He completed his PhD in the Sociology Department of Lancaster University in 2011 on British Converts to Islam. His research interests include Islamophobia, conversion to Islam and Muslim communities in Britain. Among his recent publications figures: "British Muslim Converts Performing 'Authentic Muslimness'", in: *Performing Islam* 1:12, pp. 103-128.

Peter, Frank is Assistant Professor of Islamic and Middle Eastern Studies at the University of Bern. His research interests cover the history of the modern Middle East, secularism, political religion and Islamophobia. His current project examines how secular rationalities condition Islamism in contemporary France. He has co-edited "Islam and the Politics of Culture in Europe: Memory, Aesthetics, Art" (transcript 2013) and "Los movimientos islámicos transnacionales y la emergencia de un 'islam europco'" (Edicions Bellaterra 2012; forthcoming in English at I. B. Tauris).

Rohrer, Marius has studied Islamic and Middle Eastern Studies, Political Science and Sociology at the Universities of Bern, London (SOAS) and Lucerne. He currently is a PhD student at the University of Bern, analysing the various forms of communication about Muslim claims to religious diversity in Switzerland, based on sociological systems theory. In 2011, he co-founded a consultancy for diversity management (Büro Vieltracht) where he puts this theoretical knowledge into practice. Among his primary research interests are: social theory, diversity and governance.

Schneuwly Purdie, Mallory holds a PhD in Sociology of Religion (Ecole pratique des hautes études – Sorbonne Paris) and in Applied Study of Religions (Fribourg University). She works as a senior researcher at the Institute of Social Sciences of Contemporary Religions at the University of Lausanne and at the University of Applied Sciences of Western Switzerland (Lausanne). Among other research interests, Mallory Schneuwly Purdie studies the impact of religious and ethnic pluralisation in institutions (such as prison or hospitals) as well as the incorporation of Muslim practices in urban spaces. Among her recent publications figures (co-authored with Irene Becci): "Gendered Religion in prison? Comparing imprisoned men and women's expressed religiosity in Switzerland", in: Women's Studies, 412, pp. 706-727.

Schulze, Reinhard is Professor and Chair of the Institute of Islamic Studies and Oriental philology at the University of Bern. In his research he has been focusing on the history of Islamic knowledge and Islamic religious cultures in the modern

372 | Debating Islam

age, on Islam in modern and contemporary history, on the social history of the Middle East, and on early Islamic history. His "sidelines" deal with the history of Orientalism, with Islamic ethics and with the history of science in the Muslim world.

Sian, Katy Pal finished her PhD at the University of Leeds, UK, in sociology and social policy in 2009. Her research examined the persistence of Sikh and Muslim conflict in the context of postcolonial settlement in Britain. Since then she has worked as a postdoctoral research fellow at the University of Leeds exploring the semantics of tolerance and (anti-)racism across Europe. She currently works at the University of Manchester, UK, as a lecuturer in sociology. She takes a key interest in debates surrounding racism and ethnicity studies, critical Sikh studies, Islamophobia, postcolonialism, Diaspora and South Asian identity. Katy is currently working on her forthcoming book entitled (due 2014): *Postcolonial Thinkers* (Palgrave).

Thielmann, Jörn is Executive Director of the *Erlanger Zentrum für Islam und Recht in Europa* EZIRE at the Friedrich-Alexander-Universität Erlangen-Nürnberg. Among his research interests are Islam and Muslims in Germany, the anthropology of Islam, Islamic Law, and conversion. He is currently co-directing (with Baudouin Dupret) the ANR-DFG-project PROMETEE, dealing with property and the transmission of property among Muslims. He is editor (co-edited by Ala Al-Hamarneh) of *Islam and Muslims in Germany,* Brill, 2008.

Tunger-Zanetti, Andreas is a researcher at the Centre for Research on Religions at the University of Lucerne and a member of the Group of Reseachers on Islam in Switzerland (GRIS). His research interests are Islam in Europe, religion in the public space and in the media. One of his current research projects covers the construction of immigrant religions' places of worship, another one explores Muslim youth groups in Switzerland. Since 2011 he is co-author of the country report on Switzerland in the *Yearbook of Muslims in Europe*.

Tyrer, David is Senior Lecturer in Sociology at Liverpool John Moores University. He is joint-author of *Race, Crime and Resistance* (Sage1). His research focuses on race, racism, postcoloniality, and Islamophobia. His particular interest is in the relations between states and members of racialised and ethnicised minorities. He is currently researching on Patagonia, Wales and postcoloniality. His most recent publication is (in press): *The Politics of Islamophobia: Race, Power and Fantasy,* London: Pluto.